ENCYCLOPEDIA
of
ANGLING

TIGER BOOKS INTERNATIONAL
LONDON

This edition published in 1994 by
Tiger Books International PLC, Twickenham

Produced by Marshall Cavendish Books, London

Copyright © 1985 Marshall Cavendish Ltd

ISBN 1 85501 588 9

British Library Cataloguing in Publication Data:
A catalogue record for this book is available from the British Library

Printed and bound in Italy

by Milano Stampa S.p.A. Farigliano (CN)

Contributors

Coarse Fishing: Dietrich Burkel (Wels), Neville Fickling (Zander), Frank Guttfield (Bream, Barbel, Eel, Tench), Charles Landells (Chub), Graham Marsden (Bream), Barrie Rickards (Perch, Pike), Gerry Savage (Carp), Harvey Torbett (Dace, Rudd), Richard Walker (Grayling), Peter Wheat (Crucian carp), John Wilson (Roach).

Sea Fishing: Des Brennan (Bass, Tope, Ling), Dietrich Burkel (Shark), Ron Edwards (Bass, Cod, Flatfish, Whiting, Dogfish, Sole, Dab), Gerald Green (Mullet), John Holden (Skate), Mike Millman (Pollack), Mike Prichard (Spurdog, Wrasse), Reg Quest (Conger).

Game Fishing: Arthur Oglesby (River Trout, Salmon), Fred J Taylor (Sea Trout), Harvey Torbett (Rainbow Trout).

Coarse Baits: Richard Dawes (Potato), Frank Guttfield (Sweetcorn), Bill Howes (Maggots, Casters, Worms, Groundbait), Charles Landells (Slugs), Peter Stone (Bread), Gerry Savage (High Protein), Harvey Torbett (Cheese), Paul Vincent (Paste and Crust), Ken Whitehead (Bloodworm, Hemp, Meats, Freshwater Mussel, Deadbaits), Norman Worth (Wasp Grub).

Sea Baits: Ron Edwards (Ragworm, Lugworm, Peeler Crab, Shellfish), Norman Hards (Razorshell), Mike Millman (Sandeel, Rubby Dubby), Eddie Stone (Squid and Cuttlefish), Alan Wrangles (Mackerel).

Game Lures: Bob Church (Dry Flies), Douglas Harvey (Wet Flies), Neil Patterson (New Trout Patterns), Taff Price (Nymphs), John Veniard (Sea Trout Flies, Salmon Flies, Tube Flies).

Coarse Fishing Tackle: Tony Fordham (Float Rods, Ledger Rods, Spinning Rods), Ian Heaps (Swing and Quivertip), Charles Landells (Weighing In), Billy Makin (Plugs), Barrie Rickards (Spinners), Peter Stone (Centrepins and Multipliers, Freshwater Hooks, Shots and Shotting, Swimfeeders), Deryck Swift (Catapults, Plugs), Kenneth Torbett (Nylon Line), Harvey Torbett (Knots, Keepnets, Fixed-Spool Reels), Ken Whitehead (Braided Line, Swivels, Rod Rests, Forceps and Disgorgers).

Sea Fishing Tackle: John Goddard (Wire Line), John Holden (Beachcasting Rods), Mike Millman (Rubber Eels and Lures, Pirks and Jigs, Sea Hooks, Sea Leads), Mike Prichard (Boat Rods), Ken Whitehead (Sea Booms).

Game Fishing Tackle: Stuart Canham (Fly Boxes), Bob Church (Reservoir Rods), Tony Fordham (Salmon Rods), Alan Pearson (Wet Fly Lines), Deryck Swift (Gaffs, Priests and Tailers), Harvey Torbett (Fly Leaders), Richard Walker (Fly Lines), Barrie Welham (Fly Reels).

Introductions and other editorial matter by Len Cacutt.

Introduction

Only one leisure sport is practised by millions of people, yet it has no fan clubs, no huge money-making gates, no fortune-sized transfers, and no hooligan mobs. It is our sport of fishing. Best practised purely for pleasure and relaxation, although there is a competitive side which lies in the world of the matchman. This, though, is but a small part of the sport, which includes the great salmon rivers, the quiet beauty of the estuary, the flashing, tumbling highland stream, the lowland, meandering peace of the plains river. Stillwaters, too, some vast man-made reservoirs, others lakes left by the retreating glaciers of the last Ice Age, some perhaps monastery fish-larders or tiny farm ponds — all of them, whether they hold a few tiddlers or record-breaking carp, are the province of the sportfisherman.

The sport today has numbers far beyond those of no more than 20 years ago. More leisure time, mobility (most people have cars) to reach those quiet places where public transport finds it unprofitable to operate, and the pressure of life, mean that fishing offers a few hours of escapism from the rat race.

The fish life, of course, remains the same, with the exception of fisheries where fish are seeded to replace those lost by angling or natural means, but it means that so much pressure is placed on the fish population that we really must think seriously of the future: 'Catch and conserve' should be our claim if tomorrow's anglers are to find as much enjoyment of the sport as we do today.

Any enclosed water is dying from the moment it is filled with water. If left for nature to take its course such waters eventually silt up, reed margins creep farther and farther towards each other, marsh areas take over, then vegetation, and the water is dead. Fishery management is not only an essential to all waters, for enclosed waters it is paramount. And good fishery management means that anglers can have exactly the kind of fishing they want.

A lake can be made alkaline, acidic, clear or weeded, hard-bottomed or mud, plant life can be eradicated or encouraged — all by the manipulation of natural resources and expertise.

Trout reservoir fishing has developed at an extraordinary rate. New fisheries seem to pop up every year, and gone are the days when the fly fisherman was a tweedy sporting gent who would be shocked at the thought of fishing with maggots and a float. Now, he is probably a matchman trying for a few trout while waiting for the coarse fishing season to open.

In the chapter on shot and shotting a section is devoted to the reasons for seeking alternatives for lead. The sport reacted fast to accusations that swan fatalities were caused by lead poisoning from anglers' lead shot. The figures were not wholly accepted but the sport's immediate reaction is evidence of the concern it has not only for fish conservation but for the whole aquatic ecology. It must be remembered, too, that anglers are not the only sportsmen to find their relaxation on or by the waterside.

For the sea fisherman, many old timers talk sadly of the day when they could take a boat out and return with plenty of prime, edible fish. It now seems more and more difficult to find a decent bag of sea fish consistently.

Perhaps it is due to uncontrolled, perhaps illegal, inshore commercial trawling, or the slow but steady pressure from the increasing numbers of anglers; it might even be due to natural population fluctuations acting in response to an unrecognised cycle.

There are still good fish to be had, however. So whether you seek sea fish from boat or shore, salmon from majestic river or trout from chalkstream, carp, roach and pike from one of the great fisheries, go out and savour the fresh air, the relaxation which comes from being surrounded by the beauty of coast and countryside. Sometimes the lack of fish seems not so disastrous when taken into the day's context. Then comes the time when it all goes right and you are rewarded for your efforts with that specimen you have always strived for.

Contents

Chapter 1
COARSE FISHING

This kind of fishing is certainly not 'coarse' — the gossamer-thin lines, the tiny hooks, intricate terminal tackle, plus a naturalist's understanding of the habits of our coarse fish species, all demand a high degree of skill.

In the following chapters you will read about the fine art of seeking, finding and then offering an acceptable bait to some of the most cautious creatures to be found in the wild.

At its simplest level, the angler needs no more than a rod, reel, line and baited hook. But these few necessities are but the bricks from which a large and rewarding edifice can be constructed.

You will read of ledgering, float-fishing, casting in various styles; many baits, groundbaits, and a huge range of accessories. In fact, this book covers a wide spectrum of information on these and other factions of the sport. It will lead to a knowledge of a totally absorbing sport based on understanding of fish behaviour, consideration for the countryside and an awareness that we must conserve our sporting traditions.

The best way to learn about fishing is to accompany someone who is able to fish in a number of styles, knowing which baits to choose, which size hooks best match those baits, and how to present a hooked bait in a natural manner to a fish.

Once taught, your learning is not finished. Those well-meaning but sometimes misguided people who would stop all field sports — and that includes fishing — must never be given the chance to point an accusatory finger at angling on the grounds of cruelty. And the best way to do this is to treat your fish with great care and consideration, remembering that they, like you, have a nervous system capable of reacting to injury.

Better still, develop the art of fishing with barbless hooks. At first you will lose many fish, either by poor technique in playing them or on the strike, but those that you lose will not have been harmed, and those that you bring successfully to the bank can be released without harm.

Such fishing demands skill, but that is one challenge no one should shrink from. Facing a problem and solving it is one of the satisfactions in life.

The sport of angling today is one of very large numbers of anglers streaming out every weekend to their favourite waters. And as their numbers increase so, inevitably, must the amount of fishable water available

to each decrease. Fishery management therefore is becoming increasingly more and more vital if fish stocks are not to deteriorate through overfishing.

The lone angler will find it harder to get good fishing water within reasonable distance — unless he is lucky enough to live in some quiet area close to water with a healthy head of fish.

So membership of an angling club is recommended. There will be such a club in your area and if you have any difficulty in locating one ask at your local library, police station or town hall. As a last resort, write to the National Anglers' Council, who will certainly be able to help. Their address is 11 Cowgate, Peterborough PE1 1LZ.

The cost of angling has risen — what's new? It is something the angler must take into consideration. On the plus side, today's tackle is as good as it has ever been; there are fine rods in glassfibre and carbon at very reasonable prices; reels come in many models at a wide range of prices, and the list of accessories has something for every pocket. Maggots and other baits are not cheap, but few coarse anglers can do without the 'wriggler'. The beginner should also take a few worms from the garden, they are excellent baits. Bread, too, is fine and can be used in many ways.

There are many gadgets in tackle shops that catch more anglers than fish — so start with just a few of the basic floats, a simple disgorger and a landing net. Why not a keepnet? Well, unless you are going to be a matchman, get into the habit of releasing your fish immediately after capture. Put them back a little way downstream though, if they go back into your swim they may well cause so much disturbance that other fish will be scared off.

Anglers must be aware of the law insofar as it affects them and their sport. In England and Wales, River Authorities exist to control and conserve water supplies not only for fishing but for all uses. Fishery Committees are set up to look after the welfare of the fish stocks and to control angling.

All this costs money, and some of it is recovered by the sale of fishing licences for each area. They vary in price and cover day, monthly and yearly periods. You must be in possession of the appropriate licence for the area you intend to fish. These licences carry the limits to which you are entitled and the legal season. Apart from a few exceptions the coarse season extends from June 16 to March 14.

Chub

Arm yourself with a bucket of slugs, appropriate freelining tackle and a light extending landing net; prepare to stalk your chub as you would trout, and you're ready for action

Freelining slugs for chub is one of the most enjoyable ways of fishing. The angler travels light with just a shoulder bag and a landing net, seeking out the chub in small streams and those rivers where they can be spotted. The approach is very similar to that of the trout angler.

The basic equipment is a 10-11ft hollow-glass rod, a fixed-spool reel loaded with 4lb b.s. line and an assortment of hooks from No 2 to No 4. Spare spools should carry 5 and 6lb b.s. lines. The landing net should be as light as possible—while a trout net is ideal it will be found that an extending net is needed in most areas. The new hollow-glass two-piece handles are very good and a strap can be fitted so that the net can be carried over the shoulder. The well-equipped chub stalker should also have an army surplus jacket with numerous pockets.

Bait
The most important item is the bait—and in these days of expensive high protein and special preparations, a free one is welcome. Most gardeners see the slug as a pest and you should be able to find neighbours more than willing to supply you with large brown and black slugs from their gardens, if you provide tins to put them in. If you can-not obtain slugs from neighbours, it is worth approaching a local allotment society. The Secretary will be only too pleased to give you a letter of authority and the key to the gates once you have convinced him that you are not completely mad, and really do collect slugs.

A visit in the early morning or during a rainy night will produce an ample supply of bait—the larger the better. Keep the slugs in a large bait bucket with earth in the bottom to absorb the moisture, and some food such as potato peelings or slices of melon to keep them fattened up. Should you forget the food, you will find that the slugs lose almost half their size in 24 hours. Keep the bait bucket in a cool place, out of direct sunlight. If you collect the bait some time before you need it, be sure to check it daily and remove any dead or decomposed slugs, and to

When you freeline slug for chub the name of the game is stealth and camouflage. Work your way upstream, keeping out of sight of the fish, and cast into 'chubby' areas.

replenish the food supply for the slugs.

When you go fishing, you can slip the bucket on to a dog clip at your waist. Be sure to have at least two pieces of towelling for your hands and for holding the chub. Once you have run the line through the rod rings and removed any frayed sections, you can tie on the hook. The Mustad 2/0 Beak hook with small barbs on the shank is ideal for a fair sized slug. The barbs tend to hold the slug and stop it sliding down the bend of the hook in a horrible lump. Slugs are very slimy creatures, so if you find you cannot grip one hold it in the towelling while pushing the hook through the rear end and out at the front. To avoid spoiling your clothing, wipe your finger on the towelling afterwards.

The free-lined slug

You will find the weight of the slug ample for quite a lengthy cast in places such as weirpools and far-bank swims. The great advantage of a freelined slug is that you can cast into areas which would otherwise be inaccessible. Chub in particular lie in that type of swim—under overhanging trees and bushes, platforms of debris, moored boats, and around the heavy wooden posts which protect many bridge buttresses. Thick lily beds in backwaters will often hold chub in the summer, when the slug can be cast right into the middle of them.

Polarized sunglasses are essential for spotting chub. Take a quiet walk along the river, preferably working upstream, and pay attention to all likely looking swims. In areas which look 'chubby' it is worth your while standing by a tree or some other cover for ten minutes or so. You will often see chub drifting out from cover, or lying on a gravel run at the end of a lily bed or a funnel of water running through reed mace.

The slug should be cast upstream of the fish and worked back towards them. You can control the depth at which the slug is carried by holding the rod in the air. If a chub moves over to take the bait, allow the fish to pick it up, watching for the movement of the gills which shows that the bait has been taken from the lips to the mouth. Strike sideways and you should have it. When playing a

chub you will often find that the slug has been spat out on the strike and is up the line. Other chub may try for the slug while you are playing a fish so that if you guide your fish quietly into the bank before showing yourself and netting it, you can often cast out straight away and take another fish before scaring them into cover.

How to skate the slug

Mark where the fish went and return to those spots later. Beneath overhanging trees, particularly where willows have branches in the water, it is impossible to float fish, but a freelined slug can be placed right under the tree and against the bankside. This can be done by skating the slug in the same way as you skate a flat stone across water. Make a side cast, and point the rod tip down to the water at the last mo-

Left: *Recommended by Izzak Walton, the black slug is very effective on a No. 4 or No. 6 hook. Any other casting weight is not needed because the slug is quite heavy enough to carry to the far bank.*
Right: *As this chub is netted, the bait which tempted it can be seen near the fish's mouth. No doubt that the slug is very useful chub bait.*

ment to achieve the skating effect. When a slug skates in under cover, watch the line for an immediate take. With a firm straight pull, strike at once; but with a number of tentative plucks on the line, wait until the line starts to straighten

Above: A 4lb 10oz chub is slid gently into the keepnet. It was taken from a quiet, relatively open stretch of water.

Left: When you are playing and netting a chub taken on slug do it as quickly as possible and try to keep out of sight. Slug is such a devastating bait that if you obey these rules and cast out again with the same bait the chances are that you'll catch at least one more fish before they go for cover.

before striking. Should you miss the fish, but retrieve a tattered and torn slug, put it back into the same spot at once, for the chub will often take the slug the second time around.

On the wider, streamy rivers such as the Hampshire Avon, parts of the Severn, or the Tees, you can work along the bank ten paces at a time, casting across the river and allowing the slugs to drift around between the streamer weeds. If you allow your line to bow, you will notice the plucks and then the straightening of the line. You will often find certain nondescript sections which always produce chub, due, no doubt, to unseen features on the riverbed. For future reference, mark these with a stick in the ground or a stone.

In the knowledge that you will succeed with this method, be sure to have a camera, measuring tape, and scales to record your catch. If you are really keen you might like to join the national body for chub anglers, the Chub Study Group.

Freelining

One very useful method of freelining streams and rivers is with a detachable floating crust. This is a technique to employ when having only limited success with a slug.

Quite simply, a piece of fresh bread flake is pinched on to the hook followed by a fair sized piece of crust. The crust is only lightly pinched, however, so that a flick of the rod tip makes it break free. The baited hook is then allowed to travel with the current until it reaches the best point, when the crust is twitched free allowing the flake to sink gently into the waiting mouth of a fat chub.

Invariably this method is more effective than casting a ledgered piece of bread at the fish, as no unnecessary splash is made.

When roving the banks with my stock of slugs, I find it desirable to carry with me a change of bait. Lobworm is a chub favourite, particularly if there has been recent flooding. As the river bursts its banks many worms are trapped, so nature provides groundbait in the form of thousands of worms washed downstream in a never ending supply. Using the standard tackle for freelining the slugs, tie on a size 8 hook and lower either a single or double lobworm bait into every likely hiding place of the chub. The bite is electric; the line tightens and the rod tip is pulled viciously round, so that the fish either hooks itself or breaks free before you strike.

A bait rapidly gaining favour among the chub hunting fraternity is sweetcorn. It can prove deadly, particularly among the smaller, school fish.

Summer offers the best chance of seeing, hooking and hauling out a big chub, but winter fish are stronger and in better condition. They also move around less in extreme cold. (It may be worthwhile to carry a thermometer and check the water temperature.) In winter, the best chances of specimen chub are in small rivers of character. These waters, with shallows and deeps, bends and scours, undercuts, gravels and glides call for simple ledger tackle.

Bream

There are so many variables involved in finding and catching specimen bream that only those who have taken a special interest in the species are likely contenders for a new rod record

Above: *Eric Baines with a respectable bream from the River Shannon. The bream in this river run larger on average than their counterparts in English rivers.*
Right: *Unhook a bream over a keepnet. This is necessary if a fine specimen is not to jump free and squirm back into the water.*

Most fish species have favoured areas—natural larders where they can usually be found, even when not feeding. Not so the bream—although it has set feeding routes and hotspots like other fish.

Bream are travellers, often covering large distances when following established beats, which can be likened to railway lines with stations where they stop to feed.

Small, 2-5lb fish, which gather in large shoals, need to cover several hundred yards to reap sufficient natural food, whereas big bream of over 8lb feed less often and will therefore need to travel only a short distance. It is for this reason that they are more difficult to catch.

Locate the shoals
The small shoals containing the heavier fish need to be precisely located, and this is not easy unless one knows what to look for, as most bream waters are large and featureless lakes or gravel pits.

Typical are the Cheshire and Shropshire meres known for their large bream, where I fish. Here, specimen fish are not caught by casual anglers; 99 out of every 100 are taken by those who are pas-

sionately dedicated to their pursuit.

The best location method is simple observation, based on the fact that bream have a peculiar habit of rolling at the surface as a prelude to, and during, feeding. Bream usually feed in the late evening or early morning, when you should look for their hump backs cleaving the surface. You may have to spend many hours over several weeks before you spot them, but once located, they are likely to be found regularly in the same area for a number of years.

Prebaiting for success
Prebaiting for bream pays handsome dividends, and the longer and more often, the better your chances of success. Unusual baits are not necessary; maggots, bread and worms are adequate. The choice is partly a matter of personal preference, but I use maggots and/or worms when the water has an abundance of bloodworm, and bread when the natural food is daphnia.

Prebaiting should be done in the morning if you intend to fish through the day, or the evening for night fishing. Always bait as close as possible to that time. Prebaiting is simply brainwashing. It weans

the fish away from natural food, teaches them that your offerings are safe and good to eat, and encourages the habit of looking for food at specific times.

Big bream rarely feed close to the margins, and the average distance you need to groundbait and cast is 30-40 yards. Very often, much greater distances are involved, and to throw the groundbait so far demands a good arm and a mix that will not break up in flight. I recommend an equal mix of mashed stale bread, ordinary crumb groundbait, and bran, liberally spiced with whatever hookbait you intend to use. You can use a swimfeeder while you fish, but this is not common in Northern waters, as threadlike algae can engulf bulky rigs, rendering them useless.

Frank Guttfield writes:
Bream are probably the most underrated of big fish. In reservoirs especially, bream fishing has the reputation of being a random affair, yet few really large fish are caught. Bream over 9lb are relatively common, but the more difficult to locate.

Many of the observations regarding the Cheshire meres can be ap-

AT-A-GLANCE

Specimen sizes
Notable fish lists include
common bream weighing 8lb
and over. This figure is over
1lb above 50 per cent of the
current rod-caught record
bream which weighed 13lb
12oz, taken in 1983.

Tackle, Bait, Techniques
Rod
11ft 6in glassfibre
(test $1\frac{1}{4}$-$1\frac{1}{2}$lb)
11ft 4in ($1\frac{3}{4}$lb test)

Reel
Fixed-spool

Line b.s.
3lb-6lb

Hooks
10-16 (maggot, worm)
6-10 (bread, large lobs)

Bait
Maggots, bread, worms

Groundbait
Mixed white and brown bread;
sausage rusk (in converted
blockend feeder); particle
baits, maggots, worms

Techniques
Fixed-link ledgering

plied to southern reservoirs, like those in Hertfordshire, but there are several differences. The water levels of the Cheshire meres do not normally fluctuate violently in a season, so the bream adhere to identifiable patrol routes, that can be stabilized by heavy and/or regular groundbaiting. But in the Hertfordshire reservoirs the water level can vary by up to 10ft in a year (especially as they now serve as a buffer for the nearby Grand Union Canal), discouraging the bream from establishing regular patrols.

Hertfordshire bream can be seen in May and June preoccupied with breeding in the shallows, but are less evident as the season progresses. Occasionally you spot them 'humping', rolling, or even leaping, but this suggests play rather than a prelude to serious feeding. Ironically, about 75 per cent of bream activity you *can* observe takes place in the middle of the reservoirs, well out of reach of even a champion caster.

Regular patrol routes
Locating bream in reservoirs should be based on the fact that the more regular patrol routes are controlled rather than influenced by anglers.

Regular prebaiting is usually done near popular stretches of bank, and most of the groundbait accumulates in a belt 30-50 yards from the bank, where the bream carry out a mopping-up operation.

Choice of swim
Big bream keep away from the banks by day because either the water level is high and anglers can be seen and heard, or the water level is low and anglers' movements on the stoney 'beaches' send out vibrations 100 yards or more. Towards evening, the fish are more confident and move in, feeding inside the belt of groundbait. This time has always been productive, whether in June, October or March. Dawn is also a good time in summer, but I have never tried in winter. The theory that fish gain in confidence with the diminution of the light can only be put to the test with experimental night fishing.

Individual swims do not really exist in reservoirs. It is more a matter of selecting a particular area, which will vary according to water level, weed growth, wind direction, and temperature. Other factors also influence my choice. For example,

when the water is at an intermediate level, I look for any useful cracks in the concrete base of the wall to take my rod rests.

The reservoir I fish is 60-70 acres, wooded on one side and surrounded by fields and marshes. You can hire boats or fish one third of the bank, much of which consists of concrete walls. The banks shelve steeply to a maximum depth of 22ft at high water, 10-12ft at low water, and the angler's cast will usually take him to a depth of 18ft. Although the bottom is mainly even and shingly, there are some algae patches, and here and there chunks of submerged concrete near the bank. Some non-fishing areas are reedy and make good spawning sites, but the fishable spots are unaffected by too much weed during most seasons.

Regular groundbaiting is effective, but a little in the right place often works better than a lot in the wrong place. Accuracy in placing the groundbait is preferable to a heavy, inaccurate spread over a wide area. Boats, when available, are a boon for accurate prebaiting.

Ball buoys

A buoy, made with a plastic detergent bottle, string and brick will ensure your bait is deposited in the same area. I settle for a landmark on the far bank—a chimney, tree, or position along a reed bed. I would not be without my long-handled spoon, used for lobbing out groundbait balls. Made by whipping a perforated kitchen spoon to a 5ft runner-bean cane. It places dollops of groundbait within 30-60 yards, and with hard groundbait, 80 yards. For a really stylish spoon, use half a glassfibre carp rod blank.

My groundbait ingredients are not quite the same as Graham Marsden's. I use a mixture of one part stale white bread, one part brown breadcrumb, and one part sausage rusk, but not bran, as it is not sufficiently cohesive. The consistency has to be just right; it needs to break up within a few minutes. Too hard and it takes ages to disintegrate, too soft and it breaks up in mid-air. Lob an experimental lump into the water as a test.

Attention to detail

With terminal tackle, it is the finer points of selection and attention to detail that make all the difference between hit-and-miss 'splodging' and proper bream fishing. One cannot beat a terminal feeder for accurate groundbaiting. There are a variety on the market, but none, even the Feederlink, meet my requirements. All feeders are designed for use with maggots, which creep out fairly slowly, depending on size and temperature. My feeder is not restricted to maggots as I often want to distribute chopped worms, sweetcorn, or other large particle baits, and, more important, the offerings need to be ejected fast. I convert a regular blockend feeder to a special block-link feeder, which is an open-ended feeder attached to a

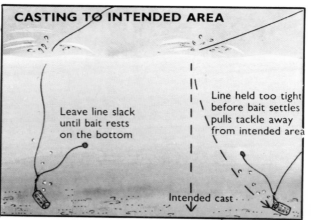

CASTING TO INTENDED AREA

Leave line slack until bait rests on the bottom

Line held too tight before bait settles pulls tackle away from intended area

Intended cast

Left: *A handy tip to bear in mind not just in bream fishing but wherever you are casting over long distances.*
Right: *A map of the waters referred to by Frank Guttfield in his search for specimen bream.*
Below: *Des Taylor with bream weighing more than 10lb. He caught it with a maggot bait from a gravel pit. Only the oldest pits hold specimen fish (weighing 8lb and over).*

swivel link, an important tackle item.

First fill the feeder about two-thirds full with maggots or other hookbait samples, then top-up with a cup of groundbait. Do not attempt to 'flick' cast the feeder as it will either come off the line or eject the contents. Instead, make a gentle, but positive sweep-cast, starting with the rod back at 45 degrees rather than vertical. When the feeder hits the water, let it sink naturally and let line run off the open spool until it has bottomed. Do not engage the clutch when the tackle hits the water, because, depending on the depth, your feeder

may come to rest well away from your baited hotspot. If there is a strong side wind, either sweep in a small section of the bow in the line before tightening, or, to compensate, step a few yards sideways before casting.

When your feeder has come to rest, tighten up very gradually, with the rod tip pointing at your terminal tackle, until you can just feel the resistance of the feeder. Then, before placing your rod in the rests, jog your tackle a few inches. This should dislodge the groundbait topping in your feeder, and the juicy offerings will spill out around your hookbait.

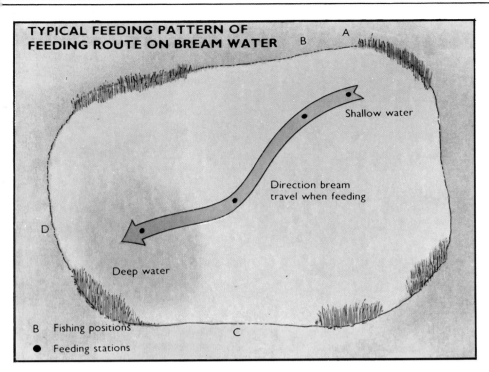

TYPICAL FEEDING PATTERN OF FEEDING ROUTE ON BREAM WATER

B   A

Shallow water

Direction bream travel when feeding

D

Deep water

B Fishing positions

● Feeding stations

C

Repeat this procedure every four or five minutes to ensure the feed is distributed. If you feel resistance, it will not have emptied.

Rod and line

I use a home-made 11ft 6in glassfibre rod with a test curve of $1\frac{1}{4}$-$1\frac{1}{2}$lb. My line is generally 5 or 6lb b.s., but even though the reservoirs are fairly snag-free, and you could use a 3 or 4lb line, the newcomer is advised to stick to the heavier line until he has the feel of casting a block-feeder.

For fishing from the top of the reservoir wall, I have a special pair of 'low profile' rod rests mounted into a 3in × 2in block of wood. This reduces the otherwise excessive length of line between the rod top and water, and with special 18in back rests I get a nice indicator 'drop' of about 1ft.

Bite indication is a problem on Hertfordshire reservoirs as one invariably has to contend with wind, drift, or both. On rare still days, I use a small dough bobbin between the reel and butt ring as a secondary indicator, but watch the bow in the line for any positive movement. Otherwise I use a dough bobbin just large enough not to be broken up by either wind or drift.

I always take great care when attaching my dough bobbin (or other bite indicator) for the bream sometimes take the bait as soon as it reaches the bottom, possibly just before. I cannot over emphasize the need to tighten-up carefully. Leap to action if you feel any movement as you attach the bobbin. Should this happen often, the bream are feeding in earnest, so dispense with the indicator and just watch (and feel) for promising tension in the line.

In the dark, I prefer an audible indicator to glow-bobbins, as these start playing tricks with my eyes after a few minutes, and lead to a headache. But I am not keen on electric bite alarms, and my method employs a strip of aluminium foil looped over the line, with a swanshot clipped to the bottom edge. Lodged on my wooden tackle box lid (or a plastic flower pot tray), it is loud enough to indicate a bite. I can then sit back and relax rather than hover over a bobbin. It is no good for registering slack bites, but then, what method is?

Once your have located feeding bream, apparently confident 'sailaway' bites can still prove almost impossible to hit. Nobody knows why we get this frustrating sort of run but a common theory is that the bream is feeding vacuum-fashion off the bottom, so the hook misses the closed mouth, enters the nose instead, and usually tears free.

To lessen the risk of nose-hooking a bream, scale down the size of hook and offering. Hooks for maggot fishing are usually sizes 8 to 12, so try 14 or 16. Anything smaller will not hold a 10lb bream. You can also fish as for carp, with an aluminium foil indicator (weighted if necessary) and the pick-up of the reel left open. Let the bream run and take several feet, perhaps yards, of line before risking a strike.

In the dark, I flip off the indicator, hold the rod, and feel the line peeling out between forefinger and thumb. On two occasions, I have had to let the bream peel off about 10 yards before I made a positive connection. If neither method works, try combining the two—scaling down hook size and letting the fish run.

Lion's share of bream fishing

There is little doubt that the paternoster rig described by Graham Marsden (or the 'fixed-link' ledger to us Southerners) and the blockfeeder, account for the lion's share of bream today. If fishing with two rods, you could even experiment with both methods—particularly if you wish to use a big bait like lobworm or mussel on one tackle. After all, when bites are coming regularly, two blockend rigs are too much to cope with.

I rarely fish a cast for more than 15-20 minutes. Fishing with two rods in this way will work-up a swim quite naturally, and every hour or so the swim is boosted with half a dozen dollops of groundbait.

White bream

The white or silver bream, *Blicca bjoerkna*, is only found in a few slow flowing rivers and stillwaters in the east of England. It is similar in shape and colour to the common freshwater bream.

White bream are similar to the common bream in habitat and diet, but tend to be more selective in their feeding and are less confirmed bottom-feeders. Bream caught in midwater are always worthy of a close scrutiny. White bream are small, reaching a maximum length of about 15in and the current British Record (rod-caught) is open at 1lb, and will perhaps be surpassed by the first angler who can correctly recognize the species.

Carp

Beware of faddists and wonder baits: in carp fishing there is no substitute for a flexible, intelligent approach, a lively respect for the species, and a first-class technique

Above: *Charlie Clay took this 17½lb leather at night when the fish venture into the margins to feed in seeming safety.*

In 1952, Richard Walker broke the British carp record with a 44lb common carp from Redmire Pool—a record that still stands. At that time, the norm in carp tackle was to use a cane rod of about 10ft and a centrepin reel or, if you were fortunate, one of the claw-type fixed-spool reels.

Nowadays, tackle and tactics are far more sophisticated. Cane has virtually disappeared from the tackle shops, although the discerning angler who can afford it may choose to build his own cane carp rod. For many carp enthusiasts, cane has

magical memories but today's angler prefers glass or carbon rods.

Davenport and Fordham were one of the first firms to offer glass carp rods back in the early 1960s. The 'D & F' rod was a standard 10ft version, but now length varies from this to as much as 13ft, with the general preference being for fast-taper versions of about 11ft. These thin-walled, purpose-built rods can cast a bait over 70 yards, while 80-90 yards

is claimed for stiffer models.

These rods are suited to the experienced carp angler, but the beginner should start with one of 10 or 11ft with a fast taper. I use a ledger rig—which as well as being a useful bottom fishing aid, is a must for presenting a floating bait at long range. The weight of the ledger depends on the distance at which you want to fish. If the carp are on the surface, say some 50 or 60 yards out, you will require a ¾oz or 1oz ledger. I use the well-known Arlesey bomb with a swivel, as this makes for free running and minimal resistance. I tie about 2-3in of line to the bomb and then attach the free end to a split ring.

Maximum casting distance

Some carp anglers prefer to use a small swivel and a ledger stop but I prefer the split ring ledger without the stop. My floating crust bait hides a No 2 or No 4 hook, though sometimes when the bait is smaller I use a No 6, allowing the running weight to rest against the hook-bait. This gives maximum casting distance, while this split-ring method also guarantees that the crust will rise very quickly to the surface, even in weedy areas, where a swivel link can become clogged.

You will need a ledger-stop to fish a small bait on the bottom at long range, but there will also be days when the carp are right under the rod tip, and this is when the art of freelining in the margins comes into its own. In 1976 I caught a 22¾lb mirror carp in 3ft of coloured water lapping a bankside clump of reeds. I had previously flicked a few small pellets of paste into the swim as an attractor and then patiently waited a couple of hours until the big carp came along and took the bait. When using two rods, I often elect to fish one at long range and the other close in. I have taken more fish at long range, but the better-quality fish often inhabit the margins, so it is well to be flexible in your approach.

As for waters, in my home county, Kent, there are several day ticket venues that boast a good head of carp. At Dartford, just off the A2, there is the famous Brooklands Lake. Here you have an excellent chance of a 20lb carp, and double-

figure specimens are regularly taken by anglers who purchase their tickets at the waterside. On the A225, which links Dartford and Farningham, is the pretty village of Sutton-on-Hone and just south of Sutton lies the productive Horton Kirby complex, where the carp fishing is superb and day permits are available on the bank.

Other Kent carp waters
Day permits are also available at Dennis Johnson's lakes at New Hythe, near Maidstone, where carp to 30lb have been taken. At Faversham, carp anglers can fish the Faversham Angling Club's School Pool and the best carp to date is a 34¾lb specimen—just one pound short of the current county record. Nationally, the Leisure Sport Angling Club offers fishing for carp on a smaller scale, and other companies offer similar facilities.

Whatever you choose to fish, there are important steps to follow if you want to catch carp. For example, if no information is forthcoming regarding the depth of the water, you will have to plumb the lake. Look for islands, as these denote the shallows which carp are known to frequent. If you discover weed beds, shallows and gravel runs, so much the better.

Reeds, lily pads and sandbanks are also popular carp haunts, and it is a good idea to watch what other carp anglers are doing. If the water is virtually free of bankside noise and heavy pedestrian traffic, the margins are a good bet. But quiet waters today are the exception, and in the main I choose to fish at long range during daylight hours and under the rod tip at night.

Now to the complex question of baits. Unfortunately, great emphasis is laid on what is used at the business end of the line, and although this is important, watercraft and technique count for a lot too. A 'killer' bait is of no use at all if it is not cast to where the fish are, and, equally, if your presentation is at fault, you will not tempt carp, the most wily of all the coarse species.

When asked what my favourite carp bait is, I reply: 'Whatever the carp are taking on the day'. I say that because today the choice of baits is so varied: one day the carp

Top: *Floating crust accounted for these four double-figure carp taken by Peter Ward.*
Above: *Winter fishing for carp can be slow and conditions muddy, but on the right water, very productive indeed.*

Below: *No netting problems for the captor of this 8½lb mirror carp. Some tricky carp swims are full of snags and have few unobstructed footings at the waterside from which to wield a landing net. Note the size of the net.*

Above: *Beside this handsome catch are potato baits of the same size as the one which caught it.*
Below: *One bait suggestion and a recommended rig.*

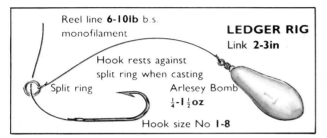

Reel line **6-10lb** b.s. monofilament

LEDGER RIG
Link **2-3in**

Hook rests against split ring when casting

Split ring

Arlesey Bomb
¼-1½oz

Hook size No **1-8**

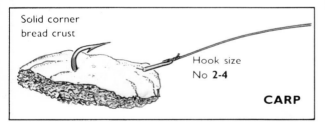

Solid corner bread crust

Hook size No **2-4**

CARP

Above: *A specimen mirror carp is brought to the net from the bank of a small water happily underrated and overgrown.*
Below right: *Kevin Clifford with three double-figure carp, the best weighing 18lb 6oz, taken from an East Yorkshire gravel pit.*

will devour floating crust as if their very survival depended on it, the next it will be high protein *à la carte* that takes fish.

To start with, there are the old-established favourites: potato, worms, bread, cheese, maggots, honeyed paste and, as already mentioned, floating crust, all of which catch carp. Particle baits—sweetcorn, beans, peas, and the like—have all become popular during the last few years. Then there are the topical high-protein baits.

Fred Wilton started anglers on the high protein gambit back in the late 1960s, since when high protein has accounted for hundreds of carp. HP, as it is known, is expensive, although there are several ready-made mixes that contain a high protein percentage available at most tackle shops.

The more successful protein baits contain casein (milk protein) and the vitamin B complex found in yeast, which is soluble in water. Protein is a top scorer in waters where carp seldom reach 20lb because of competition with other stock for natural food, where demand exceeds supply. HP will also catch carp on food-rich waters, but often will *not* score while mini-baits, sweetcorn and beans, for example, are taking fish.

When preparing high protein baits, some anglers mix with eggs instead of water. Six eggs are usually sufficient to mix 10oz of protein powder. The most widely used constituents are wheatgerm, soya, flour, casein, yeast mixture and, in some cases, gluten (as already stated there are available at least four ready-made protein mixes, each of which, when the price of each individual ingredient is taken into consideration, represents good value for

money). After mixing the eggs and protein powder to a firm paste, roll into balls and boil for about a minute. The result is a bait with a 'skin' that defeats the attentions of any unwanted 'nuisance' fish.

Protein baits are so widely used nowadays that groundbaiting is really unnecessary. Indeed, the trick is to add one or two smells of your own. I have taken to flavouring the bait with a gravy mix or soup stock. This has paid off handsomely, for I have been fortunate enough to land six carp over 20lb, with the best tipping the scales at 29lb 14oz in one season. But remember, there is not,

AT-A-GLANCE

Specimen sizes
Specimen size in carp depends, as in many sea and freshwater species, on the water or area. A 20lb fish is a specimen in a few waters, but, where the average size is small, a 10-pounder qualifies.

Tackle, bait, techniques
Rod
11ft-11½ft fast taper
11ft (1¾lb test)

Reel
Fixed-spool

Line
4lb, 6lb, 8lb (6 or 8 hooks)
10lb (No 4 carp hooks)
15lb snaggy waters

Hooks
6, 8 for particle baits
4, or low-water salmon hooks

Baits
Worm, sausage, cheese, many tinned meats, natural baits, seeds, particle baits, with flavouring or binding agents

Groundbait
All hookbaits, occasionally with swimfeeders

Methods, techniques
Float-fishing, ledgering, freelining

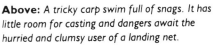

Above: *A tricky carp swim full of snags. It has little room for casting and dangers await the hurried and clumsy user of a landing net.*

and never will be, an ultimate bait.

Finally, a couple of bait preparation tips. If I want to fish a soft bait at long range I begin by rolling the mix into a dozen or so balls, each weighing about an ounce. Afterwards I put them into the freezer and leave them there until I go fishing, when I take them to the lake in a vacuum flask to preserve their hardness. They are hooked by threading the line through the hard bait with a baiting needle. The hook is then tied on and drawn back into the bait. No other weight is required and the bait—remember it weighs about 1oz—is easily cast the required distance. Now, here is the bonus: just a few minutes after coming to rest on the bottom, the frozen bait becomes soft again and even at long range the hook is set quite easily on the strike.

Alternatively, soft baits can be mixed at the lakeside. This is done by using the lake water to mix the paste—a growing habit with the carp angler—and by using a small piece of ballpoint pen tube to prevent the line splitting the bait.

17

Barbel

Hot or cold, day or night, summer or winter, barbel are there for the catching if you just know how and where to look, how and what to bait up, how and when to strike

Once the angler hooks his first barbel he will find himself equally hooked on barbel fishing. The sheer power and strength of this stubborn fighter has to be experienced to be believed. Salmon anglers who have inadvertently taken barbel all agree that, weight for weight, there is little to choose between the two.

First, when are the chances greatest? The barbel once had the reputation of being solely a summer- and autumn-only species. Of course summer and autumn are regularly productive, but late autumn and early winter can be equally rewarding for the keen angler. In fact, several of the most successful Thames and Kennet barbel experts consider October right through to early December as *the* time for the really exceptional specimens. Whatever the time of year, the key factors that control the barbel's feeding pattern are air and water temperature, coupled with flow and water level.

To some degree, the hotter it is the more a barbel feeds. In the sizzling summer of 1976, when the Thames and Kennet were as low as ever and water temperatures soared well into the record eighties, the barbel fed with predictable and clockwork regularity.

There is very little evidence to suggest that there is an upper water-temperature limit. As with most other species, settled conditions are important—any wild fluctuation in temperature, wind, flow or level is not conducive to good fishing. Here, the barbel is particularly sensitive.

In winter, the water temperature does become more critical. There has now been sufficient evidence gathered by observant anglers to establish the minimum feeding temperature. This critical level is thought to be about 5·6° (42°F) or under, but at 7·1°C (45°F) and above the chances are excellent. So the reason why November, and even December, can be so productive is that there are far more days and nights when the water temperature is within feeding range.

Left: *Mick Mulhearn with a barbel caught from the Ouse in Yorkshire. Steadily flowing water over a gravel or clay (not mud) river bed offers the best chances.*

When to fish for barbel

From January to mid-February, when winter usually begins to bite, there will be few, if any, opportunities when conditions are right. Then, from mid-February until the end of the season, the chances are on the increase, particularly for the angler who lives close to the river (or knows someone who does) and can therefore take advantage of opportunities at short notice.

Having established that the barbel is a fish of all seasons, what time of day is best? Again, it is difficult to generalize for barbel have been caught in the darkest of nights and during the brightest summer day. The general concensus of opinion among successful anglers is that barbel fishing is most consistently productive during the hour or so before, and subsequent two hours after dark.

Barbel in summer

In summer, barbel will sometimes feed on and off throughout the night, but often there will be a dead spot of, perhaps, two hours from 2300 hours to about 0100, while in the winter an evening session will invariably end before midnight. But do not fall into the trap of thinking that the feeding habits of the barbel are strictly nocturnal. The middle part of the day in summer and autumn often produces a short spell of frenzied feeding activity, but catching them then is difficult. The night-time approach is relatively simple, for the barbel at this time tends to be less cautious than in daytime. Tactics, baits and methods tend therefore to be finer and more sophisticated during the day.

Locating barbel swims comes slowly with hard-won experience. Reading a stretch of river is an art that cannot be acquired overnight. In summer and autumn, when rivers are low and sluggish, barbel tend to prefer the faster and well-oxygenated places such as weir pools. These places have often been favoured by traditionalist barbel anglers, but the fish are difficult to locate in them.

But barbel are not always found in the fastest, most turbulent water. In summer they do prefer water with a bit of 'push', but there must be a

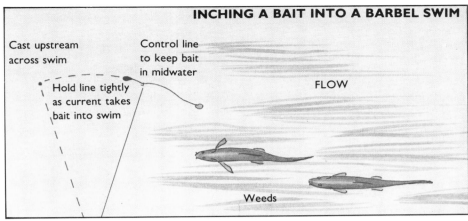

INCHING A BAIT INTO A BARBEL SWIM

Cast upstream across swim

Control line to keep bait in midwater

Hold line tightly as current takes bait into swim

FLOW

Weeds

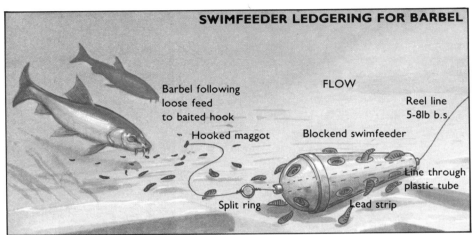

SWIMFEEDER LEDGERING FOR BARBEL

Barbel following loose feed to baited hook

FLOW

Reel line 5-8lb b.s.

Hooked maggot

Blockend swimfeeder

Line through plastic tube

Split ring

Lead strip

Top: *Steering a bait into a shallow hotspot without disturbing the fish or snagging weed.*
Above: *For precision feeding with maggots, an open or blocked swimfeeder is indispensible*
Below: *Feeling for bites with the fingers is the most sensitive method of bite detection. All the mechanical methods, floats, swing and quivertips, bobbins, all have a slight time lag for the angler. But his fingers detect the slightest twitch instantly.*

steady flow without turbulence and back-eddies. During summer, the barbel tend to steer clear of the more open stretches in daytime. In the Kennet, for instance, they are found holed up among the dense beds of streamer weed, while in the Thames they will be down among the underwater 'cabbages'. As darkness falls, the barbel will venture out into the open stretches in search of food.

Like trout, barbel prefer swift, well-oxygenated water, although they can survive in water with low temperatures and oxygen levels where trout would perish. They settle just below the trout zones.

Baits for daytime barbel

To catch these holed-up, daytime fish is not easy; stealth and delicate bait-presentation are needed. Small baits, such as maggots, are often best, and to present them effectively fine tackle and small hooks are needed—but a 3lb b.s. line and No 16 hook are of little use to heaving a 9lb barbel from dense weed. So the angler new to barbel fishing should make a start in the late evening and night, in the more open swims.

Having established the importance of a nice, steady flow, what other basic factors should the would-be barbel catcher look for? undoubtedly these fish prefer swims with a hard bottom, not necessarily gravel, and undercut clay banks are a regular haunt.

Relatively deep swims with a steady flow are usually a good bet, particularly under the near bank. Further experience will reveal that each swim has a particular hotspot.

Barbel hotspots

Like carp, barbel have the fascinating habit of rolling (and occasionally leaping), but a rolling barbel may not be a feeding barbel. However, when consistent rolling is seen it is often indication of a hotspot and sooner or later it will produce fish.

To recap: in summer, be on the look-out for swims with above-average current and, after heavy rains, the barbel will often feed well

when the level is on the way up. In winter almost the reverse situation applies: the slower-than-average stretches need to be noted. A fast-rising, coloured river is not good, but when it is fining down, and during a mild spell, conditions will be more or less ideal.

Wind, or rather the lack of it, is another factor to watch. Blustery conditions are to be avoided, while

LONG-TAILED LINK LEDGER

Buoyant bait rises to bigger barbel feeding above smaller ones

FLOW

Longer hook link up to 36in

Above: *How a standard link ledger can be modified and given buoyancy by conversion into a long-tailed link ledger. The fish responses of the moment must be considered to arrive at the extra hook length.* **Right:** *Cross section of a productive barbel swim.*

Below: *Fishing into a swim overshadowed by bushes on the River Ure. The bait is sausage meat (inset). Providing the water is deep, and pushing on vigorously, there is more chance here than in the centre of the river.*

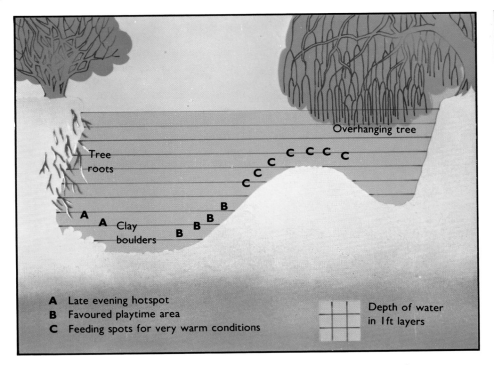

A Late evening hotspot
B Favoured playtime area
C Feeding spots for very warm conditions

Overhanging tree

Tree roots

Clay boulders

Depth of water in 1ft layers

still, muggy days or nights are often mostly productive.

Ledgering by day or night is by far the most effective method, and the beginner will be well advised to start this way. Essential tackle is an 11ft hollow-glass rod with a test-curve of $1\frac{1}{2}$lb, combined with a reliable fixed-spool reel holding line between 6 and 9lb b.s., depending on conditions. A weight attached to a 6in link and a small swivel is preferable to a weight running direct on the reel line. The distance the link ledger is stopped from the hook depends on the current, the type of bait, and the amount of weed in the swim. Usually this distance will vary between 12 and 18in, but when fishing the gaps in streamer weed you may find that it needs to be doubled.

The beginner should concentrate on well-proven meaty baits such as sausage or luncheon meat. Use hook sizes between 10 and 4, depending on the size of bait. Avoid meat baits with a high fat or gristle content; the lumps can prevent the hook penetrating. The most effective method of detecting barbel bites is to hold the rod and feel for them with line held between thumb and forefinger. At the same time, watch the rod top for movements. At night a beam from a torch on to the rod tip is a major asset and it does not appear to scare fish. But it must not be flashed on and off into the water.

For the novice perhaps the most important matter is the identification of barbel bites on the ledger, for they can vary enormously. Most barbel bites are quite characteristic and fall into four predominant types:

1. The 'rod-wrencher'. Without warning, this pulls the rod top right round almost wrenching the rod from your hands. The fish invariably hooks itself, yet occasionally it is missed, leaving the angler dazed.

2. The slow 'steady pull' that moves the tip round a few inches, sometimes preceded by a characteristic gentle 'tap-tap'. These are bites from confidently feeding barbel.

3. The sudden 'lunge'. This is a very strong, but all-too-short pull that needs lightning reflexes from the angler. A frustrating bite, nearly always missed and probably the result of the barbel feeling something suspicious. The sudden 'lunge' bite often arises from the barbel being scared by the terminal tackle. It can be caused by the use of too light a weight. Many times, the angler has been told to use 'just enough weight to hold bottom'. But in a strong flow the weight and terminal tackle will bounce along the bottom as soon as a barbel mouths the bait. So use a weight that really holds, it is less likely to scare the fish.

4. The 'vibrator'—a series of tiny tweaks and trembles on the line or rod tip when small baits are being used. Occasionally a fish will be hooked when a 'vibrator' is struck at, but the experienced angler will sometimes wait for a more positive pull to develop, for vibrating can be the prelude to a positive take and can last several minutes.

Your tackle must be powerful enough to cope with a hard-fighting barbel. The strength of this fish has led anglers who have hooked a large one to be convinced that they are playing a big salmon. Both of these species inhabit clear, well-oxygenated, strong-flowing rivers.

Crucian carp

The best crucians hide away so effectively that only copious feeding brings them out. Even then they must often be stolen delicately from the small clearings in a snaggy weedbed

Crucian carp are often found in large numbers in small, weedy ponds, but there they are invariably very small and extremely easy to catch. Although they provide an interesting challenge for younger anglers, they do not give the satisfaction which comes from hunting the big crucian—fish of 1½lb plus—found in large lakes.

Lake crucian are shy, secretive fish. They like to have plenty of cover, and the best spots to look for them are those with an abundance of weed and lilies. During the warm months of the year it is often possible to catch half a dozen or more crucian in a dawn or dusk session, using simple float tackle, casting out a bait to lie in a tiny hole cut in the weeds or alongside a margin of lily pads, and groundbaiting lightly but often. Patches of bubbles are a good indication of feeding crucian.

Groundbaiting
Prebaiting a swim for long periods prior to fishing has proved a most effective means of attracting various species of fish, yet strangely it is a method that rarely works with crucian carp. Perhaps the reason is that crucians are not great wanderers, preferring to remain in a rather limited territory. Nevertheless, modest prebaiting with sample hookbaits, a couple of hours before a fishing session, can certainly improve your catches.

If an early morning session is planned, it is well worth selecting a swim on the previous evening and introducing a mashed up loaf of bread, together with a couple of handfuls of maggots or sweetcorn. By early morning the swim should show a pronounced colour together with the tell-tale bubbles that indicate feeding fish have moved into the area.

Don't frighten the shoal by throwing in further groundbait; that won't be necessary. Simply tackle up (well away from the water's edge), then drop your breadflake- or maggot-baited hook into the middle of the largest patch of bubbles. Results should be immediate and prolonged as, by the time you arrive, the fish will be feeding with incautious abandon on bread and maggot.

Although the fishing technique is quite straightforward, however, it is not nearly so easy to pinpoint likely spots. Not all potential crucian swims contain them at the same time, for the species tends to shoal in quite confined areas, and to move together from one area to the next, according to the availability of food and weather conditions.

The most productive swims are probably those well sheltered from prevailing winds. In such a swim, in the summertime, with a water temperature between 62°F (17°C) and 68°F (20°C), there is always a good chance of catching crucian between first light and midmorning. The peak feeding period generally occurs during the hour following the sun first hitting the water. Bites tail off towards the end of the morning and usually cease completely in the middle part of the day. In the evening, after the sun has left the water, there is a second main feeding spell which lasts until full darkness.

On overcast, humid days, it is possible to keep a shoal of crucian feeding all through the forenoon, and sometimes the afternoon too, by light but frequent groundbaiting.

When the weather turns very hot and the water temperature rises over the 70°F (21°C) mark, crucian leave the sheltered swims for deeper, cooler water, and areas exposed to light winds and breezes. Swims in these parts of a lake provide par-

ticularly good fishing between late evening and early morning, and a coldish dawn offers the ideal chance of making a big catch.

As well as seeking the shelter of weedbeds and lilypads, crucians often take refuge by the dozen in a sunken tree, some of them fish of specimen proportions. Casting alongside these sunken lairs can prove to be tricky, but the spectacular results far outweigh the loss of a couple of hooks. Needless to say, the tackle needs to be stepped up somewhat to prevent the fish bolting into the jungle of sunken branches. Choose a more robust carp rod with 5-6lb line, and apply an uncompromising sidestrain as soon as you have made the strike.

By contrast, an extended spell of hot, dry, windless weather can cause a complete reversal of normal

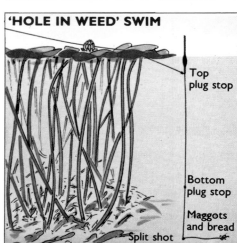

'HOLE IN WEED' SWIM

Top plug stop

Bottom plug stop

Maggots and bread

Split shot

feeding habits. In these conditions, although crucian will splash and cruise the surface above the groundbait at night, they do not feed when it is dark because the oxygen content of the water in their weedy habitat is temporarily too low. Instead, they indulge in bouts of feeding in the middle of the day, when the oxygen content is highest, regardless of the brightness and a water temperature perhaps exceeding 75°F (24°C).

Crucian carp—particularly exceptionally big specimens—are notable fighters, yet once the fast and powerful initial run has been brought under control, patience and steady pressure will bring one to the net. Indeed, a crucian will often run away from weeds and snags, rather than towards them, so tackle strength can be kept to a minimum.

A suitable outfit consists of a 12ft float rod with good tip action, a fixed-spool or centrepin reel loaded with 3lb or 4lb b.s. line, and size 10-14 eyed hooks. For night fishing it is advisable to step this up to a 10-11ft Avon-action rod and line with a 5lb breaking strain.

Crucian are caught on freeline and ledger methods, but by far the best means of detecting their sensitive bite is a float. The ideal type is a balsa-bodied, self-cocking antenna, with the antenna—of about 6in—painted black and white and tipped with a red blob for maximum visibility at dawn and dusk.

The typical crucian bite is rather like that of a small eel: the float dips, rises, moves off first in one direction and then in another, perhaps taking as long as five minutes before it finally slides under.

CRUCIAN FLOAT RIG

Left: *An antenna float is all set to transmit a crucian bite on this Berkshire stillwater.*
Below and below left: *The plug stops are set according to depth and the rig cast in at the edge of the weedhole.*

Plastic plug stop

Plastic plug stop

Plastic plug stop

Red surface band

Plastic plug stop

Cocking weight

Swivel

Split shot 6in from hook

Size 10-14 eyed hook

AT-A-GLANCE

Specimen sizes
Although at least six crucians over 4½lb have been recorded since 1972, and the British record stands at 5lb 10½oz, any crucian over 2lb must be considered to be a specimen.

Tackle, Bait, Techniques
Rod
11ft thin-walled, fast-taper (approx. 11lb test). 13ft match (for long-range float fishing)

Reel
Fixed-spool

Line b.s.
3–5lb

Hooks
Size 8 (fine-wire) to 12

Baits
Sausage paste, crust, flake, worm, maggot, particle baits, processed catfood

Groundbaits
Hookbaits

Techniques
Float, freeline, ledger

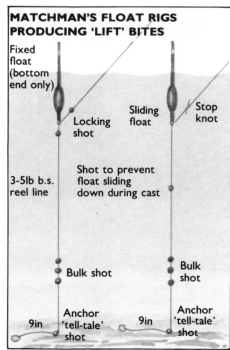

MATCHMAN'S FLOAT RIGS PRODUCING 'LIFT' BITES

Fixed float (bottom end only)

Locking shot

Sliding float

Stop knot

3-5lb b.s. reel line

Shot to prevent float sliding down during cast

Bulk shot

Bulk shot

Anchor 'tell-tale' shot

9in

9in

Anchor 'tell-tale' shot

Dace

One of the most active of our freshwater fishes, but a half-pounder is a specimen to be talked about

Dace will take most baits offered to roach at one time or another, according to prevailing circumstances. Bread baits, including paste, crust, crumb and flake, are popular, and cereals such as wheat, hemp, or tares also account for large bags, especially in winter, when insect life is less easily found by the fish. Many anglers like to groundbait the swim with hemp, while using elderberry on the hook. This is worthwhile, as the fish hang on to the bait a little longer, giving the angler fractionally more time to synchronize his strike with the disappearance of the float.

In summer, maggots, caddis grubs, woodlice, earwigs, or freshwater shrimps and worms are all good dace baits, and the angler must experiment to see which best suits existing conditions and the whims of the fish on a particular day.

Almost any float or ledgering method can be employed, according to preferences and the water fished, but the sparing use of groundbait is always useful for attracting shoals to the vicinity.

The style for large rivers
On large rivers such as the Thames, Severn, or Trent, where the stream is both broad and deep, float fishing fine and far off is an excellent style, well-suited for taking good bags. Tackle must be carefully selected: the float should be as light as possible to suit the weight of the current and the distances to be cast. It must also be heavy enough to be controllable at a distance and at the same time provide good visibility when it suddenly dips out of sight.

In such situations most experienced anglers prefer to use a centrepin rather than a fixed-spool reel. This is because it maintains closer contact with the float, permitting a more im-

mediate reaction and a swifter strike. A 4in diameter reel drum is suitable, and this must be smooth and free-running to allow the line to trickle freely off as the pull of the stream dictates. Once contact is made with the shoal, the angler can usually take several fish before the bites cease. He must then adjust his float to locate the depth at which the shoal has settled, and be prepared to repeat this throughout the day as

these fickle fish alter their level in the water.

In a shallow river, especially where the water is clear, the angler must take good care not be seen. A favourite strategy is to locate feeding shoals by eye and then select a suitable pitch well upstream, preferably with a good weedbed between the angler and the fish. A few maggots are tossed in as groundbait and the angler then wades out a lit-

Right: *Wading, with reeds behind him to break up his outline, the angler trots for dace.*
Below: *The trotting rig has an artificial caddis as bait. Two nymphs are also shown. The ledger rig is braided with maggot.*
Bottom: *The dace zone is broadly between the slow bream stretch and the faster barbel reach. But dace will also move upstream, and rarely drop downriver to where the temperature of the water may well reach over 20°C (68°F).*

RIVER NYMPHS

2 No 4

2 No 4

BB shot

Light balsa float

TROTTING RIG

No 8

2 No 4

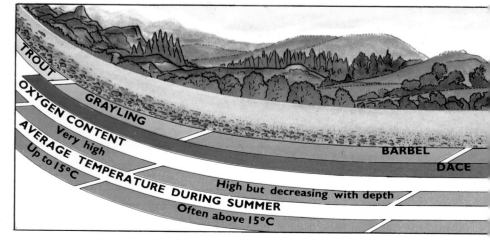

TROUT

OXYGEN CONTENT
Very high

GRAYLING

AVERAGE TEMPERATURE DURING SUMMER
Up to 15°C

High but decreasing with depth

BARBEL

DACE

Often above 15°C

tle, pegs down his keepnet in the margins and starts to fish. If he can wade as far as midstream he does so, stirring up the bottom gently to get a little colour into the water downstream. The maggots are held in a cloth bag with small holes in each end, which the angler ties to his waist to provide a regular trickle of maggots into the stream. This keeps the fish interested and on the alert to snap up offered hookbait.

Cast lightly downstream

The angler then casts lightly downstream a few yards to enable adjustment of his tackle for depth. Once the tackle is properly set, he casts downstream, trotting the bait down to the fish. As it approaches weedbeds he checks the line momentarily to swing the bait up over the weed, then resumes the trot down to the waiting shoals. Bites are fast and furious so long as the fish do not suspect his presence. He makes sure of this by retrieving line swiftly with taps on the drum, rather than by winding the handle, in order to remove hooked fish from the shoal with as little disturbance as possible.

A further alternative, both in deep, heavy water or in shallow streams, is to use ledger tackle. A light swivelled pear weight stopped by shot 18in from the hook and used in conjunction with a fixed-spool reel, enables accurate casting to the fish. In shallow waters the angler casts above the shoals, raising the rod tip so that the ledger weight rolls down toward them, although ground-baiting will bring the fish up towards the bait if necessary. The rod tip is kept in direct contact with the light line, and, fishing by touch, the angler prepares to meet the swift bites with an equally speedy strike.

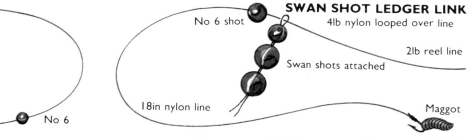

SWAN SHOT LEDGER LINK

No 6 shot
4lb nylon looped over line
2lb reel line
Swan shots attached
18in nylon line
No 6
Maggot

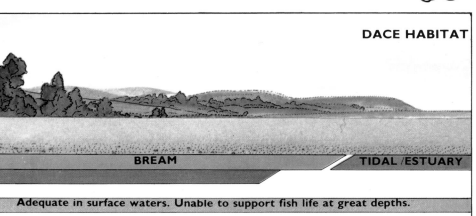

DACE HABITAT

BREAM

TIDAL /ESTUARY

Adequate in surface waters. Unable to support fish life at great depths.

Often up to 20°C and higher

Often above 20°C

AVOIDING NUISANCE FISH

The use of a bait dropper for select fishing

Loose feed thrown in to distract small fish

Bait dropper

Eel

For anglers, the eel has more nuisance value than most fish. But the rare specimen puts up a terrific fight

For many years knowing anglers have suggested that the long-standing 8lb 10oz record held by Alan Dust was not really representative of the growth potential of the eel. This belief was substantiated in 1978 by the 'surprise' new record eel of 11lb 2oz caught by Stephen Terry from Kingfisher Lake in Hampshire.

This will be an exceedingly difficult record to beat, even though there is little doubt that bigger eels exist: a 20-pounder is certainly within the realms of possibility.

It is much more difficult to single out waters that do *not* hold eels than it is to find water that do. Nearly every stretch of river, canals, lake, gravel-pit, and even the tiniest village pond will have, with certainty, an eel population.

If you are happy to catch quantities of medium-sized eels, say from 1lb to 3½lb, your best bet will be to concentrate on slow rivers, drains and canals. Slow rivers such as the Great Ouse and the Fen Drains have a big eel population, and such waters provide an ideal training-ground for the angler who eventually intends to hunt the really big ones. When I was in my teens I certainly spent quite a number of exciting and invaluable nights catching eels on the river Ouse at places like St Neot's, Offord and Little Paxton.

Productive thundery nights

In my experience, warm, clammy, thundering nights are the most productive. Avoid clear and moonlit nights: they are uncomfortable and cold to fish in and the eels do not like them either.

If you can, choose a night with plenty of cloud-cover—in my opinion the darker the better. Again, analysing my own records and those of

others, the darkest period of the night is the most productive. For carp, tench and bream there is often a 'dead' patch of an hour or so in the very middle of the night—in July and August usually between 1am and 2am or thereabouts. It is this very dead spot that has so often produced a spate of eel runs.

Having established that night fishing is essential for big eels, ledgering in some form or other is the most reliable and effective technique. On small lakes and ponds or canals where the eels can be tempted at close range, it will obviously pay to keep the terminal tackle as simple as possible, so freelining should be used if possible. However, nearly all my eeling is done at a reasonable distance—between 20 and 60 yards—so a weight of some kind is essential.

What about the basics such as rods, reels, and lines? Depending on the snagginess or clarity of the water, the rod has to be pretty powerful and I would suggest a 'stepped-up', hollow glass carp-type rod with a test curve of between 1¾ and 2½lb, and between 10½ and 11½ft in length. Accordingly, line-strength will be in the 8-13lb b.s. range. I use a Mitchell 300 for most of my stillwater fishing, and it is important in this case not to skimp but to buy 200 yards of line (in one length, of course) and fill the spool to the top

Above: *Stephen Terry with his 11lb 2oz record rod-caught eel.*
Below: *Bob Church cradles a 5½lb eel taken on lobworm from the Grand Union Canal.*

of the lip. It aids casting distance.

Whether I fish with worms or deadbaits, I stick to two basic terminal rigs. For medium-distance casting—say, up to 40 yards—I use a weight direct on the reel line stopped by a small swivel 12-16in from the hook. For longer-range ledgering where one has to 'whack' the bait out, the weight tends to overtake the bait in flight which sometimes results in twists or tangles. Here I use a weight, paternoster-style, on a fairly long link attached to a swivel,

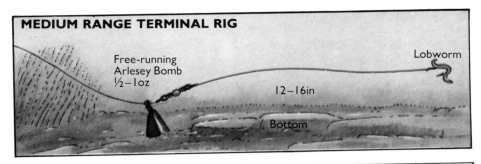

MEDIUM RANGE TERMINAL RIG

Free-running
Arlesey Bomb
½–1oz

Lobworm

12–16in

Bottom

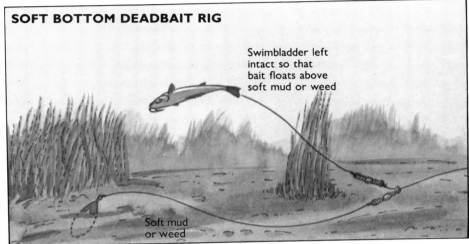

SOFT BOTTOM DEADBAIT RIG

Swimbladder left
intact so that
bait floats above
soft mud or weed

Soft mud
or weed

and again stopped on the reel line by a second swivel. I find that this rig reduces considerably the chances of a twist-up—the weight draws the bait in its flight-path.

Arlesey bombs every time
In all cases I use Arlesey bombs ranging from ½-1oz. Experience has also indicated that in the case of the link-paternoster the link strength should be slightly greater than that of the hook line. For example, if a 10lb b.s. line is used, then I attach my Arlesey bomb to 18in of 13-15lb b.s. nylon.

Some people question the use of a swivel as a ledger-stop on the grounds that it will marginally reduce the overall tackle strength. This is true, but when you are using lines of 10lb b.s. or more, it is not such a critical factor. However, a swivel is an almost 100 per cent efficient ledger-stop and as such is difficult to better. My fishing time is precious, so I cannot afford to have a bait out for hours with the weight wedged hard against it—it would reduce my chances somewhat!

Other than the basic items of comfort such as chair-beds, brollies, waterproofs and so on, it is essential

to have a large and deep small-mesh landing-net. I would suggest a minimum diameter of 24in and a minimum depth of 3ft 6in.

Bite indication is straightforward. If you are the keyed-up stay-awake type you need no more than a loop of silver foil over the line between the butt-ring and the reel; but if, like me, you prefer to nod off, or at least relax, then an audible indicator is required. Most eel fishers use at least two rods, so a pair of Heron-type antenna electric bite alarms are almost essential. Whichever indicator you use, it must put up the absolute minimum of resistance to a taking eel. Contrary to popular belief eels are very sensitive to resistance and have a very acute sense of 'feel'—even though they can very easily drag in the rod!

The golden rule is to leave the pick-up of the reel in the 'open' position so that a running eel can peel off the line without feeling any resistance. Also make sure the rods are rested (as when carp fishing) above an area that is free of undergrowth or twigs that can interfere with the line running off the spool. Play it safe and use a pegged-down plastic sheet below the reels.

AT-A-GLANCE

Specimen size
Frank Guttfield considers a 4 or 5lb eel to be of specimen size. But a new rod-caught eel record of 11lb 2oz was established in mid-1978. The author feels 20lb eels are probable.

Tackle, Bait, Techniques
Rod
10½-11½ft stepped-up carp-type rod in hollow glass, with a test of 1¾-2½lb.

Reel
Fixed-spool

Line b.s.
8-13lb

Hooks
Carp hooks, sizes 2-4

Bait
Small deadbaits—bleak, rudd, gudgeon—lobworms, foot of freshwater mussel, all threaded on to hook.

Groundbait
Chopped deadbaits, worms, freshwater mussels.

Methods, techniques
Ledgering, freelining

Bait concoctions
There are all manner of recipes and concoctions for hook baits and groundbaits, but after a great deal of experimenting I am afraid I still have most confidence in the well-proven text-book baits. These, for me, in order of preference are:
1. Small dead fish, 3-5in long, freshly killed or sometimes frozen. Bleak, rudd, or gudgeon, I am not fussy.
2. Two lobworms—again fresh, not 'off'. 3. The 'foot' portion of a freshwater mussel.

For deadbaiting I usually thread the fish on the line with a baiting needle before tying on the hook, the hook protruding out of the mouth. I then place an AA shot on the line adjacent to the vent to prevent the bait slipping up the line in flight.

Grayling

Bridging the gulf between coarse and game angling, the grayling—the 'lady of the stream'—has come to be appreciated only since pollution has made it a rarity in most waters

It is a good idea when grayling fishing to take both a long rod with a fixed-spool reel and also fly fishing tackle, a light 9ft trout fly rod with a No 5 or No 6 line. Sometimes one outfit is called for, sometimes the other, and it is then possible to change from one to the other, and if necessary back again, in the course of a day's fishing, as the behaviour of the grayling changes. The only time to despair is when a chalk-stream is running dirty; then grayling are nearly impossible to catch on any bait or by any method.

Ledgering

Ledgering is a much neglected method of catching grayling. Try it in very cold conditions, or when fishing a deep short swim or a very swirly place where controlling float tackle would be difficult. Use an Arlesey bomb of suitable size, or a string of closely spaced shot on a nylon link. There are various bite indicators which can be used, but perhaps the best is to hold the rod and feel for bites by holding the line between butt-ring and reel in the fingers. The ledger stop should be about 12in from the hook.

In some rivers, a kind of cross between coarse fishing and fly fishing catches grayling. This is the so-called grasshopper method, in which a strange device called a grasshopper is used. As that eminent Victorian angler, Francis Francis, said, it looks more like a gooseberry than a grasshopper, consisting of a heavily leaded No 6 hook with alternative turns of green and yellow wool bound on over the lead base, the whole being shaped rather like a maggot, only much bigger. It is usually fished with two or three real maggots on the hook as well, and the technique is to use a long rod and bump it about the bottom of deep places. The author cannot succeed with it despite repeated tries in Hampshire, catching only unwanted large trout. But it has a great reputation in some districts.

Flies for grayling

Grayling eat many insects and are thus very vulnerable to fly fishing. A curious folklore has grown up about fly fishing for them, involving the use of tiny fancy fly patterns, mostly garish and tied on tiny hooks and usually fished on an ultra-fine leader point. Such flies as Red Tag, Rolts Witch and Green Insect will certainly catch grayling, but when these fish are clearly to be seen taking real insects at the surface, the author feels that the best flies to use are imitations of those insects. Fish, in fact, exactly as you would for trout, with fly patterns imitating the hatching insects.

The only difference between trout and grayling is that if you strike at a take by a trout and miss, you will seldom obtain a second take from the same fish to the same fly. A grayling, on the other hand, will often give you a second and even a third chance.

Many anglers advise a special type of float, a much finer line, and a much smaller hook to catch gray-ling. These can be used but you will catch no more grayling by doing so.

In a smooth, even swim, a por-cupine quill float carrying about three BB shot is usually right; while for water full of swirls and eddies, choose a goose quill or a simple balsa float carrying four or five BB shot with a good inch of its top above the surface. Set the float so that the hook goes down the swim about 2in above the bottom and simply let it go down in the ordinary way, keep-ing the line reasonably straight bet-ween rod tip and float as you do so.

Baits

Maggots will usually catch plenty of grayling, but sometimes small red-worms will do better. The kind you want are those you find at the bot-tom of compost heaps, very old manure heaps or well-rotted lawn mowings. They are called cockspur worms and are usually about $1\frac{1}{2}$-2in long. It does not matter how you put them on the hook. Throw a couple of loose worms or, if you are using them, a dozen or more maggots into the swim every few minutes. Pieces of breadcrust or pinched-on new crumb will also often catch grayling, especially in the chalkstreams of Hampshire and Wiltshire. They seem less effective in the rain-fed rivers of the North or West Midlands, but they will catch gray-ling anywhere at times.

An alternative, when you are float fishing, is to use an artificial nymph or shrimp instead of a baited hook. Both are weighted, and the shrimp, in particular, has a lot of lead built into it, which must be allowed for when shotting the float. The techni-que when using nymph or shrimp is a little different from normal float tactics. Allow the tackle to travel a few yards down the swim, then check it firmly, which will cause the shrimp or nymph to swing up and away from the bottom. Hold the float for two or three seconds, then let it resume its normal position and go a couple of yards down the swim, then check it again, and so on till the downstream end of the swim is reached. The bite comes while the float is being checked and the ar-tificial nymph or shrimp is rising in the water; it is usually a sudden and positive take.

Above: *Bob float and redworm — traditional grayling tackle.*
Right: *Reg Righyni trots the River Nidd for grayling. These clear, fast-moving Yorkshire rivers afford the oxygen the species needs in order to thrive.*

FLOAT RIG

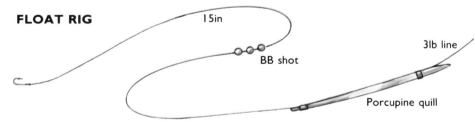

15in

BB shot

3lb line

Porcupine quill

Left: *Arthur Oglesby nets a grayling from the River Nidd, Yorkshire.*
Inset: *The patterns of artificial flies which account for catches of grayling are found in most fly boxes. Grayling, which swim deep, are less likely to rise to a dry fly (unless a tempting hatch coincides with your fishing). The leaded nymph and artificial shrimp are virtually interchangeable; their use in float-fishing is shown right.*

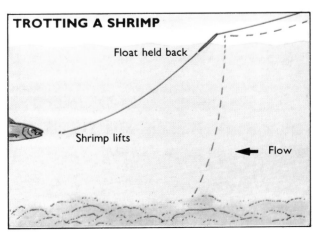

TROTTING A SHRIMP

Float held back

Shrimp lifts

Flow

Perch

A fighting beauty, the perch is probably the most popular of all our freshwater fishes. It is a worthy adversary

Few fish catch the imagination quite so much as the colourful perch, *Perca fluviatilis*, which is interesting because the perch is not one of our bigger species, growing to 4lb only rarely. It is a relatively small and crafty predator, unlike all our others. With no other species is the difference between young and old fish so marked. Baby perch are gullible to an astonishing degree, engulfing with enthusiasm lobworms as big as themselves and seemingly ignoring or unaware of bankside disturbance. On the other hand, large perch may well be about the most difficult fish in freshwater to catch, certainly with any degree of predictability or regularity.

The perch does not grow into a heavyweight so rods present no problems. For short-range fishing a 10-11ft Avon rod, carrying a line of 3-5lb line is about right, while in some circumstances it is good, but not essential, to use a long, hollow-glass matchman's rod for swinging out a lobworm on float tackle into water lilies, for example. For long-range ledgering a Mark IV carp rod is about right while a fly rod, too, can be most useful. Choice of reel is easy; any good quality fixed-spool reel, or centrepin for short-range fishing or trotting.

A worm suspended under a float is one of the traditional ways of catching perch and it is as good today as ever it was. Usually the float was a porcupine or crow quill and the angler searched likely perch lies against camp sheeting—not so common now. Man-made features, though, such as jetties, the stonework of bridges, parts of weirs or culverts seem to attract perch shoals. They also congregate near natural features such as sidestream junctions, sharp changes in slope on

Above: *Perhaps an unwise move, for the very active perch will not settle down in the folds of a keepnet for long.*

Below: *Accurate casting, plus careful tackle control are the essentials for trotting along reed from the far bank.*

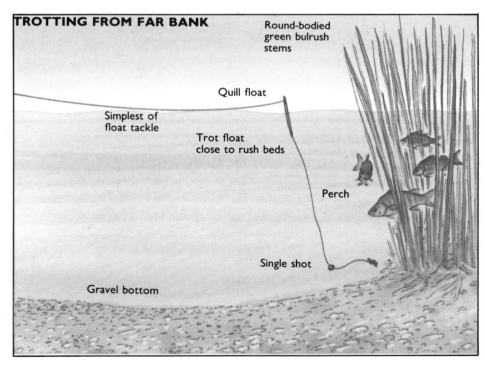

TROTTING FROM FAR BANK

Round-bodied green bulrush stems

Quill float

Simplest of float tackle

Trot float close to rush beds

Perch

Single shot

Gravel bottom

gravel pits, sunken trees and logs —anywhere other than stretches of flat, uniform water.

The roving perch angler
One of the great pleasures of perch fishing is to take a bag of worms and the bare essentials of tackle, and walk from spot to spot dropping the worm into each likely hole. If the water is relatively shallow, up to 5ft deep, it is wise to have either a self-

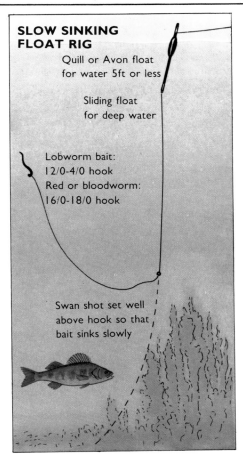

SLOW SINKING FLOAT RIG

Quill or Avon float for water 5ft or less

Sliding float for deep water

Lobworm bait:
12/0-4/0 hook
Red or bloodworm:
16/0-18/0 hook

Swan shot set well above hook so that bait sinks slowly

Left: *A buoyant, mid-water bait which does not involve the gathering of small fish as livebait is a large lobworm injected with air. Single-hooked, the worm's movements will give it an attractive and enticing 'waggle'.*

wriggle rather than a bunched-up offering. It is difficult to advise about striking. Usually the float makes a preliminary sudden dive. Wait for it to come up and then slide away. If it doesn't come up, strike!

The author has taken large bags of perch by wandering from hole to hole but it sometimes pays not to move on too quickly. One can often find a big shoal of perch and the larger specimens may only come after a lot of fishing. 'Small ones first, larger ones later', is often the rule after a quiet spell.

Sometimes it is necessary to get the bait right among the rush and reed stems. A self-cocking float is ideal, very smoothly rubbered at both ends, or attached at one end only. A bait sinking very close to the stems may be taken, while one only a foot away is ignored, probably because the perch are lurking in the weeds. On some small rivers, a long rod is an advantage for dropping baits into these positions, as it is for stret-pegging, which is also effective at times.

Now for other livebaits—small fish. Maggots will not be introduced here for the methods are the same as for any other species. One thing to remember is that when using a single maggot the arrival of perch in the swim is often signalled by a lightning dip of the float, which you promptly miss. But of small live baits, the soft-bodied fishes (minnow, gudgeon, and loach) are far better than harder or spiny baits (sticklebacks, perch, roach, rudd and so on). A big minnow or small gudgeon is ideal—one can even use roach or rudd. In fact, perch weighing anything above 3oz take small gudgeon and minnows.

Small trebles, no wire
A wire trace is not needed and for hooks you want a large single or very small trebles. Baits and tackle will on occasion be lost to pike but not to perch. It is a mistake to think that small perch will avoid live fish. They do not. When float fishing for

AT-A-GLANCE

Specimen sizes
Although many fish of over 5lb have been taken, the record stands at 4lb 12oz. A perch of over half this weight is a specimen; one of over 3lb is rare, particularly since the late 1960s when a widespread disease ravaged the species.

Tackle, Bait, Techniques
Rod
10-12ft glassfibre rod, 1-1½lb test curve

Reel
Fixed-spool

Line b.s.
3-5lb

Hook
4-12 eyed, medium shank

Baits and Lures
Lobworm, brandling, minnow, streamer and other flies, fast-vibrating spoon

Groundbait
Lobworm, maggot, caster

Techniques
Freelining, float-fished minnow or worm, long-range ledgering, link-ledgering, spinning, fly fishing

cocking float or at least the shot well above the hook so that the worm sinks slowly. When it has reached the bottom, or the end of its travel if you are fishing off the bottom, wait a few minutes and then give it a twitch of a few inches. The worm rises enticingly and then slowly sinks again. You can use exactly the same method in deep water, although here one should use a sliding float, for contact and feeling with the bait is dulled.

But which of the many different worms should you use? The lobworm beats all other baits, but at times a small red worm or, alternatively, a brandling, will work quite well. With a big lob you need a larger hook, anything from a No 12 to 4, but with tiny red worms, or even bloodworms, go as small as 16 or 18 as necessary. Sometimes perch will take a very small offering on a very small hook, and then perhaps you should be thinking about staying at the swim and working it up with maggots. Unless a longish cast is required the worm should be hooked once, so that you get a lively

perch you need a slightly larger cork-bodied float than for worming, but not above ½inch in diameter for a circular body. For paternostering with or without the float, use the tiniest of weights (perhaps a swan shot) rather than the ½oz Arlesey bombs that you would use for piking. The reel line need only be around 5lb b.s. and the paternoster link (which is tied to a swivel about 1ft above the bait) should be about 3lb b.s. and 3ft in length.

Spinning
Spinning for perch is an effective method. A wire trace is not needed. Sometimes one may need a celluloid or plastic anti-kink vane fixed on the line about 12-18in above the lure.

Pike

Like a pride of lions, young pike inhabit a home base from which to strike at passing prey. Like lions, too, in old age they lead a lonely, scavenging life, feeding off putrid flesh.

Left: *Jim Tyree with a 12½lb Waveney pike. Sometimes a strong young pike can put up a better fight than a weary old specimen.*

More folklore and complex thinking surrounds the subject of how to fish for pike than any other species. Not all of it is traditional, for a great deal of modern muddled thinking exists. In fact, fishing for pike is a relatively simple matter once you have faced up to a few home truths, unpalatable though these may be.

The prime fallacy is that the pike is a solitary beast—the lone wolf of the fishy world. It is not. Most of the time, the pike the angler fishes for—say over 5lb—is in the company, often close, of other pike. In this way, considerable areas of water may contain nothing but jack, or young, pike. Rather than the lone wolf idea, we should think of the comparison with a pride of lions. We should not compare them with a wolf pack either, for pike rarely hunt as a pack except when they corner unusually large shoals of bait fish.

Lions live as a pride with a home base. Any game which wanders through that area is safe if the lions are not hungry, but meets instant death if they are. Occasionally lions go on the rampage, hunting far and wide, and not necessarily as a pack, or even as a loose group. The pike's behaviour is very similar. Days when big pike seem to be mad to feed throughout a water, are those when their hunting urge has spread them far and wide. Most of the time they frequent a relatively small area, which elsewhere I have referred to as a hotspot.

Feeding patterns

Within a hotspot pike have feeding patterns. Considerable numbers may come on the feed at roughly the same time each day and feed for a very short period. When conditions are adverse—due, for example, to dropping temperature and barometer—only a few pike may respond to the careful angler, but again, it will be at the same time of day.

Generally speaking, these feeding periods last about an hour. In the autumn they tend to be not long after first light with a second (often shorter) period towards dark, often about 1½ hours before nightfall. In the winter the feeding period may be later in the day, often about midday, but generally the extent of feeding is less spectacular, even under good conditions, because water temperatures are lower and metabolic requirements are less.

The fact is, unpalatable though it may be, that you have to get up in the morning and fish hard and long for a day or two until you have the

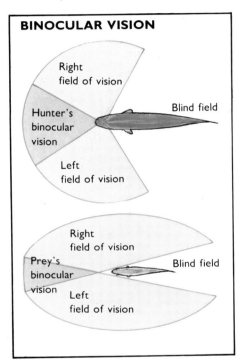

BINOCULAR VISION

Right field of vision

Hunter's binocular vision

Blind field

Left field of vision

Right field of vision

Prey's binocular vision

Blind field

Left field of vision

Above: *As it is a predatory fish, the pike needs a good field of binocular vision to help it judge angles and distances between itself and its prey. Non-predatory fish need less binocular vision because their food is static, but they have wider overall vision to help them evade capture.*

feeding pattern—always assuming that you have found the hotspots in the first place. It should be emphasized strongly that there is nothing quite like sitting in a place you know to be a hotspot, waiting for the feed—you *know* it will happen and that the prize can be yours.

All other problems of rods and tackle pale into insignificance beside those just dealt with. While not implying that there are not several good rods, reels and techniques, let me describe the extremely simple approach that has produced for me more than 600 pike over 10lb in the last 15 years.

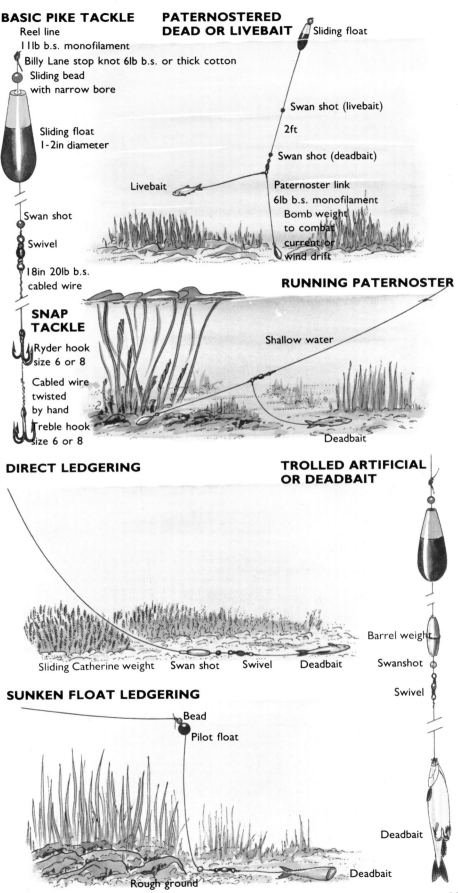

BASIC PIKE TACKLE
Reel line
11lb b.s. monofilament
Billy Lane stop knot 6lb b.s. or thick cotton
Sliding bead with narrow bore

Sliding float 1-2in diameter

Swan shot

Swivel

18in 20lb b.s. cabled wire

SNAP TACKLE
Ryder hook size 6 or 8

Cabled wire twisted by hand

Treble hook size 6 or 8

PATERNOSTERED DEAD OR LIVEBAIT
Sliding float

Swan shot (livebait)

2ft

Swan shot (deadbait)

Livebait

Paternoster link 6lb b.s. monofilament
Bomb weight to combat current or wind drift

RUNNING PATERNOSTER
Shallow water

Deadbait

DIRECT LEDGERING

Sliding Catherine weight   Swan shot   Swivel   Deadbait

SUNKEN FLOAT LEDGERING
Bead
Pilot float

Rough ground   Deadbait

TROLLED ARTIFICIAL OR DEADBAIT

Barrel weight

Swanshot

Swivel

Deadbait

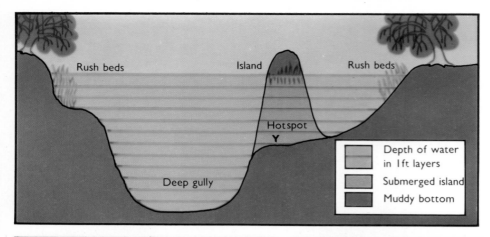

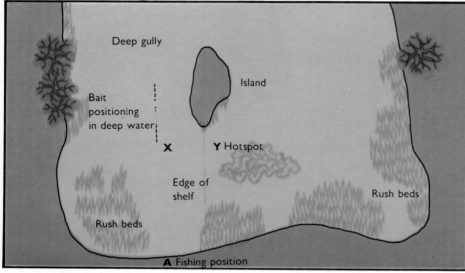

Top: *A profile of Martin Gay's favourite pike lake, Cheshunt, Herts.* **Above:** *The same lake, shown in plan view. Note hot spots, indicated by an X.*

AT-A-GLANCE

Specimen sizes
A pike of over 10lb may be regarded as a specimen in most parts of England and Wales, although 15lb is more appropriate in the Fens and the Broads, and Scottish and Irish lakes.

Tackle, Bait, Techniques
Rod
10-11ft hollow-glass stepped-up carp rod, 2-3lb test curve

Reel
Fixed-spool

Line b.s.
11-15lb; 18lb or more in snaggy waters

Hooks
Bronzed, ring-eyed, extra-strength. Trebles Nos 10-6, singles 2-1/0

Bait
Live coarse fish, dead sea fish

Techniques
Livebaiting, deadbaiting—ledger, float, paternoster-ledger, spinning or drifting with a sliding float

The pike rod

First, the rod. A model like the Mark IV carp rod is too soft, not for playing pike, but for casting the baits so commonly used in piking. However, a stepped-up carp rod is ideal. Several of these are available, in hollow glassfibre, but the best type are those with progressive action as opposed to the tip action associated with fast taper blanks.

Fast taper blanks with a test curve in the range of 2¼-2½lb have their place in piking, for example in firing 2oz weights and small baits a long distance (up to 70 yards). A slow action rod, however, will not only cast heavy deadbaits a long way (4-5oz up to 80 yards in average weather conditions) but can be used for shorter range float paternoster rigs for live and deadbaiting.

Personally, I find a 10ft slow ac-

tion rod ideal for most of my piking, which includes use of artificial baits much of the time. When spinning I would probably use lighter bait casting rods as well, but my concern here is to outline an outfit that can be used with great success and versatility for almost all styles of pike fishing you are likely to encounter.

When considering reels a ruthless approach cuts out thoughts of multipliers and centrepins, and homes in on the versatility of a good quality fixed-spool reel. I use those with roller pick-ups and able to carry 200 yards of 15lb b.s. lines. The b.s. of monofilament line that I normally use is 11-12lb, even for very big pike. Only in heavily weeded or snag-ridden waters would I go up to 14-15lb b.s., although I use 20lb line when trolling. Breaking strains under 11lb considerably increase the

risk of snapping the cast when hurling out 4oz of mackerel for 70 yards, while lines of 14-15lb b.s. drastically reduce distance.

Ancillary pike equipment

Other tackle needed by the pike angler includes a big landing net, and unhooking equipment. If used with great care a pair of long-nosed forceps or very long-nosed pliers will suffice for unhooking a pike. If the fish is sizeable, lay it on its back, sit gently astride it and with a gloved hand pull gently at the tip of its lower jaw. The pike's mouth will open easily and it is a relatively simple matter to remove the hooks with the forceps. Gags are, in my view, quite outdated and unnecessary, and all the ironmongery carried around by some anglers would be better sold to a scrap dealer.

the winter the feeding period may be later in the day, often about midday, but generally the extent of feeding is less spectacular, even under good conditions, because water temperatures are lower and metabolic requirements are less.

The fact is, unpalatable though it may be, that you have to get up in the morning and fish hard and long for a day or two until you have the

BINOCULAR VISION

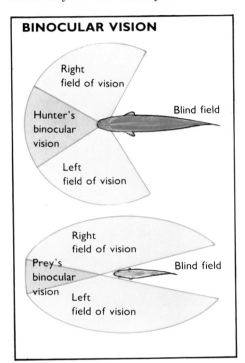

Above: *As it is a predatory fish, the pike needs a good field of binocular vision to help it judge angles and distances between itself and its prey. Non-predatory fish need less binocular vision because their food is static, but they have wider overall vision to help them evade capture.*

feeding pattern—always assuming that you have found the hotspots in the first place. It should be emphasized strongly that there is nothing quite like sitting in a place you know to be a hotspot, waiting for the feed—you *know* it will happen and that the prize can be yours.

All other problems of rods and tackle pale into insignificance beside those just dealt with. While not implying that there are not several good rods, reels and techniques, let me describe the extremely simple approach that has produced for me more than 600 pike over 10lb in the last 15 years.

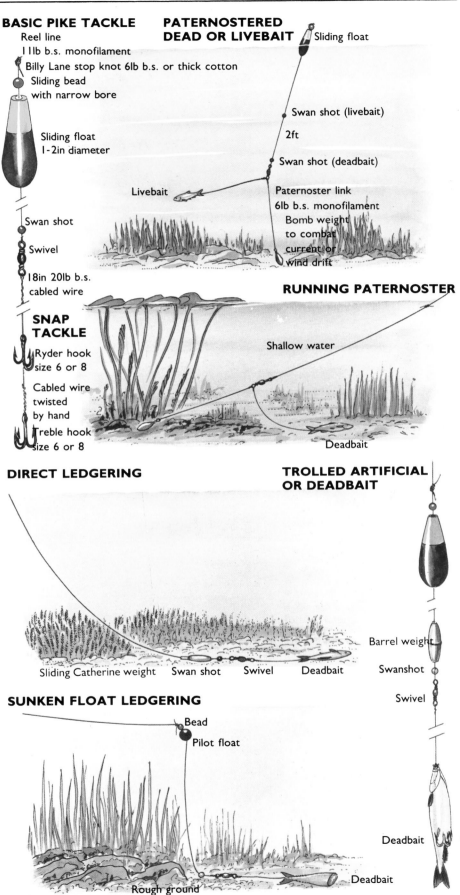

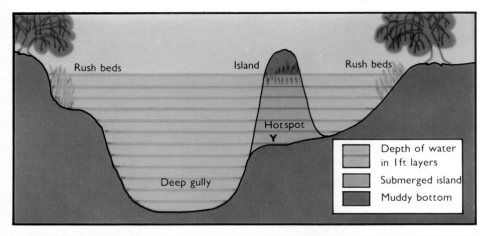

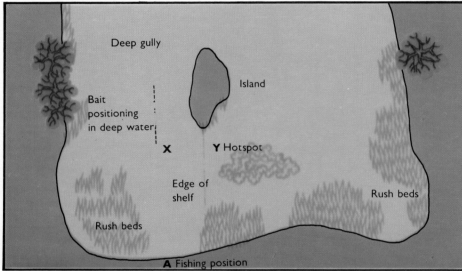

Top: *A profile of Martin Gay's favourite pike lake, Cheshunt, Herts.* **Above:** *The same lake, shown in plan view. Note hot spots, indicated by an X.*

AT-A-GLANCE

Specimen sizes
A pike of over 10lb may be regarded as a specimen in most parts of England and Wales, although 15lb is more appropriate in the Fens and the Broads, and Scottish and Irish lakes.

Tackle, Bait, Techniques
Rod
10-11ft hollow-glass stepped-up carp rod, 2-3lb test curve

Reel
Fixed-spool

Line b.s.
11-15lb; 18lb or more in snaggy waters

Hooks
Bronzed, ring-eyed, extra-strength. Trebles Nos 10-6, singles 2-1/0

Bait
Live coarse fish, dead sea fish

Techniques
Livebaiting, deadbaiting—ledger, float, paternoster-ledger, spinning or drifting with a sliding float

The pike rod

First, the rod. A model like the Mark IV carp rod is too soft, not for playing pike, but for casting the baits so commonly used in piking. However, a stepped-up carp rod is ideal. Several of these are available, in hollow glassfibre, but the best type are those with progressive action as opposed to the tip action associated with fast taper blanks.

Fast taper blanks with a test curve in the range of 2¼-2½lb have their place in piking, for example in firing 2oz weights and small baits a long distance (up to 70 yards). A slow action rod, however, will not only cast heavy deadbaits a long way (4-5oz up to 80 yards in average weather conditions) but can be used for shorter range float paternoster rigs for live and deadbaiting.

Personally, I find a 10ft slow ac-

tion rod ideal for most of my piking, which includes use of artificial baits much of the time. When spinning I would probably use lighter bait casting rods as well, but my concern here is to outline an outfit that can be used with great success and versatility for almost all styles of pike fishing you are likely to encounter.

When considering reels a ruthless approach cuts out thoughts of multipliers and centrepins, and homes in on the versatility of a good quality fixed-spool reel. I use those with roller pick-ups and able to carry 200 yards of 15lb b.s. lines. The b.s. of monofilament line that I normally use is 11-12lb, even for very big pike. Only in heavily weeded or snag-ridden waters would I go up to 14-15lb b.s., although I use 20lb line when trolling. Breaking strains under 11lb considerably increase the

risk of snapping the cast when hurling out 4oz of mackerel for 70 yards, while lines of 14-15lb b.s. drastically reduce distance.

Ancillary pike equipment

Other tackle needed by the pike angler includes a big landing net, and unhooking equipment. If used with great care a pair of long-nosed forceps or very long-nosed pliers will suffice for unhooking a pike. If the fish is sizeable, lay it on its back, sit gently astride it and with a gloved hand pull gently at the tip of its lower jaw. The pike's mouth will open easily and it is a relatively simple matter to remove the hooks with the forceps. Gags are, in my view, quite outdated and unnecessary, and all the ironmongery carried around by some anglers would be better sold to a scrap dealer.

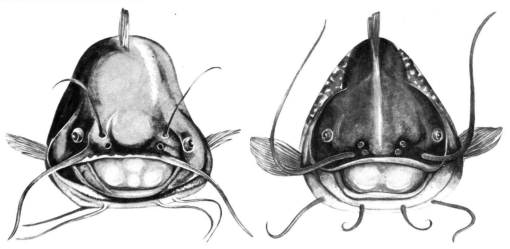

IDENTIFICATION

The Wels is often confused with the Horned Pout, an American Catfish introduced into a few waters. In fact the Horned Pout (far left) has eight barbules, whereas the Wels has only six. The Wels' barbules exceed the head length; the Horned Pout's are equal to the head length. The Wels has no adipose dorsal fin and a long anal fin; the Horned Pout has a long adipose fin and a short anal fin.

Wels

The ugliest freshwater fish in Europe — and the British record is only 43lb!

There is little doubt that the Wels Catfish is the largest inhabitant of British freshwaters: the 43½lb record breaker from Wilstone reservoir is a tiddler compared to some fish that have been seen or hooked and lost.

The Cat is sluggish in shape and sluggish by nature; it is in no way built for speed. Largely dependent on the senses of taste, feel and smell, the Catfish is predominantly a scavenger feeding on virtually anything dead, rotting or very slow moving. Dead fish constitute a significant part of the Cat's diet and so do large freshwater (swan) mussels. The gaping maw of even a smallish Cat is powerful enough to crush a mussel with ease.

The Wels in England is essentially a summer fish and has rarely been caught in water temperatures of less than 65°F. It thrives in hot conditions and appears to be most active in water temperatures between 75 and 85°F. Although Cats will feed at any time of day or night (they are the most unpredictable of fish) dark, muggy nights with plenty of cloud cover seem the most productive.

In many ways the tactics and tackle for this freshwater leviathan closely resemble those of the big eel specialist. The angler cannot afford to use fine or sophisticated tackle for these giants; brute force and simplicity are essential. The rod needs to be a powerful weapon with a test curve between 2-4lb, and it is most important that the reel fittings are reliable. A quality fixed-spool reel loaded with at least 100 yards (preferably 200) of line between 12 and 20lb is also essential.

Roach or gudgeon dead bait
Freelining with a dead fish bait is by far the most productive way to tempt a Wels. The preferred fish bait is a smallish roach or gudgeon of 4-5in long, either lip-hooked or with line threaded through the mouth. The hook size is generally a No 2 or 4 and it is important to use a really strong, reliable, sharp hook. Some specialists prefer a bait that is a few days old and 'off', while others have done equally well with freshly killed baits. Other than fish baits the freshwater mussel must rate as a very close second. Find the largest mussel possible and lightly hook it on the 'foot' together with the loose entrails. The use of a wire trace is a matter of personal preference. There have been cases where it was felt that the teeth had ground down a nylon line and eventually caused a break, but generally a line of 12lb b.s. and upwards in good condition should suffice. The landing net needs to be big.

HOOKING A SWAN MUSSEL

Above: *The shovel-shaped mouth of freshwater's largest — and ugliest — fish, the wels. It can take very large baits.*
Left: *An ideal static bait for the wels. Make sure that the point of the hook protrudes. If it is hidden in the soft part of the mussel a strike may not set the hook home — and if it pulls out you may lose an important fish.*

Roach

To tempt roach to take your bait you will have to be prepared to fish at dawn or dusk when your presence is less obvious and when this ultra-cautious species has little reason to be suspicious

Roach are very often the first species encountered by the young fisherman, but the fun of catching them grows over the years as he progresses from boggle-eyed, stunted tiddlers packed into farm ponds to those deep-sided 2lb roach with scarlet fins and silvery blue flanks —the roach fisher's ultimate goal.

Such fish, however, are usually found only in rich waters, their size determined by the environment. 'Reading a water' is therefore the key to successful roaching, whether you desire quantity or quality.

One of the most important factors is water temperature. During the summer, roach move through upper water layers and take food from the surface—they may even be caught on a dry fly. But during the winter they are loath to move more than a few inches from the bottom to intercept a bait.

Also important is water colour. In bright conditions and with clear water, even the finest tackle is quite visible. You must then be ultra-

Below: *Where the current is moderately fast, the link swivel ledger will get your bait to the fish when float-fishing fails.*

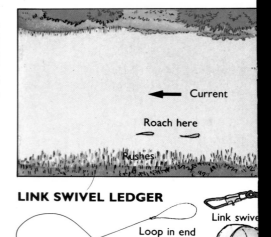

Current

Roach here

Rushes

LINK SWIVEL LEDGER

Loop in end
of hook trace

Link swivel

cautious, be as quiet as possible, and use bankside shrubbery to camouflage your silhouette. Being a shoaling fish, the roach is highly sensitive to alien vibrations, surface shadows, or anything suspicious. One frightened fish can easily lead the shoal out of the swim or make them disinclined to feed. Therefore the best roaching, particularly for larger, wiser specimens, is done in coloured water, at dusk and dawn.

Below: *Laying a trail of breadmash for the roach to follow upstream. Casts, which must accurately follow the groundbait pattern to be effective, are made downstream.*

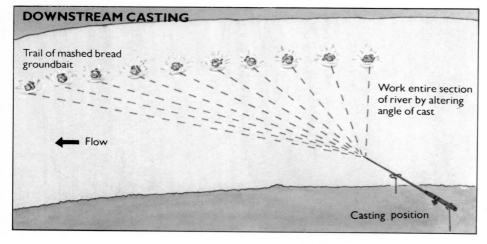

DOWNSTREAM CASTING

Trail of mashed bread
groundbait

Work entire section
of river by altering
angle of cast

Flow

Casting position

With tiny 'twitch' bites, shorten the bobbin drop to about 4in. Watch the line closely at the point where it enters the water.

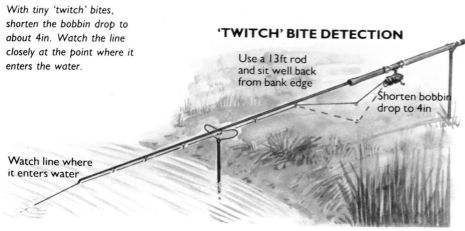

'TWITCH' BITE DETECTION

Use a 13ft rod
and sit well back
from bank edge

Shorten bobbin
drop to 4in

Watch line where
it enters water

Tackle for roach fishing
Despite the wide variety of conditions and waters in which roach are found, two rods suffice: a 12-13ft match rod and a 9ft ledger rod with a threaded tip ring for a swingtip or quivertip. The reel can be either a fixed-spool with a sensitive clutch for light lines, or a free-running centrepin. The former is probably better because long and accurate casting is sometimes called for. Two spools are needed, one with 2lb b.s. line for float fishing, the other with 3-4lb line for ledgering.

Alternatively, of course, you may decide to do away with a rod altogether and use a roach pole. In recent years their standing has grown steadily, for they present a bait very precisely. Nevertheless, most roach anglers still prefer to fish with rod and line for the pole is a technique that is very specialised.

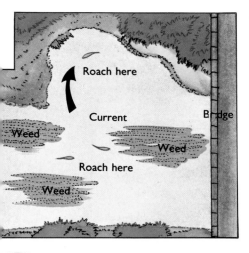

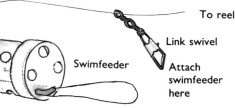

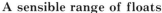

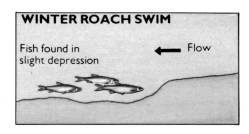

Fish found in slight depression

Flow

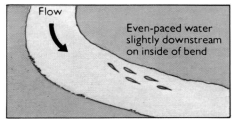

Flow

Even-paced water slightly downstream on inside of bend

Top: *In the winter, roach hug the bottom of a river and seek shelter in depressions and the inside banks of bends.* **Left:** *Not really a pretty sight, many of these fish will be injured. This 74½lb bag of roach and a few hybrids was caught from Colebrook River, Co Fermanagh.*

A sensible range of floats

Do not collect hundreds of beautiful, different patterned floats, because you will not know whether your float is wrong or your method of fishing, although nearly always it will be the latter. A sensible range would be a set of four stick floats, carrying shot from 1BB to 5BB, for trotting in slow to medium-fast swims; a set of Avons, also for trotting, but taking shots ranging from 4BB to three swan and used to combat much faster, even turbulent water; a set of zoomers or antenna floats, with shotting ranging from 2BB to 4AA for sensitive presentation in still-waters; and a few Canal Greys for ultra-sensitive work.

As far as hooks are concerned, round-bends take a lot of beating. For large baits, such as worms and breadflake, use eyed hooks from No 10 to No 6, and tie them directly on to the line. For small baits, where neatness of presentation is essential, spade ends are better. These can be tied either direct or to a hook length of 1-1½lb b.s. line when, for example, clear or very cold water deters the roach from paying attention to hooks tied to thicker line because the bait behaves unnaturally.

A good selection of split shot is also required, plus an assortment of small swivels, Arlesey bombs, and open-ended and block-ended swim-feeders for fishing far out or in fast water. The easiest spots to catch roach are stillwater lakes, pits or farm ponds. On such waters, many different techniques can be tried until you have success.

The basic technique

On a small, well-coloured water in summer, for example, start off float fishing with a 2BB quill float, with ⅛in of the tip showing and a size 14 hook holding two maggots. Begin by fixing both shots 6in from the hook and set the float overdepth to lay the bait on the bottom. Then scatter a few maggots around the float every so often and you will soon have the roach feeding.

But if bites are not forthcoming, or they suddenly stop, the loose maggots may have been taken on the way down. So push the float down the line a little and slide one of the two shot up just beneath it. Fix the other shot about 2ft from the hook. Then cast out and watch carefully as the float cocks. If the bait is taken 'on the drop', the float will take longer to settle than it should. Alternatively, bites may come a few seconds later, and the float will slide under positively. In either case, strike at once.

In windy weather, or when fishing over some distance in large lakes or pits, an antenna float rather than a Canal Grey should be used. It may be fixed either by the bottom end only, or as a slider, which is really necessary when you are fishing in very deep swims.

To reduce wind disturbance, ensure the line is well sunk by over-casting and then winding the tackle back to the desired spot with the rod tip held beneath the surface. When this is done, you can then fish in the same way as for close-range fishing —although presenting loose feed or small balls of groundbait far out calls for both a catapult and skill.

Feeding the swim

Provided water temperatures are high, roach can be expected to feed at almost any depth. So if the swim goes dead, try varying the depth until bites materialize. Alternatively, try another bait—for example, sweetcorn, a couple of brandlings or breadflake. But always use feed sparingly and step up the rate only if bites are regular.

Overfeeding a roach shoal is probably the most common reason why bites stop. A deepish hole in a small, clear-water river may contain just a dozen or so roach. Although such fish may well be large, they will not consume vast quantities of food, so building up the swim for a lengthy session with lots of loose feed is not worthwhile.

37

Left: *Hot weather, and the roach are feeding high in the water. There's a need for more caution in the angler's approach to the water, but the shoals may well be visible, and receptive even to such baits as dry fly.*
Above: *As a day's fishing progresses, roach shoals often move farther and farther out, so that by midday long-distance casting is called for.*
Right: *Forceps being used to remove the hook from a fine roach in the prime of condition. Specimens are rarely caught other than early or late and from murky, coloured water.*

Mobility and sensitive tackle

It is far better on small waters to be mobile and to use the sensitive freelining method. Use polarized sunglass to spot a shoal, then creep quietly upstream and, with just a No 8 hook holding a large piece of breadflake on the line, allow the current to trundle the bait down to the shoal. Watch the line where it enters the water if the water is not clear enough for you to actually see a fish suck the bait in. Sometimes the line will tighten quickly, the rod tip will even be pulled round, sometimes there is just a mere slow 'pluck', and

sometimes the line may even fall slack momentarily as a roach swims upstream with the bait. Whatever happens, strike quickly at any unnatural movement.

You will have trouble holding bottom in fast, deep holes, so for these pinch a swan shot 12in from the hook. Or in even fiercer conditions, such as when fishing weirpools, rig up a two or three swan shot link ledger or a running Arlesey bomb ledger and watch the rod top or quiver tip for bites.

In small rivers expect to take just one, or perhaps two, roach from a

swim and then to move on to another—a delightful and very interesting method of roaching.

Conditions are different on medium-sized rivers, however, and these are best fished with a float. As you cannot see your quarry, you must use a plummet to obtain a fair idea of both the depth and the nature of the bottom. Search for any even-paced stretch with a clean gravel or silty bottom and consistent depth. Then set up a stick float carrying sufficient shot to allow the bait a natural passage down to where you know the fish are.

two grains of stewed wheat. As the day progresses, the fish tend to rise, so trotting with smaller baits becomes the preferred method. Maggots, casters, wheat, sweetcorn, and bait such as hempseed (or other seedbaits) and elderberry, can all be deadly. But bites can often be very quick, so slow them down by feeding sparingly, putting a large grain or an elderberry on the hook. Casters are particularly good, and often sort out the better fish, but check after each cast that the inside has not been sucked out by an unseen bite.

Adjusting trotting tackle
Plan on the roach accepting the bait when it is just tripping bottom, and allow for the current when catapulting loose feed upstream. Fix the float top and bottom—then if you get no bites as the tackle trots through the swim unchecked, hold it back a little, allowing the bait to swing enticingly upwards. If roach only accept the bait when holding the float back, experiment with the shotting. Start off with two groups—one at mid-depth and a small shot 10in from the hook—and then space the weights out more evenly between float and hook.

On large, wide or fast rivers, you should change your tactics yet again. Ledgering is often the most productive method here. You can either watch the rod tip for bites or screw in a swingtip (or a quivertip in fast-flowing rivers).

Loose feed must be concentrated
Concentrate your loose feed by using a blockend feeder for strong currents or an open-ended feeder on medium to slow waters. These can be stopped 12in from the hook by a split shot, fished on a separate link via a pair of swivels, or even fixed paternoster-fashion. Try to place the tackle consistently into the same area so that a concentration of bait builds up.

Exciting ledgering
Ledgering is also useful on slow or stillwaters, particularly for larger fish which prefer the bottom. Baits can be large, such as a bunch of maggots or breadflake, and tackle should be kept to a minimum. Use just enough weight to reach the swim

Tiny hooks in cold water
In very cold water, put a tiny dust shot 12in from the hook and use smaller hook sizes, even as small as No 22, holding a single maggot or caster. You can expect only tiny bites, so shot the float well down and hit anything suspicious.

In the summer, however, bites are more positive, and larger baits can be used, particularly at dawn and dusk. Early in the morning, roach lie on the bottom, so the best method is to fish well overdepth and lay on with a large piece of breadflake, a crust cube, sweetcorn, or perhaps

or to hold bottom, set the rod low to the water in two rests, pointing at the bait, and use a ledger bobbin clipped on the line between the butt and second rod ring to indicate bites. By using a luminous bobbin, you can fish that last hour of daylight and even later into darkness, when the biggest roach show up. A more exciting way of taking a specimen roach does not exist.

By using two rods you can place one bait where you expect to find roach and use the other rod to explore different spots. Stillwater roach, even when feeding quite well, can move around quite a lot, and so during static periods do not hesitate to cover any fish which rolls on the surface well away from your swim.

Tench

Tench: where to find them, how to spot them feeding, how to stalk them, get them interested in your bait, tempt them on to your hook—and enjoy every minute of the delicate operation

Tench are found in lakes, canals, ponds (including the village duck pond), meres, gravel pits, lochs and rivers. Although the species abounds in muddy-bottomed lakes, ponds and canals, in these waters they tend to err on the side of quantity rather than quality. Generally, gravel pits and lakes produce the larger specimens, and the bigger the water, especially if it is clear, the better. The big Irish loughs produce many large tench, and every spring numerous specimen fish are taken from the famous Power Station reach at Lanesborough to where they migrate from Lough Ree to spawn. Canals, too, hold tench in large numbers, the bigger specimens mostly being found in those waterways where boat traffic is not heavy.

Although normally associated with stillwaters, tench are also found in rivers. Here, although tench are caught in summer, the best times are often when the water is high and coloured—even in winter.

Bubbling tench
When feeding over muddy or silty bottoms, tench often betray their presence by sending up patches of tiny bubbles. These should not be confused with gas bubbles, which are much larger. Tench bubbles are easily recognizable, being small and frothy in appearance and occurring in vast numbers. The size of a patch

Bill Rushmer—a specimen hunter of considerable repute—unhooks a good tench from this attractive, sheltered swim.

varies from a few inches to 3ft or more, the bigger patches usually being caused by more than one tench. Sometimes the bubbles are accompanied by small pieces of stick and other debris floating to the surface. Bubbling denotes one or more feeding tench, and a carefully presented bait cast into the area is usually taken—often before the float has cocked.

Tench eat a wide variety of baits, including maggots, bread, worms, casters, mussels, sweetcorn and wheat. Many have also been taken on artificial flies—I once took two on a Baby Doll wet fly—while there are reliable reports of specimens taken on spinners.

The number of methods which take tench is also considerable. The 'lift' technique employs a piece of peacock quill 6in in length, cocked by one or two swan shot. The shot are replaced about 3in from the hook, and the float is attached to the line by the bottom only. Best bait is crust or flake on a No 8 or 10 hook. Line strength should be 3-5lb.

As the bait touches bottom, the line is pulled tight to the float, and the rod placed in two rests with 6in of the tip submerged. An inch of the quill should show above the surface. Bites are decisive—usually the float shoots upwards then falls flat, or it may simply disappear. The strike is instantaneous. The method is most effective on hard bottoms.

For fishing over muddy bottoms a different set-up is necessary—an antenna-type float loaded with three AAA's and a No 1 shot. The latter should be placed about 15in from the hook, and the AAA's used to lock the float in position on 3-4lb line. The float is attached by the bottom only. Flake should be fished on a No 10 or 12 hook, maggots on 14 or 16, redworm on 12 or 14.

Because of the single No 1 shot on the line, the bait will sink slowly to the bottom. Bites often occur as the bait is dropping, especially if the angler is fishing over a patch of bubbles. When the bait is taken 'on the drop', the float will either disappear, or move slowly to one side, sometimes sinking, sometimes not.

If the bait is stationary when a fish bites, the float will do one of many things. It may lift, then sink

(not quite disappearing), repeating this several times before finally vanishing or moving slowly across the surface. It may lift, then go straight under. It may disappear without warning. Most times the strike should be made only when a positive movement of the float takes place, but the angler should always be prepared to experiment and strike at anything which suggests the bait is in the fish's mouth.

Sliding float

In deep water, of 12ft and over, a sliding float is necessary. For a slider to perform properly, the diameter of the bottom ring should be such that only lines of less than 6lb b.s. can pass through. Line strength should be 3-5lb. The float should have a long antenna and the shot loading should consist of about six AAA's and a No 1.

Tie a 6in length of nylon line, slightly heavier than the main line, above the float at the required depth to act as a stop knot. A plummet is then attached to the hook, the tackle cast to the spot to be fished, and the stop knot adjusted until the bait is just touching the bottom. The shot are bunched between three and six feet from the hook, with the No 1 shot 15in above the hook.

Prior to casting, the float will rest against the bunched AAA shot. The cast is made overhead and immediately the float hits the water, line is given—*on no account should the bait and shot sink on a tight line.* As the shot sink, the float travels up the line, eventually coming to rest against the stop knot. The bait is now on the bottom. The rod is then placed in two rests, with 6in of the tip submerged. When a bite occurs, the strike is made sideways.

Ledgering

Ledgering is a very successful method, especially in meres and gravel pits. The various approaches include the use of a blockend with maggots, a swimfeeder with bread or worms, straightforward ledgering with an Arlesey Bomb or sliding link ledger, and freelining.

When blockending with maggots, a Feederlink is threaded onto the line and stopped about 15in from the hook. This should be either a No 14

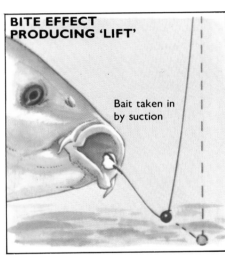

BITE EFFECT PRODUCING 'LIFT'

Bait taken in by suction

Top: *A whole freshwater mussel, hooked so that the barb is exposed and can strike home.* **Above:** *Over the years this rig has accounted for more specimen tench than any other.* **Right:** *The windbeater is an exceptionally stable variation on the lift rig.*

WINDBEATER RIG

Antenna float

Bulk shot

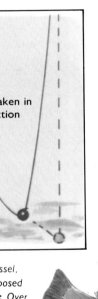

or 16, baited with one or two maggots. Each cast must be made in the same area, the continual introduction of maggots via the Feederlink in time creating a hot-spot. The cruising tench eventually finds these maggots, stops to eat them and, it is hoped, those on the hook too.

Use an indicator

The rod is fished on two rests with an indicator—a bobbin, butt in-dicator or other device—attached to either the line or the rod. Before attaching the indicator, the line *must* be pulled tight to the feeder.

Bites will vary. Sometimes the indicator will jerk up an inch, once, twice, or even three times. It may fall backwards, it may rise slowly or, as often happens, shoot up so quickly that it hits the rod with a thud. But whatever the bite indication, your own reflexes must ever be on the alert.

Deadly on hard, clean bottoms

Effective only in waters with hard, clean bottoms, this approach is particularly deadly when fished at long range—that is, where 20 yards or more must be achieved.

For swimfeeders, the set-up is the same, except that the hook size varies between No 12 and No 6, depending on the bait. Favourite baits are bread (crust, flake and paste) and worms. The swimfeeder is packed with cereal groundbait. Line strength that is suitable ranges from 4lb to 6lb.

The Arlesey Bomb and sliding link ledger rigs are used on both hard and soft bottoms. On the latter, a sliding link will result in better bites. Best baits are bread, worms, maggots and sweetcorn. Hook sizes are either 12, 10 or 8, with a gilt hook for sweetcorn. Line strength is again between 4 and 6lb.

Freelining means using nothing on the line but the hook. Best baits are lobworm and freshwater mussels, the latter fished either in pieces or whole. Before fishing, several mussels are cut into portions and introduced to the swim. Hook sizes are No 8 for pieces, Nos 6 and 4 for whole mussels (and lobworms); line strength, 6lb. Bites are detected by watching either the line or a piece of silver paper folded over it between butt ring and reel. For mussels, the pick-up of the reel is left open, the strike being made when some 3ft of line have been taken. For lobworms it is left closed.

Frank Guttfield writes:

Having gained an insight into the ways and habitat of the tench and the basic conventional methods of tempting this fish, let us now consider some of the more unusual techniques for catching old 'Tinca'. There are a hundred and one off-beat approaches, but let us look at three of the most productive and exciting methods of fishing for a beautiful and powerful summer species.

One of the most exhilarating ways of catching any fish is experienced when the angler can actually see his quarry in the water. This entails stalking the fish, and eventually putting a bait to it. It is a very selective way of fishing—there is nothing hit-or-miss about it. Once you have

found your fish the rest is up to you.

How to stalk tench

You will be aware already that the favourite tenching hours are early and late in the day, although it is important to realize that tench do not feed to a strict timetable. To stalk tench you need to be able to see them, and for this you need light. The newcomer to tenching may therefore be a little surprised to learn that some of the most exciting

Below: *The slider float is fished ideally in 12ft or more of water, evenly shotted.*
Below right: *Swimfeeder tackle and tench baits: maggots, casters, sweetcorn, brandling. The breadcrumbs are used to plug the swimfeeder.*

SLIDING FLOAT RIG

Sliding float

Stop knot

Line 3-5lb b.s.

AAA shot

3ft

No 1 shot

15in

and productive hunting can even be had in the middle hours of the day in blazing sunshine! Often the angler has no choice but to fish in these 'off-peak' hours, but if he has a flexible approach and an open mind, these daylight hours can be used well.

Tench stalking is very much a wandering game, so one needs to be able to travel as light as possible. Watercraft, stealth and caution are absolute essentials—in fact, this method demands the best of big-fish anglers. In most situations your tackle need not be elaborate—just rod, reel, line and hook, the freeline approach. A tin of lobworms, half a loaf, and perhaps a couple of swan mussels in your bag, and you are all

BLOCKEND FEEDER RIG

Swimfeeder

swivel

Stop shot

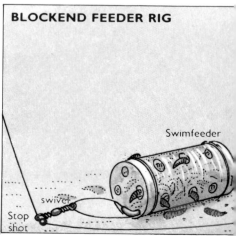

set. To get the most fun out of this kind of fishing, it pays to work in pairs. If you have a mate who does not mind crawling through stinging nettles on all fours or can shin up a willow tree like an ape, you have the basis of a successful partnership. There is nothing lethargic about this sort of fishing.

A pair of polarized sunglasses is a must for tench stalking, and a pair of plimsolls are essential for tree climbing. If your water is surrounded by trees take advantage of them and take it in turns to do the catching and the spotting—your mate, perched up a tree can give you a running commentary on what is going on down below, picking out the biggest tench in the group and giving you instruction. Sometimes the angler is fishing 'blind', relying totally on the spotter, but that only adds to the excitement. The real acrobatics start when fishing otherwise unapproachable swims from up a tree, but that is really advanced tenching!

The reader has learnt that tench feeding is not totally predictable and that they can, and do, feed at all times, although the more productive periods tend to be early and late.

Night-feeding tench
It is however, perhaps not generally realized that tench feed regularly in real earnest during the hours of darkness. This happens in particular circumstances, and there may be a number of reasons. On many of our heavily fished club and day ticket waters, any self-respecting tench would hardly venture near the banks during daylight hours. It is only after dark, when all the bankside hubbub has subsided, that tench will feel secure enough to patrol the margins and feed, often mopping up the groundbait tossed in by the day's anglers. On this type of fishery, the pattern becomes more noticeable as the season progresses, the tench growing more and more cautious as the bankside clutter increases during the day.

Water temperature
Another factor influencing nocturnal feeding is water temperature. With the rare prolonged heatwave that pushes the water temperature into the mid or upper seventies, tench do tend to go off the feed. The summer of 1976 was a classic example of this, many of the big fish being taken in the middle of the night. The ideal water temperature for tench fishing is in the region of 18-21°C (65-70°F). In a shallow lake the normal night time drop in air temperature can reduce the water temperature towards dawn by as much as four or five degrees, and this will often stir the fish into activity.

Left: *The blockend feeder rig can be made from a 35mm film cassette container. The holes must be just large enough for maggots to emerge in a slow, steady, very inviting trickle.*

AT-A-GLANCE

Specimen sizes
5lb to 7lb, depending on the average weight for the individual waters. In some areas 3lb may be very good; in others the heavier weight applies.

Tackle, bait, techniques
Rod
9ft to 13ft

Reel
Fixed-spool

Line b.s.
2lb b.s. to 8lb b.s.

Hooks
No 16 to No 2

Bait
Bread, brandlings, freshwater mussel, sweetcorn, maggot and many others

Groundbait
Worms, trout pellets, soaked maize, bread and all hookbaits

Techniques
Ledgering, freelining, float fishing

Below: *Ledgering for specimen tench in a Wraysbury gravel pit. When the fish are there, but not biting, rig for lift-bites on really fine tackle.*

Rudd

The waters with a reputation for large bags of mixed species are not the ones for a specimen hunter of rudd. Vulnerable to competition and shy of anglers, big rudd hate crowds

Rudd frequently provide a fair bag and the early season lake angler can look forward to a peaceful day when the rudd are obliging.

Surface and middle-water fishing methods are clearly indicated, and if shoals of rudd are seen well off-shore the angler must shot-up a fairly heavy tackle to provide long casting. Rudd feeding well off the shoreline are not unduly shy, but most anglers prefer to take no chances.

Fishing for rudd
A useful strategy is to cast well beyond the shoal, where the splash of tackle hitting the surface will not be noticed. The tackle is then drawn slowly towards the angler and into position over the shoal. Runs are often signified by a determined lateral and oblique movement of the float as fish take the bait along with them, rather than diving with it. In these situations a bubble-float partially filled with water often provides casting weight, permitting light shotting. Alternatively, a controller lying flat on the surface rather than being cocked like a float, allows swift bite detection on finer tackle than might otherwise be required. Whichever method is adopted, good eye-sight and swift reflexes are absolutely necessary.

When shoals of rudd do venture close inshore, great care is necessary to avoid alarming them. Fish hooked must be drawn aside from the shoal without allowing them to splash on the surface. This means employing side strain with the rod tip low until the fish can be landed.

Weed-filled haunts
In many gravel pits the depth of water may well be more than 30ft. Weed beds, invisible from the shore, are often deep rooted, but extend upwards to within 12ft or so of the surface. These are often likely rudd haunts, and the regular visitor will get to know their positions. Shoals may be feeding 10ft or more from the surface, foraging among the top of the weed, constantly changing depth and coming to the surface.

Whatever the feeding locations, the angler should use tackles as light as conditions will allow. When long casting he must make certain that his shotting is disposed along

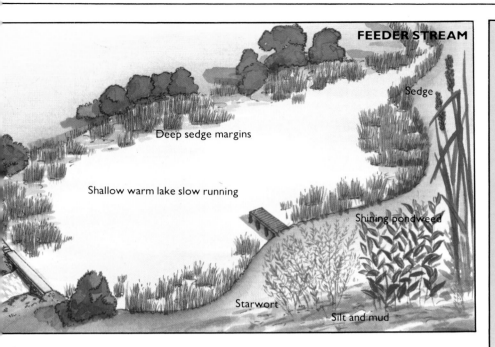

FEEDER STREAM

Sedge

Deep sedge margins

Shallow warm lake slow running

Shining pondweed

Starwort

Silt and mud

Above: *An ideal situation for rudd fishing — so long as rudd are present! The shallow margins and well weeded areas must be fished with great caution.* **Left:** *Norfolk angler John Nunn with a fine rudd. He caught the fish by ledgering close to the bed of the lake. Norfolk's Broads are fed by gentle, slow-flowing rivers offering a lot of good rudd fishing, although holidaymakers afloat have affected the fish stocks. However, there is so much fine water that good fishing is plentiful.*

the cast to prevent the hook flying back and tangling over the float or upper shots during flight. Usually it is expedient to ensure that the lowest shot is more than halfway down the cast from the float. This also enables slowly sinking baits to be presented as required.

Rudd frequently rise to a well-cast fly. The fly should be small, and almost any good imitative pattern will take fish. Nymphs should also be tried. Many anglers like to attach a maggot or a piece of white leather to the tail of the fly as an additional inducement. In conditions where rudd are rising freely this is a most enjoyable and effective way of taking fish regularly without alarming the rest of the shoal.

The fly may be fished dry, although timing the strike is sometimes a problem, or it may be fished wet, a foot or so below the surface. Wet flies should be drawn very slowly as rudd are not inclined to chase a moving bait. During the early season when fish fry are fre-

quently eaten by rudd, a small flasher-type fly, fished in short irregular jerks, is sometimes very effective. This may also account for better quality fish than ordinary bait methods, because larger, more mature fish are more prone to take fish fry at this time of year.

Free-feeding rudd

When rudd are feeding freely their presence and activity is so obvious that groundbaiting is quite unnecessary. When there are no feeding signs on the water it is advantageous to tempt them into a feeding mood, or draw feeding fish within casting distance by the careful use of groundbait. Since the rudd is predominantly a surface feeder, there is little point in using heavy groundbaits intended to lie on the bottom, and cloudbaits—used little and often—are useful.

When boat fishing on the larger waters of the Norfolk Broads, local anglers often fasten a piece of bread to a length of line attached to a stone. This is then anchored in the vicinity of reeds or weed beds, and the boat is then moved quietly away to a suitable fishing position. An alternative is to float small pieces of bread downwind at intervals, either from the boat or the shore. If there are gulls or ducks in the vicinity, the presence of bread can do more harm than good – cloudbait is then the only answer.

Norfolk rudd

Some of the best rudd fishing is to be found in many of the waters of the Norfolk Broads, which are also noted for the excellence of their pike fishing. Fishing from the bank is possible in few of these waters and the best rudd areas are the shallower reed-fringed portions where cruising boats do not venture, as the depth varies from one or two to four or five feet.

Excellent rudd are also found in the little known ponds and meres of Shropshire and the Fens of East Anglia, and perhaps the best known water is Slapton Lea, also known for large pike. Many waters contain rudd over 2lb, but their presence is never suspected until the pond is drained, or electrically fished, when fine rudd are found in the nets with hundreds of smaller fish.

Zander

If you are interested in getting the best possible fight out of a hooked zander, you need to scale down your usual pike tackle to a level which gives the fish an even chance

Above: *The zander's sharp, snatching teeth show well here. Like the pike, zander consume their prey headfirst, turning it between their incisors if necessary.*
Right: *A zander rig designed by Bill Chillingworth used to present either a live- or deadbait off the bottom so that the whole fish bait 'swims' the right way up.*

The ideal rod for zander is one similar to that used by tench and barbel anglers—one or a pair of Avon rods with modern fixed-spool reels is ideal. Alternatively, a light carp rod or pike rod is also suitable—provided it is over 10ft.

Line strength depends very much on the water. On snag-free waters where few big pike are caught, 7lb or 8lb b.s. is ideal. Otherwise, 10lb b.s. is advisable.

Few waters are without pike, so a wire trace is normally essential. Pike soon bite through heavy nylon even if zander do not. Single-strand 8lb Alasticum is strong and also very fine; other forms of braided wire are satisfactory but a little thick.

Fine wire is the best material for zander hooks. Flattening the barbs with pliers helps hook removal considerably without any more fish than usual being lost. Large single hooks, say No 1/0, or small trebles, up to No 8, may be used. Trebles

must be sharp and round-bended. When the fish are biting finickally, two No 10 hooks along the flank of a small bait may catch shy fish.

The simplest way to fish for zander is to freeline a bait on a large single hook. The advantages of this method are that the bait stays on the hook during casting, and is pushed up the line when the zander is hooked, so that it can sometimes be used again. Its disadvantage is that the strike has to be delayed to allow the zander to take the bait well into its mouth.

On the majority of occasions, the barbless hook is relatively easy to extract with a pair of forceps, causing minimal discomfort to the fish. Occasionally, a deeply hooked fish is better despatched before it is unhooked and taken home for the table.

The best baits
Baits for zander are invariably small fish or portions of fish, especially

those with a narrow cross section, which are easier for the zander to swallow. Dace, chub, or roach of up to 3oz make ideal livebait when float fishing. As with gudgeon, bleak and rudd they can be ledgered or freelined, live or dead. Frozen baits as well as fresh ones also take zander, but the former tend to be rather soft. Whether the bait is freshly killed or frozen, it should not be stale; old baits are invariably less effective.

One of the most useful baits is a piece of eel. A small 'bootlace', the sort that most anglers throw up the bank in disgust, can be cut into 2in sections and threaded with a baiting needle on to a single hook. This bait often takes good fish; moreover, you invariable get the bait back and it is impossible to cast it off. These factors are a great boon when the zander are feeding well and bait is running short.

Artificial lures will also take zander. Successful patterns include Mepps spinners, a variety of spoons and deep running plugs, all fished

FLOAT PATERNOSTER

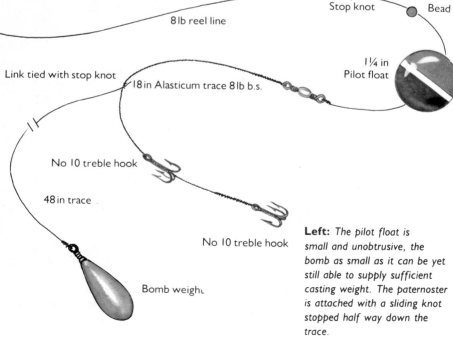

8lb reel line

Stop knot

Bead

Link tied with stop knot

18 in Alasticum trace 8 lb b.s.

1¼ in Pilot float

No 10 treble hook

48 in trace

No 10 treble hook

Bomb weight

Left: *The pilot float is small and unobtrusive, the bomb as small as it can be yet still able to supply sufficient casting weight. The paternoster is attached with a sliding knot stopped half way down the trace.*

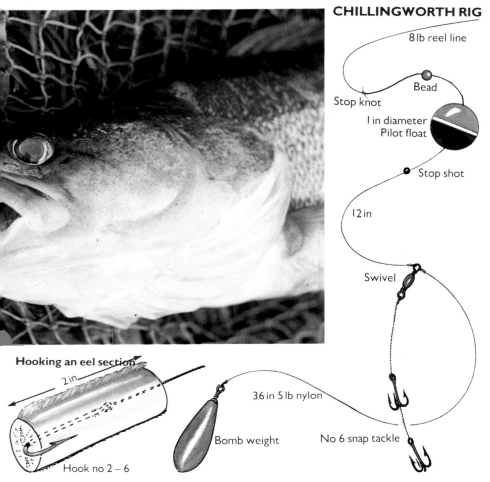

CHILLINGWORTH RIG

8 lb reel line

Bead

Stop knot

1 in diameter
Pilot float

Stop shot

12 in

Swivel

Hooking an eel section

2 in

Hook no 2 – 6

36 in 5 lb nylon

Bomb weight

No 6 snap tackle

deep and very slowly and with the
original large hooks replaced by
smaller ones, sharpened with a hone.
Wobbled deadbait is another successful zander method. A light bait
such as a dead bleak is easy to work
along the bottom.

Dead fish mounted on spinning
vanes have accounted for many
quality zander, and one popular
method is to lip hook an extremely
small fish with the treble hook of a
small bar spinner. When retrieved,
the flash of the silver or gold spinner
is the initial attractor while the fish
following a couple of inches behind
is the bait that is attacked. An instant strike will usually result in a
firmly hooked zander.

When to strike depends on the
bait, hooks and methods of indication. When float fishing with small
baits and a pair of small treble
hooks, it pays to hit the zander hard
a few seconds after the line has
started to run out. When ledgering
or freelining small baits on a similar
rig, however, indication of a run

should be as sensitive as possible so
that the strike can be made immediately. Popular indicators include tucking the line lightly under
an elastic band round the rod handle, with a square of kitchen foil folded over the line near the rod tip; an
empty line spool round the line; or a
simple tubular indicator. Whatever
method is used, the bale arm must
be open to let fish take line freely.

Forceps for unhooking
A final item of zander tackle is a pair
of forceps for unhooking. Lift the
fish up under its chin and open its
mouth with your other hand. Then,
using the forceps, pull the bait (if
still there) out of its mouth and free
the hooks. If they are deep work via
the gill covers and invert the hooks
before pulling them out.

Zander do not like keepnets and it
is inadvisable to confine numbers
together. They should be released a
few yards from where you are
fishing. Keep a big fish only long
enough to photograph.

*Zander are predatory fish, so a lure with a life-like
movement has a good chance of attracting a
hunting fish. Plugs should be fished deep and slow
for zander, sometimes called pike-perch.*

Chapter 2
SEA FISHING

If there is pleasure and enjoyment in freshwater fishing what, then, is the attraction of sea angling? Why take the trouble, as hundreds do, to rise before dawn — even in deep winter — drive up to a hundred miles to the coast and pay what can be a considerable sum to a charter skipper for the pleasure of being taken out on a cold, choppy sea?

The answer lies in an important additional factor to the sport: we have the sea in our blood and share an excitement in setting out into the alien world of the sea with its attendant threat and possible danger.

Sea fishing too provides the skilful — or lucky — angler with some splendid table opportunities: bass, turbot and other flatfish, cod, skate and mackerel. Such culinary delights in restaurants are pretty pricey these days, so a few pounds of fish are welcome in the fridge.

Pity that last fish mentioned, the mackerel! It is such a good-eating fish and trawled and caught in huge numbers on that score. At the same time, as you will read later on, it is the finest of all sea baits. Used whole for sharking, in fillets for many sea species, the head for conger, and when old, very dead, and very smelly it contributes to that horror of the squeamish sea angler, rubby dubby! A deadbait mackerel has often tempted a specimen pike too!

There are some important tackle differences between the fresh and saltwater facets of the sport. Few freshwater species are strong enough to equal the strength of the angler: salmon, large carp and specimen pike may be able to make an angler yield assuming his tackle is adequate. But such is the brute strength of, say, a 100 lb conger that it can easily defeat Man's puny muscles if it can reach its lair.

How, then, does the sea angler cope? He must follow two vital rules: get the conger off the seabed and in to open water; and his tackle — rod, reel, line, links, swivels, hook — must be able to take the considerable strain exerted by the conger's musculature.

To turn to other aspects of sea fishing. The beach caster has a skill that has been acquired by much practice in coordinating arm, eyes, the spring inherent in the long rod, controlling the spool, terminal tackle and weight, and lastly the wind, which can be very troublesome when blowing in from the sea.

Rocks, with their covering of weed holding all kinds of tasty, edible morsels for roving fish, are great places from which to fish. But a coating of slippery weed can hardly be described as a stable fishing platform. So some safety rules must be observed: never wear smooth-soled rubber boots when fishing from wet rocks; and always keep an eye on the tide, for it is no joke to be cut off by the tide when you realise that the rocks you are standing on will be covered by 7ft of sea.

Many well-organised angling clubs usually have a sea angling section. Some indeed have special classes of membership for sea anglers only. This section is run by an officer called the Sea Commodore. His title may sound grand, but he has a difficult job in organising outings, festivals, booking the best and most reliable charterboats, selecting dates with good tides. It is usually a thankless task. But bad weather, poor catches, unsatisfactory boats, even sea sickness, are *always* his fault!

With the matter of safety still in mind, a few more important things to remember: always have bad-weather clothing with you; always take some food and drink; have enough bait for the trip, don't bank on finding mackerel, and have a good breakfast before starting out.

If you have your own dinghy, never venture too far out, an hour's leisurely chug out might be fun, but if a squall comes up and the tide changes, you may find yourself heading in the wrong direction. Any craft with a mast should hoist a radar reflector. You are a small object from a large vessel and the reflector will create a visible blip on the screen. In fog, just hope someone is watching that screen!

Cod

Apart from its reputation as a fine table fish, the cod offers perhaps the most exciting fishing for the sea angler. Here we describe the best techniques for landing a really prize specimen

The cod probably excites more anglers than any other species of sea fish. It is a very abundant fish, and grows to a good size.

The rod-caught cod record stands at 53lb, although much larger specimens are frequently taken by commercial boats. The largest weighed 211½lb, and was caught off the Massachusetts' coast. On this side of the Atlantic, British trawlers frequently land cod of over 70lb.

Specimen cod—fish weighing over 20lb—can be caught over almost any type of seabed and some of the larger specimens are often taken when fishing over wrecks. The best place to catch fish, however, varies from year to year. Anyone seeking specimens therefore should watch the angling press for areas where big fish have been taken recently and, if possible, concentrate on these areas. Cod tend to remain in shoals and where there are one or two specimens, there are sure to be more.

The tackle for large cod does not have to be particularly heavy. For boat fishing, an IGFA 20lb-class rod is ideal in most cases, providing leads over 14oz are not used. If the water requires heavier leads, then an IGFA 30lb-class rod is better. In either case, the rod should be 6-7ft long and have a fast taper for a lively action, so that when the cod plunges during the fight the rod absorbs the shock. If the rod is too stiff, a sudden snatch could tear the hook from the jaw. Many cod are lost this way.

Centrepin for balance

The size and type of reel will be largely governed by personal preference. Some anglers favour the multiplier, while others favour the centrepin. My preference is for the latter, I find it balances the rod much better as it is set underneath it. The multiplier, on the other hand, is used on top, and you need either to wear a harness or to brace the reel against the left forearm (if you are right-handed) to stop a rod twisting.

My first choice of centrepin for use in shallow water of up to 10 fathoms is the Grice and Young Sea-jecta III de Luxe. If depths exceed 10 fathoms, then the larger Alvey is recommended. If you prefer a multiplier, then a Penn 60 or 65 or a Mitchell 624 is suitable for shallow water. For deep water I recommend a Penn 4/0 Senator or the Penn Super Mariner, which has a very fast retrieve. Some anglers shudder when you mention centrepin reels. They look on the centrepin as a big, clumsy walnut drum with no sophistication. But the modern Alvey reel is constructed from a light, virtually unbreakable plastic, and most recent models incorporate a smooth-action clutch operated by a lever. Although not so fast as the Super Mariner, its retrieve is faster than those of the other Penn and Mitchell reels mentioned.

When seeking large cod—and these can be found in virtually any depth from 3 to over 30 fathoms —the seabed is usually reasonably snag-free (unless you are fishing a wreck) so lines need not be heavy. For shallow-water fishing, with a 20lb rod, lines of 18lb-23lb b.s. are suitable, while for deeper water, with heavier leads, a line of 26-32lb will suit. I prefer a nylon monofilament to other lines such as Dacron. Although the stretch in monofilament reduces sensitivity when feeling bites on the bottom, I find that when a big cod is hooked, stretch is invaluable. It acts as a spring to cushion the fish's sudden plunges.

The case for wire

I have never used a wire line, but I

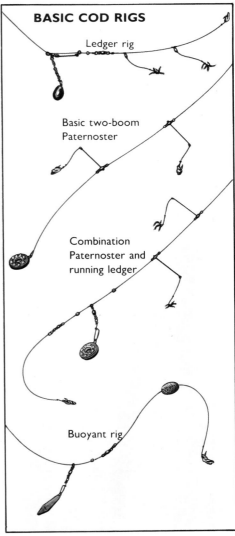

BASIC COD RIGS

Ledger rig

Basic two-boom Paternoster

Combination Paternoster and running ledger

Buoyant rig

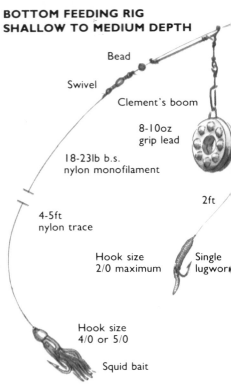

**BOTTOM FEEDING RIG
SHALLOW TO MEDIUM DEPTH**

Bead

Swivel

Clement's boom

8-10oz
grip lead

18-23lb b.s.
nylon monofilament

2ft

4-5ft
nylon trace

Hook size
2/0 maximum

Single
lugworm

Hook size
4/0 or 5/0

Squid bait

Above: *Two rigs for bottom-feeding cod — one for shallow-to-medium water, the other for deep, clean waters with a slow tide.* **Above left:** *A 30lb 8oz cod coming to net.*

have often been aboard boats where other anglers were using it, and I can see no advantage in it under normal conditions. If you should tangle with a fellow angler the unravelling of the two lines becomes far more difficult than for anglers using monofilament. But there is one occasion when wire is valuable. This is when you are fishing very deep, fast water. Here, a 3lb lead may have to be used to reach the seabed with monofilament. With wire it may not be necessary to use 1lb.

Hook size is governed more by bait size than by the gape of the cod's mouth. Most anglers believe that because a large cod has a mouth like a bucket a large hook must be used to stand a chance of landing it. This is a fallacy. Cod do not swim around with their mouths permanently agape, but open them only enough to take in food, and then close the jaws again. The smallest hook will still penetrate some part of the jaws when the strike is made.

As a general guide to size, hooks for worm should be no larger than 2/0, for whole squid 4/0 or 5/0. Whatever the bait, the hook should be no larger than is necessary to avoid the bait masking the point of

the hook. Care should always be taken when baiting to make sure that the point of the hook is completely clear of the bait. If it becomes covered, no matter how hard you strike, it is doubtful whether the hook will penetrate both bait and fish.

Most cod are bottom feeders—except when they come up towards the surface, chasing sprat or herring. Then, they are very difficult to catch anyway. For bottom-feeding fish, use a trace in conjunction with a Clement's boom, so that a taking fish feels very little resistance when moving off with the bait. The number of hooks employed at any one time is a matter of personal preference, but most anglers fishing specifically for a large cod use a single hook on a 4-5ft trace.

If the water is deep and clear, with a sluggish tide, then a French boom fastened as much as 6ft above the lead and with a hook tied to a mere 2ft of nylon and baited with squid, has proved very effective on occasions. I employed this method very successfully eight or nine years ago when there was in influx of very large cod around the Isle of Wight. The best squid is the Californian Calamara, which can be purchased

deep-frozen in this country.

Although squid and worms are the most popular baits, big cod will consume almost anything edible. I was fishing for porbeagle shark off Achill Head, on the west coast of Ireland, some years back, fishing whole mackerel fairly deep, when I got a series of very short runs. On striking I was amazed to find very little resistance, yet I had hooked a 12lb cod.

Herring strip, herring fillets and sprats have also taken their toll of large fish, as have small pout lip-hooked on a size 3/0 hook and fished off the bottom. Pout is often deadly, but if there is a fast tide run the method becomes impossible, for the pout spins in the tide, tangling the tackle. Peeler crab is another excellent bait if used over inshore boat marks or, better still, from a beach. But although most cod when gutted reveal numerous hard-backed crabs in their stomachs, this bait seems totally ineffective when used on a hook. Why this should be so remains a mystery.

DEEP-SEA RIG
CLEAR WATER, SLOW TIDE

French boom

Swivel

26-32lb b.s. nylon monofilament

6ft

3lb cone lead

Above: *Winter fishing on a Yorkshire beach.*
Left: *The squid/lugworm cocktail bait—most effective fished from a boat.*

AT-A-GLANCE

Specimen sizes
Specimen areas for cod run from Kent (boat 26lb, shore 18lb) to North Wales, where a boat-caught specimen will weigh 15lb (shore 10lb) and the Cornwall/Devon shores—specimen size 9lb.

Tackle, bait, techniques
Rod
6-7ft fast taper, 20-30lb IGFA class

Reels
Multipliers (Penn 60, 65, 4/0 Senator, Super Mariner, Michell 624)
Centrepins (Seajecta, Alvey)

Line b.s.
18-23lb nylon (shallow water)
26-32lb (deep water)

Hooks
2/0 (with worm)
4/0-5/0 (whole squid, fish)

Baits
Squid, lug, herring strip, sprat, small whole pout, peeler crab; pirks, feathers

Methods, techniques
Single-hook flowing trace with Clement's boom; feathers, paternoster, pirks

Pirks and feathers

In recent years, big catches of cod have been made on pirks and feathers. One place that is very famous for this method of fishing is the Gantocks in the Firth of Clyde. Another is the Varne Bank in the English Channel, off Folkestone. Here, the usual method is to use a heavy pirk, sometimes weighing as much as 1½lb, with three large white feathers attached above it. It is regrettable that many of the bigger specimens caught by this method are foul-hooked on the large treble hook attached to the pirk, but without a doubt feathers are very successful, particularly in deep, clear water. In mid-1978, an angler fishing at Clifden, Co Connemara, boated a fine cod of 32½lb on mackerel feathers.

For their size, large cod invariably give a most delicate bite. (In contrast, codling usually bite very vigorously, while medium-sized fish give a slower, more bouncy bite.) When a large cod first picks up the

bait the inexperienced angler is often led to believe that he has caught some undersized fish, and he will either strike too soon or move the bait before it has been taken. If left, however, the cod will slowly back away down tide giving a steady pull on the rod top. It is now that the strike can be made with confidence. More fish are lost through hasty strikes than are ever lost by delay.

The cod has many teeth, and for this reason some anglers attach their hooks to wire. This is completely unnecessary, as there is very little power in cod jaws. I have never lost a cod because it bit clean through a monofilament line.

It is important to remember that however you hooked the fish, getting it in the boat or on the beach is the next objective. Always have a large keepnet ready to hand.

Dropnetting

Landing a specimen cod from a pier or harbour is even more difficult. The best method is to use a dropnet

when the fish has been fully played out, but care should always be taken to drift the net under the fish rather than drag the fish over it. Otherwise, the tackle often fouls the bridles of the net. If this happens and the fish gives a last plunge, there is no way of easing the pressure and something has to go— usually the tackle or the hookhold.

In some years 20lb-plus cod are plentiful, in others they are scarce. This is logical when we look at the species' breeding cycles. In a good breeding season, a much higher proportion of eggs mature and this gives us a glut of small fish the following year resulting in a spate of cod weighing over 20lb, some seven years later.

Sharks

For the angler in search of big game, sharking represents the most rewarding sea fishing available in British waters. Here we describe what equipment to buy and the best tactics to use

Since sharks grow to a size much bigger than normally caught, most anglers assume that their equipment must be scaled up and that it should be heavy and strong. Consequently, many anglers buy rods and reels suited to fight and land fish many times greater than any ever caught in this country. This imbalance in tackle is further endorsed by charter boat skippers who tend to provide over-heavy tackle for the angler without his own sharking equipment.

Heavy tackle is not needed
Heavy boats rods and extremely large reels loaded with 130lb b.s. line are well beyond the requirements of any of our sharks since none make the fantastic 400-to-600-yard-runs of marlins and tuna for which such

equipment was developed. Only very long runs require such heavy lines: this is because the pressure of the water on the line during a long curving run (or its resistance as such a length is being moved through the water) would break a lighter line. Since the average angler can only produce a pull of 25lb with, say, a 7A, no angler would ever need a line much heavier than 30lb b.s. Moreover, the weight in water of any of our sharks cannot break the line, for the weight of the fish in water is only a fraction of its weight in air.

Considering the fighting qualities of the various species liable to be taken, and the weight to which they go, the following types of tackle are recommended so that each would allow the fish to give the best sport: blue shark—30lb-class tackle;

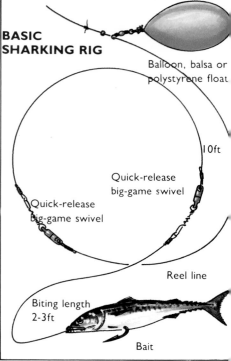

BASIC SHARKING RIG

Balloon, balsa or polystyrene float

Quick-release big-game swivel

10ft

Quick-release big-game swivel

Reel line

Biting length 2-3ft

Bait

porbeagle—50lb-class tackle; mako, thresher and large porbeagle—80lb-class rod and reel. Each one of these tackle classes can be reduced to a lower one with increasing experience in catching shark.

The terminal tackle, because of the size of baits used and the size of sharks' mouths, should consist of large 6/0 to 10/0 good-quality hooks, attached to a biting length of 2 to 2.5mm diameter braided wire, because a shark's teeth are liable to cut through anything else. The biting length, 2 to 3ft long, should be attached to a further 10ft of slightly thinner, similar wire or long-

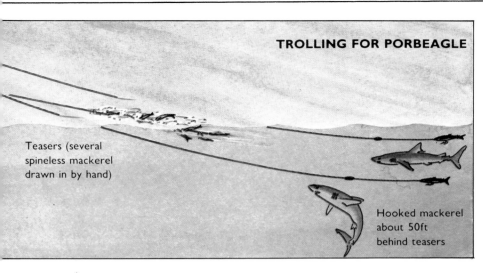

TROLLING FOR PORBEAGLE

Teasers (several spineless mackerel drawn in by hand)

Hooked mackerel about 50ft behind teasers

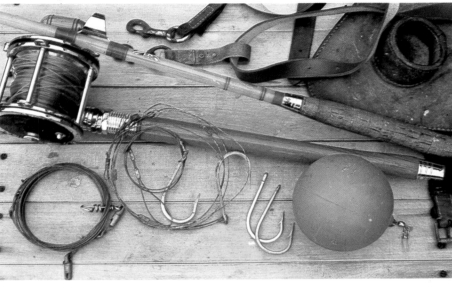

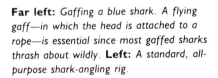

Far left: *Gaffing a blue shark. A flying gaff—in which the head is attached to a rope—is essential since most gaffed sharks thrash about wildly.* **Left:** *A standard, all-purpose shark-angling rig.*

Top: *Trolling for porbeagle using a group of teasers—usually mackerel with their backbones removed.*
Above: *Typical shark tackle—Penn 6/0 reel, wire traces, big hooks and a float.*

Top: *A specimen porbeagle and its captor.*
Above: *A 95lb blue shark, one of very many caught off the Cornish coast.*

liner's monofilament nylon to withstand the abrasive action of the shark's skin.

Bait
Bait in shark fishing consists of whole fish used either singly if the fish is large, or in number if they are small. The favourite bait is mackerel which as a shoal fish probably represents the commonest natural food of sharks. However, any other species may be used and many sharks have been taken on pouting or pollack. Various methods of mounting the bait are used with the head or tail pointing up the trace.

Each method should ensure that the bait does not come off when first taken, for sharks rarely swallow the bait at once. Natural presentation is not essential, for the movement of the bait should give off the erratic vibrations of an injured or sick fish.

The off-the-bottom rule
Since sharks are usually mid-water or surface fish, the bait should be fished off the bottom. This is achieved by attaching a float, either a balloon or square of polystyrene, to the line once the depth set for the bait has been reached. The float should always be as small as possi-

ble so as not to produce resistance once the bait is taken. This off-the-bottom rule on bait presentation is not absolute, for many sharks are taken with the bait on the bottom fished as a flowing trace.

The method of fishing depends very much on the area, the wind and tides, and both drifting and fishing at anchor are successful. In each case, the use of rubby-dubby is almost essential, especially if blue shark are sought. Any shark swim-

53

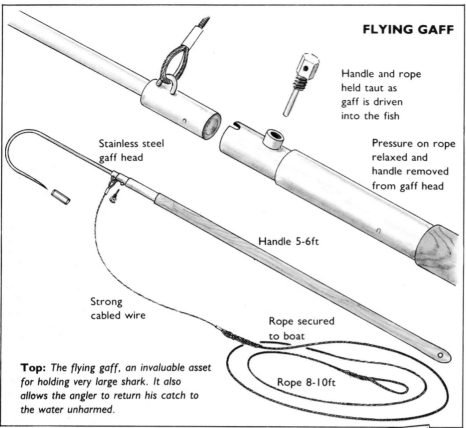

FLYING GAFF

Handle and rope held taut as gaff is driven into the fish

Pressure on rope relaxed and handle removed from gaff head

Stainless steel gaff head

Handle 5-6ft

Strong cabled wire

Rope secured to boat

Rope 8-10ft

Top: *The flying gaff, an invaluable asset for holding very large shark. It also allows the angler to return his catch to the water unharmed.*

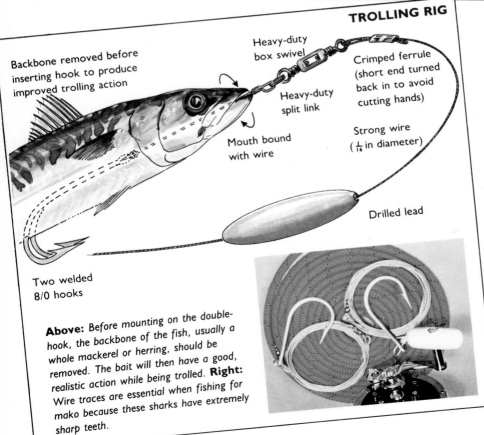

TROLLING RIG

Backbone removed before inserting hook to produce improved trolling action

Heavy-duty box swivel

Crimped ferrule (short end turned back in to avoid cutting hands)

Heavy-duty split link

Strong wire ($\frac{1}{16}$ in diameter)

Mouth bound with wire

Drilled lead

Two welded 8/0 hooks

Above: *Before mounting on the double-hook, the backbone of the fish, usually a whole mackerel or herring, should be removed. The bait will then have a good, realistic action while being trolled.* **Right:** *Wire traces are essential when fishing for mako because these sharks have extremely sharp teeth.*

AT-A-GLANCE

Specimen sizes
Four species of shark are sought in British waters, the blue shark being the most popular. Specimen sizes are as follows: blue 100lb, porbeagle 150lb, thresher 120lb, mako 200lb.

Tackle, Bait, Techniques
Rod
Blue—30lb-class
Porbeagle—50lb-class
Mako, thresher and large porbeagle—80lb-class 12ft glassfibre beachcaster (6lb test curve) for shore

Reel
To match above for boat use; 6½in side-cast for shore; multiplier for trolling

Line
30lb b.s. nylon with 2–2.5mm wire biting length of 2–3ft and 10ft wire or nylon; 31lb nylon and 10ft wire trace for shore

Bait
Mackerel or pollack

ming through its trail of fine particles will follow them to source and find the bait. The presence of the fine, oily particles of food prompts the shark into feeding.

The flying gaff
The use of flying gaffs, which have detachable handles and where the head itself is attached to or carries a rope, is essential, since most gaffed shark thrash about wildly. It is easier to control them at the end of a rope and there is less chance of injury from the handle which otherwise may break or be moved around erratically by the thrashing fish. A noose passed over the tail of the fish lying at the side of the boat can also be used to tether the fish. This is probably the best method as it always allows the fish to be returned to the water uninjured—an absolute necessity if anglers are to continue to enjoy their sport.

Bass

A 'zone beyond the third wave' sounds as superstitious and unattainable as the gold at the rainbow's end. But if you can drop a bait inside that zone, you'll find a magical reward

The secret of successful bass fishing is not fancy tackle, complicated terminal rigs or exotic baits but being able to locate the fish.

Bass are an inshore species that feed along the shallows of estuaries, over rocky ground and in surf, currents and tideways. But by far the most popular and productive angling spots are surf beaches.

Beaches can be categorized into storm beaches, which are exposed to prevailing winds and the open sea, subject to almost continuous surf, and lee beaches, sheltered and free from big waves.

Feeding zone on storm beaches

Storm beaches may be steep, with the surf breaking a short distance out, or shallow, with white water showing for several hundred yards and the pent-up surge running well up the beach before receding. Scoured by ceaseless wave action, they look devoid of fish food. This is deceptive, for sandeels, immature flatfish, crabs, shrimps and other creatures are concentrated by the surf into a well-defined area. In this feeding zone, which runs through the surf, parallel to the beach, you will find bass. It may be quite narrow but you must locate this zone and cast into it.

On steep beaches where the surf breaks close-in, the familiar advice 'just beyond the third or last breaker' will place your bait correctly. But on shallow storm beaches or on lee beaches the surf may be breaking 300 or 400 yards out, driving anglers unused to such conditions to despair. The fishing zone will be found in the first 'water table' rarely more than 80 yards out, and often much closer.

The water table is where the depth remains fairly constant despite the repeated surges and the water forms a ridge noticeably higher than the level nearby.

Wade out to knee depth and search the table by moving the bait around until bass are contacted. Fish at this distance until bites cease, then begin the search again.

Shallow storm beaches usually become steeper near the high-water mark. When the tide is almost full, the surf will shorten, and casts of 40-50 yards or less are sufficient.

Locating the bass

The task of locating bass on steep beaches is just the same. In moderate or light surf they can be fished for with lighter tackle than

Above: A handful of lesser sandeels, enough for a few casts when the bass are running. **Left:** Bass from a stormbeach. **Below:** These flasher vanes on a trolling rig give the lure more attraction.

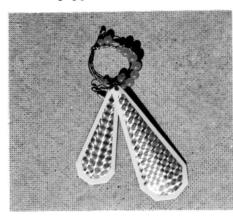

55

the shallow storm beach. Long casts are then unnecessary as bass in these conditions may be only a few yards out.

Soft or peeler crab is the most effective all-round bait for bottom-fishing, and clam, razorfish and slipper limpet are also good. Fish baits such as live and dead sandeel, or slips of mackerel or herring, will take the bass of specimen size.

In calm conditions or light surf, an ordinary casting 'bomb' without grips is adequate as it does not matter—indeed it will help in searching the water—if your bait wanders a little. In good surf, however, it will not stay in the feeding zone, and bombs with wire grips are essential for holding bottom. The breakaway type are easier to free than the old fixed-wire kinds.

Three common faults

Lack of success on storm beaches can be attributed to three common faults: not holding your rod, casting and shifting ground too frequently. Changing fishing stations or moving around on a beach pays off only if you know the beach thoroughly. If you do not have detailed local knowledge—stay put. Bass will come your way at some stage, but if you move about you may leave just before the fish reach you. Missed and undetected bites make the difference between a good and a bad day's fishing. Consequently, you should always hold your rod and stay alert. With the rod standing in its rod rests, bites may not register strongly enough to be noticed, and you may miss others because you cannot reach it in time to strike.

On lee beaches a wind usually does little but colour the water and fill it with weed. But in certain conditions, with a decent wind and wave, parts of a lee beach may develop a flash surf. Then you can fish those parts with every hope of success, for the bass will be concentrated into a narrow band. Otherwise look for the same sort of features as you would on a storm beach.

Likely fishing areas

Beaches may be a few hundred yards long or stretch for mile after featureless mile. Where does one fish? Both ends of a beach are likely

Above: Bass fishing in heavy surf on Brandon Bay, County Kerry. In recent years, this bass paradise has shown a decline in catches.
Below: Five bass rigs for use in different conditions or form different shorelines. The rough-ground paternoster, for instance, prevents the loss of an expensive casting weight on snaggy seabed rocks. Kelp stems can be disastrously effective in snagging terminal tackle.

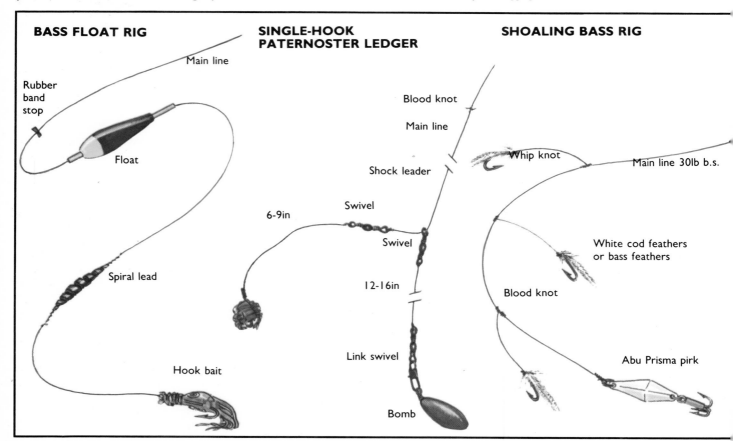

BASS FLOAT RIG

SINGLE-HOOK
PATERNOSTER LEDGER

SHOALING BASS RIG

Main line

Rubber band stop

Float

Spiral lead

Hook bait

Blood knot

Main line

Shock leader

Swivel

6-9in

Swivel

12-16in

Link swivel

Bomb

Whip knot

Main line 30lb b.s.

White cod feathers or bass feathers

Blood knot

Abu Prisma pirk

areas. If there is a sweep of tide along a beach, bass tend to swim with it so choose accordingly. One end of a beach may fish better on the flood, on the ebb or at some stage in between. Only by consistent fishing will you get to know the local pattern. Even so, weather and seasonal tides may affect this timetable. Spring tides may provide different results from neaps. At other spots fish may come at any time.

Frequently, beaches are flanked by rugged coast which may hold bass in calm conditions, but when the sea gets too rough they are driven off and can be intercepted as they hit the beach. Similarly, any spout where a current or set of tide strikes the beach is worth trying, as fish are channelled there.

Pay attention to rocks, reefs, craggy cliffs, patches of weed on a stony or pebbly bottom, and points where the surf penetrates a little farther on to the beach or appears to be a little rougher. Anything that breaks up the monotony of an otherwise featureless beach is worth examining. Look, too, at stretches where sandeels are found in the coarse sand, or where sandbanks are covered by tide. Fish in the gullies between the sandbanks, as bass are rarely caught on top of them.

The bass larder

Low water exposes rock split by pools and clean patches of sand. Weed-covered boulders and stones or fissured platforms of rock may abound. This is the habitat of the shore crab, velvet swimming crab and the larger edible crab. Blennies, gobies, butter-fish and eels are plentiful in the rock pools and under the damp weed, as are shrimps, prawns and slaters. Provided the waves are not too rough, big bass cannot resist such a rich larder.

Surfcasting tackle is quite adequate for fishing here. Long casting is unnecessary and may lose expensive tackle. Bass come in very close with the tide, nosing around in the shallows. Twenty to forty yards —less, sometimes—is usually far enough. It may seem wrong to cast right into the rough, but this is where the bass are. For fast retrieve of line over obstacles, some anglers claim that large fixed-spool reels are better than most multiplier reels.

Particularly good spots are where there is a current running onto or over a spur, reef or rock. But remember that your bait is more likely to be taken on the uptide side. It is important, after the sinker has settled, to tighten the line very gently to avoid pulling the sinker into weed or a snag.

Terminal tackle

Single-hook traces should be used, as two hooks double your chances of getting caught up. Mostly, however, it is the sinker which fouls, so when using either a single-hook paternoster or a paternoster ledger, always attach your sinker with some rotten-bottom. If you must break a fouled line, only the sinker is lost. Sparking plugs, rusty nuts or bolts, or even suitable stones will serve as disposable sinkers.

Bass feeding over rough ground bite very delicately. A paternoster ledger allows them to take line without becoming alarmed. Give the fish time to get hold of the bait before striking the hook home. If the fish is played gently at first, it usually heads for deeper water over less snaggy ground, where it can be fought more safely.

Float-fishing over rocks

In areas of high rock and deep gullies, float fishing is effective and enjoyable. As the tide floods in over the rocks and fills the gullies and crevices, the bass move in, searching for food. They may be found close-in, often in very shallow water, so keep out of sight.

Overfishing

Bass are extremely long-lived and slow growing fish, and these two factors make the species vulnerable to overfishing, whether by rod and line or by commercial fishing methods. For a number of years, angling federations and some scientific bodies have been concerned at the disappearance of the bass from parts of Ireland and Britain. Various study programmes suggest that, if present trends continue, overfishing will lead to the absence of bass from some areas of Britain's coast line for a long period, if not for ever.

There are few sea fish that enjoy

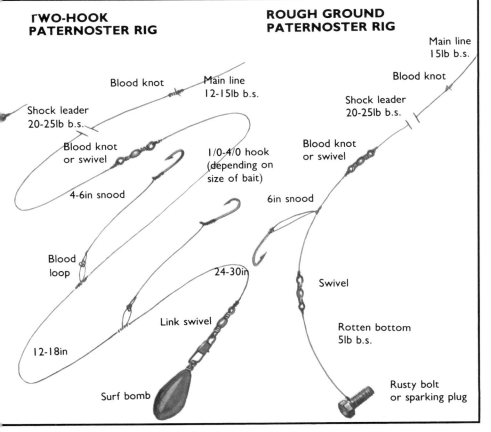

TWO-HOOK PATERNOSTER RIG

Blood knot
Main line 12-15lb b.s.
Shock leader 20-25lb b.s.
Blood knot or swivel
4-6in snood
1/0-4/0 hook (depending on size of bait)
Blood loop
24-30in
Link swivel
12-18in
Surf bomb

ROUGH GROUND PATERNOSTER RIG

Main line 15lb b.s.
Blood knot
Shock leader 20-25lb b.s.
Blood knot or swivel
6in snood
Swivel
Rotten bottom 5lb b.s.
Rusty bolt or sparking plug

ARTIFICIAL LURES FOR BASS

Killer lure

Bar spinner

Toby spoon

Rubber eel

Sandeel

Above: *A selection of popular lures commonly used in bass fishing. Bass like a fast, bright spin and may slash at a bait dropped across their path. They are also partial to slow-wobbling spoons. All the baits imitate small fish. To get the most out of bass fishing, use a light tackle: a bait-casting rod and multiplier or a 7ft spinner with fixed-spool reel.* **Right:** *Just two ways of hooking sandeel and prawn.*

HOOKING PRAWN AND SANDEEL BAITS

Sandeel

Prawn

the reputation of the bass as a fighter. In the right environment the species gives first-rate sport on rod and line. Bass fishing is usually practised from the shore or small boats close-in, but the species can be caught wherever there are off-shore reefs or sandbanks.

Spinning
Spinning for bass also embraces the use of a natural bait that is worked in similar fashion to an artificial one. A sprat or small herring that is fished 'sink-and-draw' style over known holding grounds can be extremely effective. Live sandeels are commonly used on the South West Coast.

When the bass are shoaling in-shore, boat anglers often watch for tell-tale signs of surface disturbance that indicate that bass are feeding.

As the predatory bass lunge through the swarming immature fish on which they feed, the water is whipped into a white spray. Gulls contribute to the scene with raucous screeches as they scramble to pick up floating fish left by the bass.

The boatman should drift the boat to the edge of the splashing water so that the fish are not disturbed and frightened off. A spinner cast out and drawn through the water just below the surface is almost certain

of success in most conditions.

Shorecasters
Most of Britain's bass fishermen are shorecasters, using rods that have sufficient power to cast a 4oz weight, yet with enough suppleness to feel the movement of fish and current. They rely on the bass finding the paternostered or ledgered worms that are usually offered. Crabs in both the 'peeler' and 'softie' stage of shedding the hard carapace, are a bait that can be used to great effect from rocky shore platforms where there is a mass of weed growth that bass recognize as cover for crabs.

Bass also frequent the shoreline close to rock faces and cliff edges.

Tope

With a skin as tough as glasspaper and teeth that can slice through nylon line, the tope is a tough fighting fish that needs strong tackle but a gentle touch to be landed unharmed

The tope is a strong, slim-bodied member of the shark family and is found all around our coasts. More numerous in some areas than in others, the Wash, the Thames Estuary, the Solent, Cardigan Bay, the Wexford Coast and Tralee Bay are noted tope fishing venues. The species is found in depths ranging from a few feet along the shore to depths in excess of 50 fathoms, but on the whole it is a fish found in moderate depths and is most plentiful in depths of 5-20 fathoms. The fact that it frequents shallow water facilitates the use of light tackle and permits the tope to show its superb fighting qualities.

While the tope is found over all types of bottoms it has a preference for clean ground and although it inhabits all levels of water it feeds mainly on demersal, bottom-living, species, particularly those found over clean ground. It is almost entirely a fish eater and the most popular baits used for catching tope are mackerel, herring, squid, whiting, pouting and small flatfish.

Tope are large fish running up to 80lb or more, but a more usual size is between 20 and 35lb. For that reason, sizeable baits such as a long lask of mackerel or indeed the whole mackerel can be used.

Tope are taken regularly from the shore in places. Steep-to beaches with a fair depth of water close-in offer the best opportunity, but in calm conditions the tope may be met on very shallow beaches. They run a long way up only those estuaries

Tope fishing provides some of the best big-game fishing to be found around the British Isles, though over-fishing in recent years has made the tope an endangered species.

and tidal channels that are completely saline as they have no great tolerance to freshwater. The time and place to fish is directly in the channel at low water and on the early flood tide. Tope will be found quartering little coves and bays along a rocky coast, usually at the same stage of the tide, but only persistent fishing of a particular spot will yield this information.

Shore fishing for tope

For shore fishing a beachcasting rod capable of casting 6oz is suitable. Lighter rods will handle the fish but may be over-loaded by the combined weight of bait and sinker if a heavy fish bait is used. Nylon monofilament of 18-20lb b.s. is adequate provided there is enough of it on the reel—300 yards is not too much as shore-caught tope can run a very long way when hooked. Multiplier reels are most commonly used but in some cramped rock fishing situations a large fixed-spool reel has definite advantages.

Right and below: A shocker knot or crimping will join a leader to the main reel line.
Above right: The lift aboard calls for confident, correct handling—and preferably gloves.
Far right: Cutting a wire trace with tinsnips: the fish will be returned unharmed.

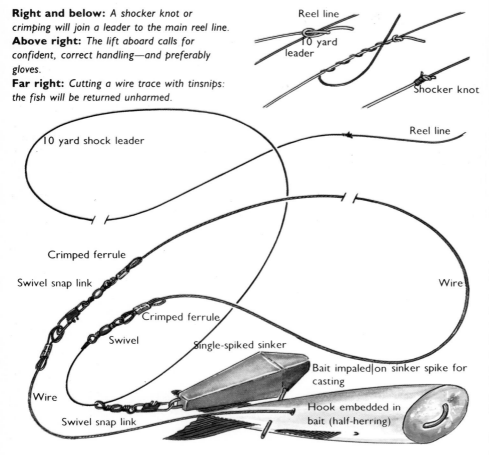

Reel line

10 yard leader

Shocker knot

Reel line

10 yard shock leader

Crimped ferrule

Swivel snap link

Wire

Crimped ferrule

Swivel

Single-spiked sinker

Wire

Swivel snap link

Bait impaled|on sinker spike for casting

Hook embedded in bait (half-herring)

How to hook tope

Tope pick up a bait and run a short distance before pausing to turn and swallow it. A ledger rig, therefore, is the most suitable terminal tackle as it allows the fish to seize the bait and move off with it without feeling drag or pressure. The fish should not be struck until it commences its second run, unless a very small bait is being used.

One method is to use an all-wire trace of 40lb b.s. Its overall length is 4ft as anything longer causes

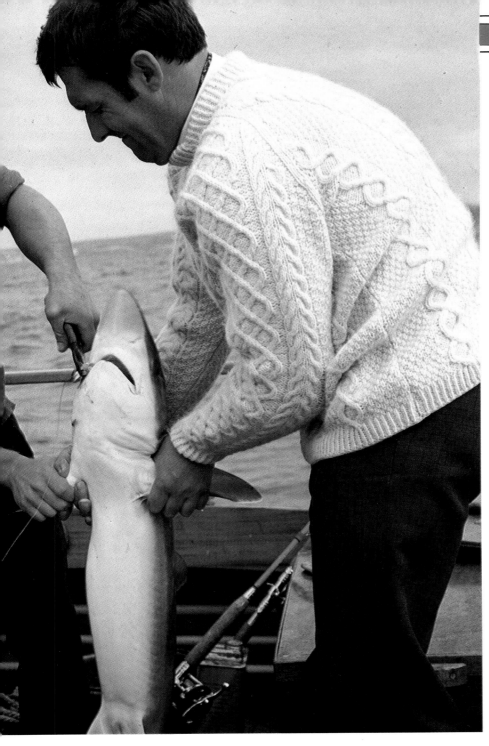

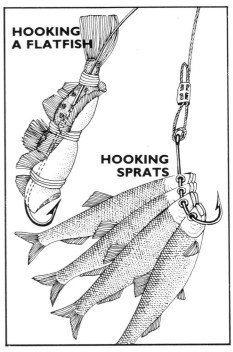

Above: *A whole dab on a hook and secured by cotton, or four sprats or other small, silvery fish used as deadbaits will attract tope.*

serious problems in casting. It is joined to a shock leader of 30lb test and then to the main line. The sinker is attached to a free running swivel on the shock leader, which permits the fish to take line freely. A similar trace is also used except that the short wire hook-link is followed by heavy monofilament of at least 40lb test. Tope have sharp teeth so a short-wire link to the hook is essential. Their skin is as rough as glass paper when rubbed against the grain, and as they have a tendency

to roll up on the trace, light nylon will part like thread. All-wire is therefore safer, but heavy nylon is preferred since it is more flexible and fishes better. It should, however, be changed after each fish as it becomes unreliable due to abrasion and chafing. Hook sizes will depend on the size of the bait used, but are normally 6/0 to 9/0. They should be razor sharp.

When casting a long trace, an old spiked sinker is used on which all but one spike is removed. The bait is

impaled on the single spike, effectively halving the length of the trace and permitting easier casting. When the bait hits the water it parts company with the sinker. A few feet of line should be wound back on the reel when the sinker is on the bottom to ensure that the trace has straightened out along the sea-bed.

Traces for boat fishing are very similar, except that heavier nylon monofilament can be used for the short-wire link—50lb to 70lb test will suit admirably. When fishing from an anchored boat in strong tides or currents a long trace may be preferred and its length can be adjusted by putting a stop (a rubber band or match stick secured by two half hitches) on the line below the free running ledger. When fishing on the drift—that is, from a drifting boat—a shorter trace is desirable. The ledger runs on the monofilament portion of the trace, making a partial ledger and when fishing over rough ground the sinker should be attached by a length of light line or 'rotten bottom'. If the trace fouls, the bottom link to the sinker should break and only the lead will be lost.

To get the best out of tope one must not fish heavy. This is un-

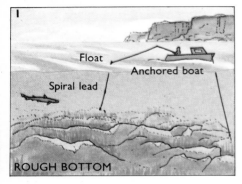

ROUGH BOTTOM

Float

Anchored boat

Spiral lead

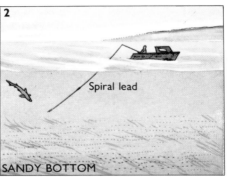

SANDY BOTTOM

Spiral lead

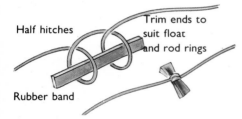

Half hitches

Trim ends to suit float and rod rings

Rubber band

Top: *Returning a tope to the sea.* **Above:** *Tope fishing from boats. When at anchor over rough ground (1) adjust the length of trace with the rubber band stopper, shown left. On the drift over a sandy bottom, a shorter trace is best (2) with no float, to avoid snagging.* **Below:** *A slider float rig with rubber band stopper for tope fishing.*

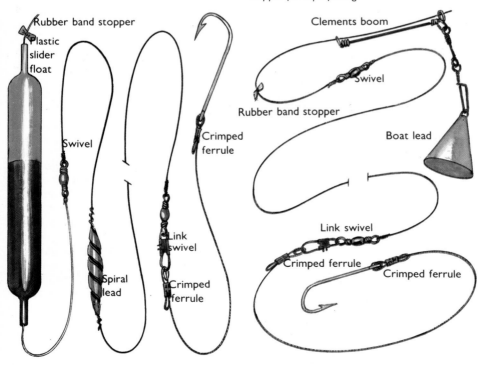

Rubber band stopper

Plastic slider float

Swivel

Spiral lead

Link swivel

Crimped ferrule

Crimped ferrule

Link swivel

Crimped ferrule

Clements boom

Swivel

Rubber band stopper

Boat lead

Link swivel

Crimped ferrule

Crimped ferrule

necessary as the tope likes to run hard and fast, particularly in shallow water and can be played on light gear. A test line of 25lb to 30lb is adequate and can be matched with rods comparable to those complying to the IGFA specifications for the 20lb and 30lb tackle classes. Multiplier-type reels with a capacity of 300 yards of line are best.

While the angler normally fishes on or near the bottom for tope, when drift fishing in depths of up to 10 fathoms or over rocky reefs he can driftline or float fish for them. These methods can at times be most effective. When floatfishing, the depth at which the bait is fishing can be adjusted to keep it clear of the reefs and avoid catching in the bottom.

Flatfish

The big, meaty turbot lies in wait for its food on the leaside of wrecks and sandbars, but the smaller, livelier plaice roams about its broken grounds and needs tempting on to the hook

Derrick Dyer's 32lb 3oz record turbot (left) and 31¼lb fish from the same Plymouth mark.

Of all the fish around our shores that provide good eating, the varieties of flatfish are the most highly esteemed, none more so than the turbot.

Famous turbot marks such as the Skerries and the Shambles Bank, which once provided excellent fishing for the rod and line angler, now only produce mediocre catches. Banks that were impossible to trawl lent themselves very well to longline fishing, and overfishing resulted.

In recent years some of the biggest turbot have been taken by anglers wreck-fishing for conger. The present rod-caught record turbot, a fish of 32lb 12oz, was boated by an angler fishing a wreck off Salcombe. When a ship sinks to the seabed it invariably lies across the flow of the current and over the years the tide hitting the side of the wreck scours out a deep hole at each end. It is in these scour holes that big turbot lurk in wait for small food fish to be swept over the hole.

Many of these wreck-caught turbot provide an unexpected bonus to the conger-hunter. But selective, serious turbot fishing is pursued over large sandbanks which sometimes come up to within three or four fathoms of the surface and fall away into depths of 15 fathoms or more. On the side of such banks big flatties lie in wait for food fish.

Although the tides over these banks may be fierce, the depth is not great, so it is rarely necessary to use leads of more than 1lb. To get the best sport keep the tackle light—a 30lb-class hollow glass rod is ideal.

If you are a multiplier enthusiast I recommend either an Ambassadeur 9000 reel, which is light and has an adequate capacity, the Penn Long Beach 60 and 65, or the Squidder 140M. For the centrepin fan the Alvey 525C 12 or the glassfibre version, the 525C 52, does the job nicely. These reels incorporate a slipping clutch mechanism and large handle.

The reel should be loaded with monofilament of between 25 and 30lb b.s. Some anglers prefer Dacron but I find this is affected strongly by the tide, and should two lines become entangled, sorting out the tackle is much more difficult than with monofilament. Wire lines are not only unnecessary but a handicap, for in turbot fishing the idea is to drift the terminal tackle away from the boat.

A Clement's boom carries the lead. The reel line is passed through the two eyes of the boom and the trace—at least 8–9ft long and of 30lb nylon—is attached to the reel line by a spiral locking attachment.

I usually fish two hooks, one attached to the end of the trace and a dropper halfway along the trace. The reason for this is that, should a fish be missed on the first bite and get away with one bait, it will often make a second attack.

The fact that a double-figure turbot has a mouth big enough to take a man's fist does not mean one should use a massive hook. The bigger the hook, the more it weighs, and a large lump of iron in a slender fillet of mackerel will do nothing but anchor it to the bottom.

Most turbot are caught on sandeel or mackerel fillet. With sandeel, a 3/0 stainless steel hook is passed through the mouth of the fish, through the gill and back into the body by the vent, with both point and barb exposed. Another method with sandeel is to use a baiting needle and thread the nylon right through the body, leaving the hook protruding from the mouth. A short length of elastic cotton is wound around the tail to prevent the fish sliding down and masking the hook.

When using the great sandeel, especially if it is a large fish, it is best to fillet from head to tail to make two baits. These fillets are mounted by passing the hook in and out at one end only.

If mackerel fillet is preferred, then a size 4/0 or 5/0 hook should be used. The mackerel is filleted from head to tail and then cut into 1in strips from head to tail to produce a long, narrow bait. The hook is then passed through and through again one end of the fillet, allowing most of the bait to hang below the hook bend.

Never worry about a fish biting short, for turbot feed on live fish and engulf the prey in their cavernous mouth. As the silver half of the fillet looks more appetizing to anglers, most usually try this first but I have caught far more fish on the blue green half of the fillet.

Whiting or pouting can be used instead. These can be fished as for mackerel unless they are small, when they are best baited whole. Many turbot have been caught by accident when an angler has fished with lugworm for other species.

As turbot generally tend to lie halfway down the side of a bank the boat should be positioned as nearly as possible on top of the bank. With a good tide and using the right amount of lead it is possible to bounce the terminal tackle away down the bank to the feeding fish.

The turbot, although spending most of its time on the seabed, will make sudden attacks from the seabed on an unsuspecting prey, sometimes rising up several feet. So the angler should be ready for a 'take' at any time while bouncing the lead downtide.

This kind of bite is a sudden snatch which should be struck immediately. No matter how strong the tide, there comes a point when the lead will hold bottom without drifting any farther down the bank. When this point is reached, and if there have been no takes, the angler may put his rod down and watch for bites. But every few minutes he should lift the rod high, bringing the tackle clear of the seabed.

Should a turbot have taken while the bait was stationary, without a bite being recorded, the fish will be felt immediately on lifting the rod tip. Secondly, the movement may encourage a nearby fish to attack.

The turbot cannot be classified as a fighting fish but a good specimen in a fast tide will put up a very good resistance. All the time the hooked fish will be trying to return to the seabed and with a strong tide it is often difficult to get its nose up. Steady pressure is needed.

Many varieties of fish surface well astern of a boat on a strong tide, but not the turbot. The habit of keeping their heads down all through the fight means that they come up virtually straight under the rod tip. However, the angler should be prepared for a final plunge for freedom when the hooked fish first

sees the shape of the boat's silhouette.

Another method of taking specimen turbot on the same kind of tackle involves allowing the boat to drift over the bank instead of anchoring. A third possibility is to slowly motor across the tide, along the side of the bank, trolling the terminal tackle with a lead heavy enough to keep in contact with the seabed. Unfortunately, this method is very difficult with more than two anglers in the boat as lines easily become entangled.

Whether trolling or drifting is practised, takes will be positive. The fish chases the bait and makes a snatch which is clearly felt.

Ron Edwards' Spotlight

My favourite boat mark is in Ireland, at the entrance to Cork Harbour, just inside Roche's Point. This is a well-known turbot bank and is marked as such on charts. Although there are numerous turbot areas around the Irish coastline, this mark produces a large number of specimens by comparison. These other areas, such as Fenit, Co Kerry, pro-

The hire-boat Saltwind II *anchors over the Skerries and the lines sweep down among the plaice, and turbot that live on the Bank. Some typical examples of prime fish in their catch of plaice are shown (inset) above right.*
Right: *Netting a flatfish aboard.*

duce considerably more, but usually much smaller, fish.

The turbot bank at the mouth of Cork Harbour is a large area and although the chart does not show either the extent of the area or the uneven nature of the bottom, I have seen as many as 20 boats fishing this mark, with virtually every boat taking fish. This bank is caused by a bottle-neck at Ram's Head which causes the ebb tide coming out of Cork Harbour to speed up, scouring sand and silt from the narrows. The tide then slows down where the estuary widens, and deposits this sand and silt on the bank.

The whole seabed seaward off Ram's Head is a mass of rivers and gullies, with depths from 6–9 fathoms within a few yards. It is on the sides of these ridges that the turbot await their prey. With shallow sandbanks on the western side of the estuary, the area abounds with sandeel and a day's supply of bait can be caught very quickly on well presented feathers.

This mark is sheltered from all the winds, apart perhaps from a due south gale, so that it is possible to fish whatever the weather. With the many ridges and changes of depth, the ebb tide causes ruffle or back-waves over a very large area and the whole surface of the sea is in constant turmoil, making it impossible to gauge the exact spot to fish by surface indications. In cases like this an echo sounder is invaluable. With this apparatus it is possible to pin-point the peak of the ridge and anchor the boat so that the terminal tackle is fished on the leeside.

Because of fast tides and because the seabed is sand and shell, the bottom is devoid of all weed so does not harbour any small life that other species may feed on.

Specimen plaice

Another highly esteemed flatfish, although much smaller than the turbot, is the plaice. The plaice can exceed 7lb but fish over $3\frac{1}{2}$lb are usually regarded as specimens. The ideal time to fish for plaice is high summer, when the weather is warm and the water clear.

Because it is unlikely that fish over 7lb will be caught, tackle can be kept very light. The size of the lead should determine the strength of the rod and the choice of lead is governed by strength of tide and depth of water. If a lead up to 12oz is to be used, an IGFA 20lb-class rod is suitable; if the lead is no more than 6oz, an IGFA 12lb-class rod.

A multiplier reel to balance these rods would be a Mitchell 602 AP, a Penn 150 or 160, preferably with metal spools or, if a centrepin is preferred, the Grice and Young Sea Jecta 111 De Luxe, which now has a carbonfibre back and is extremely light, or the Alvey 455C 12.

If the 12lb-class outfits are to be used, the reel should be loaded with

Below left: *Ron Edwards' Irish hotspot.*
Below: *Cloghane on the coast of County Kerry, a hotspot for specimen flounder and large numbers of smaller-than-specimen turbot.*

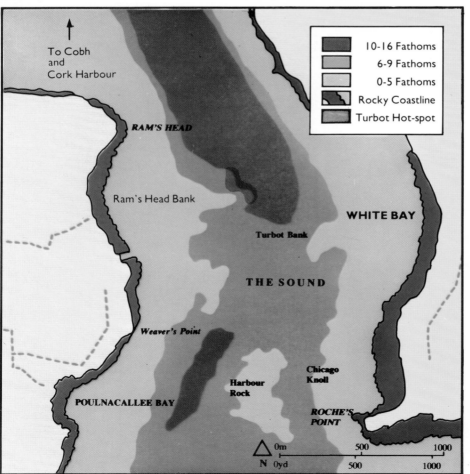

nylon monofilament of 14 or 15lb b.s. With the 20lb-class rod, 22–23lb monofilament is suitable. When the tide is running a trace should be used in conjunction with a Clement's boom or sea boom. It should be as long as can easily be handled with the rod. If you choose a 6ft rod it is very difficult to use traces of over 7ft. The number of hooks employed is a matter of choice. It is not uncommon to take two or even three fish at once, on as many hooks.

In slack water the paternoster rig is better as traces tend to become tangled when there is no tide. Slack water plaice will also come a long way off the bottom to accept a bait.

I have always found lugworms best, but big plaice can be caught on many baits, including ragworms, razorfish and peeler crab. I once caught a 4lb fish on an unbaited mackerel feather. Hooks should be kept small, especially for lugworm: a No 1 long-shank is big enough.

When using a trace in a running tide, a plaice bite is sometimes almost undetectable. For this reason it is best to lift the terminal rig 2–3ft off the seabed at regular intervals as quite often it will be found that a plaice has swallowed the bait and is lying still. Never hurry the strike. It is better to wait for the second bite and then slowly lift the rod tip, raising the tackle from the seabed. The weight of the fish will be felt and only a small strike will set the hook.

During slack water it is best to keep the terminal rig constantly on the move. This can either be done by the angler or balancing the rod on the gunwale in such a way that the rise and fall of the boat on the swells imparts a good movement to the baited hooks. The bouncing of the lead on the seabed creates attractive flurries of sand and mud.

As an added attractor, plastic spoons can be added to the trace. Plaice are very inquisitive fish and anything unusual will arouse their curiosity. A hooked plaice will make every effort to return to the seabed and will do so all the way to the

Specimen sizes
Turbot: between 10lb and 19lb (boat-caught fish), and 5lb and 9lb (shore-caught fish) depending on locality.
Plaice: between 3lb and 5lb (boat) and 2lb and 3½lb (shore) depending on locality.

Tackle, Bait, Techniques
Rod
7–7½ft 30lb-class (turbot).
IGFA 12 or 20lb (plaice).

Reel
Multiplier or centrepin.

Line b.s.
25–30lb (turbot), 14–15 or 22–23lb monofilament (plaice).

Hooks
3/0–5/0 stainless (turbot).
No 1 longshank (plaice).

Bait
Mackerel fillet, sandeel, whiting, pout (whole or fillet) (turbot). Lugworm, ragworm, razorfish, peeler (plaice).

Techniques
Clement's boom (turbot).
Clement's boom, paternoster (plaice). Anchored, drifting and trolling.

boat, in a series of plunges. In between the bursts of activity the fish will be content to keep its head down, at which time recovery of the line is relatively easy. But during its plunges, cease winding and allow the natural spring in the rod to wear the fish down. With a particularly active fish it is worth giving line.

Plaice grounds vary every year. Several spots should be tried in the vicinity where mussels are known to be, until large plaice are contacted. Then, accurate land markings should be made. You can then return to exactly the same spot on subsequent occasions and expect good catches for several weeks until either the plaice have consumed all the mussels or this delicacy has grown too big.

Whiting

The whiting, a member of the cod family, is an extremely common fish which is of great commercial importance. It also provides good sport for the boat or shore angler

For the angler, the whiting is a very useful fish—its fighting qualities are excellent for its size, and it often provides sport when little else is available. Unfortunately, many anglers seeking this quarry use rods which are too stiff and gear that is much too heavy, thus denying a hooked fish the chance to show its paces. The rod-caught (boat) record stands at 6lb 4oz, and was set by S Dearman, in West Bay, Bridport, Dorset in April 1977. The rod-caught (beach) record was set by L Peters at Abbotsbury Beach, Dorset in 1978 with 3lb 7oz 6dr. Commercial boats occasionally take fish up to 8lb, but the majority of fish caught by rod and line are under 3lb, so that very light tackle can be employed to great advantage.

Tackle
Despite the sharpness of the whiting's teeth, hooks can be tied

This 6lb 1oz whiting, just 1loz below the rod-caught record, was caught over the Skerries Bank off the coast of Devon.

directly to ordinary nylon line, for the fish lacks the power in its jaws to bite through it. The size of hook largely depends on the bait being used. For worm baits, a size 1 is sufficient, but hooks one or two sizes larger are preferable when using fish baits—mackerel and herring strip, or sprats, for example. Favoured end tackle varies from one locality to another. If the water is coloured and the tide strong, a trace proves best, for the fish will be feeding very close to the bottom. On the other hand, a paternoster is usually better where the water is crystal clear, when the fish will be found swimming and feeding just off the bottom.

During the autumn months, whiting come almost to the water's edge, giving the beach angler some

good catches. The best localities are where the sea bed is sandy and harbours an abundance of the brown shrimps upon which the whiting come in to feed. Fish are taken during the daylight hours, but far greater numbers can be caught after dark. Some of the best whiting fishing is to be had on calm, frosty November evenings.

As the sprats and herrings move inshore, so the shoals of whiting increase. At these times, whiting become more difficult to catch, as they are no longer close to the sea bed, where the angler's terminal tackle is. After making a cast he should, every two or three minutes, recover a few feet of line, thus dragging the weight along the seabed. The disturbance that this causes attracts the whiting.

As when boat fishing, the bite is usually very fierce and should always be struck immediately—before the fish makes off with the bait. If the fish are in a feeding frenzy, it is not unusual, when using three hooks, to catch three at a time. If the angler is catching pin whiting (immature, bait-robbing fish), whether it be from beach or boat, the first indication of larger whiting in the area is the disappearance of these bait robbers.

TWIN-BOOM PATERNOSTER

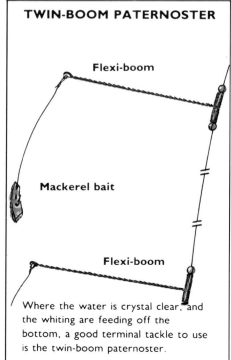

Flexi-boom

Mackerel bait

Flexi-boom

Where the water is crystal clear, and the whiting are feeding off the bottom, a good terminal tackle to use is the twin-boom paternoster.

Conger

Massive conger live long lives coiled in harbour walls or cliff crevices as well as in rusting wrecks or among reef pinnacles. So shore and sea anglers have an equal chance of thrilling sport

Conger fishing can be one of the most exciting forms of saltwater angling, whether practised from a boat or from shore. From the beginning of a trip when the bait first enters the water until the first tentative 'knock' on the line, the tension grows—for there is no way of knowing at this stage just how big a fish is mouthing the bait. Next comes the excitement of the strike and playing the fish, for this is no tame, easy-to-catch species. Even when the conger is on the surface of the water there is still the task of finally landing it.

When the angler goes fishing for a species that has a rod-and-line record of 109lb 6oz from a boat, and a shore record of 67lb 1oz, it is obvious that the tackle must be suitable for a large fish.

The choice of reel is most important. A strong multiplier or large centrepin is essential. A rod that will stand the shocks from the lunges of a big fish, yet is flexible enough to play the fish out, is also necessary.

The type of line used will depend on where the conger fishing is done. In shallow water the braided lines are extremely sensitive and give a feel of the movements of the fish.

Playing a conger from a breakwater under the ideal conditions of the build-up to a storm.
Inset: *On a large specimen, the head can be as big as a dog's and just as ferocious.*

CONGER FISHING RIGS

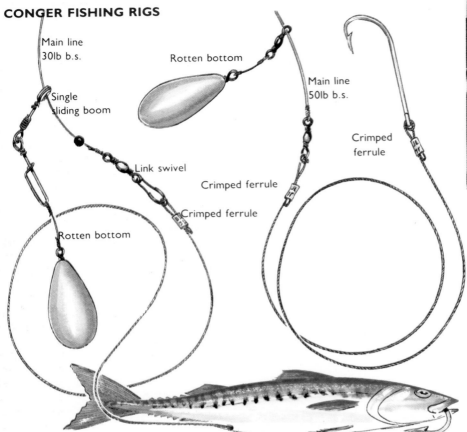

Main line 30lb b.s.

Rotten bottom

Single sliding boom

Main line 50lb b.s.

Crimped ferrule

Link swivel

Crimped ferrule

Crimped ferrule

Crimped ferrule

Rotten bottom

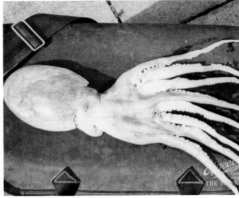

Above: *A whole squid as bait. Unlike other deadbaits, it should not be split open as its ink could repel rather than attract conger.*
Left: *Conger rigs—built for strength.*
Below: *Welsh angler John Reed fights it out with a big conger. A fighting fish must be kept from diving under the keel.*

When used in deep water where a strong current is flowing, braided lines have a tendency to belly away in the water, making it impossible to feel the fish biting. In deep water, such as when wreck fishing, nylon monofilament is the better choice, as it is more resistant to chafing, and less affected by a running tide.

Wire traces are needed, and the stronger the better, to prevent the conger's jaws from biting through the line, and also to grasp firmly when landing the fish. A conger can twist a trace around a gaff and break 60lb wire as if it were cotton thread. The wire trace should therefore be of at least 100lb strength, and about a foot long.

As a large bait is more often used, a size 9/0 or 10/0 hook is needed. The conger is more readily hooked in the jaw with a large hook. With the swivelled hooks, sometimes sold as suitable for conger fishing, the angler may find that the fish ejects the hook with the bait or swallows the bait, together with the hook, deep inside itself.

Shore fishing for conger

Shore fishing for conger produces the best specimens after dark, and autumn evenings can be very productive. The conger is found where there is deep water and a supply of food. Breakwaters, harbour walls, piers, rocky entrances to river mouths—all have produced some fine fish. Fish of over 55lb have been taken from shore marks in the Portland area, and each year sees the landing of fish over 40lb from such marks, particularly in the West Country. Groundbaiting can be very effective, and small pieces of fish will attract the conger to your bait.

Conger tackle

The best tackle when shore fishing for conger is a good rod, a reliable reel loaded with at least 30lb-strength line with a strong wire trace, and a hook at least 6/0 baited with an oily fish bait or squid. A running boom placed on the main line above the trace should have the lead weight attached to it by some lighter line, as this enables the

Below: *Boated conger remain dangerous for hours. Don't underestimate them for they retain their strength for many hours.*

angler to retrieve the remainder of the tackle if the lead gets jammed in the bottom. This is one of the hazards that conger fishermen have to endure. Wherever this sort of fishing is done—from the shore, over the reefs, or when wrecking—congers and snagging ground go together, and the angler must be prepared for many tackle losses.

When shore fishing, the best results are achieved when the rod is propped up on a rod rest or secured to the side of a wall. The reel should be set on the free spool and the ratchet engaged. The bite of a conger is very gentle—a knocking on the line. When this is observed, leave the rod alone until the line is taken off the reel at a steady rate: then strike the hook home and pump the fish as hard as possible. Try not to give line, for the fish has a habit of curling its tail around the nearest obstacle, where it is difficult to dislodge. Avoid giving line by keeping full pressure on the fish at all times. When the fish is alongside it should be gaffed as quickly as possible. Most escapes happen here.

Boat fishing for conger
Boat fishing for conger employs similar techniques, but the fish are usually larger. Wreck fishing almost inevitably produces the biggest specimens. It is advisable to leave the locations of these marks to the professional charter skippers who have the equipment to locate the wrecks, and the knowledge to anchor their boats in the right place for anglers to fish into them.

The boat has to be positioned up-tide, at just the right distance for the baits to reach the fish. A fast-taper 50lb-class boat rod, with 50lb monofilament on a heavy duty multiplier reel is recommended. You can use the same end tackle with a Clement's boom or a large swivel to which the lead weight is attached. This weight is at least 1lb and sometimes has to be heavier if the tide is a strong one. Between the end of the main line and the wire traces, use a strong link swivel which will act as a quick release if the fish is

71

deeply hooked. You should also have spare traces ready.

The bait is either a small whole mackerel or half a very large one. A small mackerel is baited-up by taking the point of the hook into the mouth and bringing the barbed end out between its eyes. Conger seize a fish-bait head first, so the hook should always be at the head end.

One very useful additional piece of equipment is a body belt or butt-pad with a socket to place the rod butt in when playing and pumping the fish.

When the conger takes

When a bite is felt, it is best to start winding your line in slowly until you feel the weight of the fish. There are

Above: *An alternative way of presenting mackerel shows the treble mounted inside the fish's head so that barbs protrude through the gills: the removal of the backbone helps to make a juicy flopping bait.*
Below: *A whole bream is bait for a specimen. The diagonal slashes free the body juices to scent the water and attract hungry conger.*

AT-A-GLANCE

Specimen Sizes
Depending on the locality, conger of 50lb to 20lb are considered specimens while boat fishing, and 25lb to 10lb from the shore

Tackle, Bait, Techniques
Rod
6½-7ft hollow glass or carbon-fibre, no ferrules

Reel
Multipliers, 4/0 to 6/0
Line b.s. 30lb-60lb
Wire trace, short

Hooks
Sea Master 8/0-12/0 offset barbs

Bait
Mackerel
Squid
Red bream

Techniques
Ledger, running trace

two good reasons for doing this. First the line will be tightened ready for the next move, and second, if the fish is only nibbling at the bait, the movement of it away from the conger will cause an even more enthusiastic attack on it.

Get the fish clear off the bottom. In most cases in deep water there is no need to strike as the fish will hook itself as it turns towards the bottom. Quite often the fish will come up quite easily. It is sometimes possible to get the fish halfway to the surface before it realizes that something is wrong and starts to fight.

If the conger dives
Make sure that the clutch on the reel is set correctly to allow line to be taken if the fish dives. When a large conger makes a determined dive for the bottom it is practically impossible to stop it, so give line reluctantly and always be ready to start pumping the fish back up again when you sense it slowing down. This can be very hard work, but the fish must be played out, or there is the chance that it will be too fresh when it reaches the surface and might break free and escape.

There is more chance of controlling a conger just beneath the surface than when it is on top of the water, and every effort should be made to play the fish out before it gets to the side of the boat. With wreck fishing there is usually a good depth of water beneath the surface, but on many reef marks this is not the case, and the fish will have to be played just below the surface.

The conger should be gaffed either in the lower part of the jaw or beneath the head. Once the gaff has been properly placed, the fish should be lifted smoothly and quickly on board. The angler whose tackle is in the fish should have his reel clutch set in case the fish avoids the gaff and plunges for the bottom again.

A word of warning: never leave a large conger to thrash about on the deck of a boat. Its jaws are very powerful and once clamped on an angler's foot will cause injury as well as the danger of serious infection.

There is a great sense of achievement in catching a large conger, and it is a form of angling that has a fanatical following both in this country and on the Continent. The British Conger Club was formed to cater for the enthusiasts and will assist any anglers who wish to try this fascinating sport.

73

Spurdog

We look here at the spurdog—a fish with few predators until it became of interest to commercial fishermen—and the smooth-hound which shares many of its characteristics

LI.145

There was a time when many anglers dreaded meeting a shoal of spurdog, as this meant that most other fish would leave the area. There are few fish in the sea that can strip an area of fishlife like a pack of spurs! Voracious in appetite, they move inshore during the summer months to release their young and eat everything they find.

The spurdog, *Squalus acanthias*, is a small member of the extensive shark group, the Elasmobranchii. Identification of the species is no problem, for there are two distinct anatomical features that distinguish the spurdog from all other dogfish common to British waters. The spurdog has two extremely sharp, curved spines on the back, one in front of each dorsal fin. These spines can wound deeply if a fish turns on the angler when handled, wrapping its body around the wrist or arm.

Distinguishing features
Another characteristic of the spurdog is the absence of the anal fin on the underside of the body, which is found between the pelvics and the tail in all spotted dogfish and smoothhounds. The spurdog is also one of the minor sharks without nictitating membranes, or third eyelids, that can be moved over the surface of the eyeball.

The fish is a dull grey-black on the upper part of the body, turning to sooty grey on the flanks, with the belly a dull white. The body is streamlined and sleek. Spurdogs are livebearers, and like all other species of shark and dogfish, copulate. The eggs are fertilized as they travel down the oviduct and a capsule forms around them that does away with the need for a placenta to nourish the embryos. The eggs then develop into embryonic fish, at which point the capsule will break, allowing the minute fish, with yolk sacs attached, to move freely within the oviducts. Generally, shark embryos live from the contents of their yolk sacs, but sometimes a nutrient is generated in the oviduct which is eaten by the developing young.

The female produces about 20 pups during the months of August and September. There is considerable evidence to show that at this time the females will separate from the male fish of the pack, travelling into shallow water to expel their young. Certainly, the sexes are rarely found in company during the middle months of the year. No doubt the separation serves to ensure the survival of the maximum number of pups. The females themselves begin to eat the immature fish immediately after they are expelled, but with the males absent enough pups survive to become adult and then plunder the fish of other species.

Mid-water trawling has done sea anglers a favour in reducing the

Above: *A hooked spurdog, though it may tangle itself in a trace and thrash about, cannot counter the heavy tackle often used on it.*
Inset, far left: *One of the day's catch.*
Below: *Charter boat in waters rife with spurdog, off Littlehampton.*

numbers of spurdog. A shortage of round fish for the commercial market, together with a growth in demand for 'boneless' species for the fish and chip shops, have made the spurdog a target for professional fishermen. The spurdog has filled this demand admirably as it has

Far left: *A spurdog caught on a surf beach. It probably followed shoaling bass inshore to prey on them.*
Above: *The head and large eye of the spurdog. Its relationship to larger sharks is obvious.*
Left: *One of the fish's two spines. These are a defence mechanism and carry no venom, but the tissue surrounding them is recorded as being toxic and wounds may require treatment.*

sweet-tasting flesh and a soft, cartilaginous skeleton.

The spurdog is not an exceptional fighter, but it can, nevertheless, cause havoc to the terminal tackle of sea anglers. Given a chance to show its ability on light gear, it can acquit itself well but, unfortunately, the spurdog is usually taken on tackle better suited to much larger fish. As a result it is hauled in, unable to put up much of a fight.

Challenge of light tackle
When a spurdog is sought deliberately on light tackle, it can really battle. Taken from the shore, as often happens when fishing a bass beach after dark, the fish will pull as hard as any bass.

The fierce attack methods of this predator and the continuous writhing of the hooked fish tend to tangle tackle. Unlike bottom-dwelling species, which suffer a decompression problem when being drawn to the surface, the spurdog has no swimbladder and will continue to thrash in its efforts to shed the hook—even after it has been brought aboard a boat. To avoid tangles, the tackle should be kept as simple as possible, with hook snoods only long enough to present the bait effectively. Long traces can only lead to massive tangles with those of other anglers.

Importance of supple wire
The sharp teeth and rough skin of the species force the angler to use wire hook links or nylon of over-thick diameter. Wire traces need not be of over-strong breaking strain as the fish does not grow to the proportions of tope. But the wire must be as supple as possible. Stiff, single-strand wire kinks readily. If you catch even one fish it can reduce the breaking strain markedly by a twisting motion that quickly places a kink in the wire. Supple braided or twisted wire will allow repeated use.

Spurdog are found close to the surface, near the bottom, and in mid-water, so paternosters or ledger rigs with a single 6/0 hook on 20lb line and a light sea rod make adequate tackle. For boat fishing use rods in the 15-20lb class. From the shore, an 11ft light beachcaster suits most situations. This gives the fish a chance to move, and the angler obtains the best possible transmission of the vibrations from the hooked fish's movements.

Many baits can be used. Almost anything will be taken. Fish baits are best, however, as the predatory instinct is finely tuned to smell when a spurdog comes upon a lask of mackerel, herring or whole sprat. When a massive pack of spurdog arrives there are times when they can be caught with hardly any bait at all! They grab at anything—a flashing spoon attached to a cod paternoster rig has been known to take them continually for a whole afternoon from a stationary boat.

Extracting the hook
Handling the boated fish can present a novice angler with a few difficulties. The best method of removing the hook involves first immobilizing the fish by standing on its tail. With the trace held out tight, the fish should be grasped just at the back of its head. The hook can then be extracted with a pair of long-nosed pliers. If the spurdog is not to be thrown back, it must be killed by a sharp blow across the snout. No fish should be left to die in the bottom of the boat.

Dogfish

Born in miniature perfection out of mermaid's purses or into their mother's wake, dogfish grow into spiney scavengers or tiger-spotted hunters and travel under a dozen different names

An angry writhing bull huss. To quieten a dogfish bend its tail round towards its head taking care not to strain the spine.

There are three species of dogfish of interest to anglers fishing British waters—the lesser spotted, greater spotted (also called bull huss) and the spurdog. The black-mouthed dogfish *(Galeus melastomus)* is also found around Britain but in deep water along the Contintental Shelf and it is not an angler's fish.

Lesser spotted dogfish

The lesser spotted dogfish *(Scyliorhinus caniculus)* is one of the commonest elasmobranchii or cartilaginous fishes native to British waters. These fish have a skeleton of cartilage while the majority of fishes have a skeleton of hard bone. Although it possesses a typical fish shape, the lesser spotted dogfish, like its greater spotted relation, is strikingly distinguished from the bony-skeletoned fish by its crescent-shaped mouth. This is situated on the underside of the head, which forces it to turn sideways to attack its prey. Another difference is the lack of an operculum or gill covering. The five gill openings are long slits,

situated behind the mouth and slightly forward of the pectoral fin. The upper half of the body is a reddish brown colour covered in hundreds of small black spots with one or two darker blotches. The underside is a creamy white, but when left exposed to the sun after capture large red blotches appear. The skin also differs greatly from bony fish in that, instead of having large overlapping scales, the scales are hundreds of minute pieces of bone embedded in the skin. The angler catching one of these fish should exercise great caution as the skin of the dogfish is extremely rough and can inflict a very painful graze.

The crescent-shaped mouth has small, pointed teeth which bite and tear food. Just in front of the mouth are the very large nostrils which may account for its very strong sense of smell. It certainly needs this faculty as it has very poor eye-

sight and so seeks its food mainly by scent. In this way it can detect any dead organisms in its vicinity and so act as a scavenger.

As the dogfish is so widely distributed, every angler is bound to catch one sooner or later. The easiest way of extracting the hook without coming to harm is to either subdue the dogfish with a blow on the head or to hold the tail and fold it towards the fish's head, holding the two together, and so immobilizing the fish while the hook is extracted.

Breeding habits

The breeding habits of the lesser spotted dogfish differ greatly from the bony fish in that the dogfish family possess male and female sex organs. In the male fish, part of each pelvic fin is modified as a clasper with which the female eggs are fertilized internally. The female of the species lays her eggs in pairs. These are about 2-2½in long by 2in wide, with four long, curling tendrils—one at each corner. With these tendrils, the female anchors her eggs to growing seaweed or other objects on the seabed.

The lesser spotted dogfish matures at a length of about 24in and a weight of about 1½lb, but rarely exceeds a length of 3ft and a weight of about 2½lb. The British rod-caught record fish weighed 4lb 8oz and was taken from Ayr Pier in Scotland in 1969. The species is abundant all around the coast of the British Isles, and is found in both deep water and in shallow water near the shore. Although it sometimes inhabits water over rocky ground, it favours sandy, gravel or muddy bottoms. Most of its feeding takes place on the bottom, but it will sometimes swim near the surface to steal herrings, sprats and other fish from drift nets, often getting caught itself in the process. The basic diet consists of shrimps, small crabs, hermit crabs, molluscs, and any small or dead fish that come its way.

Greater spotted dogfish

The greater spotted dogfish *(Scyliorhinus stellaris)*, also known as the nurse hound or bull huss, is far less common in British waters than its smaller relative. It is again distributed all around our coasts but

DEEP WATER

Molluscs

Squid

Dead fish

Hermit crabs

HOOKING A SQUID

is found in numbers only along the South Coast and around Ireland. Generally, it prefers deeper water and a rocky seabed.

Apart from being a larger fish, it differs from the lesser spotted kind in that, as the name suggests, it has bigger, but fewer, black spots on the reddish-brown upper half of the body. It also tends to have a rather broader snout, but neither characteristic is a certain means of distinguishing one species from the other. The only reliable aid to identification lies in the difference between the nostril lobes or flaps. The nostrils of the lesser spotted variety are covered by a single flap, whereas the greater spotted dogfish has a separate flap for each nostril.

The greater size of this species —the record rod-caught fish weighed 21lb 3oz and was caught off Looe, Cornwall, in 1955—means that, while sharing a similar diet with its smaller relation, it can also consume much bigger prey. The greater spotted dogfish has been known to eat fish as large as the thornback ray.

The species mates, eggs being fertilized internally, as does the lesser spotted species. The eggs are larger, measuring 4-5in by 1in, and have long tendrils on each corner by means of which the eggs are secured to the seabed. The newly hatched fry measure about 6½in.

Both species of dogfish can be

Above: Huss feeding in deep, murky water can be taken on ledgered fish strip, or squid if it can be presented in a natural way **Below right:** *More lesser-spotted dogfish are found feeding in shallow water though other kinds do also.*

taken on a very wide range of baits. The stronger the smell of the bait, the better. When fishing from a boat, a sack of rubby dubby tied to the anchor is used to send a strong scent of fish offal down on the tide to attract any dogfish.

The lesser spotted dogfish is a very useful fish for the competition angler as it hunts in packs and can be caught in numbers. If three hooks are used, three fish at one time can sometimes be taken. The bait should not be too large for this fish as it has a smallish mouth. When hooking a fish strip—mackerel or herrings are often used—a piece about 3in in length by 1in in width should be used with a 1/0 hook. On a strong tide a running trace of about 7ft is recommended, while on a slack tide the paternoster rig pays off.

The bite is slow and bouncy, and very distinctive. Do not strike until the fourth or fifth pull in order to ensure that bait and hook have been swallowed. The dogfish is slow-moving and sluggish, and indeed seems incapable of achieving any real speed. Once hooked, this fish's fight is unmistakable. There is a backward pull, followed by a move

SHALLOW MURKY WATER

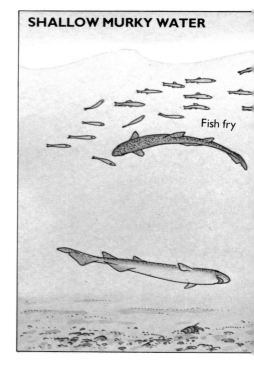

Fish fry

Left and above: *Rough and spined dogfish need very careful, decisive handling to avoid painful grazing or even deep lacerations of the skin. Both these holds are correct.*

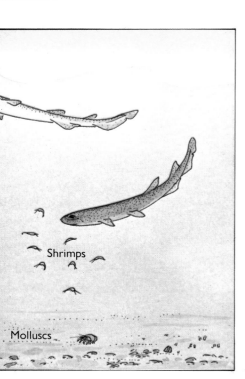

Shrimps

Molluscs

is on cold winter nights during an incoming spring tide, as the fish likes the security of a good depth of water. Among the best places to fish for them is the 18 mile long Chesil Beach on the Dorset coast, and the North Cornish headlands of Trevose and Towan. The British Record shore-caught spurdog of 16lb 12oz was taken as Chesil in 1964.

Shore anglers often make large catches of the lesser spotted dogfish, particularly in the west of Ireland. In shallow water, catches are better after dark than during the day'time, although when the water is coloured there are exceptions to this rule. It would appear from this that the fish does not. like strong sunlight, for this perhaps has an adverse effect on its already poor vision.

Bouncy bites
Shore-caught fish behave in exactly the same manner as those taken from a boat, except that the bouncy bite is more pronounced (particularly if the rod stands on a monopod rest), making the angler think something much bigger than a 2lb dogfish has attacked his bait. This can be very irritating to the bass angler after a sporting fish, or to the tope hunter who might have taken considerable pains to cast an immaculately presented mackerel bait a great distance only to have it mutilated by small dogfish.

The greater spotted dogfish, by virtue of its greater size, puts up a much better fight than the smaller variety, although the bite is very similar. Once the strike is made, however, the similarity ends. On a strong tide this fish is capable of a short run, and takes full advantage of the flow for this. The jaws are lined with sharp teeth, which the fish often uses to chafe through the nylon hook length and so gain its freedom. For this reason, a short snood of wire is recommended.

Baits
Reliable baits include whole small squid and large fish baits. A whole mackerel, intended for tope, presents no problem to this dogfish. The strike should be delayed to give ample time for the bait to be swallowed, for all dogfish have a habit of letting go at the surface.

towards the boat, and this sequence is repeated all the way to the surface. Remember that very often the angler is convinced that he has hooked the fish only to find that it has merely been holding the bait, which it releases on being hauled up.

The spurdog *(Squalus acanthias)* is very numerous in British waters, where specimens up to 21lb 3oz have been caught. It can be easily distinguished by the 'spurs' or spines, in front of each dorsal fin. Great care must be taken when handling the species, as these spurs can inflict severe lacerations.

Also called Picked dogfish or Common spiny dogfish, the spurdog is given to hunting in packs. Meeting up with a pack is either a blessing or a disaster, depending on your point of view: they snatch at just about every kind of bait without the slightest caution. Unlike the bull huss and lesser spotted varieties, the mouth of the spurdog makes very short work of a nylon monofilament trace, so light wire is usually used by specimen hunters.

The fish will often seek its prey close to the shore which gives the beach and rock angler the chance of a good catch. Most of the top action

Mullet

The delicate bite and timidity of mullet have made them the sea shore equivalent of the carp. Anglers become obsessed with the species simply because it is so difficult to catch big fish

The thick-lipped mullet is as straight-forward to catch as most other species. Its natural foods are algae and plankton, but it is also an opportunist feeder, eating any food available in sufficient quantities. For example, in harbours, where scraps, fish offal and bread are thrown into the water, the mullet have long since given up their natural diet and have become pre-occupied with this 'new' food.

Harbours are therefore one of the best places for mullet. Not only are the fish conditioned to take a food which anglers can use as bait, they are also used to noise from boats and people, and are not as wary as fish in estuaries and tidal creeks.

Survey the harbour at low and at high tide, looking for food traps. Fish-loading bays and inlet pipes are often good areas. Boating marinas composed of floating pontoons are also good, if permission is granted to fish from them. If it is, keep your tackle off the gangway. Clutter only angers boat owners and is the reason you often see 'No Fishing' notices on such places.

It is worth questioning the locals. They will not only know the best places but also the best times to fish. Some harbours fish most productively on flood tides, others on the ebb or at some times between tides. Only experience or local help will tell you when.

The ideal tackle for harbour mullet is a light 12ft freshwater rod, a fixed-spool reel loaded with 100 yards of 6 or 7lb b.s. line (depending on the amount of snags) and a sliding-float cocked by five or six BB shot 6in from a short-shanked, side-twist No 8 hook, honed very sharp. Some anglers use a paternoster rig with a No 8 hook on a 4in snood. The snood is attached 9in-1ft above a $\frac{3}{4}$oz lead.

Crabs break up the groundbait balls into little pieces which attract the mullet shoals. Fish the hookbait 9in-1ft above the groundbait so it is near the mullet but away from the crabs, which would strip it.

As soon as bites start, hold the rod in readiness all the time and meet definite bites with an instant firm strike to put the hook home in the fish's thick rubbery lip. More fish are lost through halfhearted striking than anything else. But make sure your slipping clutch is set to give line, for mullet are extremely hard fighters. The hardest bites to hook are 'lift' or 'flat-float' bites produced by a fish coming towards you. These call for concentration and instant striking on the first sign of the float lifting.

Shotting near surface
Sometimes mullet come to the surface to feed on flotsam or bread that has floated up from the groundbait. When this happens, quickly slip the shot up the line tight under the float and cast to the feeding fish. This way the shot cannot sink the floating crust bait, but you have enough weight to cast. There are few more exciting sights to the mullet angler than a big fish sucking in a surface bait and then diving with a great swirl as the reel screams.

SHORE

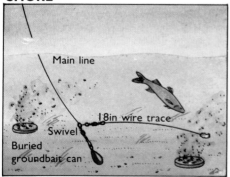

HARBOUR

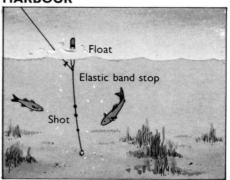

ESTUARY

Above and left: *Groundbait for mullet can be tethered in perforated tins, or anchored. The three illustrations above show rigs for shore, harbour and estuary fishing. The terminal tackle and lead for the shore fishing style are exaggerated in size for the sake of clarity. Mullet fishing, especially for large specimens, is one of the great angling challenges. The species can be totally frustrating, yet enticingly obvious by their movements.*

Ling

A novice fisherman's first deep sea boat trip to a chartered wreck or reef is an almost guaranteed pleasure thanks to the shoals of suicidal ling which infest these deepwater marks

Most newcomers to deep water wreck and reef fishing, probably began by catching ling. It is a prolific species with a wide distribution, but the greatest numbers are found at deep-water marks at the western end of the English Channel and Southern Ireland. A very powerful fish, the ling reaches a maximum length of 6½ft, and weight in excess of 100lb. Anglers seldom come into contact with ling of more than 45lb, and so far only five have broken the 50lb barrier. The British Record stands at 57lb 2oz—a fish caught from a wreck lying south west of Cornwall's Dodman Point.

The number of ling that inhabit wrecks is phenomenal; but some idea can be gained from the catch of 6,200lb made by eight anglers in a two-tide session about 24 miles south west of the Channel Islands. Fishing over a virgin wreck follows a very definite pattern. The first assault will remove several thousand pounds of fish in the 15-25lb class. Successive visits result in fewer fish, but the average weight will be much greater. Until the ling have been drastically thinned out, conger and other species that live on wrecks hardly show among the catches. The hulk may be alive with eels but only the odd one will be caught

Left: *A magnificent 34lb wreck ling.*
Below: *Gaffing and boating a ling—a job for two, however small the fish.*

the first four times the wreck is fished. They are outnumbered.

The ling *(Molva molva)* is a member of the cod family, although at first sight one might think it more closely resembles the conger. It has a long, slimy, eel-like body but the head and back are broad and its coloration, spineless fins, barbules and very small scales are telling indications that it is a member of the great family of the Gadidae.

Habitat and size

It is essentially a deepwater species, and while small fish may be found close to the shore, adult ling are rarely found in depths of less than 15 fathoms and are taken commercially in depths up to 200 fathoms. They are most plentiful in depths of 20-60 fathoms. The ling has a great liking for rough and rocky ground, particularly deep-fissured reefs rising steeply from deepwater. A demersal or bottom-dwelling species feeding almost entirely on other fishes, the ling spawns offshore in deepwater from April to June. It was once considered a mid-summer and autumn fish but with the development of wreck fishing, the angling season is now all year round.

Tackle and bait

When fishing over rough ground from a drifting boat, an ordinary paternoster trace will suffice. The lead or sinker should be attached by some 'rotten bottom' in case it catches in the bottom. Only the sinker will be lost if it is necessary to break

will make short work of light nylon traces, so heavy gauges are advised for terminal rigs. Extreme care should be taken when you are unhooking the fish as the sharp teeth can inflict nasty wounds.

Seeking ling

When fishing from an anchored position for ling, a simple ledger rig is very effective. As conger are found on the same ground it is advisable to use a short 6-9in wire link to the hook, for conger are likely to sever an all-monofilament trace. When fishing on the drift there is a risk of conger taking the bait. Wire is also recommended when wreck fishing as ling will be found on the bottom together with conger. If you are seeking ling, another hazard when fishing wrecks are the banks of very large pollack. The difficulty here is trying to get a large bait down without it being taken.

A big fish bait is more easily got down when fishing from an anchored boat. Anchored uptide of the wreck, the bait can be worked downtide without encountering the pollack and coalfish. When fishing on the drift, however, artificials such as 20oz pirk will get down through the depths very quickly—usually too quickly for the marauding fish in midwater. Pirks are very good for taking ling and the addition of a lask of mackerel to the treble hook of the pirk can prove very productive.

Specimen ling

However, there are exceptions to this general rule—in particular in the western end of the English Channel, as far east as Portland Bill, where numerous shipwrecks of both World Wars lie in very deep water on a flat sandy seabed. These massive rusting hulls, with a twisted maze of superstructure, have a great attraction for many fish. Conger, ling, pollack and coalfish all take up residence in them. Such wrecks provide very good fishing for the amateur fisherman as they are avoided by the commercial trawlermen's nets and immature fish are thus able to grow to maturity in relative peace. In these ideal conditions, ling grow to specimen size very quickly, for sheltered from the tide they expend

out, and this can be quickly replaced. Hook sizes should be 6/0 or larger, depending on the size of the bait. If fishing specifically for ling, large baits are advisable because pollack and small conger living on the same type of ground will go for the smaller baits. For ling, a whole small herring or the whole side of a mackerel is very attractive bait.

The take is usually deliberate, so wait until you feel the weight of the fish before striking. Should you miss, drop the bait back down quickly to the fish. Ling are fierce predators that will snatch again at a bait that has been whipped from their jaws, if given the chance. They do not run when hooked but fight

Top left: *These three specimen ling are of uniform size and probably came from exactly the same part of the wreck they inhabited.*
Above: *Catch from waters off Hoy Island in the Orkneys. Note the butt pad—an item of tackle vital to comfortable 'pumping'.*
Left: *The Eddystone Reef is famous for its specimen fish—including ling.*

strongly and stubbornly. Like many species with swimbladders, when brought up quickly from deepwater on heavy tackle they come up more easily after the first few fathoms.

However, heavy tackle is not necessary and when taken on light tackle they fight vigorously all the way to the boat. They have a very impressive mouthful of teeth which

Above: *Snapping and thrashing on the hook, a ling of any size needs careful handling.*

the minimum physical effort needed to satisfy their appetite, so that fish weighing between 30 and 40lb are commonly taken.

When drift fishing, where conger are not expected, it is possible to fix the hook to the line by making a 10in loop at the end of the trace, effectively making a double length of monofilament above the hook. Although fish have very sharp teeth, and could possibly sever 20 or 30lb monofilament, they are unable to bite through this double line.

Despite their size, ling are relatively easy to land. They fight vigorously to begin with but once raised from deep water their swimbladders become extended because of the change in water pressure. Inevitably the fighting qualities of any fish in this distressed condition is greatly impaired and the ling is no exception. In fact, if taken from a depth of about 40 fathoms, it will often lie almost motionless and exhausted when raised to the surface.

Landing the catch is an operation where many good fish have been lost by an over-anxious angler jabbing excitedly with the gaff. The angler should remain calm. A slow, deliberate, upward stroke in the region of the head is all that is required. If the gaff is kept moving the fish can be swung aboard in a single positive movement, cleanly and without undue fuss.

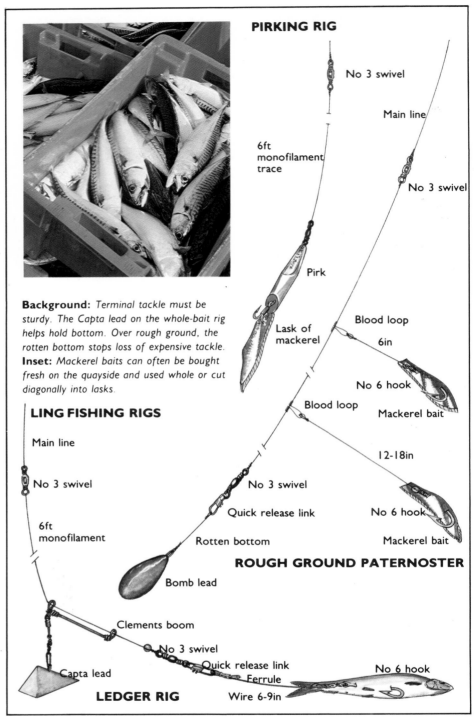

Background: *Terminal tackle must be sturdy. The Capta lead on the whole-bait rig helps hold bottom. Over rough ground, the rotten bottom stops loss of expensive tackle.* **Inset:** *Mackerel baits can often be bought fresh on the quayside and used whole or cut diagonally into lasks.*

PIRKING RIG

No 3 swivel

Main line

No 3 swivel

6ft monofilament trace

Pirk

Blood loop

Lask of mackerel

6in

No 6 hook

Mackerel bait

Blood loop

12-18in

No 3 swivel

Quick release link

No 6 hook

Rotten bottom

Mackerel bait

ROUGH GROUND PATERNOSTER

LING FISHING RIGS

Main line

No 3 swivel

6ft monofilament

Bomb lead

Clements boom

No 3 swivel

Quick release link

Capta lead

Ferrule

No 6 hook

Wire 6-9in

LEDGER RIG

Successful Red Gill

The Red Gill PVC sandeels are very successful lures for fishing wrecks. These can be fished as a single lure on a following trace, in tandem, or in threes in paternoster fashion. If a feather jig is used it is advisable not to have more than three feathers either baited or unbaited. When fishing with multiple lures one can hook two or three heavy fish at the

same time, but unless very strong traces are used, one lure is almost inevitably broken. Single lure fishing enables the angler to use lighter gear and so derive far more enjoyment from his sport.

This lure has accounted for many large ling from the South West coast. It must be fished deep, for ling inhabit the seabed in the area of rocky pinnacles.

Pollack

Reefs and wrecks are the obvious places to go in search of monster pollack and rod records, but shore fishermen and open-water anglers differ on what counts as a 'specimen' fish

For the pursuit of specimen pollack, the angler must be aware that pollack fishing is divided into three seasons: spring/early summer, summer/autumn and winter. There is a definite migration of fish according to season. Few fish frequent shallow water or the great reefs during the coldest months of the year. Instead they migrate to deep water in the Atlantic. In late April the first few return, and numbers build up rapidly, reaching a peak on the reefs in late August.

During high summer, pollack provide good sport for boat fishermen, but until mid-October those fish coming close to land are rather small. Fish that live in deepwater wrecks are present throughout the year, but the population dramatically increases from the beginning of November, when the residents are joined by migratory shoals.

Many wrecks beyond the 40-fathom line, about 20 miles offshore, hold thousands of large fish during the winter, and provide spectacular sport. Between December and March the females grow heavy with roe. A pollack weighing 18lb in December may, by the end of February, be close to the British boat-caught record weight of 25lb. There are three kinds of boat fishing: inshore, offshore, and reef

and wreck. Each demands a completely different approach and to find specimens in numbers requires quite a lot of dedication.

Light-tackle pollack fishing in shallow water is exciting during the autumn and early winter. In the western English Channel from Torbay to Land's End, pollack up to 14lb are caught within a few hundred yards of land—sometimes in less than four fathoms. While specimen fish can come from any patch of rocky ground, fishing off prominent headlands, where the tide runs strongly, is the best bet for consistent sport.

Among prime marks are Berry Head, Start Point, Bolt Tail, Rame Head and Queener Point, Chapel Point (Mevagissey) and the Gwineas and Manacle Rocks. From late October very large pollack hang around harbour estuaries and it is not unusual to contact them at night on the flood tide in tidal rivers. Good examples of these rivers are the Tamar, Fowey and Helford.

For inshore fishing, most experts favour a 10ft fast taper, hollow glass spinning rod, matched with a small multiplier loaded with 10-12lb b.s. monofilament. It is essential to choose a soft line with a small diameter. End tackle for anchored or drift fishing is a 12ft trace worked

from a single wire boom—commonly known as the 'flying collar' rig.

Moody pollack hook themselves
Most inshore pollack are contacted close to the bottom during daylight, and the popular method of fishing is to allow the baited hook to reach the fish and immediately begin a steady retrieve. Very few pollack, big or small, take a stationary bait, so it is vital to keep it moving at all times to give a lifelike appearance.

Shallow-water pollack are moody fish. At times they strike savagely, taking the bait well down without hesitation. More often, the first indication of the pollack's presence is a gentle pressure on the rod, followed by a more pronounced pull, before the tremendous power-dive so characteristic of the species. Striking is unnecessary, as the sheer speed of the dive against the multiplier's drag is sufficient to drive the hook home.

The combination of shallow water and light tackle makes even an eight-pounder seem a giant. In shallow water, pollack do not suffer distortion to the swimbladder through change of water-pressure, so they are able to make a series of line-stripping runs, but it is their downfall when hooked in deep water.

Unless the drag is set accurately to match the line's breaking strain, the fish will certainly succeed in breaking free—this is always a big hazard when fishing close to shore, and it has been responsible for the loss of many fine specimens.

Keeping a thin profile
It is important to maintain close contact—at no time should the line be allowed to slacken. If it does, the fish will dive deep into thick kelp and you may lose it when the terminal tackle snags. Some idea of a specimen pollack's fighting capabilities in the shallows can be gained from my own best fish of 12lb 10½oz. It took 25 minutes to beat on spinning tackle.

Sliding-float fishing from an anchored dinghy is also effective, particularly in a strong tide-run. The float—a thin-profile pattern 8in long—is quickly whisked away by the run of water, so a large amount of ground can be worked. The usual practice is to let the float run at least 200 yards before starting a slow retrieve. Unfortunately, pollack weighing more than 6lb are seldom caught on float gear, but it is a method that guarantees a fair bag.

Trolling for pollack close to shore is a method which is effective in the Alternatively, small ragworm bunched together are taken greedily. Many of the largest specimens have fallen to these baits. Fish-strip gets little response inshore and should be used only as a last resort.

The cream of pollack sport is found on the concentrations of rock that make up the deep water reefs off Devon and Cornwall. Any conversation concerning fishing for pollack will inevitably touch on Ed-dystone, Hands Deep, Hatt Rock and Wolf Rock.

Each reef is a maze of gloomy canyons and soaring walls of rock clawing towards the surface. Life of all kinds abounds, providing an endless supply of food for big predators. Here the specimen pollack is king, and, on a rich diet, males and females reach over 20lb.

The Eddystone Reef
Fourteen miles south of Plymouth and nine from Cornwall's Rame Head are the rocks of Eddystone.

The Eddystone light stands on the

The rock ledges at the tip of Portland Bill make a productive fishing mark for the pollack specimen hunter.

highest rock, but the reef extends above and below the water for nearly two miles in every direction. The rocks are red gneiss, a very hard rock found at only two places in England—at the Stone itself and two miles away at Prawle Point on the Devon coast.

The best fishing is on a dull day as red gneiss has an unusual mirror-like quality which reflects sunlight underwater. This seems to deter the fish from feeding.

Big pollack are a feature of the Eddystone Reef. Specimens of 14lb and more are commonplace in autumn and winter, and during the summer months large shoals of 6-8lb pollack roam the reef.

At the north east of the reef is a

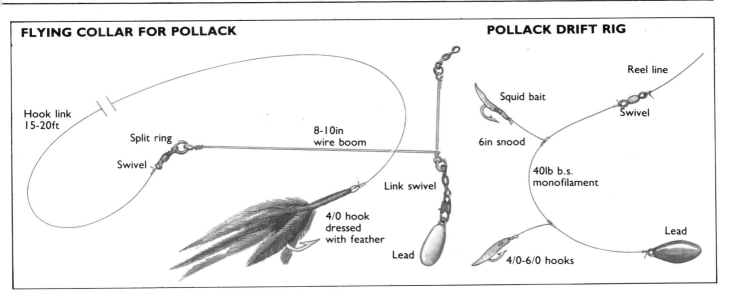

FLYING COLLAR FOR POLLACK

Hook link 15-20ft

Split ring

Swivel

8-10in wire boom

4/0 hook dressed with feather

Link swivel

Lead

POLLACK DRIFT RIG

Reel line

Squid bait

Swivel

6in snood

40lb b.s. monofilament

Lead

4/0-6/0 hooks

group of rocks at a depth of 20 fathoms, rising to within 10 fathoms of the surface. Here, many specimen pollack weighing over 12lb, and occasionally even more, are taken.

Another good spot is located a mile from the lighthouse on the south side, where a massive pinnacle of rock rises 68ft from the bottom, although there is still 60ft of water above it at low tide. King rag works particularly well, but big mackerel frequently fall to the feathers and baits intended for pollack.

Despite their size, fishing for large reef pollack with heavy tackle is completely wrong. Pollacking requires no more than medium-weight gear, which can consist of a two-handed spinning rod or a 20lb IGFA-class boat rod—although the latter is a bit heavy for the discerning angler. Many enthusiasts use an 11ft hand-made, one-piece, hollow glass rod with an all-through action. Used in conjunction with a multiplier and 15-18lb b.s. monofilament, it has maximum sensitivity in detecting light bites and is perfect for playing large fish.

As in shallow water, experts fishing rough ground use the 'flying collar'. It allows very long traces and baited hooks to be dropped at a fast pace through any depth of water without their tangling with the reel line. The boom can be purchased, or made from an ordinary wire coat-hanger.

Once the eyes have been twisted at all three points of the boom, split rings are added. These connect

Above: *Reef tackle. The wire boom is for rigidity: the hook link is monofilament and need not be any thicker than 15 or 18lb b.s. to withstand a pollack's bite.*

swivels to the reel line, the long trace is particularly important, as big pollack revolve on their way to the surface. Without the swivel the trace becomes hopelessly twisted, and needs replacing after each single pollack capture.

Allow the boom to run to the bottom and then retrieve steadily for 60 turns of the reel. This procedure is repeated until the bait is taken. Once the pollack has taken the baited hook, it will bend the rod with its desperately determined dive.

A plastic version of the wire boom is now on the market. The reel line runs through two guiders on the top edge to a swivel, which joins the long trace. With this boom, rigging-up takes seconds. It performs well enough, but should really be bigger.

The single hook and long trace of the flying collar rig increases the quality of sport, as the fish can quickly work up top speed. When there is a good flow of water, such as during a spring tide, you can use a 20ft trace. In a moderate run, however, you can reduce the length by as much as 50 per cent.

An appetite for currents

Long study of the pollack's eating habits shows that a fast run of water encourages it to feed freely. In slow-moving water and in the slack top and bottom of a tide, few bites will

materialize, but, as the tide strengthens, the pollack will begin to hunt around for food.

Medium-weight tackle allows the use of a small lead even in deep, fast-moving water. With 18lb b.s. monofilament it is possible to get away with a 6oz lead, which makes for comfortable fishing and does not hamper the fish's movement.

I mentioned earlier the desirability of retrieving line through 60 turns of the reel before letting the bait sink back to the bottom. Most pollack on a reef will be somewhere within that range. By counting each revolution of the reel-handle and noting the number when a fish is hooked, the exact feeding-level can be determined. Valuable fishing time can be saved in this way, by working only the productive zone. Naturally, it will alter as the hours pass, but it is a simple matter to maintain contact.

A pollack hooked on a long trace usually surfaces close to the boat. As the boom cannot pass through the rod-rings, the fish must be gently drawn to the net by hand. The majority brought from deep water are incapable of further fight at this stage, so there is little chance of their escaping.

Whether or not you intend to eat it, a pollack should always be lifted from the water with a wide-mouthed net. Gaffing is uncertain and damages the fish.

While any part of a large reef is likely to hold several fish, there are always hotspots. Many charter skippers have precise knowledge of these, and find it comparatively easy to anchor in a position that will place baited hooks exactly where they are most needed.

If the reef is unfamiliar, move around until a high pinnacle is pinpointed with the echo-sounder. The anchor is then dropped well uptide, as the boat will move back a long way before its anchor takes effect. Baits then run over the top of the pinnacle and end up on the sheltered side of the rock, where many fish will be found—especially in fast tide conditions. Pollack tend to stay out of fierce water.

Although king ragworms are not found in deep water, they make deadly bait for reef pollack, and take most fish between May and mid-July. Detailed records compiled over a 10-year period show that, except for live sandeel, worm surpasses other baits by a large margin. Consequently, pollack purists spend hours digging for worms. The popularity of the bait for reef fishing has led to overdigging and shortages at many places, and giant worms of 12-18in are now extremely difficult to find.

King rag are offered on a 4/0 hook to which a few red and white feathers have been whipped. Half a dozen white or red beads are threaded on to the trace to rest against the hook's eye. These embellishments induce a take when other baits and unadorned hooks are left untouched.

By the end of July pollack take mackerel, squid-strip and all manner of livebaits. Anglers seeking specimen fish should livebait with small mackerel, hooked through the body behind the vital organs or in front of the dorsal fin. Pouting also make livebaits but, being susceptible to water-pressure, they are usually in a poor state and incapable of displaying much activity when returned to the bottom.

Artificial eels
If large livebaits are used, allow time for the pollack to get a firm hold of the bait fish before striking. It is also important to raise the hook size to 6/0 and employ a 20lb-class rod to cope with both bait and catch.

In recent years artificial eels of various kinds have become popular baits. They are undoubtedly useful,

but their full effectiveness is restricted to periods of big tides.

Successful reef pollacking requires a sensitive touch as, quite often, the fish only mouth a bait without making a determined attack.

Wreck fishing for pollack is spectacular, but its sporting level depends on the method used. Pollack run much larger on wrecks than on reefs, and the concentration of fish is considerably greater. Even a small wreck, standing just a few fathoms high, provides shelter for vast numbers of fish.

During the summer the flying-collar technique is widely used from a drifting boat, as few skippers bother to anchor if they are after pollack. Tackle is a 20lb-class 6½-7ft hollow glass boat rod matched with a medium-sized multiplier and monofilament line. Braided lines have no stretch, but their resistance to water demands the use of much larger weights, and spoils the sport.

Working from an anchored boat means slower sport, but is more enjoyable. You can settle down to uninterrupted fishing and, by increasing or decreasing the amount of weight, establish a spot where the big fish are feeding.

Unfortunately, fishing at anchor with medium-weight tackle is possible only during neap tides and on the first days of the build-up to spring tides. The most productive wrecks lie in deep, exposed water, which can roar along in big tides. To combat a five-knot tide, increase gear to the 50lb-class and use 2lb of lead.

At the other extreme, light-tackle wrecking for pollack is becoming popular on wrecks during the smallest tides. Several British anglers have set IGFA world records for pollack (*Pollachius pollachius*), with a line standard of 6lb for men and 12lb for women.

A strange discrepancy
Across the Atlantic, where the IG-FA is based, *P. virens*—the coalfish of British waters—is referred to as pollack. Ludicrously, British records for *P. pollachius* appear in American lists for *P. virens*. Such a situation must be cleared up without delay, and separate lists established.

Catching specimen pollack of over 18lb on 6lb line requires a high level

AT-A-GLANCE

Specimen sizes
Boat: Devon, Cornwall 16lb; Dorset 15lb; IOM 14lb; CI, Hants, Scotland, Ireland, IOW 12lb; W, S Wales 10lb; elsewhere 9lb. **Shore:** IOM 7lb; N Devon 6½lb; CI 6lb

Tackle, Bait, Techniques
Rod
10ft fast-taper, hollow glass spinning rod; 6½-7ft 20lb-50lb class hollow glass boat road; 11ft one-piece hollow glass

Reel
Multiplier

Line b.s.
6lb-18lb monofilament

Hooks
4/0, 6/0

Baits
King rag and feathers, prawn, mackerel, pouting, sandeel and other livebaits, squid-strip, artificial eels

Weights
6oz-2lb

Techniques
'Flying collar' with single hook and long trace; light wrecking, sliding float, trolling.

of skill as well as the right rig. In experienced hands, the one-piece 11ft rod comes into its own, its length and sensitivity allow very large fish to be played out. This type of pollacking can be done only with a few people fishing at the same time otherwise lines will snag.

Good bait presentation is vital when fishing ultra-light over wrecks. Mackerel or squid-strip should be cut into strips 8in long and 1in wide, tapering to a point. The hook is positioned at the thin end. But live sandeel is still the best bait of all.

Wreck fishing during the winter with heavy-duty paternoster rigs and pirks often results in catches up to the record weight of 25lb.

Skate

Skate are widely distributed around our coasts, and to catch them you need patience and muscle. They offer the angler a wonderful opportunity to tackle monster fish

Sea fishermen perhaps hunt skate because they offer the chance of a monster fish from waters in which a catch of more than 100lb is rare. Skate is not a great sporting species, and it may be that they are fished, as mountains are climbed, because they are there.

Skate fishing varies little from Scottish and English waters to the marks of Eire. Almost all of it is from an anchored boat under the command of a professional skipper whose job it is to put you over suitable ground. Years ago, a boatman worth hiring could almost guarantee a fish or two, but today the skate marks have been so ravaged by both commercial and sporting

fishermen that success is a reflection of excellent luck, rather than skill or know-how. Established fishing grounds are around Scotland—Ullapool, Scapa Flow and the Western Isles—and over the Irish Sea in Kinsale, Westport and Valencia but it is a rare stretch of coast that has never produced at least one specimen. Skate travel with the tide and are much more active in warmer months than in autumn and winter.

Without good bait, the odds against hooking a skate are long indeed. The species preys upon all kinds of fish, crustaceans and worms, and successful fishing baits are those which exude a powerful scent and are big enough to with-

stand the predations of smaller fish and marine creatures which attack before a skate locates the tackle.

A waiting game
Among skate fishermen it is generally agreed that fresh mackerel and herrings are best. Both are extremely juicy baits which result in showers of blood, fatty droplets and fragments of meat, spreading a scent lane. This is very important where the skate are scattered over a large area.

Skate fishing is a patient waiting game: half a mackerel or even a whole fish is certainly not too big to ensure that when the fish eventually comes along, enough bait is left on the hook to spark its interest. The effectiveness of the bait depends on its freshness. Stale bait might well be a complete failure except where the skate are accustomed to fish offal, as they are in the vicinity of commercial fishing ports.

Feeding habits

Skate feed relatively slowly. It is debatable whether this behaviour reflects natural caution or is due to clumsiness in shuffling the enormous flat body over the prey. Whatever the reason, a bait that is correctly mounted helps the angler. While it is seldom necessary to hide hook shank and trace wire inside the bait, neat packaging at least ensures that the hook point ends up in the skate's jaw, and is not buried in a mass of squashy bait.

The skate has formidable jaws that literally grind hooks to powder and great care is needed in the selection and construction of the terminal tackle. The hook must be strong, forged, and with a brazed eye. The preferred size is between No 6/0-12/0, but there is much in favour of the smaller hooks because they are far sharper. A needle-sharp point and neat barb are essential to drive the hook into the muscles.

The trace, incorporating a simple running ledger, needs to be short

—2ft of cable-laid wire of 150-250lb b.s. are knotted and sleeved to the hook and to a big-game swivel. Attached to the other side of the swivel is 2-6ft of 80-100lb b.s. nylon monofilament to provide a buffer against abrasion and some insurance against sudden jerks, which nylon, being more elastic than Dacron, is better able to absorb. A Clements boom and sinker are threaded onto the nylon and held at the correct distance with a stopknot, then a second swivel is tied on. The main line, 50-80lb b.s. Dacron, is secured by the usual combination of doubled leader and Policansky knot.

Good skate rods are inevitably powerful with the emphasis on lifting ability rather than fishing sensitivity. Hauling a big skate off the sea bed is tough work even without burdening yourself with a rod that makes life more difficult due to

Below: A 136½lb skate caught on whole mackerel. **Far right:** This skate weighted 141lb and was boated at Stornoway, Outer Hebrides.

SKATE RIGS

Below: Mount a sizeable strip of herring on to a Mustad Sea Master and crimp the hook to cable-laid wire. Attach a second trace of nylon monofil of 80-100lb b.s. holding a Clements boom. Link this trace by a heavy-duty swivel to 50-100lb b.s. reel line.

Bottom: Hook a Sea Master crimped on to cable-laid wire of 150-250lb b.s. into the back of a mackerel and bind the bait to the hook and the wire with Alasticum. Crimp the wire to a barrel swivel and attach a long trace holding a Clements boom to it.

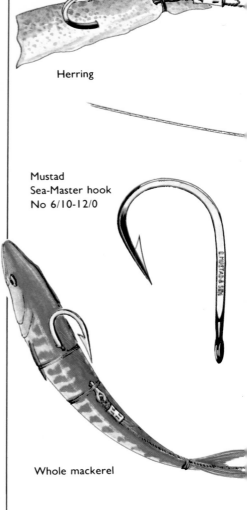

Herring

Mustad
Sea-Master hook
No 6/10-12/0

Whole mackerel

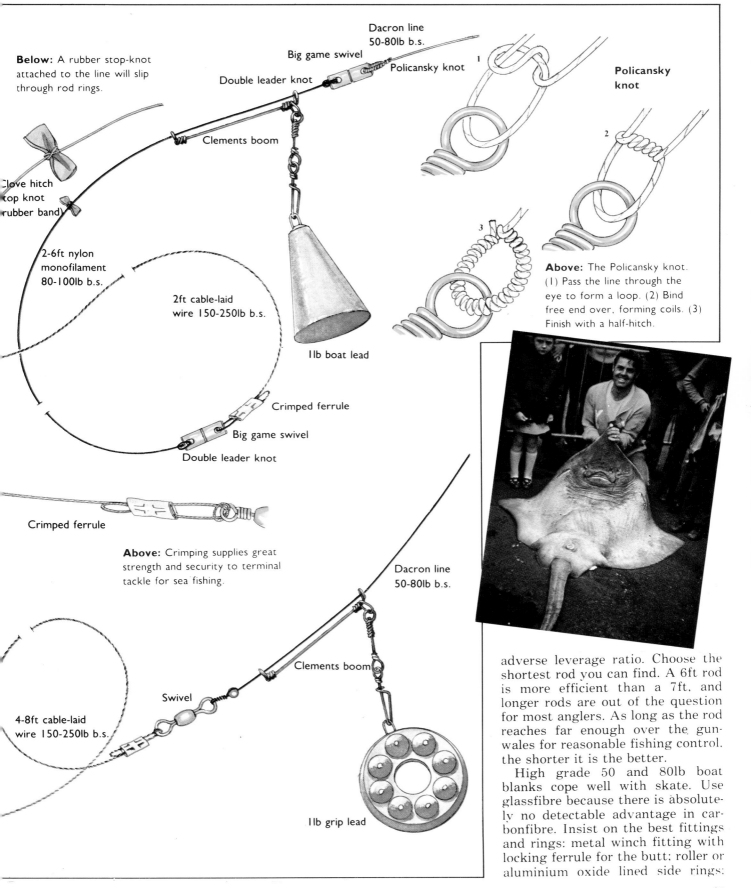

Below: A rubber stop-knot attached to the line will slip through rod rings.

Dacron line 50-80lb b.s.

Big game swivel

Double leader knot

Policansky knot

Clove hitch stop knot (rubber band)

Clements boom

2-6ft nylon monofilament 80-100lb b.s.

2ft cable-laid wire 150-250lb b.s.

1lb boat lead

Policansky knot

1

2

3

Above: The Policansky knot. (1) Pass the line through the eye to form a loop. (2) Bind free end over, forming coils. (3) Finish with a half-hitch.

Crimped ferrule

Big game swivel

Double leader knot

Crimped ferrule

Above: Crimping supplies great strength and security to terminal tackle for sea fishing.

Dacron line 50-80lb b.s.

Clements boom

Swivel

4-8ft cable-laid wire 150-250lb b.s.

1lb grip lead

adverse leverage ratio. Choose the shortest rod you can find. A 6ft rod is more efficient than a 7ft, and longer rods are out of the question for most anglers. As long as the rod reaches far enough over the gunwales for reasonable fishing control, the shorter it is the better.

High grade 50 and 80lb boat blanks cope well with skate. Use glassfibre because there is absolutely no detectable advantage in carbonfibre. Insist on the best fittings and rings: metal winch fitting with locking ferrule for the butt; roller or aluminium oxide lined side rings;

always specify a double roller tip; and choose the comfort and control of a soft, fairly wide diameter foregrip. Double-whipped rings are tougher than a single plain wrap.

Recommended reels
The reel has to be very strong rather than large. Skate may run, but seldom as far as sharks. Line pressure is immense, however, and the spool must be able to withstand it without collapsing. Big game multipliers and heavy duty centrepins are essential, as is a reel saddle to reinforce the winch fitting. The shoulder straps of the full harness clip to the reel so that most of the weight is transferred from the arms to the shoulders and back.

Once anchored over promising ground, the angler simply lowers his bait to the seabed and waits with the reel out of gear. Skate feed slowly, and to strike too soon invites a complete miss or hooking the fish in the wing. Give it time to get the hook well down, then strike hard. Keep up the pressure because the skate will hunch down on the bottom using its body as a sucker. You have to pull harder than the fish can, and that is backbreaking work. Playing a skate is a tug-of-war.

Many anglers say that one good skate is enough to last a lifetime.

Above: *The rod curves low and the shoulders, arms and back begin to ache as a large Irish skate is battled to the boat.*
Below: *Hooking a whole crab or its body with the legs trimmed off: either is excellent bait for skate or larger rays. The legs, of course, should not go to waste but they should be bound together with elastic and presented as a bunch of tasty morsels for rays. Take great care when unhooking, for the jaws of these fish can inflict severe crushing wounds on fingers.*

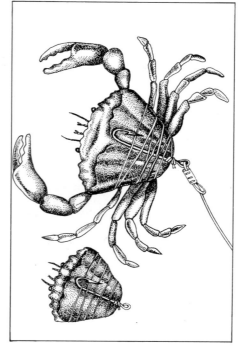

For the most part skate fishing is brutal fishing that requires only patience and a strong back. But as long as big skate haunt our coastal waters anglers will fish for them because to land a big one is still an achievement few can boast of.

Skate are rare in many of their former strongholds. Rod and line fishing endangers stocks—in fact it may be more of a hazard than commercial fishing. So, bearing in mind that skate are poor eating anyway, put them back alive. It is best not to boat them in the first place: none of the cartilaginous species withstand manhandling and are best cut free while alongside the boat. The wingspan can be approximately measured and is closely related to the weight of the fish.

Sole

Over a hundred years ago, stagecoaches rushed fish from the Kent coast to the tables of London's rich. With numbers now declining, the sole has once again become a rare delicacy

A close-up of the Dover sole's head showing the rounded snout, glove-puppet mouth and fringe of highly sensitive feelers running along the underside of the head.

The sole, *Solea solea*, perhaps so called because of its footprint-like outline, is one of the most highly esteemed food fishes to be found in British waters. Belonging to the *Heterosomata* (flatfish) group, the sole, like most other members of the flatfish family, swims on its left side and has both its eyes on the right or upper side of its body.

Coloration
The colouring of the right side varies acording to the type of seabed on which it lives. It may be almost all black or a light, sandy brown, with darker patches and speckling—although there is always a very dark spot on the tip of the right pectoral fin. The left or underside is usually pure white. The eyes, which are smaller than in most fishes, are set very close together. The mouth is small and curves downwards, and the snout, which is also rounded, projects beyond the mouth, giving the fish a rather disgruntled expression. Except for the underside of the head, the whole body is covered with small overlapping spiny scales. This makes the fish very rough to the touch, particularly when rubbed from tail to head.

The sole is often called the 'Dover' sole, a name which stems from the time when the gentry of London paid great prices for it. A regular and fast stagecoach service from Dover carried, among other things, locally caught fish to the capital.

Other names have also been given to the sole. Small soles, under 1ft long, are often referred to as 'tongues' as they resemble an animal's tongue. Fish of between 6oz and 8oz are called 'slips'. Try holding a live one of this size and the reason for the name quickly becomes apparent. Large specimens of over 3lb are nicknamed 'doormats'.

Distribution
Favouring warmer water, the sole is to be found throughout the English Channel, the Irish Sea, the West Coast of Ireland and the southern half of the North Sea as far north as the Firth of Forth, becoming scarce farther north. Spawning takes place in most areas from the end of March until early May. Many fish move inshore to spawn, particularly into estuaries. A female fish of 1lb will lay over 120,000 eggs, but at least 95 per cent of these eggs are eaten by other creatures before they have had time to hatch. The eggs, which are pelagic, have a diameter of 1-1.5mm and take between six and ten days to hatch, depending on water temperature. The larvae develop into the adult fish shape at about ½in long and adopt the customary demersal life-style.

Sheltered early life
During its first summer, the sole spends its life in sheltered estuaries, often ascending major rivers, such as the Thames and Humber, for considerable distances. In fact, soles are quite commonly caught as far up the

Thames as Gravesend. By October in their first year, the young fish have grown to about 2in, but their growth rate slows down during the winter. Rapid growth does not begin again until the following March, but by August the fish are over 4½in long. Male fish mature when about 8in long, on the East Coast, and 9in long on the South Coast, while females mature at 10in and 11in.

Soles live offshore in deep water during the winter, but move inshore, particularly into river estuaries, during early spring. There they inhabit sand or mud-and-sand bottoms, often in very shallow water. During daylight hours they partially bury themselves in the sand, feeding mainly at night on the many marine worms found on this type of seabed.

As summer turns to autumn, the sea temperature falls, so the sole migrates back to deeper water, some fish travelling great distances. In Ministry of Agriculture, Fisheries and Food tagging experiments in the River Blackwater in Essex, fish tagged in May were recaptured from the Dogger North ground, off Flamborough Head in Yorkshire, in the November of the same year. The following May most of the recaptured fish returned to the Blackwater, suggesting that many of the fish return to the same area year after year.

In very cold waters the fish congregate in the deepest parts of the North Sea, and it is then that commercial trawlers make their heaviest catches. The colder the winter, the bigger the catches, for when the water temperature is very low, the sole becomes lethargic and does not bother to bury itself in the seabed. Consequently it is easy prey for the standard otter trawl. Otherwise, commercial fishermen, especially the Continentals, employ beam-type trawls that literally dig the fish out.

Accidental catches

While the sole is much sought after by commercial netsmen, very few anglers fish for it specifically. Indeed, many rod-and-line-caught specimens are taken by accident rather than design. Some anglers claim that the sole is a very difficult fish to catch on a hook, but this is a fallacy. Despite its peculiar-shaped

HOOKING A WORM

mouth, it can take a baited hook quite readily, provided a very small hook and small bait are used

As the sole is nocturnal, the angler should begin fishing at sunset, when the fish are just beginning to feed. The areas from which the shore-based angler is most likely to make good catches are shallow sandy bays (particularly near river mouths), shingle beaches which run off into sand or mud towards the low water mark, and river estuaries.

One particularly famous area is the stretch of beach between Dengemarsh and Dungeness in Kent. On beaches such as this, the most productive period is usually one hour either side of low water—when distance-casting is totally unnecessary and is, in fact, very often a disadvantage as most of the fish are lying within 30 yards of the shingle. It is only when the angler is forced back up the beach by the incoming tide that more distance should be given to the cast so that the bait reaches the sand at the base of the shingle. Similarly, when

Above left: *The lemon sole,* Microstomus kitt, *is related to the halibut.*
Above: *After death, the eyed side of the Dover sole quickly turns a dark sepia.*
Left: *Small pieces of ragworm are all that's needed as a sole bait: larger pieces would be too big for the fish's relatively small mouth. A broken worm also oozes milky body fluids into the water which adds to the bait's attraction. Alternatively, you might try mussel or shrimp—both are reputed to work well.*
Below: *Sole tagged and released in the Essex Blackwater were found at Flamborough Head, Yorkshire the same year—proof of a remarkable pattern of inshore, north south migration.*

fishing river estuaries, if the edge of the main channel can be reached with, say, a 40-yard cast, it is pointless to cast farther as most of the fish will be found along the shelving bank.

Sole records
Although the shore-caught record sole is a fish of 5lb 7oz, caught by L Dixon from an Alderney, Channel Islands, beach in 1980, most fish encountered when rod and line fishing are under $2\frac{1}{2}$lb, with the majority between 8oz and $1\frac{3}{4}$lb, so heavy gear is completely unnecessary. As most sole fishing is done on quiet summer nights, the lightest possible beachcasters can be used with a line of under 15lb b.s. If the venue demands long casting, then the nylon-type paternoster rig should be used to achieve a good distance, but in other areas a stainless steel paternoster gives the best results. Soles, like all other members of the flatfish family, are attracted by glitter.

Hooks should be long-shanked to make unhooking easier, as the fish usually gorges the hook. The hook should be no larger than a size 6. The best bait depends on the worm commonest in the area. For instance, if there are extensive lugworm beds in or near the fishing area, lugworm is the obvious bait; if the main worm in the area is ragworm, then this

should be used before buying any others.

Best baits
Because of the small size of the hook, small pieces of worm should be used. Too much bait on the hook will cover the point and result in missed fish. A medium-size blow lugworm will bait three hooks, and a large king ragworm is sufficient for perhaps a dozen. In estuaries where maddies (small ragworm) are the favoured bait, then one, or perhaps two, fills the hook nicely; but always make sure the point is left exposed for quick penetration. The lead should be as light as possible to hold bottom, and if there is a strong cross-tide then a spiked lead should be used, preferably of the breakaway type with swivelling gripwires.

Bait 'nailed' to seabed
When boat fishing for soles, it is best to have the bait 'nailed' to the seabed, for whereas other flatfish will come well off the bottom to accept a bait, soles prefer the bait tight to the seabed. The best way of doing this is to use a trace leaded at intervals with swan-sized split shot. Because of this, longliners invariably catch a lot more fish than anglers with rod and line, despite the fact that the longline is crude compared with the sophisticated tackle of the angler. As in beach angling, boat fishing hooks should be a long-shanked size 6, and the strike should be delayed until the sole attacks the bait a second time.

Sole for the table
Like all sea fish, the sole should be gutted immediately, but its flavour is enhanced if the fish is refrigerated for one or two days before being eaten. Like game, it matures. The fish should also be skinned before cooking and this is best done after it has been kept for one or two days. Trying to remove the skin on a fresh sole results in much of the flesh being pulled away from the bone; but after 24 hours it becomes a much easier operation. Fishmongers usually skin a sole from the tail towards the head, but the layman will find it easier to start at the head and strip back. Fish preparation is easy once you have the knack.

Wrasse

Wrasse find their food and shelter in the recesses of a broken, rocky coast where they may seem within reach but can tantalize any angler trying to winkle them out

Wrasse are not difficult to find around Britain, particularly on the West Coast where the water is slightly warmer and the shore more rocky than elsewhere. But to fish for wrasse successfully, a keen knowledge of the fish and its behaviour are a necessity.

To find a wrasse fishing spot, look for deep water close inshore—at least two fathoms at low tide. Depth does not play a major role, however, as many ballans in the 5-6lb size range have been caught in no more than 3ft of water. A rocky coastline with vertical cliffs, interspersed with sheltered, broken ground where vegetation can grow, is ideal. In

Float fishing is certainly the most exciting method as it gives the angler something to watch. Your response to bites can be quick and positive and your bait can be fished over a wider area.

The ideal spot
Imagine a rocky shore with indented gullies, into which the water surges at the pattern of swell and wind. Using float fishing tackle, a bait can be put into the many possible feeding areas along such a shore with far less risk of it becoming snagged than a tethered bait on a cast ledgered rig. Float fishing allows an angler to find a fish rather than ex-

A SIMPLE LEDGER RIG

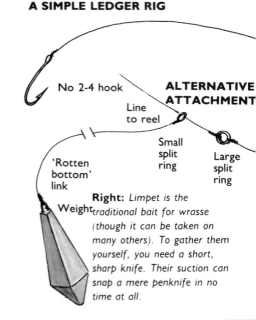

No 2-4 hook

ALTERNATIVE ATTACHMENT

Line to reel

Small split ring

Large split ring

'Rotten bottom' link

Weight

Right: Limpet is the traditional bait for wrasse (though it can be taken on many others). To gather them yourself, you need a short, sharp knife. Their suction can snap a mere penknife in no time at all.

FREE SWIMMING FLOAT

TETHERED FLOAT RIG

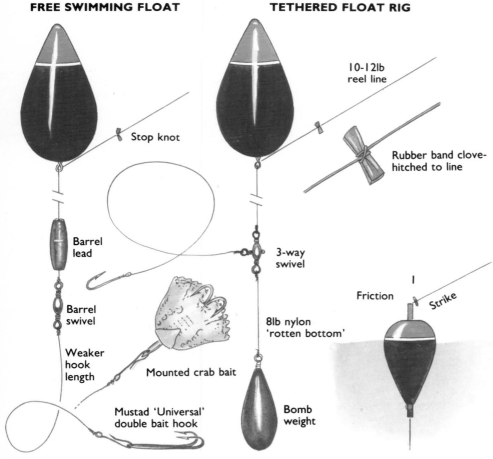

Stop knot

Barrel lead

Barrel swivel

Weaker hook length

Mounted crab bait

Mustad 'Universal' double bait hook

10-12lb reel line

Rubber band clovehitched to line

3-way swivel

8lb nylon 'rotten bottom'

Bomb weight

1 Friction Strike

2 Strike

3 Stri

Friction

Friction

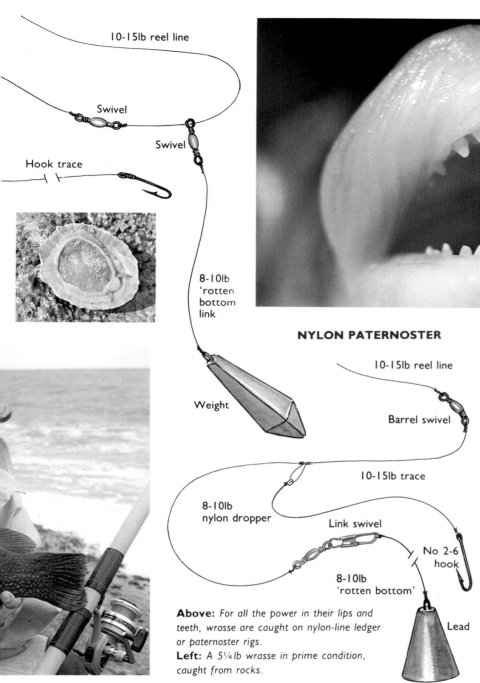

10-15lb reel line

Swivel

Swivel

Hook trace

8-10lb 'rotten bottom link

Weight

NYLON PATERNOSTER

10-15lb reel line

Barrel swivel

10-15lb trace

8-10lb nylon dropper

Link swivel

No 2-6 hook

8-10lb 'rotten bottom'

Lead

Above: *For all the power in their lips and teeth, wrasse are caught on nylon-line ledger or paternoster rigs.*
Left: *A 5¼lb wrasse in prime condition, caught from rocks.*

Above: *The mouths are capable of tearing mussel barnacles off the rocks.*

bait, then rushing into the nearest weed or broken ground. A pull then results in a lost fish and probably lost terminal tackle as well. With a rotten-bottom, all you should lose when pulling free is the weight.

When float fishing, there are times when the bait should be trotted and times when it should be kept stationary over a known wrasse hole. For trotting, use a free-swimming rig and for stationary holes, a tethered rig (see diagrams). With the latter, the float bobbing up and down with the waves can drop the lead into crevices or thick seaweed, so a rotten-bottom is again used in order that the rig can be salvaged if it becomes fouled.

Wide range of baits
Baits for wrasse are legion, but there can be no doubt that peeler and soft crab are the best. King ragworm, harbour and tidal river ragworm, and to a lesser extent, lugworm, attract them, followed by mussels, cockles, scallop and limpet. Hermit crabs also make excellent bait. Most anglers know the wrasse's reputation for tearing limpets off rocks, but these do not figure highly in the fish's diet. The author has caught many wrasse on them, but more often resorts to adding a lugworm or a small fragment of ragworm to form a cocktail.

Left: *Where there is a known hotspot, the float can be anchored with an old lead, using rotten-bottom. There are advantages of reduced friction in using the inverted float.*

TWO BASIC SEA FLOW ATTACHMENTS
1. On striking, friction centres on top of float stem.
2. As float pulls over, friction transfers to foot.
3. Friction is much reduced by line running through ring.

pecting it to come out in search of a bait. Furthermore, wrasse can see well, which is yet another reason for choosing a rig that swims a bait to and fro with the current.

When there are clean patches of sand and mud between the rocks, and you know where these are, then it is possible to use a ledger rig. Nevertheless, a rotten-bottom of lesser breaking strain should be used between reel line and lead. Wrasse have a habit of grabbing a

Dab

Though thousands of tons of dab are trawled every year from accessible inshore waters, millions more remain, buried up to their eye-sockets in sand, ambushing everything edible in sight

Because of its love for shallow water bays the dab is frequently encountered by the shore-based angler. In many localities the dab is fished for exclusively, as it feeds freely during calm settled weather conditions unlike the codling and whiting which prefer heavy surf, resulting in uncomfortable angling conditions.

The bait need not necessarily be fresh. In fact, badly blown lug will invariably catch more fish than will fresh, the big disadvantage being the difficulty in keeping such a soft bait on the hook while casting. Ragworm is another very good bait, particularly if the water is clear, but again only small sections of a worm should be used. During the late

Terminal tackle should be kept simple; a two or three-hook paternoster rig will take plenty of fish and the angler gets no bother with the terminal tackle tangling or becoming twisted when casting. When fishing from a shelving beach great distances in casting are not required as dabs will oblige by coming almost up to the water's edge in search of food. The bite is usually of the short rattling variety and may be confused with a small pouting bite. It is best, therefore, to wait for the second or sometimes third bite before making your strike.

Dab's favourite bait

Although not predominantly a shoal fish, the dab appears to move around in small groups. Having taken the bait, for example, the struggles of the hooked fish attract other members of the group to the remaining baited hooks. When seeking dabs from a boat, the ideal location is an area of the seabed with a sandy bottom and an easy tide. The best conditions are during settled weather, with calm seas and clear water. Fish can be encouraged into the area by lowering a rubby dubby

bag full of mashed-up shore crabs to the seabed. Dabs are partial to the squashed crabs and the abundance of food will keep the fish in the area of the baited hooks. Worms—particularly stale ones—are a favourite bait both in shore fishing and from boats, where stale worms do not have to stand the rigours of beachcasting. Slipper limpet and hermit crab tails are also good.

Tackle

The best rig for boat fishing for dabs is undoubtedly a pat-trace, consisting of a short two-hook trace, which will waver in the tide, and a third hook which fishes about 30cm off the seabed. Dabs will often take a bait that is well off the bottom, hence the need for this top hook. Again, small hooks and small baits are the order of the day. If the bait is too big it will only result in many missed bites. Once the baited rig has been lowered to the seabed and no bite has registered after a few

minutes, the rod top should be raised 2 or 3ft.

The movement of the bait often encourages the wary fish to make a grab at it. If a bite is missed, allow the tackle to return to the seabed immediately; the fish will usually makes another attack on the bait. If this happens, delay the strike, allowing the fish plenty of time to swallow the bait and hook.

The best sport will be had as the main tide run eases just before a slack water period, and again immediately after slack water as the run builds up again. Many areas that produce consistently good catches of this flattie during the summer months tend to tail off during the early autumn. This usually heralds the arrival of the whiting and cod. It is very noticeable that big catches of dabs are never made if either of these species are prolific. The slower moving dab is unable to compete with the speed of the whiting for the available food, and in the case of the cod, the dab itself provides food.

The dab is not fished for commercially to the same extent as plaice. The reason for this might be that the flesh is softer and does not keep as well as plaice. A large dab in good condition, however, gutted immediately after capture and eaten the next day, is considered to have a superior flavour to the plaice.

PAT-TRACE RIG

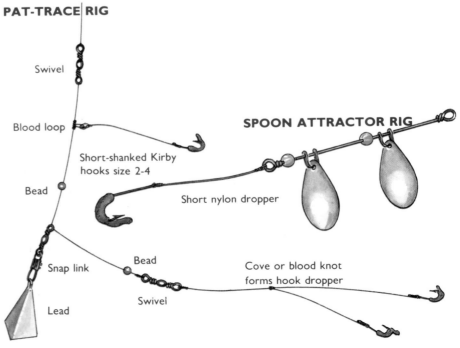

Swivel

Blood loop

Short-shanked Kirby hooks size 2-4

Bead

Snap link

Lead

SPOON ATTRACTOR RIG

Short nylon dropper

Bead

Swivel

Cove or blood knot forms hook dropper

Chapter 3
GAME FISHING

A great deal of totally unnecessary snobbery became associated with game fishing about a hundred years ago. It may have arisen from country landowners jealously preserving the trout streams and salmon rivers that ran through their often very large estates. Only those at their social level — and above, of course — were allowed to fish there.

Many of these gentlemen anglers were highly literate for the period and having the time to spare to take an interest in the natural history of rivers were able to write about the sport as they knew it. Their experiences with trout and salmon, the flies with which they were caught, fill many shelves of sporting libraries. Some are full of wonderful advice, some of little value in practical terms.

One subject which aroused great interest was the use of the artificial fly to catch game fish. The angler was expected to be knowledgeable enough to recognise what emphemerid fly the trout were rising to, and then to be able to tie a life-like imitation from silk, feather, fur and a long-shanked hook.

Game fishing is the pursuit of an Order of fishes, all of which possess behind the dorsal fin a fleshy protuberance given the name of adipose fin. Its function, even today, is not clear, for it does not act like a fin, nor does it have finrays. Perhaps it is a residual organ.

Salmon, sea trout and brown trout all have the adipose fin. The rainbow trout too of course, even though it is an introduction from American waters. In Britain it breeds only rarely in the wild, and is reared in fish farms to be stocked in game fishing reservoirs. In America there is a migratory form known as the steelhead.

One other fish, the grayling, also has the mark of the 'upper class' fish, the adipose fin. Unfortunately this beautiful fish, named long ago as the Lady of the Stream, has evolved to spawn alongside and at the same time as the coarse species. It is, therefore listed among them.

What, then, is different about game fishing? It is largely practised with the artificial fly and whippy fly rod. The line has weight of its own, so nothing else is added to cast the practically weightless lure. Throwing the fly out is done by using the spring inherent in the fly rod and the weight of the fly line. The technique of fly casting is not difficult, but it must be taught properly. It is a form of fishing that is rarely static, the fly being cast out, worked slowly back, and recast.

Salmon fishing, done with fly, lure, prawn, spinner and even worm, is an expensive sport. To fish a beat on a classic river costs hundreds of pounds, plus very expensive hotels, ghillies, and the tackle and accessories of the sport. For salmon, some licences are also costly, but in Scotland anglers should check with riparian owners about rights.

The spread of game fisheries has made fly fishing for trout readily available to thousands of anglers who would otherwise have not been able to partake: now it is often just another adjunct to their usual float and ledger styles in the coarse season.

Strict limits on size and the number of fish to be retained are laid down everywhere. Anglers are required to complete a form giving details of their catch. This is because reservoirs are stocked and fish taken away must be replaced. The term 'Put and Take' fishery describes it well.

Some enormous rainbow trout have been bred by a process of selective breeding. Fish of 20 lb and more, a weight undreamed of not long ago, have been hooked and brought to the bank. Anglers say these monsters have put up a tremendous struggle, so being pond-bred does not seem to affect their strength.

In summary, there is more game fishing available now than there has ever been, and stillwater trouting is the reason for it. Specialist long-distance casting techniques have been developed to reach the large trout kept out to deepwater by the pressure of angling.

To tempt them, many new fly patterns have come along, mostly imitations of nymphs and small fish. The Polystickle is typical of these.

For some time, salmon authorities have been claiming that the numbers of fish running in from the sea have been diminishing. Part of the blame must lie with the industrial pollution of salmon rivers leading to a decline in water quality.

Another factor is the increase in illegal netting at sea and poaching in rivers. Fines and convictions are applied whenever possible, but there is always a shortage of enforcement officers and long stretches of riverbank go unpatrolled.

River trout

If you learned your fishing on a reservoir, the sight of river trout can be a disappointment. But once you have hooked a specimen, no stocked water will ever hold the same appeal

Get to know your fish, its weaknesses and foibles. Watch its reaction to other trout which stray into its territory. Does it compete with them for food? Greed has seen the downfall of many a good fish. And always bear in mind that you are taking on a special kind of quarry—one that has seen all the mismanaged attempts to extract it from the water and that will scornfully retreat the moment you have the slightest laspe of concentration or expertise.

In dry fly fishing, the biggest cause of failure with sophisticated trout is undetected drag. It is, of course, helpful to have some idea of the fly on which the fish is feeding and to be able to choose a reasonable facsimile to put on the leader. But the paramount factor is a presentation that makes the fly look like a natural insect alighting on the water's surface film.

Drag—the ultimate deterrent
Some years ago I was casting over one or two very good rising trout. The casting was careful and dextrous, but, although none of the fish was alarmed and they continued feeding on the naturals, there was not one which would condescend to take the artificial. I could have concluded that I was presenting the wrong fly, but when I carefully withdrew to a small bridge just upstream, the fish were still rising

boldly to naturals I had imitated.

It was then that I snipped the artificial off my leader and dropped it on to the water so that it would float down over the fish. A good trout promptly came and took it as though it had been looking for that fly all day. That it would subsequently spit it out seconds later was of no account. What is more, other trout in the vicinity rose to and took three more artificials chosen at ran-

Trevor Housby with a 7½lb brown trout taken from the River Test—perhaps the most famous of trout rivers. The fly is still in its mouth.

dom and dropped on to the water. Pattern had nothing to do with the problem. It was all allied to the fact that, when presented from the bridge, the flies were untethered to a leader, line or, ultimately, to me. Drag was the enemy!

A specimen trout knows all about drag and may well locate itself in a lie where drag can be easily detected, but not easily overcome, by the angler. One trick which may be tried is to cast so accurately that the fly is dropped on to the nose of the rising fish. This calls for great skill and is often best attempted as the rings recede from an earlier use.

Usually one of two things happens. Either the fish takes the fly with a greedy grab, or it bolts for cover as though the devil himself had been after it. Properly attempted, though, it enables the angler to cover the fish before drag occurs. Additionally, it does not give the fish much time to scrutinize the fly and decide that it is not the real thing. The technique has caught some good trout, but it has frightened many more.

Many trout are caught just before or after a very prolific hatch of naturals. At the peak of the hatch, there are often too many naturals for fish to bother with the artificial.

Sometimes, the best way of securing a specimen is by the use of the nymph. This may be tantalizingly passed in front of a feeding fish before the main hatch of naturals occurs. But always bear in mind that the specimen trout is most likely to take your fly when you least expect it to do so.

All the good wild trout that I have caught have demanded the utmost skill. We need all the skills of the hunter if we are to get on to terms with such fish. Practice casting until you can drop an artificial fly into a soup plate at 20ft and so that it alights like thistledown. Learn to move with the stealth of a cat and always aim to spot your specimen before it sees you. Bear in mind that it only takes one cast to catch a fish.

Barry Potterton writes:
River trout sport in the South can be divided into fishing chalkstreams, the rivers and streams of Wales, Devon and Cornwall, and the few other southern rivers which have not fallen foul of pollution or water abstraction. Chalkstream fishing has been discussed on pp. 337-339.

The rivers and streams in Wales, Devon and Cornwall are mainly fast-flowing spate rivers which hold a natural stock of wild brown trout. They may well hold the odd rainbow trout if the river has been stocked and they may also have a seasonal run of salmon and/or sea trout.

These rivers can be fished with fly, but I will concentrate on spinning and worming in the three different water conditions that one is likely to meet: clear water at normal level (which is most common), low-water, and a coloured spate.

Spinners and spoons
Clear water at near normal level is the most appropriate condition for light spinning. Rather than a spinning rod, I like to use a Mark IV Avon or reservoir trout fly rod, both of which have extra length and play fish better in fast water. I use a Mitchell fixed-spool reel loaded with 100 yards of 6 or 8lb b.s. nylon. My favourite baits are a small Mepps spinner, a fly spoon or a very small Devon minnow.

The height that the bait fishes in the water is most important, and this is determined by the overall weight of the end-tackle. Too little weight and the bait will skate across the surface of a fast stream. Too

Quite different, a brown and a rainbow caught from the same river on very light fly tackle.

much weight will cause continual snagging on the bottom.

Weight can be added to end tackle by putting shot or swan shot 18in above the bait. In the case of a snaggy bottom, shot should be added until the bait fishes at a good depth, perhaps even touching the bottom once or twice as it is fished across the stream.

If the bottom is relatively snag-free, use a simple paternoster set-up, incorporating a three-way swivel, which allows the bait to ride just above the bottom. The short perpen-

dicular length of line should be about 8in long and of less breaking strength than the main line—so that you do not lose the lot if your weights become snagged. Use swan shot or smaller shot because these are easily changed and can slide off the short length if they become snagged.

Reaching deeper pools
Fish down and across the river with just enough overall weight to feel the bottom once or twice as the bait swings round. Good-sized trout are most likely to be found in these deep pools, so look for a position where the main pool and flow of water is

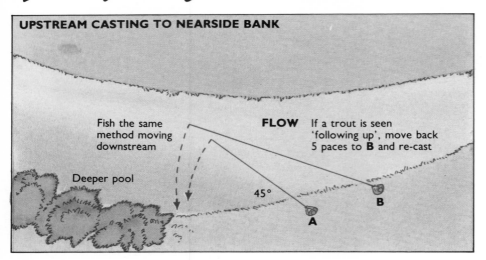

UPSTREAM CASTING TO NEARSIDE BANK

Fish the same method moving downstream

Deeper pool

FLOW If a trout is seen 'following up', move back 5 paces to **B** and re-cast

45°

A

B

AT-A-GLANCE

Specimen sizes
Water and parentage are all-important in determining specimen sizes for brown trout: hatchery-bred fish should weigh 10lb, natural fish betwen 1lb on upland becks and 4lb on rich rivers

Tackle, Bait, Techniques
Rod
Mark IV Avon, reservoir trout fly

Reel
Fixed-spool/fly reel

Line b.s.
6-8lb

Hooks
6-14 spade-end (worms), 10-12 (livebaits)

Baits
Dry fly, wet fly, nymph, Mepps spinner, Devon minnow, fly spoon, marsh worms, lobworm head/tail

Techniques
Dapped or floated dry fly, wet fly, nymph, paternoster spinning, roller ledgering

towards my bank. Start fishing the very top of the pool with short casts down and across at an angle of about 45 degrees. This ensures that you are fishing with the correct weight.

Tasteless worms
Worming for wild trout is every bit as skilful as fly fishing for 'stockies'. In a river with varying currents and depths, straightforward trotting of a float and worm is not practicable. I prefer to fish an adaptation of a rolling ledger down and across the current. This gives the worm a natural movement with the current, taking it into the pool itself.

Top left: *How to fish an awkwardly shaped pool, using the river flow direction.*
Left: *Keir Muter during the lift off the water while fishing the North Tyne.*

Sea trout

Daytime fishing for sea trout is a matter of luck; night-time specimen hunting a matter of detailed preparation, intelligent speculation and the steely nerve needed to fish in the pitch dark

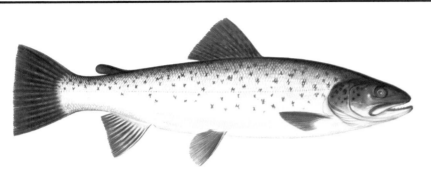

While anglers continue to argue about whether or not a sea trout feeds in freshwater, most of those with experience agree that though they feed they do not forage.

If something looking like food floats overhead, passes by in the current, or even remains quite still in the sea trout's immediate vision, the fish might investigate. It might move nearer, it might even take the food but spit it out immediately.

Big sea trout are more inclined to do this than immature fish, which makes them all the harder to catch. Specimen-hunting for sea trout is almost impossible, unless the river holds more specimens than small fish to begin with.

There are—or were—rivers where ten-pounders were common and where fish almost double that weight were on the cards. The Conwy is one such river and at one time expert night-anglers thought little of taking several huge fish there. We hear little about these rivers now. Perhaps they hold as many specimens, perhaps as many are caught, but less is being said or written about them nowadays.

Falkus' teaching

I caught my first sea trout by accident in the Hampshire Stour and later I took seven from the Scottish Dee while salmon fishing by day. With the ghillie at night, using regular fly tackle, it was a different story, but I never really felt close to sea trout fishing until I met and fished with Hugh Falkus, who showed me fish that made me tremble with excitement. From then on I was hooked on sea trout, particularly specimens.

Do not misunderstand me. I am interested in, but never expect to catch, the ten, twelve and fourteen-pounders that I have seen in that marvellous little spate river in Falkus' Cumbria. A five-pounder from that water calls for celebration and, from such a river, is well worthy of the name specimen. Many smaller fish will be caught before even a five-pounder comes to net. That is what makes it a challenge and the challenge is what makes Hugh Falkus, master sea trout angler, insist that you fish after dark. Wait, he says, until you know it is too dark to see and then wait another half an hour before fishing.

Falkus' methods with the fly are well known to most sea trout anglers. I have used his flies and techniques in many other spate rivers—as far north as the Outer Hebrides, as far west as Carmarthen, and in Ireland. They have also worked for migratory rainbows in the northern USA.

For the techniques discussed here, two or three rods and two kinds of reel are required. A 10-10½ft fly rod, with matching line and fly reel, is used for flies and lures. A floating line, a sink tip and a high density sinking line (No 7 is likely to be most useful)

should meet most fly fishing needs.

Freelining a lobworm calls for a ledger or spinning rod of about 10ft and a fixed-spool reel bearing a main line of 6-8lb and a slightly weaker leader ahead of that.

It is not easy to be selective about size when going for sea trout, especially at night, and I can only repeat the advice given to me many years ago by Falkus: there is never a time when the chances are absolutely nil; with fish in a pool there is always the chance of a big catch.

Systematic fishing

With settled conditions, or in a river rising slightly, Falkus advises that pools are fished systematically one way and back again, using a floating line tipped with a teal blue and silver sea trout fly pattern.

This pattern is called the Medicine. It is tied on a low-water salmon hook and is lightly dressed. Later, a large sunk lure on a sinking line is put through the same procedure, though of course the fishing action is entirely different. A small double hook, again lightly dressed and fished slowly through the pool, sometimes accounts for fish when they tweak the fly.

The accepted fly-maggot combination, where two maggots are attached to a regular flasher, often results in missed fish. Instead, Falkus' Secret Weapon is employed when fish peck at, rather than accept, the fly or lure. The maggots are loaded on the forward single and the sea trout, which makes a half-hearted gesture at intercepting them, is invariably hooked on a tail-end treble.

At some time during the darkest part of a black night, the surface lure is put to work. This is positively the most dangerous of contraptions as it whistles past the ear like an angry hornet.

The lure causes a wake as it travels across and back over the surface of the still pool and if any method is likely to attract the biggest sea trout in the pool, then this, correctly practised, is it. Often the sea trout rises from the depths, misses the lure completely and crashes down on it, giving the impression of an almighty take. But unless by sheer chance the fish is briefly foul-hooked, there is no fur-

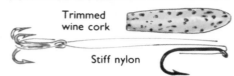

SURFACE LURE FOR SEA TROUT

Trimmed wine cork

Stiff nylon

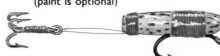

Body whipped on and varnished (paint is optional)

ther contact and the fish is lost.

Sea trout have been known to attack the surface lure several times during one cast and there have been times when several casts in succession have brought a reaction. When a big fish gets lined up correctly and is actually hooked, sea trout fishing becomes something more than an equal tug-of-war.

I like to try all methods but I prefer to fish with the worm because I regard it as the most effective (though also the most difficult) of sea trout techniques.

I have never practised anything more demanding anywhere in the world and yet, when I know fish are present, I keep trying all night. Those huge sploshes that indicate some kind of irritation from a big sea trout set my pulse racing and I try to figure out where my bait is and what it is doing. With a little pull on the water, the bait can be made to move around slowly in search of fish, sinking gently under its own weight, even though it occasionally snags on rocks.

Lobworming skills
With a slight pull on the water, it is possible to feel which way the worm is travelling and how it is behaving. With little or no pull to help you keep in touch, freelining with a single lobworm that has to be cast almost to the far bank can be tricky.

It is essential to keep in touch, for you must feel the slightest indication of a take or pull. Sometimes the line will slacken and all may appear lost, but the sea trout may have swum towards your bank and may still be in contact. Sometimes the line will strip off the spool slowly, indicating a positive take.

A premature strike usually results in a slack line and a mangled and rejected worm. Striking too quickly may also result in lost fish because the thin membrane at the 'scissors' of the sea trout's mouth pops, leaving a large hole from which the hook is very easily dislodged.

Feeling your way
It is a non-stop business. Cast, retrieve slowly, do not let the bale arm close, for you want the fish to run off with the bait unhindered. Remember that drawing in slack line

Above: *During the cast this surface lure whistles past your ear like a hornet. But it can produce takes when all other methods fail.*
Right: *Three sea trout lures tied by famous anglers: on the left by Arthur Oglesby, in the centre by Hugh Falkus and on the right by Dick Walker.*
Far right: *How to fish a fly through a series of promising lies.*
Below right: *Late run sewin of 7lb taken from the River Tywi near Llandeilo, Wales, in October.*

by hand, with the bale arm open, can cause incredible tangles. You cannot cast and let the bait settle to await the sea trout's pleasure or it will become snagged in the rocks. Ease the bait over obstacles, feel for the slightest touch, and learn to recognize the difference between a pull from a fish or rock. It is very difficult and frustrating in the dark, but it is the best way.

In complete blackness even a 6lb line is invisible and the gentle action needed to keep the bait moving allows a certain amount of slack to accumulate near the reel. It needs nothing more than one turn of the handle to trap this surplus line and a bird's nest results.

It is better to do this gentle drawing and bait manipulation by gathering the line above the first rod ring. It is a bit of a stretch but it does keep contact and prevents a muddle around the bale arm.

Eels have been present in every sea trout river I have fished, and they alone require that the bait be kept on the move. They are more active on some nights than on others and there are occasions when, after rebaiting a dozen times, you wonder whether fishing with worms is worth the effort. Then the pool suddenly becomes alive with leaping sea trout, with perhaps an eight-pounder among them, and there is

no way you are going to quit.

Some years ago I acquired some luminous plastic tape which I attached to things I was likely to need when fishing in the dark. Charged in advance by a torch beam, these pieces of tape were useful on my landing net arms, to show exactly where I had to draw a hooked fish. Low-powered beta lights are now used for the same purpose and, though they are more expensive, do not need recharging.

One night I cut a 1in strip of

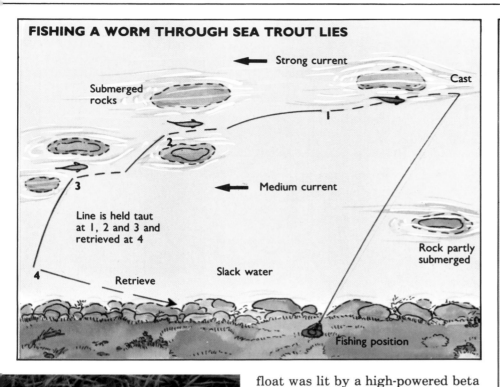

FISHING A WORM THROUGH SEA TROUT LIES

Strong current

Submerged rocks

Cast

Medium current

Line is held taut at 1, 2 and 3 and retrieved at 4

Rock partly submerged

Slack water

Retrieve

Fishing position

luminous tape and put it on the hook with two lobworms. Until that moment I had not had the slightest sign of a bite; then I caught three sea trout in succession.

Two nights later, in very low-water conditions—these little spate rivers drop very quickly—I caught two more by the same method. I often wonder if there are certain conditions when something luminous attracts sea trout.

I once tried to fish worms after dark on float tackle. The tip of the float was lit by a high-powered beta light and as it travelled downstream an enormous sea trout leaped at it and threw it clear of the water.

Anglo–American hybrid
Studying the sunk lure, as tied by Falkus, and seeing illustrations of what is it was meant to represent, reminded me of a fly by my American friend Ted Trueblood. He called it the Integration because it was tied of black and white bucktail. When retrieved in fast water it looked remarkably like a long-bodied creature such as a brook lamprey.

The first attempt at using them brought two good takes and two lost fish and so we developed the Integration-with-Stinger, which has a small treble incorporated in the dressing, well behind the forward single hook. One of my biggest sea trout from Wales was taken on it in the early hours of the morning. That fish, however, was hooked on all three points of the treble and on the single hook forward as well.

Integration jig
A later development was the Integration jig, for which I have great hopes. The problem of fishing a sunk fly under the far and vertical bank of a rocky spate river caused me to consider the American idea of the jig. I have caught many fish on jigs. The

AT-A-GLANCE

Specimen sizes
There is no official record for sea trout, but the BRFC minimum qualifying weight is 20lb. A fish of over half that figure is certainly a specimen, while, on some waters, a five-pounder deserves the title.

Tackle, lures, techniques
Rods
10-10½ft fly rod (with matching line)
10ft ledger/spinning rod

Reels
Fly reel; fixed-spool reel (spinning, freelining)

Line
Floating, sink-tip, high-density (No 7); 6-8lb b.s. (with weaker cast) for spinning

Flies and lures
Teal blue and silver (in Medicine pattern) on low-water salmon hooks, the Falkus Secret Weapon; large sunk lures; surface lures

Baits
Worm, maggot

Techniques
Fly-fishing; spinning; freelined lobworm

majority have been American fish, but if trout, catfish, crappie, bluegill, walleye and pike respond to them, why not sea trout?

I tested the jig on the River Cothi in Wales, where several fish were hooked and then lost, but only because the hooks on which they were tied were soft-wired. There was no mistaking the fact that they worked, but opportunities to put them to further use have been few and far between.

Fishing for sea trout, above all big sea trout, is seldom predictable, and frustrations pile up throughout the season. Then comes that new idea, that incredible success that turns you into a sea trout addict. From then on you are looking always for a better specimen than the last.

Rainbow trout

A fine sporting fish which at times can be maddeningly coy, rainbow trout have gained the respect of trout fishermen everywhere since first introduced in the last century

The rainbow trout, *Salmo gairdneri* is a native of the Pacific coast, rivers and lakes of the North American Continent, ranging from the Bering Sea in the north, to the southern Californian coasts in the south. Since 1884 the species has been introduced to suitable waters all over the world with varying degrees of success. In Britain it has rarely bred successfully and in most cases now exists only as a result of continual restocking from fish farms which have successfully bred the species by modern stripping techniques.

Native habitat

In its American habitat the rainbow fills a niche comparable to that occupied in Britain by our native brown trout. Similarly it exhibits numerous variants (each once believed to be a distinct species) and provides a similar range of migratory and non-migratory fish. Its growth rates vary widely according to type and environment, and it provides excellent sport for anglers. Brown and rainbow trout, are however, of a quite different species—although related to the *Salmo* genus.

Generally a far hardier fish than the brown trout, the rainbow can withstand high temperatures, low oxygen levels, and murky waters. It is also a far more active fish, being a free riser to the fly and living and moving in loose shoals, with a strong urge to migrate upstream for spawning, falling back into lakes or lower reaches for the rest of the season. At the extreme it is anadromous, like sea trout, migrating from dense to less dense water to breed.

In appearance it is similar to the brown trout apart from a distinctive wide lateral band of iridescent magenta along the middle flanks. It is usually black spotted, and the spots, unlike those of the brown trout, grow more quickly. Rainbow trout grow to a larger maximum size than the brown trout. It also spawns later than brown trout, and is therefore in excellent condition in British rivers and enclosed waters at the very end of the season.

An early season rainbow taken on a black lure. Before the arrival of natural flies, lures are generally the best bait to use.

The history, literature and taxonomy of rainbow trout in North America is every bit as confusing as that of its British cousin, the brown trout. Nineteenth century American and European zoologists identified and named a variety of species of trout. In Europe, for example, Gunther described some ten different species each with its own scientific name, while in America a similar number of trout were similarly identified, described and named by various authorities.

Classification

During the early part of the present century the zoological view that a species should be regarded primarily as a breeding unit, despite minor physical differences, gained ascendency. It was shown under laboratory conditions that all the known British trouts were able to produce fertile progeny when cross-bred. More than anything, this led to their re-allocation to a single species *Salmo trutta*. The same sort of study of species in America resulted in an all-American trout being classified into the species *Salmo gairdneri*. All trout were subsumed under this heading with the single notable exception of the brook trout, which in fact turned out to be a char and now enjoys the separate specific title of *Salvelinus fontinalis*.

Above: *Rainbow trout in the 'wild'—which are not stock fish put into waters from fish breeding ponds—rarely achieve the high growth rates produced in prime waters such as Avington. This rainbow is typical of a naturally bred fish.*
Below: *A fine 8lb 12oz rainbow caught on an Appetiser fly from Siblyback Reservoir.*

In America, however, the char is still commonly known as a trout, but can be distinguished from the rainbow by its green-brown colour with lighter 'worm-track' patterns on the back, and reddish tinge on the underside. Examination of the vomerine bone on the upper palate will also provide distinguishing features. Rainbow trout have single rows of teeth set in a 'T' shape. Chars, on the other hand, bear only a group or cluster of teeth on this bone. The North American brook trout has also been introduced to some waters in Britain and these should not be confused with either brown or rainbow trout.

Feeding habits

Rainbows normally feed on a very similar diet to brownies. When young they exist on daphnia, cyclops and other infusoria, but once past the alevin stage quickly graduate to shrimp and insects, and on to snails and fish fry in addition within a year. Not only are rainbows more prone to rise than brown trout, but they are far more active in their search for food, ranging between the bottom and the surface continuously and taking good advantage of midges, nymphs, mayflies and their larvae, and in the evening on sedges and daddy long legs. In waters where coarse fish fry are plentiful, rainbows soon get used to supplementing their diet with such delicacies. It is not unusual for anglers to find fish of 14in with roach of three of four inches in their stomachs. Such fish become as predatory as pike, and as rainbows move in loose shoals they are sometimes seen driving shoals of small fish into the shallows where they hunt them down voraciously.

When to use the dry fly

At the other end of the scale, rainbows often rise freely in boisterous weather, feeding well on the surface during high winds, following the wind lanes in large groups and fearlessly rising under the bows of the angler's boat. They will often cruise upwind in such conditions, dropping into the depths when they come to the far shores, and then feed earnestly either in mid-water, or on the bottom.

In calmer weather, when the surface is like a millpond and the angler despairs of getting his wet flies to work without creating a heavy wake, the rainbows will often rise maddening at midges and other small flies on the surface, ignoring the wet flies offered by the fisherman. Then the dry fly is often useful. Takes are sudden, and the rainbow is usually moving fast when it hits the fly. Smash-takes occur in these conditions, even when the cast is realistically heavy. It behoves the angler to ensure that his rod is not left pointing at the fly.

Lures and flashers

When the fish are dour and not showing, the angler must fish the water, covering as much territory as he can to get fish moving, or locate moving fish. A lure is sometimes successful and several patterns should be tried at various depths and different speeds. Sometimes the angler is reduced to 'scratching the bottom' with a weighted lure fished slow. Alternatively, a flasher fished fast may be used. Rainbows can often be tempted when high water temperatures have caused the brown trout to go completely off feeding. They will also move quite fast from comparatively deep water to a tempting fly realistically fished on or near the surface, following it until it is about to break surface.

The buzzer rise

When the buzzer rise occurs in the evening, fish will sip delicately at the nymph or smash at it, leaping out of the water and landing on the nymph with a boil. In late summer, when the sedges are on the water, rainbow trout will take both boldly and hearteningly.

When fish are hooked high in the water they will often leap and splash on the surface from the moment they are hooked. Sometimes it is essential to get the rod point down into the water to sink the line so as to absorb their acrobatics.

Though deplored by some trout purists, the introduction of rainbows has made fly fishing available to many more anglers, and most reservoir anglers welcome the rainbow and the exciting sport it offers in a hundred subtly different ways in different conditions. It can be as coy as the brown trout, and loves to cruise on the surface on hot days, sipping in the green pea-soup which the

Above left: *The adipose fin which seems not to serve any function.* **Above:** *The head of a rainbow with a hook still lodged in the angle of the jaws.* **Left:** *A 15lb stock fish which fell to a sunken wet fly.* **Below:** *A typical three-fly team for use when trout fishing on reservoirs.*

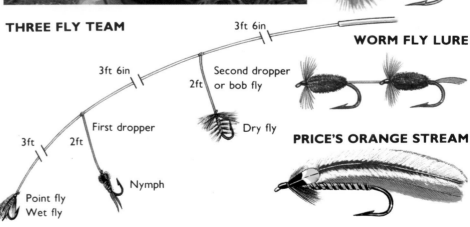

THREE FLY TEAM

3ft 6in

3ft 6in

Second dropper
or bob fly

2ft

Dry fly

First dropper

3ft

2ft

Nymph

Point fly
Wet fly

WORM FLY LURE

PRICE'S ORANGE STREAM

water often becomes in these conditions. Then it can be maddeningly difficult to tempt.

Rainbows are very suitable for introduction to reservoirs because they live only for four or five seasons, and can be stocked in a range of sizes. In most farm conditions a one-year-old fish may be between 4 and 8in, attaining between 6 and 12in in its second year. A third year fish may be between 9 and 16in,

and a fourth year fish between 14 and 20in. These are average figures and can be exceeded with suitable feeding and water conditions. A few years ago a 10lb rainbow was exceptional.

Recent rainbow introductions at Avington fisheries, where 20lb fish are being produced on high-protein diets, indicate that selective breeding has improved future catches, even larger fish can be expected.

Salmon

An introduction to the four major techniques of salmon fishing
—spinning, worming, prawning and fly fishing. Anyone who
masters all four can enjoy sport throughout the game season

For most experienced salmon anglers the epitome of skill in their sport comes, perhaps, in the months of May and June when the salmon are in a playful mood and will condescend to take very small flies fished on a floating line. This style of fishing is not as complex as it may appear, and by far the most challenging aspect of the exercise is to be on the right river at the right time and place. This injects a degree of chance into the success or failure of salmon fishing and there are few short cuts to assist the novice.

Small flies, floating lines

Fly fishing with small flies and floating lines is one of the easiest and most successful forms of salmon fishing providing that the water temperatures have been sustained over the 10°C (50°F) mark for a few

Below: *A salmon angler on the River Avon at Bicton in Hampshire.*

days, the water lacks an excess acidity and is clear and not excessively deep. The Aberdeenshire Dee is a classic example of a fly river, but there are many others where similar conditions are found.

Basically the fly is cast across the current and slightly downstream. The angler may have to wade to successfully cover known lies, but the object is to make the fly pass over the lies slightly submerged and as slowly as possible. The take from a fish may appear as nothing more than a slow but solid draw. In any event it is a grave mistake to strike and it is quite normal for the salmon to hook itself as it pulls the fly. A hooked salmon has a few ideas of its own and the angler may expect to struggle with a fish for roughly one minute for each pound it weighs.

It cannot be stressed too strongly that the primary requirement is to

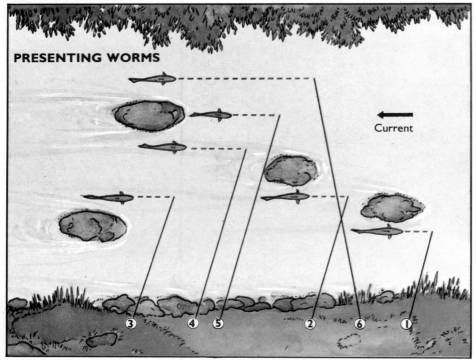

PRESENTING WORMS

Current

③ ④ ⑤ ② ⑥ ①

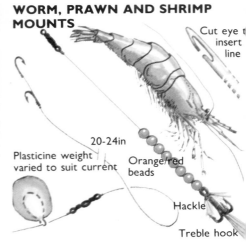

Cut eye t insert line

20-24in

Plasticine weight varied to suit current

Orange/red beads

Hackle

Treble hook

know the salmon lies, and what to do and when. Casting or placing the fly may be quickly learned, but it may take years to know an area.

Above: *Six stations to cover the whole swim.*
Below: *Another stretch of the Avon — a southern, chalk-based river — at Winkton. Here the fishing is strictly controlled.*

therefore of paramount consideration. The angler must assess current strength and depth and then choose a bait which, when cast across the current, will swing round at good depth without fouling the bottom and, in all but semi-stagnant water, without winding the handle of the reel. Good salmon baits are to be found in the wide range of Devon minnows, and the myriad of spoon baits on offer are available in a wide

Spinning technique

Undoubtedly, the form of salmon fishing that requires the most practice is spinning with a double-handed rod and a fixed-spool or multiplying reel. This technique must account for the lion's share of all salmon caught, but it is often overused and abused and there are some rivers where its continued use may do more harm than good. It is a useful technique to apply in the early spring when the water is cold and deep and when the fish are reluctant to move far from their lies. At such times it is barely possible to make the bait move too slow and deep. Of course, it is not much fun to be continually hung up on the bottom, but if the right weight of bait has been chosen it should be possible to cast it across the current and have it swing round without winding the reel handle. The current is generally strong enough to make the bait revolve. Any form of reel handle winding before the bait is out of the current and dangling immediately downstream will make the bait move too fast and too high in the water.

Choosing the weight in the bait is

PRAWN SPINNING RIG

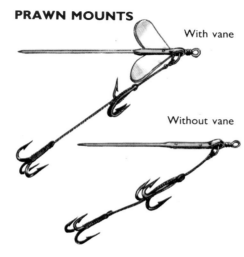

Reel line   Swivel   Leader   Spinning vanes   Prawn or shrimp

Anti-kink weight

Above; below right: *Prawn and shrimp can be used with spinning tackle or a float.*

Left: *These are lightweight baits for late spring, when temperatures have risen.*

choice of colours. During the colder months there is rarely a call for baits smaller than 2in long.

Other methods

Although spinning and fly fishing form the basis of most salmon fishing techniques there are several other legitimate methods which the angler may resort to when the going gets tough. It is possible to limit all salmon fishing to small flies and floating lines in late spring and summer and big flies and sinking lines for early spring or late autumn. However, worm, prawn or shrimp have many a time saved an otherwise blank day or week. At certain times and seasons the use of these

Right: *To be on the river at the right time is one of the essentials of salmon fishing. But having got there, your fly, line and the speed of current become irrelevant, and you must learn their correct permutations.*

Below: *Autumn fishing on the River Tweed at Innerleithen—an angler to be envied.*

PRAWN MOUNTS

With vane

Without vane

natural baits can be very effective, but there are still too many anglers who will resort to them without trying other more sporting methods.

It should not be implied that fishing with any of these natural

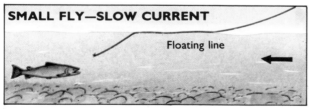

SMALL FLY—SLOW CURRENT

Floating line

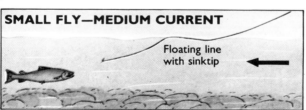

SMALL FLY—MEDIUM CURRENT

Floating line with sinktip

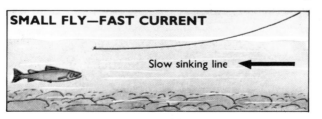

SMALL FLY—FAST CURRENT

Slow sinking line

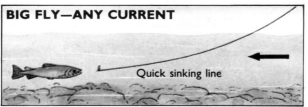

BIG FLY—ANY CURRENT

Quick sinking line

baits is easy. There is a sense in which successful fishing with a worm or prawn is more difficult than fly fishing, but there are times, conditions and situations when they might prove too effective and spoil the sport for others.

The same basic requirement for good weight assessment is necessary for successful worm fishing. The worm has to trundle over the bottom of the river and if the weight is too heavy there will be frequent hang-ups. If it is too light the worm may not get to the bottom.

Worm fishing

The best time for worm fishing is, perhaps, after a recent flood when the water is still coloured and higher than normal. The salmon may be laid quite close to the bank and there is again no substitute for knowing the waters. Whatever happens the angler must be at great pains not to strike at the first bite he detects. A salmon will frequently play with the worm for several minutes before rejecting or pouching it and moving off. The angler should, in fact, feed line to the gentle tapping movement given to the line; and he should not make a firm and decisive strike until he feels definite movement from the fish. This is perhaps one of the most exciting aspects of worm fishing.

Shrimp and prawn

The roving shrimp or prawn can be very deadly sometimes. In Norway, a popular way of prawn fishing involves a sink-and-draw method with heavy weight banging on the bottom of the river. Extensive knowledge of the river bed is required to bounce the prawn skilfully over all the likely water and the angler must expect frequent and irritating hang-ups. Usually when the prawn is taken it is with a bang, but there can be times when it is taken lightly. Unlike worm fishing, however, every suggestion of an enquiry should be dealt with by the angler with a firm and decisive strike.

Spinning prawn

Another successful way to fish the prawn is with it mounted on a spinning flight. Sometimes it may be fished as any other spinner, but it can be used to good effect by letting it drop

LEAD WIRE RIG

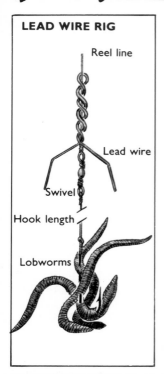

Reel line

Lead wire

Swivel

Hook length

Lobworms

SPINNING SHRIMP OR PRAWN

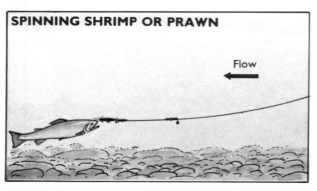

Flow

FLOAT FISHING WITH A SHRIMP OR PRAWN

Flow

AT-A-GLANCE

Specimen sizes
Tay, Spey, Wye 40lb; Ness, Tweed, Nith, Dee 30lb; Esk, Eden 25lb; Scottish Islands 10lb; Tywi, Teifi, Dee, Usk 20lb; Avon 30lb; Severn 20lb; Eire 25lb.

Tackles, baits, techniques
Rod
Double-handed, 9ft salmon spinning rod
Salmon fly rod, 12ft-14ft

Reels
Spinning, multiplying, closed-face, fixed-spool

Line
9-12lb b.s. (spinning)
Fly lines: sinking, sink-tip, floating, to match rods
Casts 9-12lb b.s.

Fly/lure sizes
According to season and water conditions

Baits
Spoons, Devons, plugs, flies, sprats, prawns, shrimps, worms, tube flies

Techniques
Spinning (sink-and-draw, harling, trolling), fly

Top left: A spiral of lead wire above the swivel can stop hooks snagging the bottom.
Top centre: Prawning for salmon with spinning or float tackle.
Left: A selection of traditional salmon flies.

downstream with nothing more than the current making the bait rotate. In very sluggish water, when the fish are confined to the deep holes, the small shrimp may be merely cast across the current and retrieved in very slow jerks. Sometimes it is possible to see the salmon come and inspect the shrimp and there may well be more salmon which want to play with the bait than there are which take it firmly.

For most of the season, therefore, it is the angler who makes his fly or bait move slowly who will have the highest number of successes. But there are times when a small fly fished fast near the surface will pay high dividends. This happens chiefly when the water temperature is quite high—and there are not many situations in the waters of the British Isles where this occurs.

The big build-up of salmon begins in early September, as late-running fish move in from the estuaries to join the spring and summer fish prior to spawning. Spinning, worming and prawning can all be deadly at the end of the year, to such an extent that many fisheries restrict the final few weeks of sport to the fly rod. If the water is low, early sport comes from the lower reaches, where even inexpensive tidal stretches give an excellent chance of success in dry weather. But if there is rain, the fish will run quickly, even through the middle reaches.

Chapter 4
COARSE BAITS

It is safe to say that if it is edible, and will stay on a hook, it's a bait. The range of possible coarse fishing baits therefore is enormous and at one time or another everything that can be mounted, wrapped around or squeezed onto a hook has tempted a fish to inspect it. For a fish, taste and smell are closely linked senses because of the watery medium in which they spend their lives.

No doubt primitive man watched fish which rose to airborne insects that had become trapped in the surface film; he saw smaller fish being chased and eaten by larger ones; and when berries fell off trees and worms ended up in the water to be snapped up he realised that this was a means of capturing food.

Fishing, then, first for food then as a sporting pastime, has accompanied man to the present day, so no wonder that we are able to use so many different baits. Izaak Walton liked to use worms, and knew that the lob was favourite, but he also fished with the smaller ones found in dungheaps and compost.

For perch, the worm is paramount; it is irresistible to those little stripeys which hurl themselves at a wriggling worm dangling in midwater. And a small perch can give a bite that is often taken to come from a much larger fish.

The common bluebottle's offspring, the gentle, if left to multiply unchecked would smother the Earth in a very short time. So perhaps we anglers do our ecology a favour by using them in vast numbers as bait and also in caster form as an attractor.

For years, it has been the practice of many anglers especially matchmen, to add colour to maggots in the form of commercial dyes. One of these dyes, Chrysodine, has come under suspicion that it may cause cancer in humans. After investigation, ICI advised anglers not to use any dye for colouring their baits and now many tackle shops no longer sell either the dyes or the coloured maggots.

All kinds of insects, airborne, terrestrial and aquatic, can be used as bait and while it must be doubtful if some are ever met by fish under normal circumstances the fish do take them when offered. But, then, fish never see a loaf of bread, yet a soft pinch of flake pressed onto a No. 10 or 12 will often lure a fat roach into taking it. In a number of forms — crust, paste, flake, sometimes with protein additives — bread is a good, reliable bait.

A number of seedbaits are popular, most of which stay well on the hook, a point which beginners find comforting, for there is nothing worse than sitting and fishing away, then deciding to reel in and inspect the bait, only to find the hook bare.

Of the seedbaits, hemp probably heads the popularity list. This bait not so long ago was proscribed on the suggestion that it was unfair. It was claimed that the dope element associated with hemp so affected the fish that they became literally (no pun intended) hooked on it. It is rubbish of course. The addictive element in hemp is not found in the seed, but it took a long while before the truth prevailed. But there are still some waters where hemp is banned.

Bloodworms are a very effective bait, highly attractive to fish. They are not real worms, but the larvae of gnats and midges. Not often available commercially, these tiny creatures must be collected by the angler himself — and a dirty, time-consuming and messy business it is. A special rake-like tool is used to scrape the bloodworms off the mud layer where they are found.

Many foods from the larder can be used as coarse baits. They range from cheese in a number of forms, beans, pasta, potato, all kinds of tinned and preserved meats, and fruit. The small, parboiled potato became famous as a big-carp bait in the 1950s and is still one of the carp fanatic's favourites.

Fish eat fish, so we can use this cannibalistic trait to good advantage. Livebaiting was once widely practised but is going out of favour, partly on the grounds of respect for all fish and a dislike of causing any unnecessary suffering, and partly because we have found that a well-fished and presented deadbait is just as effective. Pike specialists use quite large deadbaits for specimen hunting; ledgering with whole mackerel or herring is standard. But some years ago the Vincent brothers took things further. They used pike up to 5 lb as bait for large Broads pike, and caught a 30-pounder. It was dramatic confirmation of the size of fish a large predator will take.

Only one rule of thumb need be used when considering coarse fish baits: try anything that will stay on the hook. It might work, and if it doesn't, see what you have in your sandwiches. Many an angler has happily sacrificed his packed lunch because he found that the fish liked it too!

Maggots

When all you've caught after a long day's fishing is a cold, then its time to review your choice of bait. Maggots are good bait for many kinds of fish, and breeding them yourself is easy

The maggot is the most popular coarse fishing bait used in Britain. Almost all our freshwater species may be taken on it, major competitions have been won on it, and it has also accounted for some record fish.

Maggots are small, easy to buy, transport and use. Not so long ago they were cheap, but prices have risen steeply. Maggots now cost about £1 a pint. They are sold this way because pint beer glasses were once used to scoop them up for sale.

The maggot is the larva, or grub, of the fly. The maggots of the bluebottle, greenbottle, and common housefly are the ones which are used by the angler.

There are four stages in the life-cycle of a fly: egg – grub – pupa – fly. The female of the common housefly lays between 120 and 150 eggs at a time and deposits several batches during its lifetime

Maggot breeding

Breeding maggots is big business. Millions are sold every week by tackle dealers all over the country. Professional breeders use bluebottles for mass production of the ordinary maggot. The common housefly's maggots are known as 'squatts', and being smaller than the bluebottle larvae they are used as 'feeders' thrown in to attract fish. Maggots

from the greenbottle are called 'pinkies'. These are also small and used as 'feeders', but may be used on the hooks when circumstances require very fine tackle.

Commercial fly houses holding the breeding stocks are maintained at constant temperatures of 21.1°C-23.9°C (70-75°F). This enables maggot production to meet the year-round demand.

Maggot breeding starts when meat or fish is placed in the fly house so that the breeder flies can lay their eggs. When this is done the meat is said to be 'blown'. The meat is then removed from the fly house and placed on trays in long sheds. When the maggots hatch they begin to feed and grow. On reaching bait size they are transferred to another tray filled with bran or sawdust. As they wriggle through this they are cleaned and then ready for despatch, usually in large biscuit tins, to tackle shops. There they are kept in fridges to prevent them reaching the pupa (or chrysalis) stage too soon.

Maggots are usually sold in sawdust or bran. To improve their taste

remove them from the sawdust or bran and transfer them to a clean bait box containing custard or blancmange powder, flour, or a similar substance. As they crawl through this they become well-coated and tiny specks flake off in the water to add an extra attraction for the fish.

The 'gozzer' is a very soft, white maggot, the larval form of a type of bluebottle, reared mainly on pigeon carcass, pig's or sheep's heart. After five or six days of feeding, these should be given a final bran 'bath' and left until required.

A very succulent maggot, the 'gozzer's' powers of attraction are highly valued.

Coloured maggots

To increase the attractiveness of maggots to fish, they used to be dyed a variety of colours, and could be bought coloured orange, yellow, red or bronze. Tackle dealers supplied Chrysiodine R for dyeing them orange or bronze, Auramine O for yellow, and Rhodamine B for red. These dyes may be used in one of two ways. First, the maggots can be col-

oured by raising them on foodstuffs treated with a small amount of the dye. The second method is best for maggots that have already been cleaned, as they are when bought. For this, sprinkle dye on them and stir well, then leave for one to four hours according to the depth of colour desired. But Chrysiodine is suspected of causing a skin disease and it is recommended that it should not be used in this way.

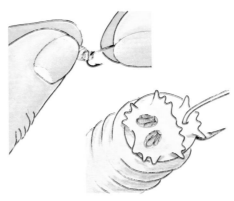

Above: *Hook the maggot through the vent at the blunt end. This will allow it to wiggle attractively to tempt the fish.*

The 'annatto' is a special colour-fed maggot whose yellow colour comes from the dye used to colour butter. Gozzers and other extra soft maggots produce the best results with this dye. Annatto is bought in roll form and must be cut into slices and mixed into a thin paste with water before use. The best time to introduce annatto is when the maggots are about half-grown. Spread the paste on the meat and replace in the bran. When the maggots stop feeding they are ready.

To prevent your maggots from turning into chrysalids, or casters, before you want them to, when the weather is warm, place them securely in a plastic box with extra bran and store them in your fridge where they will become cold and still. Make sure the lid of the box is securely closed, but remember that maggots need air, so ensure your bait boxes are ventilated with pinholes.

Lastly, if buying maggots from a shop, be sure they are fresh and do not include remnants of last week's stock. They should be shiny and wriggle vigorously.

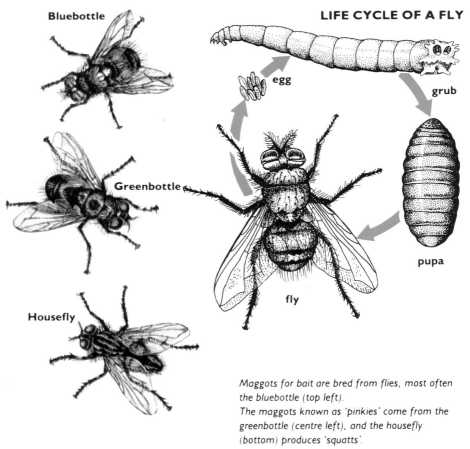

LIFE CYCLE OF A FLY

Bluebottle

egg

grub

Greenbottle

pupa

fly

Housefly

Maggots for bait are bred from flies, most often the bluebottle (top left).
The maggots known as 'pinkies' come from the greenbottle (centre left), and the housefly (bottom) produces 'squatts'.

Casters

Hailed by many as the new 'wonder' bait of recent years, casters need to be firm and dark red to ensure success. For this reason many anglers have turned to producing them at home

The chrysalis, or pupa, of the fly is known to anglers as a caster. At this point in its life-cycle (from egg to grub, or maggot, to pupa, to fly) it is an excellent bait. First made popular by match anglers in roach waters, some experts consider casters to be the most important new bait adopted in recent years. Although the maggot remains the most popular general bait, the time may be near when the caster will have replaced it. As well as roach, chub and dace are partial to it and it has accounted for bream, gudgeon and tench. When first introduced to a stretch of water the fish may be uninterested but, once sampled, every caster is likely to be taken. The fish probably gets its food more easily from the insect at this stage of its lifecycle than it did when it was a mere maggot.

Casters can be purchased from a tackle shop or bait dealer and kept in a refrigerator for about a week.

Above: *Casters and maggots laid out at the swim.* **Below:** *To hook a caster pierce the head with the point of the hook and sink the bend and most of the shank into the bait.*

HOOKING A CASTER

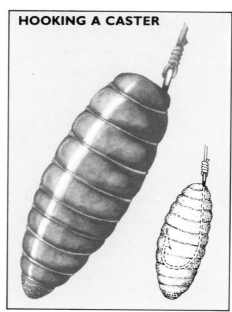

Home production can work out to be more expensive than buying them ready-bred, but the angler needs chrysalids (or casters) as sinkers: too fast a metamorphosis and the caster becomes a floater, of no practical use except as a means to check on the presence of fish in unknown water. The keen angler who needs a constant supply, therefore, will want to produce his own, in order to control the speed of change. After a little trial and error the angler can have casters in perfect condition and colour in the quantities he needs as and when he wants them.

Whether you buy casters from the dealer or raise maggots yourself, you will need about five pints of maggots to produce three pints of good quality casters—enough for a match or a day's fishing.

For large casters, choose large maggots. To test for freshness if you are buying the maggots, look for the food pouch—the small black speck under the skin. This pouch carries all the food the insect needs to complete the stages of its development to a fly, and should still be visible.

It takes a fresh maggot, one that has just been taken from its feed medium, five to six days to turn into a chrysalis with the temperature at between 65° and 70°F (18° to 21°C). To slow development, put the maggots, in a plastic box, into the refrigerator for three days—more in very hot weather, less in cold.

Tip the maggots on to a sieve to be riddled and cleaned, then into tins of dry sawdust, so that maggots and sawdust cover the bottoms of the tins to a depth of not more than a couple of inches. The maggots should now be kept in a cool place: a garage or cool outhouse is ideal.

After about 24 hours the first of the casters will be seen. Once this stage is reached put the contents of the tins on to a riddle over a larger container and the maggots will wriggle through, leaving the already-turned casters on the mesh. Any dead maggots that you find amongst them should be thrown away.

Return the live maggots to their tins. Repeat this inspection and selection process every 7 or 8 hours. Each batch of casters can be rinsed in water to remove bits of sawdust, drained on the riddle, sealed in plastic bags and placed in the refrigerator, at not less than 34°F.

Removing floaters
By rinsing the casters, any floaters can be removed at this stage. Damp casters can sour in the refrigerator and some anglers prefer to omit rinsing at this stage as a final check should may be made before setting off, or at the waterside.

If you do not want to use the refrigerator for collecting the bags of casters, you can put them direct from the riddling into a bucket, just covering them with water and adding to their number as they develop. Floaters can thus be eliminated as they appear and the bucket kept in the same cool outhouse as the tins of maggots.

Whichever method you use, you will find that the casters vary in colour. Casters of a uniform dark red colour—the favourite—can be achieved quite simply. On the evening before use, wrap all the casters in a wet towel and leave in a bucket overnight. Next morning all the casters will be the same colour.

The choice of hook size will be governed by the size of the caster. The biggest you can use will probably be a 14, but generally a 16 or 18 will be necessary. The hook must be buried in the caster. Hold the caster between thumb and forefinger and, with the hook in the other hand, pierce the head of the caster with the point. Turn the hook very gently into the caster and, with some of the shank still showing, lightly tap the top of the shank until the hook sinks into the caster.

Casters may be fished singly, or in twos, threes and fours. In deepish, fast flowing water, casters are best introduced as groundbait. Where there are plenty of fish and they start to take, you can put as many as two dozen casters in every cast. Casters can also be used in combination with other small bait, such as worm tail, hempseed or tares. When groundbaiting the swim with a mixture of hemp, it is essential to make sure the casters are fast sinkers.

When fishing deep water at long range, a quantity of casters can be mixed with a cereal groundbait to resemble a 'plum duff' with crunchy casters worked into the groundbait ball. Thrown into the top of a swim by hand, the ball will drop quickly to the bottom before breaking up—an ideal groundbaiting method when ledgering casters. Little and often is always a good maxim when groundbaiting with casters because it is easy to over-feed the swim.

When fished singly, casters need fine and delicate tackle. An easy casting rod is advisable when fished far off—too vigorous a cast will flick the bait off the hook. Quality casters are thought to be a good roach bait on any canal or river. With the approach of autumn they can be unbeatable on some waters.

Casters work best on clear waters, so when a river is coloured it may pay to revert to the maggot.

Just a word of warning – don't overfeed your swim with casters, for they are a filling meal for hungry fish. If bites are not coming, it is a mistake just to throw in more casters, your fish may be quite happy to munch away down there!

FROM MAGGOTS TO CASTERS

Top: Five pints of maggots give a day's supply of casters.
Above: In five or six days most of the maggots turn to casters. Remove all dead maggots (right).

Bread

If you want a cheap, plentiful, easy to use and highly effective coarse fishing bait, try bread. Most species can be taken on it, and it's especially good for caching carp and tench

Above: *One of the standard bread baits used by carp fishermen is the floating crust.*

Use a stale, thin-sliced white loaf to make paste. The fist step is to remove the crust from the slices.

Take the bread out of the cloth and knead it until it becomes a firm, smooth, non-sticky paste.

Bread is not only an old-fashioned bait but also a very successful one. In recent years, and on many waters, it has been neglected, perhaps because its uses are not fully understood. Four different baits can be made from a white loaf —flake, crust, balanced crust and paste. The first two of these come from a new loaf, the fourth from an old loaf, the third from both.

Flake

Flake is the name given to the crumb of new bread. The crumb of a two-day-old loaf is difficult, if not impossible, to place on the hook. When removing the crumb from the loaf a light touch is essential. Take hold of the crumb and lightly pull it from the loaf: it should be like a sponge with one edge sealed between thumb and forefinger. With the other hand take the hook, push the shank into the 'sponge' and gently pinch the crumb over it. Both

the bend—or part of it—and the point of the hook will be exposed. The two sides of the crumb must be joined together with the minimum of pressure. If the sponge falls apart the bread is too old: one light edge-pinch should be sufficient to keep it together. If the flake is pinched too tightly the bait will be hard and unattractive.

The size of flake, and therefore the size of hook, depends upon the fish you expect to catch, the water you are fishing and the time of year. Chub, barbel, carp and tench during the early part of the season, and big roach in waters not too heavily fished, can all be taken on a No 6 hook. For bream, chub in winter, roach in some waters, tench, grayling and crucian carp, use a No 10. For dace in heavily fished waters, or in winter, use a No 12; in exceptional

circumstances, when for example, the fish are shy or in very cold water, use a No 14.

Many anglers dislike flake because it is difficult to cast. The cast must always be a soft one, smooth and unhurried. Generally a sideways cast is best, or when fishing close in, an underhand one. When proficient, overhead casts can be made without bait and hook parting company in mid-air.

An advantage of flake is that, whether trotted or ledgered, small particles constantly break off, thus attracting fish from downstream into one's swim.

Crust

Crust must come from a newish loaf,

Soak the trimmed slices in a bowl of cold water, making them soggy but not so wet that they disintegrate.

Wrap the soaked slices in a clean cloth (such as a tea towel) and squeeze them firmly to remove all excess water.

The finished paste. Some anglers mix additives such as aniseed, brown sugar or custard powder into their paste.

Bread paste should be moulded around the shank and bend of the hook, leaving the point exposed.

weight must be given to the bait, so just before casting the crust is dipped into the water for a moment. This is called 'dunking'.

Hooking the crust

Opinions differ as to which side up the crust should lie. To make the bait hang crust side down take the crust and the hook, push the hook into the crumb side, out of the crust, then back through the crumb until both bend and part of the shank of the hook protrude. The opposite actions will make the bait hang with the crust up. About half the shank with the point and barb should always protrude from the crust. A hook slightly larger than the thickness of the crust must be used. If the hook is completely buried, the wet crust is liable to fall or cast off.

Crust will catch fish in all seasons but it is especially useful in winter, fished stationary close to the bottom. The distance it is presented off the bottom is determined by how far the weight is stopped from it: 6in from the crust and the crust will be fishing about 6in off the bottom.

In June and July crust is especially good for tench, fished either under a float, 'lift' style, or simply ledgered. It can be fished in rivers, trotted and ledgered, and floatless on a weightless line. In stillwaters, ledgered and floating crust has probably accounted for more carp than any other bait.

Ledgering

Ledgered bread crust is one of the deadliest of baits for chub, while smaller pieces of crust will take tench, roach and even dace.

Crusts tend to be buoyant, so for ledgering the weight should be stopped very close to the hook to hold the bait near the riverbed: an Arlesey bomb is ideal and should be stopped an inch away from the hook.

The size of the ledger depends on the size of the bait and the flow of the river. Ideally, the weight should be such that the crust should just stay held in position in the current.

Don't be afraid of using really big chunks of crust for chub fishing, especially in summer. A chub will soon make short work of a wad of crust the size of a matchbox, it has a very large mouth.

not more than two or three days old. The loaf should be kept in the shade, because once hardened the crust is useless. Depending upon the species being sought, sliced and unsliced loaves can be used. For roach, dace and grayling, a cut loaf is best: where larger pieces are required for such species as chub and carp, an uncut loaf is necessary, especially when using floating crust.

The best way to cut the crust from an unsliced loaf is to insert the point of a sharp knife into the side of the crust. Cut through the crust in the shape of a square. When you pull the square of crust away from the loaf, a chunk of the soft flake beneath it will also come away.

Floating crust is very popular among carp and chub fishermen. The crust must be soft, so the baking of the loaf and its freshness are very important. Hard, brittle crust is useless. Some fastidious anglers order specially-baked loaves, but this should not be necessary if you choose a loaf which has been baked to a light brown colour.

Crumbly or too-hard crust from stale loaves is also useless, breaking up as the hook is pushed through it. A fairly large piece of crust, say 1½in square, is often used with a cast of 20 yards or more. For distance-casting the corners and edges of the loaf are, for a given size, heavier than the flat areas and therefore cast better. When no floats or weights are used, however, some

Cheese

Strongly scented and easily moulded to the hook or mixed with cheaper ingredients as a groundbait, cheese is attractive to most non-predators and even, now and then, to perch and pike

For most purposes Cheddar cheese makes an excellent bait—but it must be fresh. On occasion, softer cheeses such as Stilton or Danish Blue are also very good.

Understanding wives and mothers do not object to anglers removing small pieces of stale cheese, but taking the fresh Cheddar may raise a few eyebrows. Removal of the Stilton or Danish Blue is apt to put a definite strain on any relationship.

The thoughtful angler makes his own arrangements to purchase cheese before he goes fishing. But however you obtain it, it is well worth trying this versatile bait.

Fresh Cheddar can easily be moulded into a putty-like consistency. This should be done as and when needed, the cheese being flattened between the finger and thumb and then folded around the hook and shaped firmly in place.

Chub and barbel
Traditionally, cheese is an excellent barbel and chub bait. It also takes good roach and dace. Much of its effectiveness depends on the fact that the flavour drifts down on the current, awakening the olfactory responses of distant fish and bringing them up to the hook. For this reason, cheese is more effective when used in rivers and streams than in stillwater, and clearly the stronger the flavour the better the attraction. This is not to suggest that cheese will not catch fish in lakes but merely to imply that stillwater fish are less likely to pick up the scent.

For chub or barbel, walnut-size pieces on sizes 4, 6, or 8 are about right. In slow or sluggish waters this can be used on the bottom without using any weights. In faster water, however, it is necessary to use a ledger weight such as an Arlesey bomb to hold the bait down, once in position. A few smaller lumps of cheese should be thrown into or upstream of the swim at intervals during fishing. Groundbait too should be liberally laced with cheese powder as this helps to hold shoals in the area of the hookbait.

If the angler has been careful to work unobtrusively, and provided he has chosen his swim well, chub and barbel will often take a cheese bait within a few minutes of it being cast into position. Should it not be taken soon, it still has the advantage that it holds to the hook well and does not need retrieving to check if it is still there.

Roach and dace
For roach or dace, pieces the size of peas on size 10 to 14 hooks are used. In suitable swims a ledger might be used but the favoured practice is to swim the stream with standard float-fishing tackle. Again bites are usually positive. Though durable, cheese is soft enough to allow good hook penetration when the time comes to strike.

The much softer cheeses, such as Stilton and Danish Blue, when mature, are sometimes too soft to be moulded on to the hook. If so, mix the cheese well with a good stiff bread paste. The cheese imparts sufficient flavour to the paste to provide a tasty bait for many species.

Cubes of cheese
As an alternative to moulding the cheese on to the hook, it is possible to cut it into small cubes of a size to suit the hook. The hook is then either pressed firmly into the cube or threaded through it. In either case the hook point must be very close to the surface of the cube, even protruding. Some smaller cubes are thrown into the swim as attractors.

The versatile cheese slice has gained a lot of friends over the last few years. You can use either the white or yellow variety, cut into slivers, to fish running water where it dances and shimmies through the swim in a most attractive way. It attracts bites from all species of fish—the roach in particular being susceptible to a thin strip of tasty cheese lowered tantalizingly below a lightly shotted stick float.

Different shapes cut from the slices sink and fish quite differently from any other bait, and bites can come at any time during the bait's introduction to the water. A big chub, for example, may appear from nowhere to grab a halfpenny-sized strip of cheese almost as soon as it hits the water.

Sliced cheese is equally effective when used in conjunction with a bread punch. On stillwaters this is an advantage because the shapes don't come into contact with the angler's hands. Lay the slice on a flat surface, press in the punch, and insert the hook lightly. During summer months, crucian carp are spellbound by punched cheese, and very often a tench or two show up.

Perch, pike and trout
Surprisingly, although cheese is regarded as best suited to non-predatory species, it does occasionally take perch, or even pike and trout. There are on record the captures of a 22lb pike and a 10lb 12oz Kennet trout on ledgered cheese. During the early season, when chub and barbel both take fish baits such as minnows, it is sometimes useful to mould the cheese on the hook in the shape of a spinner so that it will revolve as it lies below the ledger. Here, it is necessary to insert a swivel between the ledger and the hook link.

Other predators, such as barbel and chub seeking moving prey may respond to a piece of cheese spinning just off the bottom. The noted Avon angler Bill Warren, who died in April 1978, took more than 200 chub of 5lb-plus from his river—all on cheese paste. If you are fortunate enough to secure a worthwhile trout on cheese it may well make up for the fact that you plundered the best Danish Blue from the fridge before leaving home. And you may also be forgiven for doing so!

Worms

Cheap, versatile and plentiful, earthworms are one of the most effective baits available to the coarse fisherman. But for best results you need to know how to look after them properly

Earthworms have been used as a bait for fish for a thousand years and more, and today they are just as effective. All species of freshwater fish can be caught on worms, and indeed several record fish have fallen to this bait. Even the salmon or trout may be taken in this way, sometimes deliberately, sometimes by chance.

The redworm

The redworm is a smaller species, not usually over 4in long, and is a useful roach, dace, bream and perch bait, although any species of worm may appeal to all freshwater fish. This worm is found in compost heaps, and under large stones or rotting logs; any sizeable object in the garden could conceal enough worms for a good day's fishing.

The brandling is of similar size to the redworm but is distinguishable by a series of yellowish rings around its red, often shiny, body. It can be collected from manure piles or compost heaps. The presence of a compost heap will, of course, mean a regular supply of worms. If the wormery is tended by adding potato peelings, tea leaves and vegetable waste, the worms will grow much bigger and probably breed there, thus supplying a constant store of bait. Where grassy conditions are suitable, worms can be dug at the river bank. Be careful to fill all the holes in and not leave places which other anglers can stumble over.

Cleaning and toughening

Although very effective on the hook, most worms become soft and lifeless very quickly in water and often drop off the hook during casting out. Their quality can be improved to overcome this by allowing the worms to work through a good soil for a few days prior to use. Sink a box in the earth, providing small holes in the bottom for drainage. Place the worms on a bed of soil (a dark, loamy kind is best) and cover with sacking. In wriggling through the soil they will scour themselves to emerge brighter and so more attractive to the fish. They will also be tougher, and will stay on the hook longer and wriggle more enticingly. 'Faddist' used to recommend that worms be kept in fine red sand or brickdust, suggesting that this gave them an added colouring as well as making the texture of their skins much tougher.

Alternatively, a bucket containing sphagnum moss (obtainable cheaply from a florist) provides a medium for cleaning and toughening your worm bait. They will burrow through the moss, which should be damp but not wet. To keep worms fresh immediately and during use, put them in clean moss and place in a linen bag. Tins and jars should be avoided, for they do not allow the worms to breathe properly. Remember also to weed out dead and dying worms, for one dead worm in a bait tin tends to trigger off an extremely fast mass mortality among the rest.

Hooking the worm

It is important to hook a worm correctly, for this ensures that it stays on the hook and that it will wriggle naturally to attract the fish. A whole worm can be hooked anywhere along its length. If necessary, pierce a long worm several times and feed it along the hook. Tails or pieces of worms should present no problem and stay on the hook. In general do not try to cover the hook, for a worm is a very tempting bait and, if lively, will probably wriggle enough to expose part of the hook anyway.

Apart from using a single hook, there is the two-hook rig known as pennell tackle, and the two- or three-hook Stewart Tackle. These multiple-hook rigs are best when the whole of a big lobworm is used.

Look after worms, they are an all-purpose, all-weather angling bait.

Lobworms may be gathered from a lawn, but if the grass is long it may be difficult. Cricket pitches and close-cut sports fields will also yield lobworms in plenty if access, at the right time, is available to the angler. The best periods are after dark and following a heavy dew or shower.

Below: *All freshwater fish are attracted by earthworms but roach, dace, bream and perch are particularly susceptible to the smaller, brighter coloured redworms.*

COMMON BAIT WORMS

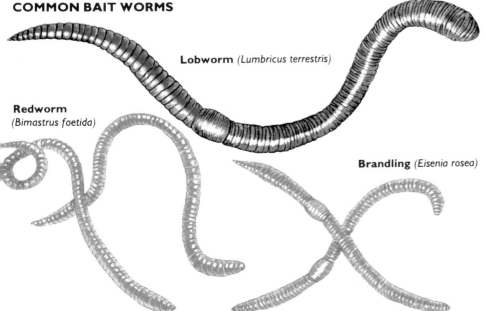

Lobworm (*Lumbricus terrestris*)

Redworm (*Bimastrus foetida*)

Brandling (*Eisenia rosea*)

Paste and crust

One loaf can produce a versatile range of very attractive baits for most coarse fishes

Breadpaste is one of the oldest and probably most successful baits. Correctly mixed—and surprisingly few anglers can do it properly—it is a very effective offering, capable of catching most species at all times of the season.

Paste must be made from an old loaf, four days old at least. The loaf is prepared by removing the crusts then cutting it into slices an inch thick. Take one slice and dip it into a bowl of water, removing it almost immediately. Placing it into the palm of one hand, knead it into a paste with the other hand. Keep kneading until all the lumps have disappeared and it is soft. Now repeat the procedure with each slice in turn until you have sufficient for your fishing needs.

Put all the balls of paste together and knead the mixture, making sure that the texture is right by adding water if necessary. The texture is most important. The paste should be soft but not tacky. Should any stick to your fingers, mix another slice to a slightly drier consistency and work in. The final kneading should be made immediately prior to fishing. Place a piece on the hook, cast and retrieve. If it remains on the hook during the retrieve it is too hard; if it flies off during casting it is too soft. Adjust it accordingly.

Mixing the paste
Mixing paste should be done over a clean bowl, for if the bread is right it will crumble. (If it doesn't it is not

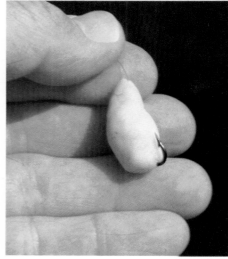

Above: *Ledgering breadcrust for chub.*
Left: *Balanced crust—a tough, castable bait.*
Right: *Floating crust for carp or big chub.*
Below: *Breadpaste on the hook. It can be given interesting colour (and perhaps scent) by the addition of custard powder or dye.*

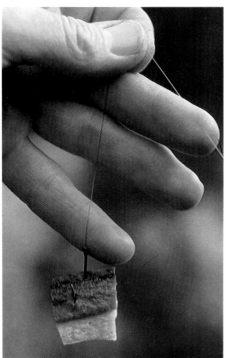

old enough.) Pick up the fallen pieces and mix them in with the paste. New—even fairly new bread—will not make good paste; the results are glutinous, slightly grey in colour and contain lumps. Stale bread does not go lumpy, the texture is constant and it retains its whiteness.

When mixed, the paste should be kept in a clean plastic box, wrapped in a clean cloth. At all times it must be shielded from the sun; if not, a thin crust will form, rendering the outside useless for fishing.

Paste additives
At one time it was recommended that oils and aniseed should be added to the paste to make it even more attractive to the fish. In my experience, however, this is not necessary. Nevertheless, there is one additive that has been found to be very successful—custard powder. Sprinkle some custard powder in a bowl, place the paste on to it and mix thoroughly until the paste is bright yellow in colour. Both the smell and colour attract fish, especially roach, bream and dace.

A favourite trick of Northern canal anglers is to add a few crystals of maggot dye to the bait as they press the mix together.

The angler is now equipped with paste that is white, custard yellow and perhaps other shades. It is quite extraordinary how the fish react to these variations of colour in different weather and water conditions.

Some anglers mould their paste on to the hook in a pear shape. While this does not prevent fish eating it, the author prefers to use it rough, simply pinching it on to the hook lightly with the minimum fuss. The less paste is handled, the better.

Hook sizes suitable for breadpaste range from 4 to 20 depending on the fish sought. For roach, bream, dace and grayling, 14 to 20 are right; chub, bream, tench and sometimes large roach need size 10; 8 for chub and barbel; 4 or 6 for carp.

Casting with paste
Because paste is a very soft bait if properly mixed, great care must be taken when casting. While overhead casts can be made without paste and hook parting company, in most situations a sideways cast is preferable. To ensure that the paste remains on the hook, the cast must be a smooth one: the least jerk and the bait will either fly off or partially dislodge itself from the hook. Most trouble arises when casting into wind when a more powerful cast is required. This should not deter the would-be paste fisherman, however. A powerful cast does not necessarily mean a jerky one. Keep it smooth and no trouble will arise. Smooth cast or not, the hook must be the same size as the bait; if it is not this will only encourage the paste to come adrift. It is probably safe to say that it is the problem of keeping paste on the hook which stops so many anglers from using it.

Balanced crust
One very effective, yet comparatively little-used bait is balanced crust. This comprises a carefully judged mixture of bread crust and paste. Mainly a stillwater bait, balanced crust is popular for carp fishing over mud or weed.

It is most important to get the right proportions of the ingredients. If properly balanced, the bait takes a minute or two to sink and, when it does, sinks slowly, finally coming to rest on the surface of the mud or silkweed without actually sinking into it. When the bait does settle, the line should emerge from underneath, thus making it almost impossible for a fish to touch it with its lips as it takes in or investigates the bait by mouthing it.

To make balanced crust, a piece of crust is taken from a new loaf and placed on the bend of the hook. The paste—made up to the consistency described earlier—is then moulded round the hook shank. Too much paste and the bait will sink too quickly and may become partially submerged into the mud or weed.

Balanced crust is a 'big fish' bait and calls for big hooks to match, ranging from 2 to 10. For carp 2, 4 and 6 are suitable; tench, bream and chub need size 8, roach size 10. Should fish be biting shyly, 10s will suffice for all species with the exception of carp. The hook size should be such that the point and part of the bend protrude from the crust, with the paste added until it is level with the top of the shank.

Groundbait

Knowing where to place your groundbait is part of the secret of successful coarse fishing. There is a wide range to choose from, but making your own is cheaper and can achieve better results

Groundbait is put into a swim to attract and hold fish and is very useful, if not essential, in producing results in most kinds of coarse fishing. Made-up groundbaits range from heavy mixtures, which sink to the bottom rapidly in a fast current, to 'cloudbait', which make the water attractive to fish and are used in slow currents or stillwater. More simply, groundbait can be samples of the hookbait thrown in loose—worms, maggots, casters, hemp, and others, or combinations of these, are commonly used.

Making your own groundbait
Bags of dry groundbait, mixed and ready for use, can be bought from tackle dealers but, unless one buys in bulk, it is generally cheaper to mix your own. You can then make up groundbait to suit differing water conditions and your own personal preferences.

The basis of most groundbait mixtures is stale bread, prepared by breaking it up or mincing and then soaking it in water for an hour or two, or overnight if very hard. When soaked, drain it as much as possible and make into a smooth paste. This can be made into small balls for throwing into the swim. Numerous ingredients can be added to the basic mix and their use is to some extent determined by the type of fish sought and the water condi-

tions. For example, bran, semolina, chicken meal, sausage rusk, barley meal, boiled and mashed potato, clay, peat, crushed egg shells, samples of the hookbait, and other additives are used. These substances are especially useful in extremely fast water and when hook-bait samples are needed on the bottom. The extra weight takes the groundbait to the bottom before it is washed away.

Cloudbait for slow water
In a slow flowing water, light cloudbait can prove effective. This is prepared by cutting bread into thick slices and allowing it to dry out. To speed the process heat the bread in a domestic oven, then crush the dry crisp slices to a fine powder and sieve out all lumps. At the waterside the powder is dampened to the preferred consistency and made into small balls for throwing into the area to be fished. As they sink slowly these will break up and cloud the water. This effect can be heightened by using milk instead of water. The addition of semolina will improve the mix when wet and bind it for lobbing into a distant swim.

It is well worth experimenting with both flavouring and colouring for groundbaits. Some fishes find added honey, for example, very attractive. Flavour can be introduced in the form of oils of aniseed,

lavender, fennel, verbena, pilchard and others. Powdered egg and milk are also useful. Other additives will enhance both flavour and colour. Among these are blancmange and custard powder, flour, sausage rusk, crushed biscuits and hempseed. Fishing can sometimes be improved by colouring the groundbait to contrast with the hookbait.

Tasty 'maggot pie'
'Maggot pies', probably first used by Norfolk anglers for groundbaiting a swim when ledgering, are based on a cloudbait mixture (either bought or made up), which is poured into a large flat vessel at the water's edge and wetted to the required consistency. Feeder maggots are then added and orange-sized balls are made and thrown into the swim. If expense is no trouble, the mix can be made heavier for fast flowing water by the addition of boiled mashed potatoes. In general, about 1lb of potatoes is used to 4lb of cloudbait. For a long day's fishing, or a big match, make about 10lb of the groundbait and add a half a gallon of feeder maggots. For very fast water it may be necessary to add clay or even pebbles.

'Black Magic' is the name given to a dark groundbait. It is prepared by working in a proportion of lawn peat to the bread. The peat should be dried and sieved finely before mixing, and the final groundbait mixture should be dampened at the water's edge as needed.

Liquid groundbait
A liquid groundbait, unusual yet sometimes effective when fishing lake margins with floating crust for carp, can be made from well soaked bread mashed and mixed with water or milk. This is dilute enough to simply pour into the water.

Right: *With well placed groundbait, fish will remain in the hookbait area.*
Far right: *Indiscriminate groundbaiting is bad fishing. It must first attract fish then hold them. Correct positioning is determined by water flow and depth. Your hookbait must always be placed in the action zone.*
Left: *Groundbaiting two separate areas — one close in with loose feed to keep the fish interested, the other across the water with groundbait while ledgering for bream.*

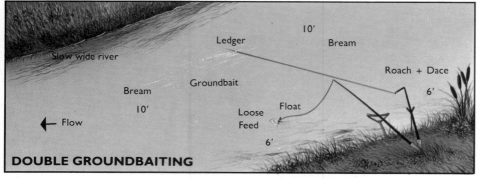

DOUBLE GROUNDBAITING

Trout pellets, which are used to feed and fatten fishery bred trout, are rich in protein and send trout into a frenzy at feeding time! Most fish will take the pellets, but crushed and mixed with breadcrumbs they make an excellent high protein groundbait that has been successful with carp and tench.

Luncheon meat is a highly successful hookbait for chub and barbel, and groundbait for use with it should contain meat. Sausage meat works well enough, but minced meat is better. Either can be used on its own or added to an ordinary groundbait.

Double groundbaiting

Most anglers bait only one area from any one bank position. But baiting two separate areas, one close in and one far out, is an interesting and effective method of hedging your bets when fishing larger waters.

The diagram at the bottom of this page shows how this technique can be applied to a slow, wide river. For much of the season, roach and dace shoals occupy the margins alongside the shelf, but bream are to be found far out in the deep middle section. By double groundbaiting, you go after either roach and dace or bream, whichever produces the best bites.

For a session starting early in the morning, a sensible plan would be to rig up both ledger and float rods, but first to ledger the middle for bream over a groundbait carpet of cereal and hookbaits. At the same time the near swim, just two rod lengths out, should be loose fed with casters. After an hour or so, if the bream prove uncooperative, you could then switch to the float rod and trot down for roach or dace. You would now be fishing a swim which had been regularly fed and if fish are feeding you should get good sport.

Above: A selection of commercial groundbait including the heavy mixtures which sink to the bottom. The bottles at the back contain flavourings and dyes.

Below: Adding sausage meat to close up the end of a swimfeeder containing sweetcorn — an effective groundbait for attracting carp, tench and bream.

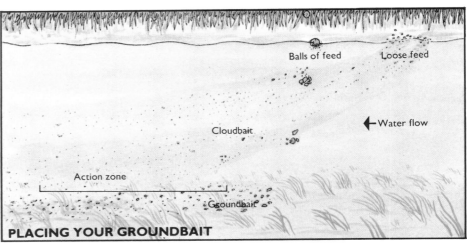

Balls of feed   Loose feed

Cloudbait

◄— Water flow

Action zone

Groundbait

PLACING YOUR GROUNDBAIT

Potato

First popular with specimen carp catchers, potato is now used to take tench, roach, chub and bream. Its big advantage is that while deterring smaller fish, it attracts some really large specimens

Cooked potato, presented in a variety of forms, is favoured as a bait for large carp but is also attractive to bottom-feeders in general and sometimes tench, bream, chub and barbel. The occasional larger roach will take a potato but one of the bait's advantages to the carp fisherman is that smaller fish will usually be deterred by its size and will leave it to the specimens. The attractiveness of potato to large carp is perhaps attributable to its curiosity value and, despite a notorious cautiousness, they will investigate a potential food not normally found in their natural environment if careful groundbaiting is used to allay their suspicions.

Pre-baiting with potatoes is favoured by some anglers, particularly carp catchers. Use a handful of small potatoes thrown into the same swim or swims at the same time every day before a fishing session. A good groundbait can be made up from ordinary or instant potatoes mashed up with scalded bran. This mix, or small par-boiled potatoes similar to the intended hook bait, can be introduced to a swim on several occasions for up to a fortnight before fishing.

Preparation

To prepare the bait, select smallish potatoes—from about large marble to golfball sized. Leave the skins on and boil them for about 15-20 minutes. It is important not to cook them too much for they will fly off the hook on casting or will break up in water if too soft. They should dent slightly under gentle finger pressure when cooked enough. They should then be peeled carefully or scraped before being used on the hook. The peeled and tinned variety make a good substitute and need less preparation as they are already part-cooked.

Ledgering

Ledgering is the usual method for presenting potato to carp. A freelining technique is used, for the bait has its own weight and so does not require weights to assist casting or to get it to the bottom rapidly. Sometimes the weight of the potato will cause it to sink into mud on the bottom where the fish cannot see it. In this case use a slice cut from a potato prepared in the same way. This will lie flat on the bed and if cut large enough it will still deter the smaller fish.

To hook a potato, thread the line through it, using a baiting needle. Better, sink a short piece of plastic tubing through the bait and pass the line through it. This will prevent the line cutting into the potato with the force of the cast, which often has to be a long one. Then tie on a suitably sized hook (some use a barbless model or cut the barb off the regular kind) and pull the hook back into the potato gently so as to prevent fragmenting when casting.

POTATO BAITS

Potato is particularly effective for carp and can be presented whole, chipped, sliced or made into balls. Small new potatoes (fresh or tinned) are ideal, though instant mashed is favoured by some.

Potato slices

Par-boiled potato

Potato chips

Instant potato

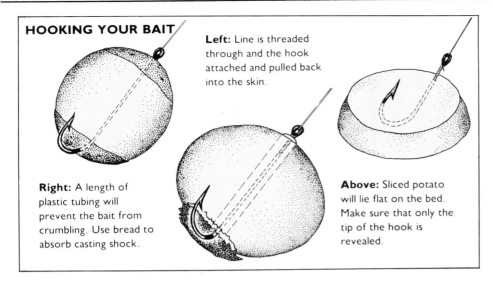

HOOKING YOUR BAIT

Left: Line is threaded through and the hook attached and pulled back into the skin.

Right: A length of plastic tubing will prevent the bait from crumbling. Use bread to absorb casting shock.

Above: Sliced potato will lie flat on the bed. Make sure that only the tip of the hook is revealed.

Effects of casting

To further cushion the effects of casting, leave patches of peel where the point is to penetrate and where it will emerge. Alternatively, use an ingenious method devised in recent years. After tying an eyed hook, the bend is sunk into a round piece of bread crust and then the potato is brought down firmly on to it. This pad of crust will absorb the shock of the cast, which would otherwise jerk the hook back into the potato, possibly breaking it up.

Although a large, eyed hook is preferred by many carp anglers, a hook-to-nylon can also be used by threading the loop through the bait and then pulling the hook back into the potato.

Remember to take a good supply of par-boiled potatoes on a fishing trip as they will sometimes fly off the hook or break up whatever precautions are taken. The bait must also be changed after taking a fish. Keep the cooked potatoes in water until ready to use on the hook as this prevents them from turning brown. A screw top pickling jar is ideal for this purpose.

Like many baits, the potato is worth experimenting with. Potato chips, lightly fried so as not to be too soft, have been used with some success for carp, although more often in Europe than in this country. A potato paste can be made from mashed potatoes bonded with an additive such as the scalded bran or bread-crumbs used in the ground-bait. The important thing once again is to achieve a consistency that will keep the bait on the hook during casting and while being fished.

Proven carp catcher

All baits—and potatoes are no exception—are subject to fashion and in some cases, mere fad. There are some anglers who stick to one bait for a season or two and then for no apparent reason, switch to something completely different. Of course, there is always room for experiment, but at the same time the most reliable baits always come back again—and potato is nothing if not a proven carp catcher. In any case, it only takes one angler to have a successful session using potato for the news hungry angling press to persuade its readers that potato is the 'new' wonder bait. And with more anglers using it, more fish will be caught.

Fishing with potatoes has accounted for the capture of some of our largest carp and remains among the best methods.

Used on their own, potatoes can be a bait that will tempt some of the largest carp. But one of the great pleasures in fishing is to try those unusual experiments that very often succeed where normal procedure has failed.

Along with your small, par-boiled potatoes, take a tin of thick black treacle. When the potato has been mounted on the hook, dip the potato into the treacle so that it receives a good, sticky coating. It could be a winner.

Potato balls made from instant potato mix

Granules (or Powder)

Tinned potato in kilner jar

Bloodworms

The difficulties of collecting, preparing and fishing these tiny baits is amply rewarded by the catches they bring, but baiting up on this small a scale is a precise art

Although many anglers may never have used bloodworms, few will be strangers to them, having seen the small, bright red larvae in a rain butt or garden trough. Here, they live either in the thin layer of silt at the bottom, or burrow into the thin green alga that lines the side. Warm weather will bring them out into the open where they progress through the water by a series of violent body contortions.

Their bright red colouring comes from the presence of haemoglobin in the blood—the pigment also found in human blood and that of all the higher animals. However, there are some species of chironomid that are green or yellow, and some which are completely colourless.

Collecting bloodworms
The largest bloodworms will be found in stagnant water. Those that inhabit running water are somewhat smaller in size and are referred to by the angler as 'jokers'. The traditional instrument used for their capture is a long firm pole some 5ft in length. To one end of this is fastened a thin strip of pliable aluminium at least 1½ft long. This strip can be bent into various angles to suit the depth of water that is being searched, and the scraper is sliced through the top surface of mud a short distance out from the bank, with an even motion that traps the worms by folding them over its leading edge. After each sweep the worms can be gently slid off the scraper into a tin or plastic box. The whole action is rather like scything grass and takes practice to perfect.

Storing lively bloodworms
They should be stored separately in moist, black garden peat which has been crushed and broken until it is a fine dust. Not only will this keep the larvae alive and active, but also pro-

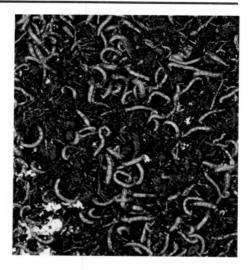

After the worms have been carefully washed under the tap, they can be stored and transported in moist, black, crushed peat.

vide a binding medium for those that are going to be used as groundbait. The peat forms a black carpet across the bottom of the swim which is, in itself, an attraction. If hookbaits are kept for any length of time, they should be packed into damp moss and stood in a refrigerator where they will normally remain useful for several weeks.

Hooking bloodworms is an art. Naturally, only the smallest hooks, sizes 20 to 22, will be fine enough to match the small bait. Hooks should be mounted on ¾lb or, at the most, 1lb b.s. hook links. The easiest method of hooking is to lay the bloodworm on to the thumbnail, then pierce one end of the worm with the point of the hook and gently ease it over the barb. Good eyesight is important if you are to avoid splitting the worm open, and some anglers resort to a watchmaker's eyeglass as an aid.

When a long pole is being used to present the bait, a barbless hook is by far the best for the job as it causes minimal disturbance to the

outer skin of the worm, thus preserving the natural colour and juices that fish find so attractive.

Need for small floats
The float is a very important item in bloodworm fishing. Often the bait will be taken 'on the drop' and, if the angler is counting on small fish to make up his weight in a competition, he will be fishing a mere 12-18in below the surface. This means that the float must be small, require very few shot to cock it, and that these shot be mounted into, or immediately below, its body. Above all, that part which shows through the surface must be as thin as possible so that the smallest touch on the bait will produce an immediate response.

Tight-line tactics
A tight-line tactic pays excellent dividends with bloodworm fishing, and the roach pole is probably the best instrument by which to apply it. Its easy style of casting will also prevent undue strain on the bait, which is so delicate that it will usually be thrown off the hook by a long-distance cast.

By presenting the bloodworm on delicate pole tackle, the French National squad have walked away with more world championship victories than any other country—often taking fish that surprise English anglers with their sheer size. Carp up to 5lb are not uncommon and when you consider that a size 24 hook and a ¾lb line have led to their downfall you will begin to appreciate just how devastating this pole/bloodworm combination can be.

The bloodworm is not merely a match fisherman's bait for small fish. It is equally successful with large fish and many specimen hunters seeking carp and tench have found it produces excellent results, especially on hard-fished or difficult waters.

Several bloodworms mounted on to the hook in a ball, or used as a cocktail bait with a single maggot, make up a mouthful that few fish seem able to refuse.

Thus all the trouble and care needed to collect and use the bloodworm is more than worth while – if you are allowed to fish them! So remember to check before using them.

Slugs

Slimy and grotesque-looking, despised by the gardener—that's the much-maligned slug. But freelined it's a killing bait for the most wary chub and free for the collecting besides

Great grey
(*Limax maximus*)

Most people think of the slug as a slimy and unpleasant creature which must be treated with distaste. To the hard-working gardener it is a major pest, eating young green shoots. But for the big-fish angler the slug is almost a thing of beauty and a bait that will attract even the most wary chub.

There are over 20 species of slug to be found in Britain. They can be considered as snails that have lost their shells, for the internal anatomy of a slug is very similar.

The best slugs
For the angler, the best slugs are undoubtedly the black, *Arion ater,* the great grey, *Limax maximus,* and the red, *Arion ater rufus.* Most of the other British slugs are too small to use as a big-fish bait.

As slugs tend to lie-up when frosts appear in late October or November, one must construct either a holding area or a place where they can be allowed to breed. By far the best way to keep them is in an aquarium. This will enable you to see what is going on inside without having to disturb the inmates.

An ideal size is an aquarium measuring 48in×8in×15in. It should have as a cover a well-fitting lid of ¼in plate glass.

Place about 6in of garden soil in the bottom and make sure that you have a few good-sized lobworms in it as well. On top of the soil place some small pieces of plywood, about 6in×6in. The food for the slugs is placed on these slabs.

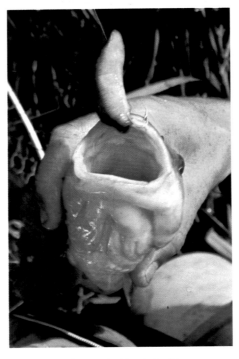

Your slug will be attacked by chub without any preliminaries, resulting, more often than not, in neat lip-hooking.

As slugs like to hide during the day you must prepare somewhere for them to go, so put a couple of inverted flower-pots on top of the soil.

Keep moisture down
The atmosphere in the tank is kept moist by the tight-fitting lid. This creates rather too much moisture, so if the aquarium is kept propped up at one end the moisture will filter down and form a pool which should be siphoned out from time to time.

It is important to keep the pool of condensed water low since for some reason the slugs tend to crawl into it and drown. Therefore it is best if the 'sluggery' is kept in a garden shed or garage, for the smell of decomposing slug is very potent.

On a rainy day, place them on the lawn for a 'run'. But keep an eye on them for they can move surprisingly fast and disappear into the grass.

Food for the slugs can be all kinds of household waste, greengrocery and garden cuttings. Add potato-peelings and greens such as cabbage.

Check the tank regularly and remove any dead slugs. When the tank is established and the slugs are feeding well, they will probably breed. So in late October or November place some sheets of newspaper on the soil. The slugs will lay their clusters of small white eggs on the paper, and some on the insides of the inverted flower-pots on top of the soil.

After the eggs have been laid, remove the slugs. They will soon die as they only live about a year. Any rotting food must also be taken out. Now cover the sides and top of the aquarium with polystyrene sheeting to keep in the warmth.

When spring arrives, very small slugs will be seen. Often, the tight lid and condensation attract tiny flies and mites. The young slugs will feed on these, but get them 'weaned' on to potato-peelings and green-stuffs as soon as possible.

A few fresh slugs from the garden ought to be put in, but it seems that some species cannot get on together. The large black slugs do not live with the red. So keep to one sort which you can find locally. The slugs should be about 3in long by May and in June they can be fattened up for the summer's fishing.

Fattening them up
Three days before you go out on a fishing trip, get a whole melon and cut a small hole in the tough skin. If you place this in the sluggery they will crawl in and gorge themselves, often leaving nothing but the melon's tough skin. The largest slug I have bred using this method is one that measured an incredible 7½in long. Perhaps this should be listed in a famous book of records?

Hempseed

Hempseed is possibly the best bait for coarse fish such as roach and dace, but many people have problems with it, if only because they can't keep up with the speed of the bites

Acclaimed by the match fisherman and other anglers as a 'superbait', banned by some clubs as unsporting, condemned for years as a water pollutant, suspected of drugging fish—controversial hempseed has been all of these.

Good quality hemp, available at a reasonable price nowadays from most tackle dealers, is big, black, and should be free from dust or husks. A pound is ample for a normal day's fishing. Before use it should be washed carefully in cold water, immersed in a clean pan of cold water and then brought to the boil. To emphasize its blackness a large lump of household soda can be added, together with two teaspoonfuls of sugar to hide any acidity. Having boiled, allow to simmer and carefully watch until one side of the seed opens and a white kernel protrudes slightly, showing that it is

PREPARING HEMPSEED

Rinse the raw hempseed under a fast-running cold tap

Leave the seed to soak overnight in a bowl of clean water

Rinse the soaked seed in cold water again the following morning

Put the seed into a large pan of water and bring it slowly to the boil, stirring constantly with a wooden spoon

Reduce the heat and allow it to simmer, but don't leave it unattended in case it overcooks

When about half the seeds have split, revealing the white kernels, remove the pan from the heat

Leave the seed to drain and cool in a sieve

Alternatively, rinse the hot seed in cold water, then leave it to drain

A third method is to stand the sieve in a pan of cold water, then let it drain

fully cooked. Boiled beyond this point it will disintegrate and become totally useless.

Keep the seed damp
Now sieve the seed and wash it under a cold tap until thoroughly cool, otherwise the cooking process will continue. Finally—and vitally important—store the seed in an airtight, watertight box, keeping it sealed until it is required. If you fail to keep hemp wet it will float on the water, bring fish up to the surface and eventually, as it carries downstream, take them with it out of the swim doing no good at all.

It is no exaggeration to say that half of the hempseed used by anglers is wasted. A large quantity thrown into the water for groundbait overfeeds the fish, drastically reducing the chances of hooking them. When a swim has been selected, start by covering the palm of the hand with seeds and throw them well upstream, and repeat the process once or twice while tackling-up. The float should be adjusted by trial and error until the hook swings an inch off the bottom of its passage through the baited swim.

Hooking hemp
Hooks for use with hemp should be small—from size 10 downwards—and made from fine wire. Special hooks, with the back of the bend flattened to allow a single hemp grain to be easily mounted were available at one time; some anglers today flatten their own with a small hammer and a fine punch. The effort taken to do the job is amply repaid with time saved in re-baiting the hook whilst fishing.

Select a large seed, hold it between finger and thumb, then squeeze it and push the bend of the hook into the open side through the white kernel. Gently done, this should hold the seed on the hook. If the seed drops off, it will indicate that the hemp has been overcooked. With each cast it will probably be necessary to re-bait the hook, a tiresome procedure that, as will be seen later, can be avoided by the use of artificial hemp or alternatively a suitable substitute.

At every cast to the head of the swim, throw in no more than 8-10 loose grains, aiming them right on the tip of the float. Once they hit the water, tighten any slack line between rod tip and float and prepare yourself for some of the fastest bites imaginable.

The smell and taste of hempseed are potent, and the use of a groundbait mixed with water in which it has been boiled will often have roach, rudd, dace, chub, bleak, bream and the occasional barbel snatching frantically at the hookbait. Often, because of the nature of this bait, the float will have dived under and the seed be released before the less experienced angler has had time to strike. In this situation, you can continue using hempseed as a groundbait but with a larger hookbait, such as elderberries, both fresh and preserved, currants, or tares, one of the seeds used in pigeon feeding. These larger mouthfuls usually succeed in persuading a fish to hold on long enough to the bait to allow a strike that will drive the hook home.

Occasionally, the quick bite that is not followed through can be caused by the fish attacking the lead shot on the cast, which closely resemble hempseed.

If you have the patience, you can separate the biggest and blackest of the seeds as hookbaits, and use the rest as groundbait

Before hooking, you will have to open up the seed between thumb and forefinger by squeezing along the line of the split

Seeds can be put on the hook by gently but firmly clamping the split around the hook-bend

Another way is to ease the point into the kernel until it emerges from the 'eye'

Only correct cooking enables you to hook hempseed securely

Meats

Although meat baits and meat-based groundbaits are no longer a rarity, many are deterred from using them by problems of cost, hooking and presentation. Here are some of the solutions

At the turn of the century the angling press was astonished by the report of a man who had caught a fish on a sausage out of his luncheon pack. It was, the experts said, an exceptional happening. No one should consider catching a fish on a meat bait. There was only one form of bait used at that time with any association to meat, and that was greaves, a waste product of tallow obtained from candle manufacturers and used both as hook and groundbait at Thames weirpools to catch barbel.

Today, meat baits—pure meat and not merely by-products—are commonplace, and barbel, roach, bream, chub, tench and carp are regularly caught on them throughout the year. Much of the present day angler's success is the result of the modern preparation of meat products which are packed with a consistency that not only allows easy mounting on the hook, but also a slow break-down in the water allowing flavour and smell to remain around the lure.

Luncheon meat

The best known and most used of the meat baits is undoubtedly luncheon meat. The tinned types are easily carried and provide a hefty chunk of meat from which substantial sized cubes can be cut. Blind buying of the first tin on the shelf is not advised. There are many cheap varieties of luncheon meat which have a very high fat content, and this means a soft cube of hookbait that will either break away from the hook during the cast, or fall apart within a few minutes of lying in the water, especially if the swim lies in fast water.

A few extra pence will purchase a good meat mix that should be kept refrigerated until required, and thereafter kept as cool as possible while the angler is fishing. Once the

tin is opened, keep the contents out of the sun and packed away in an airtight box. Drop any unopened tins held in reserve into the shallows at your feet—probably the best refrigerator on a warm day.

Mounting the bait

Mounting cubes of bait onto the hook requires care. Choose a hook too big rather than too small—sizes 8-4 are usual—and push the point of the hook slowly into the centre of the cube before threading it round onto the bend, making sure that the barb shows. To prevent the bait from jerking free on the cast use a small portion of green leaf or fine clear polythene folded double. This should be pushed over both point and barb to act as a platform behind the cube, and into which it will press during the thrust of the cast. It will not effect the hooking properties,

and will save endless re-baiting.

There are variations on the luncheon meat theme, such as Spam, Prem and liver sausage, but avoid Continental processed meats that are highly seasoned, usually with garlic. Corned beef is excellent, but tends to shred quickly.

Sausage meat

Sausage meat is another excellent meat bait, but it should be stiffened with breadcrumbs or, better still, sausage rusk, until it assumes the consistency of putty. Another deadly bait is sausage meat mixed together with rusk and soft cheese with a little plain flour to harden the balls once they have been shaped into bait-sized pieces.

Tinned pet food, especially cat foods with a high proportion of fish in their ingredients, hit the headlines a few years ago as a deadly carp bait. Preparation of the bait for the hook is messy, and requires a little trouble, but results are usually worth the effort. Ideally the tin should be opened at the bank, hook-sized lumps moulded, and these dipped into boiling water to form a hard glaze over the surface which helps hold them in place during a cast. Obviously some soap and a towel are essential items when using this method, otherwise the whole of one's tackle smells very strongly by the end of the day.

The use of pork rind or strip has been in vogue for some years now in America, where it can be purchased uncooked, vacuum-packed and ready for the hook. The strips are hooked into the treble of a spinning lure, and it is claimed that baits treated with this addition of two or three worm-like strands towed astern really tempt the big fish.

The other way of using bacon strips is to hook-mount them as one would a worm, on a single large hook, and slowly reel this without a float and with the minimum of weight through areas where predators are found.

Where to fish

Meat has a better chance of success in waters where it has been accepted for a number of years, and some species take it more willingly than others. Probably the natural place

HOOKING LUNCHEON MEAT

HOOKING PORK RIND

for its use is when fishing for barbel and chub in a weirpool, where luncheon meat is best.

A solitary piece flung just anywhere into the pool and left is hardly likely to be effective. Back up its use with groundbait. Fast water that washes away free offerings or bait from the hook, is a dead loss.

Choose an edge of the pool, preferably as close to the sill as possible and at one side of the main flow of water. Depth is decidedly useful, and if there is an undercut to the structure so much the better— an eddy will probably be created holding the bait in one place. Make several trial casts and search for the slack water that always lies at the head of a pool before baiting.

Other places
Other places where meat will often do well are above the weir—where the river and navigation channel divide producing deep water under the rod—and where erosion has taken a bank away, leaving a deep cut and slow stream. Lock cuttings are worth a try, but there is always a risk of too much attention from eels, especially in the autumn.

Other natural places to try are where human food is most readily available—such as near boatyards and houseboats moored along the banks of a canal.

Above: *Mixing blood with a cereal-based groundbait – do it on the bank, not at home.*
Top right: *The leaf prevents the cube tearing free in the cast. The point need not obtrude.*
Above right: *The aim is to imitate a worm.*

To use meat on its own as a groundbait would obviously cost a fortune. The solution is to use a little, and to eke it out with cereal bait to give bulk. Raw mince is a good, cheaper, substitute. A pound left uncooked and thoroughly mixed in with pulped bread, sausage rusk or even bran, can go a very long way.

'Flaked' corned beef
Corned beef can also be 'flaked' then mashed into a cereal base to provide a taint of the whole hookbait. Ideally, the mixing should be done on the day you fish, in order to avoid the bait becoming rancid.

In recent years, a number of cereal mixes with dried meat in them have appeared on the market as dog foods. These are cheap and effective and need only be soaked overnight before use. In an emergency they can be rehydrated immediately before use by covering with boiling water, then left to cool before packing. Kept moist at the bank, this bait will sink naturally and is particularly useful for swimfeeder work.

The cheapest meat additive to

groundbait is blood. A pint bottleful from a local abbatoir, refrigerated until needed, can bring most coarse fish that are gross bottom-feeders into the swim. Mixing before arrival at the bank is not recommended.

Bloody porridge
Use a plastic bucket, tip the cereal base into this and then add the blood in the same way that water would be added. A thick porridge consistency should be aimed for, and the bucket should be kept covered with a damp cloth to prevent drying out.

An alternative, especially with sausage meat, is to roll a large supply of very small balls that can, if necessary, be catapulted into a distant swim.

Fish that accept meat baits generally do so avidly, and the angler should always be prepared for the bite. Rods left in rests are in danger of being pulled onto the bank, and floats left unwatched can lose the angler fish after fish. By far the best way of using meat in all of its forms is with the ledger, and the rod should be hand held, with one rest only giving support along the upper third of the rod itself. Watch the tip of the rod carefully: when you see it bounce you should then strike immediately. The name of the game with all meats is to try every meaty item in your larder.

133

Freshwater mussels

Well camouflaged and easily overlooked, droves of meaty mussels creep even now through your local fishing water on big yellow feet which carp and tench find irresistible

Although there are some 26 different types of freshwater cockles and mussels in the British Isles, only one specimen is of value to the coarse fisherman—the swan mussel. This big mussel, frequently six or more inches in length, is found in numerous lakes, reservoirs, ponds, canals and slow-flowing rivers, where it lies in the muddy shallows, especially near reed and rush-fringed banks or where overhanging trees give it cover of darkness.

Mussels congregate together, and move slowly by means of a foot that protrudes from the thick end of the two shells when they are held open. They feed by filtering water through two tubes or syphons and retaining floating particles of fine weed and minute animals. Often the angler is not aware of their presence because their shells are dark green and yellow, two-thirds buried in the bottom and the top third covered with moss. They are, however, excellent bait for tench and carp, and although time and trouble must be spent in finding and preparing them, the reward in terms of fish caught is well worth the effort.

Searching for musselbeds is a waste of time. It is far better to look along the banks for broken shells that diving birds have captured and opened—something they are unable to do on the water. Once the shells are discovered it is necessary to wade and feel for the upright head of the shells that protrude above the bottom. Despite the disguise provided by weed growth, the smooth oval shapes are unmistakable as the hands rub against them.

For a serious day's fishing, some 30 to 40 shells should be collected from a site well away from the swim

Only the careful use of a knife will preserve the contents as intact as this. Every part of the creature should be used.

you intend to fish. It is a good idea to store them in a sack, and later sort them into big specimens that can be kept in a box of damp weed for use as hook bait, and smaller ones for groundbait.

Opening a mussel

Opening mussels can break fingers unless a little care is taken. The halves of the shell are held together by a series of extra tough sinews situated on the lower part of the back where the thick edges join. These sinews must be severed first, and any attempt to prise open the shells at the back or through the thin front edges will probably cause the knife to slip. You should hold the mussel firmly in one hand with the hinges upward, slide the knife along the join, and gently sever the hinge;

both halves of the shell will then fall easily apart.

The knife can now be slid around the inside of the shell to release the 'body', most of which consists of a thick, yellow piece of flesh at the foot. Do not throw the shells away—pound them into small pieces and add them to the groundbait bucket. Naturally the shelled mussels and broken pieces will need some stiffening before they can be thrown into the swim. Damp sausage rusk or soaked new bread are two of the best mediums to use.

Mussels as hookbait

Some authorities say that the groundbait should be prepared at least 48 hours or more in advance of the day it is intended to fish, so that the bait will be 'high'. Mussels used as hookbait, it is sometimes suggested, should be opened and left in the sun to dry and turn rancid. Experience has shown, however, that little is to be gained from this practice, except an increase in the numbers of eels that will be hooked. The smell of fresh blood in the groundbait coupled with the bright pieces of broken shell lying on the bottom are all that are needed.

Larger mussels used for hookbait should be opened as required, and the yellow fleshy foot removed and mounted on a big (size 2 or 4) hook. Turn the hook once through the body and push it well past the barb to give a good hold.

Although ledgering is the accepted way to fish the bait, laying on, especially during the midday period when fish are inclined to mouth continuously rather than pick up the whole offering, has a lot to commend itself.

Do not forget that mussels are a bait that will attract fish, especially when the groundbait has been treated with blood or oil, and every effort should be made to keep the groundbaited area as close to the bank as possible.

Although freshwater mussels are found in shallow water, deep swims, up to and over 12ft, are ideal. An even better chance of success can be expected if the swim has been raked and cleared of weeds so that the groundbait is clearly displayed on the river or lake bed.

Wasp grubs

Every scrap of a wasp nest can be used as bait: the juicy queen grubs as hookbait, smaller ones as loose feed; the honeycomb structure on your hook and the residue scalded into groundbait

For float fishing in clear, fairly fast-flowing river water, there are few deadlier hookbaits than wasp grub. From late August onwards sport is often hectic and bites so positive they are hard to miss.

So effective has the bait proved to be that its use is banned in many contests. It is even barred completely on some controlled waters, so always check before using it.

Fishing the bait is simple, finding it a bit more difficult. A lot of anglers are just too lazy to take time to go out and collect this quite remarkable bait, and you will need at least three nests for a good day's fishing. Even so, wasp nests are more easily come by than many anglers think.

Collecting wasp grub
Wasps are not the most clinically particular creatures. Where there is muck, there you will find wasps. Strange as it may seem, there are more wasp colonies per acre in towns than in the country. I've collected, in one evening, as many as ten nests from city parks.

Evening is usually the best time for wasp spotting. To find a nest, pick a likely area of wasteland, banks or hedges, then watch. If you see a wasp idly meandering, stopping here and there, ignore it. If you see one flying straight and with purpose, mark mentally the direction of its flight path; the nest is rarely more than 100 yards away.

Another wasp will soon come along the flight line. Follow it fast, and as far as you can. It may beat you, but the next will probably lead you to the nest entrance. This is usually underground but rarely deep down. Found in soft earth, often under a hedge or bush, nests are round or oval in shape and made up of layers which make it look very much like a papier-mâché structure.

The next problem is in removing the nest while avoiding painful stings. Reassuringly, a wasp sting is not as dangerous as that of the honey bee which carries a venom akin to that of a cobra. The danger in a wasp sting comes usually from the bacteria injected at the same time—so take care!

Although cyanide-based insecticide compounds are on the market (Cymag is the most efficient), their general use cannot be recommended. Unless stored and used correctly, they can be dangerous (you will have to sign a poison register to obtain them) and safer proprietary insecticides are preferable, although not so effective as Cymag.

Whether you use a cyanide-based mixture or another type, it should be applied using a large tablespoon tied firmly to a 3ft stick. Put one spoonful as far into the nest entrance as possible and make sure that you are upwind of the nest so that the noxious fumes blow *away* from you.

Succulent grubs on the point of hatching. Only the best go on the hook and can prove killing.

Another spoonful is sprinkled around the entrance. All this is best done in the early evening when all the wasps have returned. Block the entrance with a clod of earth and wait for at least two hours, preferably overnight.

The nest should be removed as carefully as possible, since every bit of it can be used by the angler. Dig round the nest, scraping away all loose earth and lift it out whole.

In comparison with the maggot, wasp grubs are big, creamy and soft. The biggest and plumpest were destined to be queen wasps; they also make the best hookbaits. Remove and lay aside all you want for this purpose from their tube-like homes in the centre of the nest.

The smaller grubs and any damaged ones are then scalded, along with the nest of 'cake', for use as the attractor groundbait. This can be used mixed with breadcrumbs or on its own. It is also worth trying as hookbait once in a while.

Presenting wasp grub
Wasp grubs are best used with float tackle of the kind suited to fishing bread flake. Bob Morris became Severn Champion using wasp grub bait to take a record 55lb of chub from the breamy lower end of that river. His secret was to put a piece of bread flake on the hook every half dozen casts or so. This often tempts the bigger chub which tend to lie at the rear of the shoal.

Now and then it is necessary to fish wasp grubs hard on the river bed. Most fish take 'on the drop'. There is no mistaking the bite, particularly with chub. With a size 10 or 12 barbless hook, all that is needed is to tighten line quickly—and your fish is on.

Apart from the Severn Championship win, wasp grub has accounted for a record-breaking Trent Championship victory. It will tempt most species. Single grubs on the hook will lure roach, and at least one carp of over 20lb has fallen to a ledgered grub in the past.

As soon as a tinge of colour creeps in to cloud the water, sport comes to a halt. The reason for this is not yet fully understood. Possibly the suspended sediment dulls the fishes' taste or smell.

Sweetcorn

Lightly cooked, thawed from the deep-freeze or straight from a can, sweetcorn makes a costly groundbait, but a deadly hook-bait for carp, tench, chub, barbel and many other coarse fish

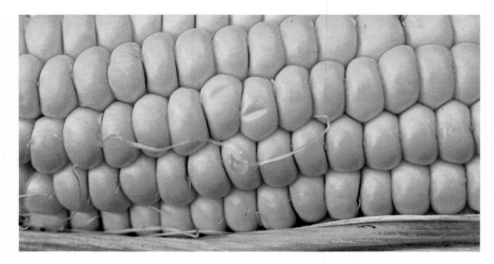

Top: *Copious prebaiting on a large still-water. Hotspots should be carpeted with grains.*
Above: *One or as many as four grains can be hooked on eyed or spade-eyed hooks.*

Among big fish enthusiasts, as well as the match angling fraternity, particle baits have been much in vogue for the past five or six years. But there is nothing new about them. Some, like maggots, casters, hemp, and boiled wheat, have been used for decades. But sweetcorn is relatively new (at least in Britain) and has had a great impact on the big fish scene.

Carp fishing specialists began to experiment with this deadly bait in the early 1970s, although there is little doubt that other enterprising anglers used it long before. The author, for one, caught tench on sweetcorn in the early 1960s, and it is very unlikely that he was the first. Certainly American anglers used corn long before us.

Not only carp take corn

Carp are particularly attracted to sweetcorn, but there are several other fish for which it is equally effective. Other than the predators, most fish, including tench, rudd, roach, bream, chub, dace and barbel, can be 'educated' to take it readily.

Sweetcorn's greatest attractions are its availability and its convenience. In its ready-to-use, canned form, it can be put on the hook without any preparation. Alternatively, you can buy fresh or frozen corn which is just as good after a little preparation. Whole corn-on-the-cob needs cooking and de-cobbing, while frozen loose corn needs boiling for a few minutes to soften it. But if you intend pre-baiting with large quantities, you can make a significant saving by buying bulk and boiling up as required.

Nevertheless, the canned corn is still the most popular form, but do give the environment a thought before taking cans to the waterside. It is more convenient and less anti-social to open the can at home and empty the corn into a plastic bait box or other container. In fact, there are now a few environmentally conscious clubs that ban cans of all types on the river banks and punish infringements with expulsion.

Sweetcorn keeps quite well, but in hot weather treat it like maggots and keep it in the shade if possible. Drain off the 'juice' and give the corn a quick rinse under the tap before putting it in your bait box, for it becomes sticky and slimy in hot weather. Removing the juice does

not detract from its effectiveness as a bait. Corn can be frozen after use, too; it is expensive, so do not waste. With care, it can even be re-frozen.

Sweetcorn grains range in size from that a match-head to that of a large pea. So all manner of bait sizes and hooks can be used—from a single small grain on a No 18 to six or seven large grains hiding a No 4 or No 2 carp hook. Compared with other particle baits, few grains are needed to cover the hook.

It pays to use eyed hooks or spade-ends with a prominent spade. These help to keep the corn on the shank. With whipped-to nylon hooks there is always a risk of the corn sliding up the line, resulting in false bites and snagged hooks. Some anglers favour gilt or gold hooks, but the author has found them no better and uses bronzed, eyed hooks.

The big question with corn is how much free bait to introduce into a swim. This is a very controversial subject, and the views of experts vary, particularly when it comes to 'educating' carp and tench in stillwaters. The general plan, however, is to encourage big fish to feed intensively over a small area.

High protein baits

The excitement has long since died away that greeted the arrival of high protein baits. But genuine advantages do spring from knowing where and when to make sparing use of HP

High protein (HP) is not a magic formula bait that will guarantee big fish catches. But used wisely and correctly on suitable water, it will succeed where other baits have failed to tempt fish.

The originator of high protein baits was Fred Wilton of Snodland in Kent. As long ago as 1967 Fred had already achieved success with his high protein preparations on a Kentish water that proved to be the ideal experimenting ground. Fred's idea was to provide the undernourished carp with a vitaminized, high protein diet far superior to the food chain the lake could supply, since the water was overstocked. He reasoned that, after a long and heavy groundbaiting programme to introduce and to familiarize the bait, it would be taken instinctively.

Waters with insufficient food
As has been said, this was on a water where the carp failed to achieve their weight potential simply because there was not enough food to go round. The lake in question—and there must be scores of waters in other places with similar characteristics—was inhabited by carp to the occasional double figures, plus pike, roach, tench, perch and literally thousands and thousands of silver bream. 'Silver slimies' (as they are known) are of no interest to the carp hunter even if the matchman or pleasure angler takes some delight in them. Fred overcame the risk of 'nuisance' fish picking up the bait by using eggs to mix the compound instead of water. The paste, dry weight about 10oz, was then rolled into balls of 1oz and boiled for one minute. This produced a tough, rubber-like skin on the outside of the bait ball and defeated the attentions of the unwanted species.

Initial recipe
This initial recipe consisted of Phillips Yeast mixture (approximately 43% protein) and contained the vitamin B complex which is water soluble; wheatgerm, similar but with a slightly inferior formula and only 31% protein, Farlene baby food and Pomenteg, a groundbait additive. It was made up as follows: 6oz of wheatgerm (Bemax), $2\frac{1}{2}$oz of PYM, $\frac{1}{2}$oz of Farlene and 1oz of Pomenteg.

When the number of catches fell off in January, casein (milk protein), with calcium, was introduced in place of the Farlene and Pomenteg, and catches immediately improved. Calcium caseinate is 90% protein and this put the overall value of the bait up from 31% to 46% protein. The winter campaign that year fetched 72 carp, 13 of which were double-figure fish.

It has been proved that HP will catch big carp; the author has taken several 20lb fish using it. He remains certain, however, that the expense of buying individual ingredients is not justified by big carp returns. On big-fish waters, high-protein-using carp men have sat behind lifeless lines while a 'layman' using luncheon meat has pulled out a 28lb carp. And remember, the use of high protein baits is expensive.

Today, there are very few waters left where the carp have not seen high protein. If you know one, you are lucky! Consequently, the problem of an expensive groundbait programme can be dispensed with.

It is now often a subtle preparation that will put carp on the bank. The present-day carp angler also uses HP in particle form, and the latest vogue is to include a smell additive. This can range from a soup stock to a teaspoonful of vanilla essence and generally these have proved very successful. But once again, the usefulness of any ingredient lasts only as long as it continues to attract carp. The carp is wily and quickly learns what to avoid.

If you want to see fish climbing on each others' backs to feed on high protein, visit your local trout farm. The trout are fed on a high-nutrient diet to ensure a fast growth rate—and they love it! Ground-up trout pellets make a useful carp special when mixed with soya flour (44% protein) and milk powder. One such mixture contains 5oz of pellets, 2oz of soya flour and 2oz of milk powder (Casilan). Where fishing for carp in a water that contained the odd trout, the author caught four mirror carp to $14\frac{3}{4}$lb and three rainbows—all on trout pellet paste!

Follow the recipe carefully
Another tried and tested high protein mix comprises 4oz of Purina cat food, 2oz of soya flour, 2oz of Phillips Yeast mixture and 2oz of Casilan. Mix thoroughly and then add six standard eggs—remember to whip the eggs first—then roll into roughly 1oz balls. Boil for one minute and allow them to cool. If you have followed the recipe carefully you should end up with a firm bait that will catch big carp.

Particle high protein
To make a particle high protein bait requires a bit more patience. The mix is made as before, but there follows the lengthy task of rolling the paste into $\frac{1}{2}$in strips. These are immersed in boiling water for 30 seconds and allowed to cool.

It is as well to groundbait with the particle offerings as you fish. This will often attract fish into the swim. Particles often tempt other species, however, so be prepared for big roach, bream and tench.

Given ideal conditions, high protein bait should prove a top scorer, but never go to a water without an alternative bait.

Deadbaits

The accelerating trend away from livebaiting has resulted in a wider variety of deadbaits being used, with more imagination, by anglers concentrating on more species than simply the pike

The gradual acceptance of dead fish as a highly successful pike fishing bait during the late 1950s will be recorded by angling historians as a fortunate turn of fate. Prior to this, pike fishing took place with a live bait, which meant catching and conveying fish until they could be mounted and used on snap-tackle mounts—a method which entailed considerable inconvenience for both fish and fishermen.

Against this style was a growing lobby of anti-blood sport agitators who were pressing for prosecutions against those who used live fish, alleging cruelty when hooks were mounted into them. River Boards, strengthened by new legislation, were introducing bye-laws prohibiting the use of livebaits because of the risk of spreading disease where baits were transported and used in strange waters. Finally, conservationists were raising their voices at the number of immature fish taken and used for livebaits, stressing that this denuded waters of future breeding stock.

Deadbaits are just as successful as livebaits—at times even more so—and there can be no element of cruelty in mounting them for fishing. They can be easily carried, and need not be freshwater fish, thus silencing the conservationist objections. The angler also has a choice in the size of bait, from a small sprat weighing ounces, to a large mackerel weighing over a pound. Certain freshwater fisheries allow a limited number of fish to be removed as baits, and where this is legal, naturally they may be killed and used to augment the variety.

Keep deadbaits frozen

All deadbaits are best deep frozen until required, and they should be graded into species and according to size, then bagged and frozen in small batches so that enough for a day's fishing can be removed and defrosted with the minimum inconvenience and waste. Time and trouble spent in freezing each fish straight away will pay when it comes to mounting the bait, and during casting, when twisted fish can often affect both the distance and the accuracy.

Fishing with static deadbaits is by far the most common technique, and it requires a rod soft enough in its action to cast a dead weight over a long distance. Fast-taper, tip-actioned rods will snatch the bait from its hook in casting. Whether a multiplying reel or a fixed-spool is used is largely a matter of preference and cost. But it is worth remembering that heavy baits, constantly reeled in and cast during the day, impose a great strain on the line: and the multiplier has fewer line angles along the rod.

Match the line to the rod

The weight of the line used in deadbaiting is equally important, and care should be taken to match it to the rod. Lines that are too thick strain the rod and restrict casting distances: those that are too light will strain and are liable to suddenly snap during the cast.

Unlike livebaiting, the majority of deadbaits are fished on, or close to the bottom. If ledgering is adopted as the style of fishing then there will be little problem with end tackle —the weight of the bait will rule out the need for a large supply of ledger weights stop beads and so on. But many anglers prefer to use a float, maintaining that with it they can see exactly where the bait is lying and note its slightest movement. A further argument for float fishing a deadbait is that any drift across the surface will ultimately move the bait, and this slow movement can often be used with advantage.

Naturally, when a float is used, it must be capable of sliding up the line, with a stop knot (a short length of nylon tied with several overhand loops) fixed on to the line to check the float at the correct depth, and a small weight fixed above the trace to cock and prevent the float jamming below the surface after it has been cast. Unless the intention is to allow

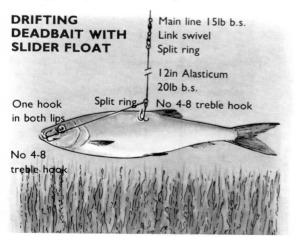

DRIFTING DEADBAIT WITH SLIDER FLOAT

Main line 15lb b.s.
Link swivel
Split ring

12in Alasticum 20lb b.s.

Split ring — No 4-8 treble hook

One hook in both lips

No 4-8 treble hook

Left: *This rig can be drifted a foot or so above the bottom, keeping the fish horizontal and lifelike. It also keeps it above the weed tangle so that feeding fish can see it. Mackerel are best for use with this method as they stay rigid. This bait does not look natural to the human eye, but a feeding predator can be fooled by it.*
Right: *Two methods of mounting herring on trebles for pike fishing. When the idea of offering herring as deadbait for large pike was first suggested, special rigs and mounts had to be devised because of the weight of the bait.*

the bait to drift, then the smaller the float the better.

There are innumerable deadbait hook rigs which can be used, some with four or five treble hooks that take time and patience to mount. Generally, the fewer hooks the better. Fine-wire trebles, sharpened and checked for temper, can easily be mounted on to cabled Alasticum. Their size should match the bait being used because small trebles combined with a large bait obviously reduce the chance of hooking on the strike, and large trebles on a small bait make the whole rig cumbersome.

Probably the most popular rig is the deadbait snap-tackle. Two trebles, equal in size, are mounted on to a trace, their spacing varying according to the size of bait used. One treble is mounted close to the tail, the other into the side in front of the dorsal fin. The trace is then fed under the gill cover and out through the mouth, and tied to the line through the medium of a swivel. If extra-long-distance casts are to be made, then three or four turns of nylon round the body will help to prevent it breaking away from the hooks during the cast.

A lifelike drifting rig

A useful drifting deadbait rig is made by securing a split ring into the eye of a treble. To this is attached a short length of trace that terminates with a similar-sized treble and another separate length of trace, which finishes with the link swivel for attaching the reel line. The bait is mounted with one hook of the end treble through both lips, and two hooks of the split-ringed treble through the back of the fish at the dorsal fin. Mounted in this way, the bait hangs like a livebait, and when fished in mid-water moves freely with any surface drift.

Carrying deadbait rigs needs care if a mess is to be avoided. Barrie Rickards solved the problem with his balsawood log. This cylinder of soft wood with end pieces allows trebles and traces to be safely secured, and when slid into an empty tin, will not snag other items of tackle. Baits themselves are best put in leak-proof Tupperware boxes.

A deadbait is only as successful as

Barrie Rickards's Balsa Log. This was the name given to the original idea for safe and efficient storage of traces. The well-known pikeman kept it in a box, away from other tackle items which always seem to gather together by themselves and end up a hopeless jumble of trebles, nylon, swivels. The specimen hunter's idea really does speed up preparation at the bankside.

its angler allows. Cast carelessly into the water in the hope that it will be discovered, it is generally unproductive. The water should be studied, plumbed if possible, and varying depths noted on a simple sketch chart.

One method worth using over submerged weedbeds is to inflate the belly of a whole fish with a little air, using a hypodermic syringe. A very small amount is needed to make it float just 3in or so above the bottom. To ensure that just enough air has been injected, drop the bait into water at your feet and watch for its position against the bed.

Although most deadbait fishing is regarded as a static, or possibly a drifting style, dead fish also make excellent 'wobbler' lures. They have all the attraction of spinners plus an

ease of casting that puts long distances within range. An added bonus is the cost of wobble baits; they can be used as an alternative to expensive spinners.

Giving a deadbait its 'wobble'

Naturally, wobbled baits must be mounted so that they can be retrieved head first through the water, and the simple snap-tackle rig outlined earlier, modified by mounting it so that the tail section is pulled forward into a curve, will provide an ideal slow-wobble and combined twist. To help keep it down on the bottom, use a thin length of lead or zinc pushed into the mouth and passed into the stomach of the bait. Once in place, the bait can be given a curve and the shape will be retained by the metal strip.

After casting, the bait should be allowed to sink to the bottom before the retrieve begins. Turning the reel in a succession of slow turns with a stop every few seconds will cause the bait to adopt a rise and fall pattern that few fish can resist. The strike must be immediate, and no time allowed for turning.

Chapter 5
SEA BAITS

At first it would seem that the range of baits for the sea angler is nowhere near the number available to the coarse fisherman. The latter has so many different foods, fruits and animal baits that the list seems endless.

So what is there in the sea? Bear in mind that most fish eat what they do not from any conscious action but from inherited instinct.

There are the main standbys of the sea: the lugworm, and that colourful fighter the mackerel. It easily leads the favourite bait list.

Our chapter on the lugworm covers the matter adequately, and the nastier, pincer-armed ragworm is also included in its relevant section. Both these marine worms occupy a prime place alongside the mackerel.

Another bait, liked by the sea angler but to most non-anglers appearing like something out of a horror movie is the squid. The species used as bait is, however, not that giant which gives battle with whales, but a smaller animal, imported into Britain and not found in our waters.

So take a stroll along a rocky shore, stand amid rocks covered with seaweed and dotted by small pools and you will be surrounded by sea baits of many kinds. Lift a tangle of kelp or bladderwrack and you will see colonies of winkles and limpets; both make good baits for the angler who likes to fish off rocks.

There will be mussels, clinging to the rocks by their anchorage, a series of tough threads called a byssus. A bunch on a hook, held fast by thread, will tempt the wariest cod. Muddy areas, such as those off some East Anglian beaches, will hold a multitude of cockles and in the clean sand the razorshell will hide, embedded fast and held there by its muscular foot.

There are other, less well known animals found along the shore that the angler should try. Sea mice, nothing to do with the rodent house pest, are really worms with flattened bodies, their segmentation clearly showing a relationship to the worm family.

The whelk prefers deeper water, but it can be found at low-water mark during spring tides. This gasteropod has a strong, tough and fleshy foot which stays very well on a hook. Professional longliners know this and use the whelk to great advantage on hundreds of static hooks strung across the tide.

A relative of the whelk, the periwinkle, needs to be used in bunches, but its body releases a substance into the water that acts as an attractor to hungry fish.

Associated with rocky shores are those delightful pools

— oceans in miniature — full of life in many forms. But splashing about in one is not the best way to see what life it holds. Sit quietly, with the sun before you so that your shadow is not thrown across the water, and just watch.

Shrimps and prawns will scuttle from side to side; shore crabs of all sizes scamper sideways; limpets covered by water relax their powerful grip and extrude a fleshy arm. Even small fish left by the retreating tide, such as gobies and blennies (of which we have many species) can be caught and will provide useful baits for inshore bass and small pollack.

The sandeel is also a great bait. Live, it is almost irresistible to a roving bass in the swirl of estuarial water, and even when preserved can tempt many a big fish.

This introduction to the chapter on baits for the sea angler cannot end without mention of lures and feathers. Many seaside boatmen ply for hire and offer sea fishing trips. But the holidaymakers who sit in tight rows are given nothing but handlines bearing a heavy weight and a string of six gaily coloured feathers. These are lowered into packed shoals of marauding mackerel and with great excitement six fish at a time are hauled aboard. The holidaymakers think they have been really fishing, but it is no more than harvesting. The way to fish for mackerel is to use a light rod, line of no more than 5 lb b.s. and a single flashy spinner. When you have your mackerel hooked on this gear it will fight all the way to the boat, but have that chance which all sporting instincts should allow.

Cod also take feathers, but for this larger fish they are white, usually from chickens, and only three hooks are used because three cod at a time is more than enough to cope with.

The American sea angler has for years used a wide variety of plugs, lures and gaily coloured artificial baits. Until a few years ago British anglers were content to use a spinner now and then, and thought themselves daring when the Redgill, Eddystone and other imitation eels and sandeels became available.

Now, a lure originally from Norway is the in-thing for deepwater cod and pollack. Called the pirk, it can weigh up to 2 lb and in consequence is expensive, a factor to consider when trolling over snaggy ground. Some grotesque lures look like no creature extinct or living, called popping bugs they attract pollack when trolled over the fish's hunting grounds.

Mackerel

The mackerel, one of the easiest of fish to catch, has increased in importance as a food fish following the scarcity of herring, but its oily flesh also makes an excellent bait

Of all the fish species inhabiting Britain's coastal waters, there is none with a more mixed reputation than that enjoyed by the mackerel. Although some rate them highly for a variety of reasons, there are those who dismiss them as 'dirty eaters', or as being too easy to catch or not worth eating. But as a fish bait, a fresh mackerel has no equal.

What makes the fish so attractive as a bait? In short, it is the mackerel's abundant body juices, rich in oils and vitamins, a characteristic shared with the herring and salmon. Fish are able to detect these juices by the sense of smell which all species, to a greater or lesser degree, possess. Because of its attraction, it is important that mackerel is used only when it is in prime condition.

Feathering

Mackerel may be taken in various ways, although the majority are caught by boat anglers using sets of hooks dressed with feathers. 'Feathering' is a good method, as up to six hooks can be used and, on occasions, a greedy mackerel will be caught on each, thus providing a plentiful supply of bait. Some fishermen advocate other methods, such as highly efficient sets of Norwegian lures, in which metal alternates with rubber tubing cut to imitate the eel.

No matter how efficient the lure may be, however, it will not produce results if fished at the wrong depth. It is important to remember that the mackerel, not possessing a swim bladder, can move surprisingly fast and so a shoal can change depth very rapidly. If several anglers are on board it is advisable for them to fish at different depths until a shoal is located. When very calm conditions prevail, as is often the case at

first light, watch for sudden turbulence on an empty patch of sea—this could well be caused by mackerel just below the surface.

Mackerel as bait can be fished in a variety of ways, and methods of presentation attractive to most species can be found. Two important considerations must be borne in mind, whatever style of fishing is to be employed. First, the bait size and presentation should be appropriate to the quarry and its manner of feeding; secondly, the bait and hook should be matched in size.

Apart from its other advantages, the mackerel's shape and bone structure make it an ideal bait form. It can be cut in different ways according to requirements. The section adjoining the caudal or tail fin provides on each side a near-triangular patch known as a 'lask' or 'last'. This is recommended for bream, whiting, and other small species. Remember, though, that while various species may be of roughly similar size, their mouths are quite dissimilar—a fact to be considered when selecting hooks and cutting

Two trolling rigs which can be used when fishing with mackerel as bait. The upper rig uses two single hooks arranged in tandem and sewn into the belly of the fish, and the lower one uses a double hook.

bait to match. An over-large bait can mask the barb so that hooking the fish becomes virtually impossible.

Alternatively, a side or flank can be offered, either whole, halved or sliced into strips to resemble small fish. To hook a half-side or strip of mackerel, drive the hook right through the fish and then twist this to allow the hook to come through again in a different place. This ensures that maximum benefit is gained from the oily flesh.

A whole side of mackerel can be held in position and presented in an attractive manner by whipping a small hook on to the trace a couple of inches above the main hook. The top of the bait is then supported, the lower portion being free to move with the current to simulate the motion of a small live fish.

Mackerel heads

A mackerel sliced diagonally across its body from just below the gill cover on one side to a point near the vent on the other, makes an ideal tope bait, as indeed does the head complete with entrails. To obtain the latter, the fish should be cut around the 'shoulders' so that the head comes free with the innards attached. Here again, the important thing is to exploit the fish-attracting juices. This bait is excellent when float-fished. To secure it, pass the hook through the head of the mackerel adjacent to the eye.

Conger can often be lured by a whole mackerel. Use a baiting needle to draw the hook into position. Some anglers draw the hook up to the vent, others prefer it to protrude from the bait's flank. Whichever method is used, slash the skin in several places to release the blood and oily juices which predatory fish

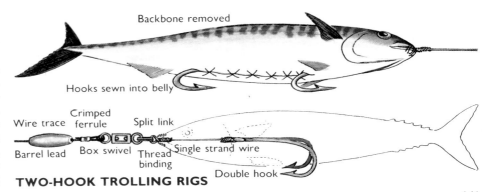

Backbone removed

Hooks sewn into belly

Wire trace
Crimped ferrule
Split link
Barrel lead
Box swivel
Thread binding
Single strand wire
Double hook

TWO-HOOK TROLLING RIGS

find highly attractive. When using large baits of this kind, the tide's motion will frequently cause them to spin and to impart an amount of twist to the trace. To overcome this, use at least one swivel between the reel line and the hook.

For most sea anglers the mackerel is a summer species. This leads to an obvious question: what does one use when fresh mackerel are not available as bait? In some areas, the South West for example, mackerel are caught professionally throughout the winter, weather permitting, and can be bought fresh from fishmongers. In other regions, though, when the fish have travelled to inland fishmongers via the wholesale market, by the time they reach the angler, they can be very wrinkled, unattractive specimens – not an attractive bait.

For anglers with a deep-freeze, a great saving can be made by catching early morning mackerel and then freezing them for later use. But fish which have been dead for hours, and lying in the sun in an open boat, do not freeze properly for when unfrozen they will rapidly deteriorate into a soft and useless mass. At one time the alternative solution was simple—use herring. This species was cheap and plentiful. They are

PREPARING MACKEREL

Right: When fishing for large fish such as cod, where large hooks are needed, a whole side of fresh mackerel is ideal bait. The hook should be threaded through it.

Far right: A side of mackerel cut into strips will bait about a dozen hooks.

Below: Mackerel heads can be injected with pilchard oil as an added attraction for conger.

Below right: The main attraction of mackerel lies in its rich and oily flesh.

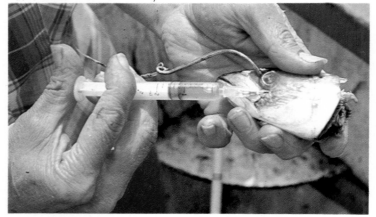

RUNNING LEDGER RIGS

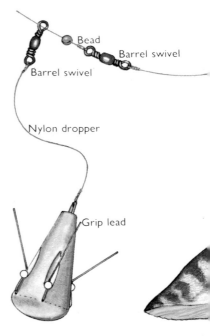

Hook

Tail end

Thread binding

Bead

Barrel swivel

Kilmore boom

Crimped ferrule

Wire trace

Bomb lead

Left: A mackerel tail, fished on a running ledger with a wire trace, is one of the standard methods used by anglers concentrating on conger. When a mackerel head is being used as bait for conger, the hook should be inserted through the mouth, with the point protruding from between the eyes. Small mackerel can be used whole.

Right: Using a lask of fresh mackerel on a running ledger. Note the 'Breakaway' casting lead.

Bead

Barrel swivel

Barrel swivel

Nylon dropper

Grip lead

still an excellent bait, but overfishing has led to a scarcity and consequently to high prices.

Having dealt with the mackerel as a bait, let us return briefly to its defence in other spheres. The mackerel is not a 'dirty eater' but is a predator which chases and kills other fish, although there is a period during spring and early summer when plankton become the main part of its diet.

Competition for food

That mackerel can be easy to catch cannot be denied. This is certainly true of most, if not all, shoaling species. The competition for food can be so great that individuals will throw themselves on anything attractive, as witness the savagery with which a pack of spurdog will dispute possession of a bait, or the way whiting will snap at potential food. The larger the shoal the greater the competition. However, large shoals are not as common as they were.

A mackerel long-since caught and stale is a sad offering as a table fish. But one fresh from the sea is a real delight full of terrific flavour.

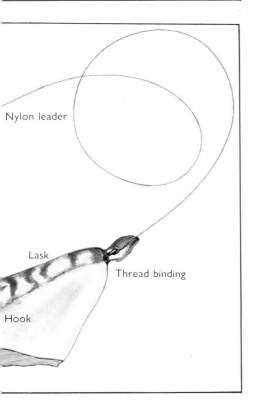

Nylon leader

Lask

Thread binding

Hook

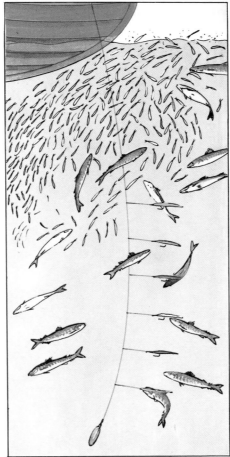

The illustration above shows one situation in which a six-hook rig will take six fish every time. If the rig can be lowered alongside a shoal of small food-fish, the feathers will be taken for members of that shoal by larger predators feeding at its edges. The need for well spaced fishing positions on the boat is obvious: on an overcrowded boat even if the reel lines are weighted sufficiently not to bow overmuch — can result in tangling.

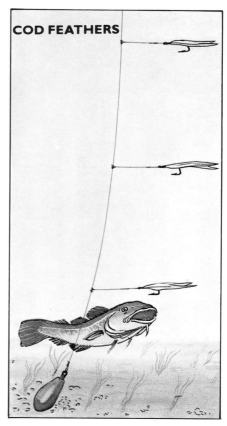

COD FEATHERS

Ragworms

Of the many kinds of ragworm found on the seashore, none is more eagerly sought after by the angler than the King ragworm. Few fish can resist it and as a bait it is second to none

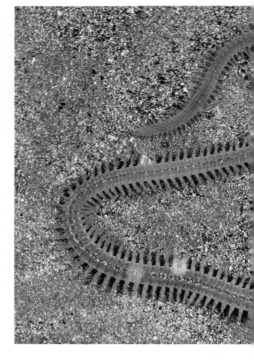

Just as the soil of the countryside is a home for many kinds of earthworm, so the seabed provides sanctuary for many kinds of marine worm. One of the commonest species is the ragworm, of which several kinds exist.

The ragworm differs from the lugworm in that it tapers very gradually from head to tail and is much fleshier. Most ragworms are bright red and all varieties have hundreds of 'legs' down each side of the body. The head is armed with a pair of bony pincers which the worm can thrust out and retract at will and a large worm can inflict a painful bite on the unwary angler.

Where the ragworm is found
King ragworm is probably the most common and the most sought-after for bait. The angler can obtain two large, or several smaller baits, from a good-sized specimen which can be over 2ft long. The worm is found close to the high-water mark but the nearer one goes to the low-water spring-tide mark, the more prolific it becomes—although this varies from coast to coast as does the worm itself. The best localities are estuaries where there is a mixture of river mud and shell, where it lives in a U-shaped burrow, the sides cemented with mucus from its body. Once it has dug its home the worm can propel itself through the tunnel with its many 'legs'. The bait-digger seeking this worm treads the ground carefully, watching for a waterspout pushed up when the burrow is compressed by his boot. If worms are scarce it pays to locate both entrances to the tunnel and remove the soil between, looking for the tell-tale burrow. In some areas you may have to dig to a depth of 2ft or more to secure the worm. Where there is an abundance or worms, and each foot-

fall produces several jets of water, 'trenching' is the best method. A good day's supply of bait can be obtained from one hole.

At spawning-time the king ragworm changes its bright red colour (with a pale green back) into a slate green and, when broken, exudes a slimy, milky liquid. During this

Below: *Ragworm vary considerably in colour, but are usually green-yellow, tinged with red.*

COLLECTING AND PRESENTING RAGWORM

Below: Large ragworm may be mounted by passing the hook through the mouth and along the body to emerge at the side. Smaller pieces may also be used.

Right: To extract the ragworm from its mucus-lined burrow, locate both entrances to the tunnel and remove the soil between Grasp the ragworm firmly and ease out carefully. Too strong a tug will cause it to burrow.

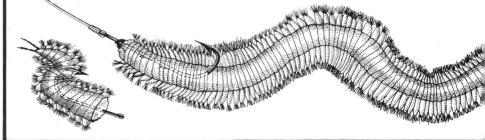

season, which varies from area to area but is usually in spring, the worm is of very little use as bait. One interesting fact, however, is that during the breeding season, large numbers of worms leave the safety of their burrows and swim freely in the sea. If, as often happens, there is a sudden onshore wind, great numbers are thrown up by the breakers onto the beach, either to die in the sun, or be swallowed by seagulls.

All worms deteriorate very quickly in high temperatures and, once dug, they should be dried and cooled as soon as possible. Whole, undamaged worms should be wrapped singly in newspaper and stored at 2°C in a refrigerator, where they can be kept in good condition for more

Left: *Growing up to 1½ft in length, the king rag. Nereis virens, has a vicious bite*

than a week. Damaged worms should be separated and used first. But if keeping is not important—perhaps all the worms are going to be used next day—they will keep perfectly in a box of vermiculite (insulating granules).

Mounting the bait

King ragworm can be an extremely effective bait, particularly for bass and pollack. For these fighting predators, worms up to 1ft long can be used whole. Secure just the head on the hook, leaving the rest trailing. Mounted in this way it is very life-like and pollack and bass rarely bite short. They have insatiable appetites and take the whole worm into their mouth before making off with it. The largest worms can be cut in half and baited in a similar way. Other species that prefer ragworm to lugworm are flounder, thornback ray, and sharks such as dogfish and smoothhound.

White ragworm is a variety which has become very popular over the past few years, particularly with beach anglers. It is smaller than the king ragworm, one 8in long being a good specimen. Because it is a very localized worm it cannot be dug in sufficient numbers to ensure regular commercial supplies.

The white ragworm lives in sheltered bays where there is an abundance of soft yellow sand, although it is sometimes found in the same area as king ragworm if there is fine surface gravel.

Preserving the white ragworm

The white ragworm does not keep as well as the king ragworm and the most useful preservative is a plastic bucket full of fresh seawater. As well as being much smaller than its cousin the king ragworm, the white ragworm is also more delicate, and a fine gauge wire hook is recommended to avoid damaging the worm.

Rockies are another small member of the family and, as the name implies, they are found in chalk rocks among deposits of mud and sand in sheltered bays. These deposits tend to fill the natural crevices in the chalk outcrops and the worm lives in these, so that a pick-axe is more useful than a fork for prising this bait from its habitat.

HEAD

Left: Top, or dorsal view of the head of the king ragworm in its protruded form. The eyes can be seen as four dots just before the body segments begin.

Lugworms

Buy them, dig them, fish them, preserve them—lug contribute to the diet of so many inshore fishes that you can make killings all year round with whole or mangled worm baits

The lugworm, *Arenicola marina*, is one of the most popular of all baits used in sea angling, particularly with anglers fishing the East Anglian and Kent coasts. It is a smaller species than that other very popular choice of sea anglers, the King ragworm, but when used from beach or boat it can be one of the deadliest baits for cod.

A good percentage of the sea fish found around the coastline of the British Isles will usually take this bait readily and, besides being ideal for cod, it is useful for the small varieties of flatfish—plaice, dabs and flounders.

Lugworm vary in size from 3in to 7in, although few reach the greater length. Being a 'wiggleless' worm, it is used almost exclusively for bottom fishing. As the body of the worm deflates the instant it is pierced, most anglers bait at least three worms at a time and quite often double the number on a hook. This is very much the case on the East Coast where beaches of 150 yards plus are common. The lugworm is almost useless as a bait in association with a single-hook, long-trace method so much favoured by South Coast boat anglers after pollack and coalfish. It is not a popular bait either along the English Channel coast of Devon and Cornwall. This can be largely attributed to the presence of the giant King ragworm which grows to more than 2ft long. Many inland sea anglers prefer to buy a day's supply of lugworm from their local tackle shop, but anybody can easily dig an adequate supply for himself.

The best environment
The lugworm prefers sheltered beaches with a good depth of top sand and where the sea has a low salinity. River estuaries, therefore, provide the best environment. One never has to travel far along the British coastline to encounter such habitats—Whitstable, Dale Fort, St Andrews, Millport, the south coast of the Isle of Man, Clew bay on the West Coast of Ireland, are just a few of the many well-known areas where

Though Chesil Beach is a mass of pebbles, a short way offshore the waves scour lug out of bare sand, attracting a variety of fish.

the lugworm can be dug in numbers. Size and colouring can vary considerably from area to area—in some cases there is a marked difference between the worms dug from the same sandy bay—due to environmental factors.

The common lugworm is often known as the 'blow' lug to differentiate it from the black lug which is very thick-skinned and requires gutting to prolong the time it will keep, and from the Deal yellow-tail, a worm peculiar to the south side of the Stour Estuary in Kent.

Lugworm live in a U-shaped burrow in the sand, the entrances of which are marked at one end by the tell-tale spiral casts and at the other by a depression in the sand known as the blow hole, though which the worm draws its food. Into the tunnel fall particles of sand mixed with water and organic matter, all of which the worm eats. The organic matter is digested and the sand is excreted, forming the cast at the other end of the burrow.

For digging the common lugworm the ordinary flat-tined potato fork is the best tool; a spade chops too many worms in half. Lugworm casts are found on any sandy beach below high water mark but, normally, the nearer to the extreme low water mark the greater the number of casts to be found and the bigger the worms. If the sand is covered in casts no more than 2 or 3in apart, then worms can be dug by trenching, that is, digging the sand as one would the garden. However, if signs are few and far between, 'singling' is best. This involves removing the sand between the blow hole and the cast, thus uncovering the worm after about three forkfuls. The burrow is lined with mucus from the worm's body, giving it a bright orange colour rather like rust, and enabling the angler to see exactly which way the burrow is running at each forkful.

The worms should be removed to a clean wooden box or plastic bucket. Never use a galvanized pail as the zinc kills the worms very quickly. When sufficient worms have been dug, they should be washed in clean sea water to remove all particles of sand as well as any worms pierced by the fork. These should be put into

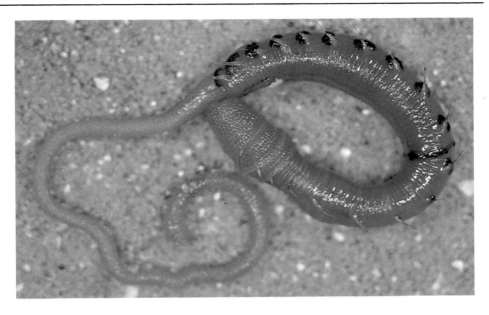

a separate container for, although they will live as long as the whole worms, the blood exuded by their wounds seems to have an adverse effect on the others.

The Deal yellow-tail
The Deal yellow-tail is probably a sub-species of *Arenicola marina*, although many authorities believe it to appear different simply through environmental factors. However, the worm behaves entirely differently from the common lugworm. The cast, instead of being a haphazard spiral, is perfectly symmetrical, and the worm burrows to a greater depth than the common lug.

The yellow-tail is generally larger, and when dug appears very limp, seeming, to the uninitiated, to be dead. It also has the peculiar habit of coiling itself into a circle when held in the palm of the hand, whereas the common lug will only bend slightly. The best way of keeping the yellow-tail—its name derives from the bright yellow stain it leaves on the hands—is in clean sea water.

Black lug
Another sub-species is the black lug, which is even bigger than the Deal yellow-tail and has a very thick skin. It often lives in a mixture of mud and sand, where the most successful way of obtaining it is to use a small, long-handled spade, digging straight down from the cast and following the trail until the worm is sighted.

Roll them in newspaper
Immediately after digging, the intestines and blood should be squeezed out through the head end and, to keep them in perfect condition, the worms should be rolled singly in sheets of newspaper. The black lug is large enough to provide several small baits from a single worm, although for cod fishing a whole worm should be threaded on the hook. Because it is tough, it makes an ideal bait for beachcasting.

Common lug can be threaded either singly or doubly, depending on size, when beach fishing for cod, but for boat fishing it is usually better to hang them from the bend of the hook, just passing the hook in and out of the body where the sandy tail section joins the fat part. The number of worms put on a hook depends, first, on the size of the worm and, second, on the size of the fish expected. When fishing for varieties of small flatfish, a largish worm may be broken in half to provide ample bait for a small mouth.

Lugworm country
Lugworm, however, is much used by anglers fishing the Atlantic side of the Cornish and Devon peninsula, where large numbers of lugworm can be found. The Padstow estuary, the shoreline of Constantine Bay and the vast Bridgwater Bay in Somerset hold millions of lug. It is also located in quantity at many places on the Welsh side of the Bristol Channel.

Peeler crabs

When a peeler crab steps backwards out of its eyes, legs and skin, it represents a soft, vulnerable victim to gulls, cod, bass—and the angler out early enough to reap a day's bait

Crabs have their skeleton on the outside of their body and their muscles and organs inside. Growth is only possible by changing shells, and this is done by growing a new, larger shell, which has at first to be soft in order to fit beneath the existing hard shell. When the new, soft shell is fully formed, just before the old one is discarded, the crab is known as a 'peeler'.

Common shore crab
Of the many varieties of crab found around our coasts, the best, and most widely used, for bait is the common shore crab *(Carcinus maenas)*. The young crab starts life from an egg which hatches in the upper layers of the sea. At this stage the larva bears no resemblance to the adult, but in a few weeks it undergoes five moults, after which it sinks to the seabed and takes on the characteristic form of a crab.

During the crab's early life moulting takes place frequently during the summer months, when the water is warm, but the process occurs less frequently in winter and as the crab matures. At the half-grown stage it sheds its shell two or even three times a year, whereas the adult changes its shell very infrequently—probably every second year.

Immediately after casting off its shell the crab becomes what is known as a soft-back or soft crab. It is defenceless and so hides itself, but a new shell begins to form straight away. After a few hours the shell is like parchment but the crab is still not at its best as a bait.

The colour of the common inshore crab varies greatly according to its locality, but it is most often a greenish-brown, sometimes with distinctive markings on the top of the shell or carapace. The crab approaching maturity adopts a much redder hue.

A deadly bait
Peeler crabs are highly attractive to all sea fish but are especially deadly with bass and cod. Inshore boat fishing and beachcasting will both produce good results with this ir-

Above: *Peeler crab in the process of moulting. The crabs peel by walking backwards out of their shells, shedding eyes, teeth, gills and stomach lining. The old shell can be seen here perched above the new, soft one; the new leg is also visible.*
Below: *Crabs can be hooked in a variety of ways or bound with elastic to the hook. The legs alone are too good to waste, but the claws should be discarded. The weight of a whole crab lends casting distance, but you cannot be too rough or the crab will tear off the hook when you cast.*

resistible bait. The cod is greedy and is relatively easy to hook, but the bass will often suck the bait from the hook and so demands the angler's full attention.

Many anglers hold that the peeler crab is the supreme sea fishing bait, while others criticize it because of the preparation needed. With care, however, several fine pieces of bait can be obtained from one crab. First remove the eight legs and two claws from the body and then, using the thumbnail, remove the carapace. With the aid of the thumbnail, or a knife, remove as much of the shell from the underside as possible.

Small baits
The crab can be used whole, depending on the size but, more often, the body is cut crossways in two or quartered to provide four small baits. Anglers often discard the legs and claws but these, hooked in a bunch like worms, can prove a deadly bait. By carefully removing the four segments one at a time from the legs with a gentle twist and a pull they can be peeled off. The claws can be dealt with in the same way.

When starting a day's fishing it is advisable to leave the peeler crabs in a bucket of sea water for a while as this makes them softer and easier to peel. Beachcasting crab puts considerable strain on this soft bait and so the whole body or segments should be tied to the hook with elastic thread or wool. It is annoying to see it fly off the hook on the cast.

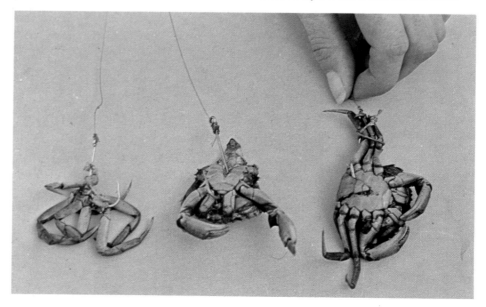

Squid and cuttlefish

The Cephalopoda—squid, cuttlefish and octopus—are ideal sea baits for a variety of species. Here we talk about using squid but the techniques would apply equally to cuttlefish or octopus

The flesh of squid, cuttlefish, and to a lesser extent octopus, makes excellent bait to tempt many species of sea fish. They belong to the class Cephalopoda, and are cylinder or sac-shaped molluscs with suckered tentacles surrounding the mouth and joining the head. The eyes are conspicuous, and the mouth is equipped with horny jaws like a bird of prey's beak.

The squid is most commonly used as bait, as its distribution in the Atlantic, English Channel and North Sea brings it within range of trawlers operating at ports dotted around the coastline and can be bought in most tackle shops.

Two ways of mounting squid on the hook. On the left, mounting the tentacles; on the right, mounting the whole squid.

Advantages of squid bait

Squid is the cleanest bait to use in sea fishing as the flesh is firm, cuts cleanly and easily, and can be presented attractively in a variety of ways. Above all it keeps well, and a supply laid down in a freezer can stay perfectly fresh for two years. This applies if you follow simple rules. The squid must be thoroughly cleaned by severing the head and cutting evenly down through the centre of the body to the tail. It should then be opened and laid out flat, and the stomach removed in one easy movement. With care you can do this without bursting the ink sac which has an acid content that is irritating to human skin. Squid wings are useless as bait and can be thrown away. Finally, it needs thorough washing using two changes of fresh water, and then the bait is ready for freezing.

Squid have a 'quill' or backbone closely resembling plastic, while the shell of the cuttlefish is a familiar sight on beaches.

Change a frayed bait

As the squid is so tough, it is possible to catch several bream on the same strip of bait. As soon as the edges show signs of fraying, however, it must be changed. Hundreds of conger eels to 100lb are also taken on squid head, or a whole squid hooked through the body and ledgered close to a wreck or on rough ground. Similarly it is a great favourite with the ravenous ling.

A strip of squid about 10in long and 1in wide cut to resemble a fish, makes a fine trolling bait for bass. Mounted on a long-shanked hook and worked astern at about three knots, it will dart about in a realistic manner and soon find a taker.

For shore fishing on storm beaches, squid is ideal bait as it stands up to long casting and can take any amount of battering from heavy surf. Many flatfish enthusiasts use it extensively as a bottom bait for turbot, plaice and dabs, although it has never been much good for flounder.

During the winter months, monster mackerel in South West waters have a definite liking for a thin strip of squid, and give great sport on light tackle.

Sandeels

Once a summer bait, sandeels are so versatile that anglers now use aquaria for year-round supplies. Live, dead or in lasks, sandeels can be spun, trolled or float-fished to deadly effect

The sandeel is not only one of the best baits for sea angling, but a very important part of the food chain for most species of fish. Three varieties are found in British waters: the greater sandeel *(Hyperoplus lanceolatus)* which can be easily identified by the black spot on the sides of the snout, the sandeel *(Ammodytes tobianus)* and the smooth sandeel *(Gymnammodytes semisquamatus)*.

They have elongated bodies and no spiny rays in the fins. The upper jaw is extensible and shorter than the lower; the tail forked and separate from the dorsal and anal.

When and where to find sandeel
Sandeels shoal in very large numbers but are seldom seen in daylight as they lie buried in the sand. They emerge after dark, and the light from a torch will often reveal what appears to be a solid shimmering mass in the shallow water of sandy estuaries. Sandeels are generally caught by towing a fine-mesh seine net from a small rowing boat off sandy beaches, or by digging and raking in the sand on the beach. The latter is best done at low tide right at the water's edge, as the eels like to hide in very wet sand. If there is a freshwater stream running down the beach this is a good place to search.

The speedy sandeel
Most sandeels are dug for at night when it is customary to work by the light of a pressure lamp. Once an eel has been lifted out of the sand it must be picked up immediately as it has the ability to tunnel back extremely quickly. In fact, a 7in eel, when placed on very firm sand, can disappear beneath the surface in less than two seconds.

Collecting by hand will produce about 30 eels in a couple of hours—more than enough bait for a day's fishing. A seine net, however, will trap as many as 10,000 eels in a single run of less than half an hour. The net is weighted at the bottom with rolling leads and supported by cork floats which keep it upright and level with the surface. It is paid out from the stern of a rowing boat which slowly describes a circle about 50 yards out from the beach. One end of the holding rope is kept onshore by a member of the three-man team, and when the net has been completely laid, the other end is brought ashore. The seine is then pulled smoothly in until the bag is clear of the water.

Baiting up with sandeel
To bait up with a sandeel, hold it firmly but lightly between the fingers and thumb, throat outwards. Put the point of the hook through the bottom lip and nick it into the soft skin of the belly just behind the head—this is the normal way of offering it in a fair run of tide. When fishing in slack water, however, it is often better to simply hook the eel through the top of its body, in front of the dorsal.

Hooks for sandeels
Hooks must be long in the shank, needle-sharp, and fine in the wire—a description that fits the Aberdeen perfectly. Live eels must be offered on a very long trace, which allows them to swim around in a natural manner. The movement is enhanced if nylon monofilament with a b.s. of no more than 12lb is used.

Trolling with live or dead sandeels over rocky ground can be a rewarding business. and big catches of pollack and bass are made. Of the many species partial to sandeel these two predators head the list, and even medium-weight fish of these species completely engulf a fair-sized eel in a single attack.

For shore fishing from rocky stations the live eel is best used with float gear, but the float should be sufficiently large to withstand the eel's thrashing without going under.

The eels can also be offered as a spinning bait if you are fishing deep water from rocky ledges. This is common on the north coast of Cornwall for bass, pollack and mackerel, but there is no doubt it is a great bass bait when fished live.

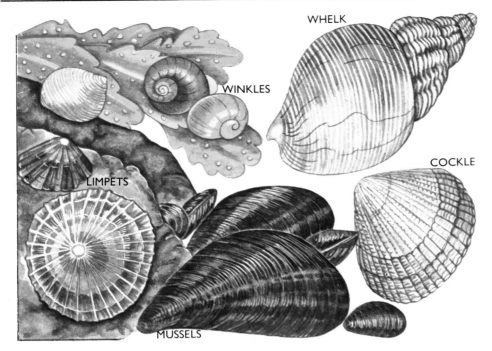

WHELK

WINKLES

COCKLE

LIMPETS

MUSSELS

Shellfish

Mussels have been a popular bait with sea anglers for many years and rank as one of the best baits for flatfish. But cockles, limpets and even whelks have their attractions too

The mussel, which is a bivalve, or two-shelled creature, has been a very popular bait for years, particularly on the East Coast. It is very easy to gather but it does require some preparation as it is virtually impossible to bait with the seed mussel upon which the fish are feeding.

Cockles as bait
Cockles are another variety of bivalve which will take many different species of sea fish. They are used extensively in Scotland, particularly on the Clyde. Cockles may take longer to gather as they have to be raked out of the sand in their preferred habitat of sheltered bays without strong tides or heavy surf. This bait requires no preparation other than the opening of the shell and the removal of its contents. Rather than cracking them open with a heavy blunt instrument, which will damage the animal inside, it is better to take a cockle in each

hand, and where the shells are hinged, lock one into the other and give a sharp twist. This breaks the hinge on the weaker of the two and allows the creature inside to be hooked out with the thumbnail. It is not a very large bait singly, but half a dozen or so on one hook make a very respectable offering.

The limpet is another mollusc, cone-shaped and dark brown in colour, which the angler can gather himself. They can be detached by prising them off with a knife or similar implement. The animal is then exposed and removed from the shell with the thumbnail, to reveal orange disc-shaped flesh and a blackish patch. Used singly on a small hook it is a good bait for flatfish, particularly dabs, while several on a large hook will attract most other species. Unfortunately, its soft texture means that it cannot withstand forceful casting and is likely to be mutilated very rapidly

by any crabs in the vicinity.

The winkle, a member of the snail family, is among the smallest of the univalve molluscs. It can be found on most coastlines below the high-water mark and prefers a rocky bottom with good weed covering. The shell is smooth and ranges in colour from brown to black.

The main problem is that of removing the fish from the shell. If boiled first, this is done with a pin, but with a live winkle it is necessary to crack the shell with a hammer or any other blunt tool. As they are small, several winkles are needed to make an adequate bait, but their toughness means that they remain on the hook for a long time and are not thrown off on the first cast.

Whelks
Whelks are not really sought after as a bait by anglers, although commercial fishermen often bait their longlines with them very effectively. Their success, however, can probably be attributed to the fact that a longline is left for several hours undisturbed and that the whelk is so tough that it will remain on the hook until eaten by a fish. For the rod and line angler it is best as a bait for cod and pouting as these two species are not particularly fussy.

Gathering limpets for bait presents few problems for the angler. They are common on the East Coast, the South East and the Channel coasts.

Limpet beds are usually found near the low water mark on average spring tides, with the most likely areas being sheltered, sandy bays and estuaries. After an onshore gale many colonies are thrown up on to beaches where they soon die from the heat of the sun.

As their name implies, slipper limpets must be extracted by slipping each specimen off the back of the one underneath, using a blunt bladed knife. This exposes part of the flesh, which is usually bright orange. Remove the flesh, together with the black tongue, from the shell, again using a blunt bladed knife. As large specimens are only 1½in long, three or four should be used on a hook. A single limpet, however, may be used when fishing for smaller species of sea fish, such as dabs.

Razorshells

Popular among shore anglers as a bait for bass and flatfish in summer, razorshell are wary creatures that require skill and cunning if you are to gather enough for a day's fishing

GATHERING RAZORSHELL

To collect razorshell for bait, walk slowly backwards and watch for signs as the animal breathes after you pass.

Among the animals that bass and sea cod feed upon as they follow the incoming breakers are a number of molluscs of the bivalve group (two-shelled animals). These creatures include the rock-borers, the gapers, the piddocks (which include the notorious 'ship-worm', the teredo) and the razorshells—the name being derived from the likeness of the elongated shell to an old-fashioned 'cut-throat' razor. In all these animals the long narrow shells are open at each end, and have a long 'hinge' joining the two shells.

Four species

There are four species of razorshell found in the sand and mud of the British coastline, the largest of these being the pod-razor, *Ensis siliqua*, whose shell grows to 8in long and 1in deep. The three other razorshells are the grooved razorshell, *Solen marginatus*, and two other species not having popular names, *Ensis arcuatus* and *E ensis*. Both are very similar in appearance but the latter is smaller, often having a reddish brown foot. The grooved razorshell inhabits muddier areas than the other species, and is found up to 18in deep in the muddy sands of the south west coast of England.

All razorshells live in mud or sand and move rapidly downward when

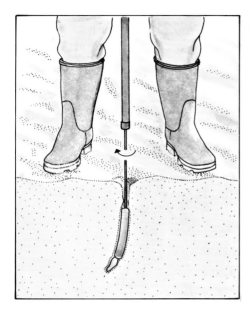

Thrust a spiked stick into the depression, turn it to hook the sides of the shell, and withdraw the razorshell from its burrow

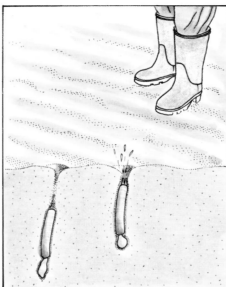

Another method, also preceded by walking backwards, is to use a wedge-shaped stick to prevent the shellfish burrowing.

The bait can then be gathered by using a trowel to dig the creature out. Be careful of the shell's very sharp edges.

vibrations reach them through their surroundings. They remain in the vertical position with their muscular foot at the bottom, where it is swollen by blood to anchor the creature down. From the top end, which is in fact the rear of the razorshell, siphons extend from beneath the surface to extract small food particles from the water. Oxygen present in the water enables the shellfish to breathe.

How to locate razorshells

The presence of razorshells can be detected by the small jets of water thrown up from the siphons and the small depression the animal makes in the sand or mud. Collecting them demands quick reflexes and adroitness, for they can burrow quickly beyond the reach of the spade.

For anglers, the most commonly found razorshell is the pod-razor, largest of the British species. Gathering them is an acquired skill, for when disturbed they disappear downwards extremely fast and burrow even further by extending the foot to grip the sand, then using their strong muscles to pull the shell downwards.

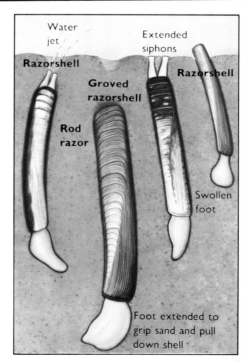

Above: *The four species of razorshell found on the beaches of Britain. They can all be used as bait.*

The traditional method of gathering razorshells for bait is by the use of a tool about 3ft long with an ar-

rowhead point. One must approach the area so as not to create the vibrations which will send the animal burrowing downwards. The 'spear' must be thrust down the hole into the shell's two halves and twisted so that the point grips the sides of the shell to prevent further burrowing. The razorshell can then be withdrawn quickly.

Sprinkling with salt

Digging with a fork or spade must be fast and accurate, but the angler seeking a supply of bait quickly may well spend more time digging than fishing if he is not long-experienced in the art. It has been suggested that if the depressions marking the razorshells' positions are sprinkled with salt, the animal is irritated and forced up to the surface.

To extract the animal from its two hinged shells, carefully cut through the hinge with a sharp knife. Do not prise open the two shells along the unhinged side as this will damage the creature. The attractiveness of the razorshell as a bait lies in its meaty foot, but the whole animal is hooked with the foot supporting the softer organs.

Rubby dubby

Though evil smelling and not for those with a delicate stomach, a rich concoction of old mackerel mashed up and mixed with fish offal, blood and bran, makes a killing groundbait for sharks

Rubby dubby, a word coined in Cornwall in the 1950s when shark fishing began as a sport, was borrowed from American big game anglers. In America, 'chumming'—throwing chopped up pieces of fish into the water—had long been used to attract tuna and other species of giant game fish.

The best dubby is made from oily pilchards, herring and mackerel, pounded to a pulp with a blunt instrument. Fish offal and unwanted fish are constantly added and some skippers introduce bran to thicken it up. Blood collected from slaughterhouses is also a popular ingredient but contrary to belief it does not stay in a liquid state, due to it being a coagulant. It then resembles jelly, and is a useful additive to existing rubby dubby. Occasionally it is kept separate and after a good stir ladled directly into the sea with an old saucepan. Under the rules of the International Game Fish Association and the Shark Angling Club of Great Britain, the use of blood, flesh, and the guts of mammals for 'chumming' or 'rubby dubby' will disqualify a catch, so if you have a world or British Record shark in mind, make sure none of these are used on the boat.

Conventional dubby is placed in stout meshed bags or in small sacks and suspended over the side of the boat at bow and stern, a length of rope holding it just beneath the surface, where constant wave action keeps the oil and particles of fish flowing. Every so often the bags are bashed heartily against the side of the boat to help things along.

'Rubby dubby trail'
Once in the water the 'rubby dubby trail' gradually builds up. Pieces of flesh sink quickly or slowly, depending on their oil content, while the

Above: *This is the basis for a bucketful of rubby dubby — a mess of ancient mackerel. Beginners should keep well clear! But shark think the aroma attractive.*
Below: *Maurice Cleghorn, oblivious to the aroma, happily mincing old mackerel during the preparation of rubby dubby. Pilchard oil is another ingredient to the noisome recipe.*

oil droplets stay on the surface. On rough days it is quite remarkable how this trail smooths out the sea. If the trail is 'fed' regularly with fresh bags of dubby it becomes deeper and wider, forming almost a solid lane of attraction, leading a shark straight to the baited hooks.

Quite a few rubby dubby barrels are started at the beginning of the season. The mess is topped up each day; after a couple of weeks it is said to be of superior quality, guaranteed to attract sharks.

Groundbaiting
While the Cornish version is used mainly in British waters for sharking, many skippers operating bottom fishing trips attach a bag of fish guts and mashed flesh a few feet from the boat's anchor rope. When the hook bites into the bottom, the tide flow carries particles of flesh back under the craft, thus attracting fish into the vicinity of the baited hooks. This variation really comes into the category of groundbaiting, and of course by comparison with a sharker's dubby is not at all unpleasant. Dubbying as used in shark fishing is a certain way of attracting mackerel. Drop a set of feathers into a slick that has been working for as little as ten minutes and the chances are that each hook will hold a shining mackerel.

It should be remembered that land predators always hunt upwind. Fish react the same way, and search for food uptide. It usually takes about an hour for the rubby dubby to do its silent but deadly work.

Shark boats leave harbour around 9.00am allowing two and a half hours to reach the ground, set up the drift and get the dubby in the water. It takes a further hour for a useful slick to build up, and half an hour for the shark to swim up it. Quite often a reel will 'sing' punctually at one o'clock.

Each boat has its own characteristics: those with large wheel-houses and high prows catch the wind rather more than craft with a lower profile. In certain wind-on-tide conditions some boats overrun the slick, and others side-slip, creating an undesirable bend in the trail. When this happens a fish can easily swim past the baits and continue hunting.

Chapter 6
GAME LURES

When discussing baits and lures for game fish one thing must be clarified: why should one restrict one's choice of bait for, say, salmon on ethical, practical or any other grounds when the coarse fisherman can use anything edible, with the exception of the odd banned bait? And those exceptions are usually based on ignorance and misunderstanding.

It might seem unfair but there is logic in the game angler's concentration on the artificial fly. The salmon family, which of course includes the trout and its lowly cousin the grayling, are predators. They chase, catch and eat aquatic animal food in the form of other fish, insect life and the many flying insects that for one reason or another fall onto the water.

In summer, many larvae of flying insects are responding to the growing warmth of the sun and the lengthening hours of daylight. Prompted by their body clocks they crawl up reed stems into the air, shed their dull larval skin and emerge as winged flies.

The very reason why one Class of them is called the Ephemeroptera is that, literally, they live for a day, their life *is* ephemeral. They mate, then die within hours, their spent bodies fluttering down to twitch briefly on the surface film.

The trout are waiting, also prompted by their own inherited timing mechanisms. They gobble the flies in their hundreds and thousands, for they are full of useful protein and predators need it for strength and speed.

For hundreds of years anglers have watched this annual feast, and thinking naturalists that they were they decided that the best thing to do was to imitate nature. And the great Victorian angler/naturalists spent their lives creating close imitations of those flies from feather, fur and silk.

Today, the game fisherman follows tradition, but at the same time has developed a huge range of other kinds of artificial lures. The original imitation fly was a wet pattern, the wings were swept back and it was fished below the surface. The dry fly, an object of much study, has its wings tied so that they stand upright, the air trapped there keeping it on the surface.

But the modern angler now has imitations of the nymph and larval forms of aquatic insects, and also ties flies to resemble small fish. The artificial nymphs are fished in short, jerky motions from the lake bed towards the surface, even at times left on the bottom and given

a twitch now and then. They imitate larvae crawling about. In fact, this form of fishing is not far from ledgering, but no game fisherman would admit to it! And to be fair there is a subtle difference.

Each game fish has its own particular artificials: there are brown trout, sea trout, salmon, rainbow, even grayling flies. In fact there are many, many books on fly patterns, far more than on any other kind of fishing.

The problems of what to offer trout as bait can become matters of enormous argument. If one reduces fishing to its basic *raison d'etre* one should use the bait which you know will result in landing the fish. But, then, why make it difficult by trying to fool the fish by offering it a whisp of feather and fur? If it will take a worm more eagerly, is it not logical to do so?

But searching deeper into the artificial's motion on and under the water perhaps we are assuming too much deliberation by *Salmo trutta*, which never has and never will be able to make a conscious decision. All its actions are reflex, genetics having decided the structure of its central nervous system and therefore the extent of its inability to select option A or B as a matter of free choice.

When the angler's fly settles gently on the surface, its creates tiny waves, recognised by the angler as a small circle of spreading ripples. The trout's eye sees it too, but the fish also responds to the vibrations created in the water and the shape of the artificial as it lies on the surface. If all these indications are right, that is, doing what the natural fly does, the trout's primitive brain triggers off an instant feeding response and the fish gulps feather, fur and hook.

Lastly, why does the salmon fall to the artificial fly, the prawn, spinner or worm, when biologically it is supposed to be moving up-river with a single intent — to spawn in the reeds from where it originated some three years ago? We do not know the answer, all we know for sure is that salmon are caught by those methods.

The daftest reasons why salmon take lures have been put forward: 'The fish is curious'; 'it is irritated by the lure'; 'we've got our biology wrong' and so on.

Wise anglers keep their theories to themselves and just go fishing, content just to know that salmon can be tricked by a bunch of feathers, a twist of lurex, some dyed fur and that hook nestling in the middle.

Dry flies

The range of dry flies available to the game fisherman is vast. Knowing which one to use to tempt trout to the surface calls for patience, skill and an expert eye for reading the water

Dry fly fishing has always been regarded as the supreme art in fly fishing circles. This is particularly so on rivers and chalkstreams where matching the hatch is only the beginning of the problem and where presentation has to be considered as well. But dry flies also play an important part in reservoir and lake fishing where trout are attracted by insects on the surface.

Favourite season
Of all the periods during the season when trout rise to a dry fly, the favourite is the time that the mayfly hatch. The huge flies emerge from the water in such large numbers that the trout literally gorge themselves to capacity, and the better fish rise freely. On these occasions almost any artificial pattern representing a mayfly will take fish. Unfortunately the mayfly only hatches in running water and in a few privileged lakes, and so it does not affect the dry fly fisherman everywhere.

Early in the season the hawthorn fly hatches in large numbers and very good catches can be made with the aid of a Black Gnat. Again this mostly applies to running waters, but vast numbers of hawthorn flies were noticed at Rutland Water. Although the fish were not rising to them at that time, they will probably do so in the future.

In late summer, one of the most popular flies that hatches on every water is the sedge. These medium sized flies start to hatch in July and August and are present throughout the day, and in vast numbers at nightfall. If weather conditions are good and flies are hatching, a pattern representing a sedge can be very effective, for the 'spent' sedge falling back upon the water is the fly most likely to attract the attention of the trout. But they are by no means the only ones. Throughout the year there are hatches of buzzers, the dreaded caenis, which is too small to be imitated, and a number of Ephemerids such as the olives. These insects all hatch from the water and return there to lay their eggs, and this is when the trout will rise to them.

Land-borne insects
In addition to these insects, there are also the land-borne kind which live and breed on dry land but are often carried on to the water by winds. Naturally these flies are more important to the reservoir angler because the large expanses of water are too much for the insects to fly across while maintaining a battle with the wind to stay in the air. When they fall into the water they make a meal for lurking trout.

Of the insects that hatch on land, the daddy long legs is the one which, year after year, adds to the larder of the trout. In the late summer the daddy long legs hatch in vast numbers in the bankside vegetation, and being fairly weak fliers, are easily carried onto the water when the wind rises. The trout then cruise the margins and wind lanes taking the daddy long legs with a great swirl or splash, and fantastic sport can be had with a natural or imitation fly.

The other land insect that really interests the trout is the flying ant. On rare occasions, a swarm of these insects is blown on to the water and the trout feed heavily on them, so it is wise to have an imitation in the box, just in case. The same also applies to bees and grasshoppers, but there are few recorded patterns of these insects. When trout are seen taking them the angler must be ready to tie an acceptable imitation.

Dapping
There is another type of dry fly fishing which is most successful on large stillwaters—dapping. It is in fact a very old method regaining

popularity. Although used mostly on the big Irish loughs it is fast becoming popular on the larger English reservoirs.

Dapping requires a rod of at least 13ft—a coarse rod will do fine for the purpose. Fill a centrepin reel with nylon of about 8lb: to this attach approximately 10 yards of special dapping floss. Finally your leader is a couple of yards of 5lb or 6lb nylon: a good selection of bushy hackled dry flies and a bottle of silicone floatant and you are ready to fish.

It is possible to dap from the bank but this is primarily a method to use from a broadside drifting boat. Tactics are simple: allow the wind to lift the floss line as you hold the rod ver-

Below left: *The flies recommended in the article and tied by David Collyer are, left to right: Pond Olive, Black Ant, Hacklepoint Coachman, Sherry Spinner, Walker's Sedge, Lunn's Particular, Iron Blue, Drone Fly, Black Gnat and Daddy long legs.*
Below: *A fine brace of rainbow and brown trout. Brownies of this quality are usually bottom-feeders and your only chance of catching them on the dry fly is likely to be Mayfly time or when the 'daddies' are blown on to the water in fair numbers at the back end of the season.*

tically. As you lower the rod watch carefully as the fly rests gently on the water. If no rise occurs, lift and repeat. When a trout boils at the fly, pause for a couple of seconds before striking otherwise you will find you keep pulling the fly out of the trout's mouth before it has taken properly.

Most essential, of course, is a good wind. Once you master the method you may wish to try dapping with a natural insect. This is perhaps the most deadly of all methods as the Irish gillies will tell you. They use a bunch of three mayflies or daddies impaled on a No 10 hook. But the best fish catcher of all is undoubtedly the dapped grasshopper.

Patterns of dry fly
In almost all instances where trout feed on land-borne insects, the rule is not to move the fly. It is not possible to simulate the vibrating motion of their legs and in any case they are soon dead or exhausted and then lay still. An imitation is far more likely to succeed if it is cast out and then left. Regarding the patterns of dry fly that are needed, every angler should include in his collection the following: Tupp's Indispensable, Mayfly, Sedge, Black Gnat, Grey

Duster, Iron Blue, Daddy Long Legs, Sherry Spinner, Pond Olive, Lunn's Particular, Flying Ant, Drone Fly, Greenwell's Glory, Royal Coachman, Wickham's Fancy, Silver Sedge, Kite's Imperial, Grey Wulff, Grey Duster, Lake Olive and perhaps appropriately Last Hope, which was originated by John Goodard to represent the Pale Watery dun or similar, light coloured river insects.

These are only a few of the many hundreds of dry flies available. The tremendous growth of fly fishing, and the advent of the relatively cheap package holidays abroad, has led to English fly fishing enthusiasts travelling all over the world, notably the United States, Canada, Alaska and even New Zealand. This has resulted in many flies with origins far from our reservoirs and, to a lesser extent, rivers.

Unless treated with a floatant, dry flies will quickly become waterlogged and need frequent changing. This is especially true of the wool bodied types. But the invention of Permaflote by Dick Walker and Arnold Neave means that you can fish the same fly all day without a change, unless, of course, a fish has taken it, when it will need a change. One word of warning—it's best to treat the flies and leave them to dry thoroughly before use if you want the best results from them.

Retreiving a fly against a current will 'drown' a fly. But with Permaflote, after a false cast or two, you're back in business.

The leader is best left untreated with floatant. Degrease it with mud or one of the commercial leader sink preparations: there's nothing so guaranteed to scare trout as a floating leader.

A fly that you have changed should be left to dry thoroughly before replacing it back in the fly box or you are likely to introduce rust to your other flies. Either stick it on one of the sheepskin patches on a fishing waistcoat or lightly stick it in your hat, taking care not to crunch the hackles.

Dry flies have probably the biggest literature in all fishing subjects. Once you become interested, your only aim is to tempt a fat trout with a fly tied yourself.

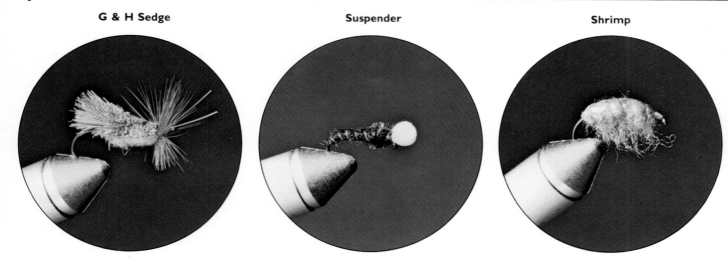

G & H Sedge   Suspender   Shrimp

New trout patterns

Many of our familiar patterns have evolved by way of random experiments:
recent revolutionary additions have been the
result of radical rethinking and of research into trout behaviour

You must be careful when defining what is, or what isn't, a 'new' trout pattern. Many new artificials are merely tinkerings with old ideas; a change of body colour here, a change of feather fibre there.

Trout patterns that break new ground and that are unique in both concept and construction are few and far between. And in recent times—perhaps the most exciting and prolific in the entire history of fly-tying—only a handful of patterns can truly claim to push forward the boundaries. Such a fly is the Muddler Minnow. Although not a new pattern, its influence is still as strong now as it was over 20 years ago when it was first devised.

Many people believe that the Muddler Minnow got its name because of the way it moved in the water. They say it confuses the trout into taking it. This is not true. The Muddler Minnow was a direct attempt by its creator, Don Gapen, to tie an exact imitation of the flathead Cockatush minnow (related to the carps)and only one of many found in the Nipigon River in Northern Ontario, nicknamed 'muddlers' by the locals.

The G & H Sedge
Arguably the most buoyant of all dry flies (deer hair is hollow) and certainly the most revolutionary sedge pattern ever to have fluttered from a fly-tying vice, the G & H Sedge is one of the very few all-British patterns to have enjoyed enormous impact in America (normally, it is the other way round).

Place a long-shank No 8 or 10 down-eye hook in the vice. Tie green silk in at eye and wind it to the bend, leaving a double length to be used later as the underbody. The body material of deer hair is spun on Muddler-style. Several spinnings of this hair are necessary, each new one pressed close up to the last until the hook is completely palmered with deer hair. Clip this hair to give the correct sedge silhouette when viewed from below.

Tie in two rusty dun cock hackles at the head. Leave the stripped butts protruding over the eye as antennae. Clip the top of the hackle. Finally, dub dark green seal fur on to the length of silk left at the bend of the hook. Pull it taut under the trimmed deer hair body and whip it in at the eye.

The Suspender
Developed by Neil Patterson to keep hatching nymphs hugging the surface film in fast flowing rivers, the Suspender was adapted for stillwaters by John Goddard.

A small ball of ethafoam, trapped in a pouch made from a woman's nylon stocking or tights, is attached to the head of the hook. The ethafoam acts as a float keeping the imitation 'suspending' motionless —head in the surface film, body dangling down—in exactly the way trout see the natural midge pupa poised to hatch out the adult. Before the Suspender, a midge pupa artificial had to be kept moving to prevent it sinking out of the surface film, or greased up which meant that it sat on the surface horizontally and not in the natural position.

Cut out a small ball from a block of ethafoam. (The padding from in between the walls of a padded envelope does just as well.) Push it into a small square of stocking material and attach it to the head of the hook with two or three turns of silk. Having done this, continue to tie a midge pupa using the standard 'buzzer' method, using a seal for the

USD Paradun

USD Polyspinner

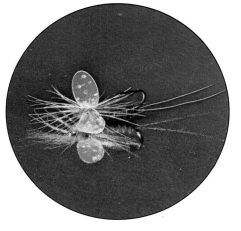

Funneldun

colour of the natural on the water as body material. The Suspender does not require a hackle at the head.

USD Paraduns

Without a doubt, some of most significant developments of the last five years have been made on rivers, notably, the work of the fly-tyer John Goddard, and his co-writer Brian Clarke. In their recently published book, *The Trout and the Fly*—an expedition into the world of the trout using underwater tanks and cameras—Goddard and Clarke made a detailed study of natural and artificial flies as seen from the trout's point of view.

Their expeditions resulted in a long and demanding check-list of how a dry fly should perform if it is to seduce the trout into taking it without the merest hint of suspicion.

One of the observations they underline is that a dry fly should float hook-up in the air, rather than dangling unappetisingly below the surface in full view of the trout.

Upside down flies

In order to meet this criterion, they devise a series of upside down flies called USD (upside down) Paraduns. These were presented by carefully positioning hackle tip wings and parachute style of mounting the hackle. This ingeniously and elaborately made the fly float hook up in the air.

Their Paraduns and Polyspinners (using polythene for wings with pin-prick holes to imitate the action of light on the veins of the natural) are of immense beauty, delicacy and

realism but require an extraordinary degree of dexterity to create them.

In the wake of Goddard and Clarke's research, an upside down fly devised by Neil Patterson comes most of the way, if not all, towards meeting the Paraduns' goals. Named the Funneldun on account of the process involved in tying in the hackle, it calls into play very simple fly-tying procedures and does not require the high quality cock hackles normally needed to tie a dry fly.

The Funneldun

The Funneldun is a straightforward, hard wearing and cheap fly to tie and incorporates an entirely new approach to tying a dry fly.

Place an up-eye hook (14-18) in the vice. Wind the silk in at the eye. Dub in a small thorax over the turns of silk right up against the eye.

Take a ginger and grizzle cock cape and select one hackle from each zone where you would normally consider the hackles too large. Tie in these two hackles (shiny-side facing the bend of the hook, the tips curving forward towards the eye), about one-third of the way down the hook behind the thorax. Wind the ginger through the grizzle and tie in the butts at the bend side of the hook. The hackles should be sloping slightly forward towards the eye rather than at right angles to the hook.

With the silk behind the hackles, 'funnel' the hackles forward with the thumb, first and second fingers of your right hand. With your left hand, wind a few turns of silk over the hackle roots to hold the hackles sloping at an angle of 45 degrees

pointing forward towards the eye.

Wind the silk towards the bend (a little dubbing can be added) winding in a bunch of grizzle whisks as you go as tails. Wind these tails in so they finish a little way round the bend of the hook. Whip finish at the tail. Finally, with the fly still in the vice, clip a small V out of the top of the hackle. This will ensure the Funneldun lands on the water hook in the air ten out of ten chucks.

The Shrimp

Popularized by Goddard and Clarke, the Shrimp brings a degree of simplicity into an art that is becoming increasingly fingersome as fly-tying standards rise by the year.

Pioneered by Bob Preston who used it to fish deep-lying trout on the Wiltshire chalk streams, the Shrimp is a crafty way to conceal weight —large amounts of it—in the guise of a tasty food parcel that sinks a hook down to trout at great depths.

At the bend of the hook (size 8-14), tie in a length of gold wire and a strip of plastic doubled up that will later form a shell back. Plastic money bags from banks make excellent backs as they don't contract when tension is put on them. Build up strips of wine bottle lead on the back of the hook or wind lead wire round the hook shank—to form the characteristic hump back. Mix 95 per cent olive seal fur with 5 per cent sunrise pink, dub it on to the silk and wind it over the body. Rib with the wire and pull the plastic strips over the back of the fly and tie in at the head. Whip finish and tease out the dubbing to represent legs.

Wet flies

When trout are feeding below the surface of the water, wet flies and nymphs come into their own. Just as in dry fly fishing, the variety of patterns at your disposal is legion

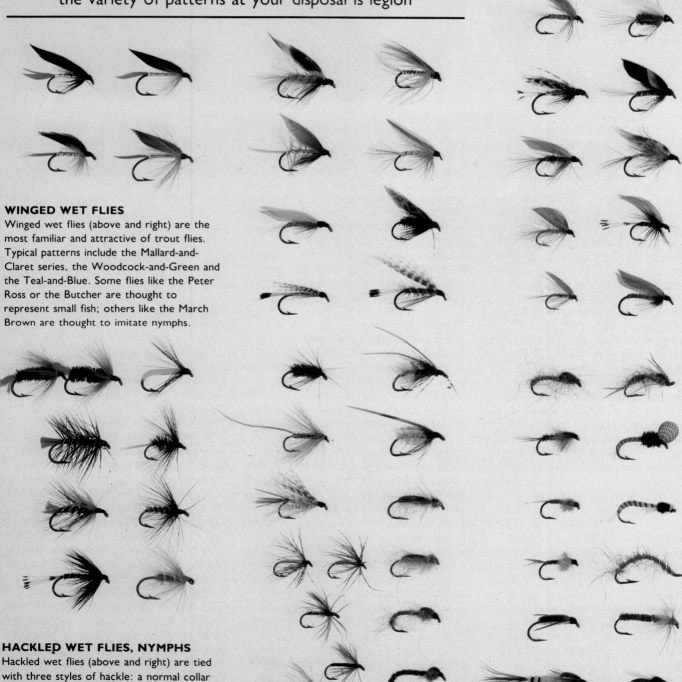

WINGED WET FLIES

Winged wet flies (above and right) are the most familiar and attractive of trout flies. Typical patterns include the Mallard-and-Claret series, the Woodcock-and-Green and the Teal-and-Blue. Some flies like the Peter Ross or the Butcher are thought to represent small fish; others like the March Brown are thought to imitate nymphs.

HACKLED WET FLIES, NYMPHS

Hackled wet flies (above and right) are tied with three styles of hackle: a normal collar hackle; 'Palmer tied'—spiralled the length of the body; and 'spider'—a sparse shoulder hackle. Nymphs (right) simulate larval, nymphal or pupal forms of insects.

In contrast to the dry fly which is intended to simulate an insect floating or alighting on the water, the wet fly represents some small insect or creature living and moving actively below the surface.

The dry fly usually represents the winged fly only, but a wet fly may represent the insect at any stage of development except the egg. It *may* imitate a half-drowned winged fly or even the critical transition stage when the pupal nymph is struggling to hatch into the adult stage and break through to the surface. It can also represent the free swimming or crawling larva, or the partially developed nymph darting among the lower layers or ascending towards the surface. Other creatures simulated by many wet fly dressings include water spiders, shrimps, snails, beetles, and fish fry.

Difference between wet and dry
The fundamental difference of function between wet and dryflies is in the manner of tying and in the softer, more absorbent, materials used for wet flies. Wet flies must sink, and generally fairly quickly. Soft, easily wetted hen hackles or the larger, softer, cock hackles are used, both to provide a clean entry and to give a semblance of limb movement when the fly responds to the vagaries of the current, or when it is retrieved. If the fly is winged, the wings are tied sloping rearwards, almost horizontally over the hook shank. This also assists entry and streamlines the fly in the water.

Swift sinking is essential for those flies intended for deep fishing. In this event the body is weighted with lead or copper wire to get the fly down quickly to the right depth.

Palmer tied flies
Any fly tied today with a full body hackle is known as 'Palmer tied' after the original Red Palmer, one of the oldest known British flies and one of the simplest to tie.

In its early tyings, the body consisted simply of red wool with a large, soft, red cock hackle spiralled around the body from the eye to the bend and ribbed with a spiral of flat gold tinsel.

The killer Black Zulu is tied in the same manner as the Palmer, and has a black body, black full hackle, silver tinsel ribbing and a little red tag of wool at the tail. Both patterns are excellent, both are tied without wings, and in a way represent a sort of halfway stage between the wet and dry flies because both can be fished dry by the simple expedient of oiling them first. They are also valuable as 'bob' flies, which are tied to the top dropper on the leader and made to skate across the surface, bobbing from wave to wave, as the tail fly is fished sunk. Bobbed flies will often be taken by fish in the last stages of retrieve, almost alongside the wading angler.

Spider or shoulder-hackled flies
Palmer flies also include a number of winged flies, such as the Invicta and Wickham's Fancy. These have shoulder hackles and are found in almost every angler's fly box.

When a winged fly is made with a somewhat sparser hackle tied with one or two turns only at the shoulder, it is called 'shoulder hackled'. If this sparse tackle is used *without* wings, the fly becomes a 'spider hackled' fly. A fairly bushy example is the Black and Peacock spider, useful when fished deep for fish feeding low on snails. An even thinner hackle is used on the Black Pennel, the Snipe-and-Purple, and the more recently developed Phantom Larva. Many nymphs are also tied with small spider type hackles at the shoulder.

Throat or beard hackles
The barest possible hackle effect is obtained when seeking to represent the limbs, antennae or external gills of many larval forms. Either the spider-type hackle is stroked downwards and fastened under the throat, or instead of using a hackle, a *false* or *beard* hackle is used by separating some fibres and tying them as a little bunch under the throat.

Beard hackles are used by many anglers to tie wet flies because they provide a slim outline, reduce shoulder bulk, make winging easier and save on hackle materials, without in any way reducing the effectiveness of the fly. Good examples are the Coachman, and the Cinnamon-and-Gold.

Winged wet flies
Winged wet flies are probably the most attractive and best known of all traditional lake flies. The Mallard-and-Claret and its series exemplifies the type and consist of mallard wing combined with golden pheasant tippets for a tail, a beard hackle, a body of red, claret, green or blue wool or seals' fur, ribbed with gold or silver tinsel or wire. Substituting wings of woodcock, teal, or partridge instead of mallard, and playing similar permutations on body colouring, gives us the Woodcock-and-Green, and its series, the Teal-and-Blue and its stablemates, and the Partridge-and-Orange. The permutations on this theme alone offer a very wide range of subtly differing colours and outlines.

Nymphs
Nymphs are probably the most important of all wet flies and properly used account for more fish than any other group.

Wet fly action
Whatever the type of fly used, its success often depends more on its action and movement in the water than its resemblance to the original. When trout are feeding freely, the actual pattern of fly is sometimes not important. But when fish are highly preoccupied with a particular insect, the angler must use all his ingenuity to discover what it is and how best to present its imitator. Speed and depth of fishing are often vital.

Unlike his dry fly counterpart, the wet fly man may fish two or three flies on the leader, the extra flies being attached on short nylon legs, or droppers, attached to the main leader at intervals. He must select his pattern so that the tail fly fishes deep, the middle fly in midwater, and the bob fly on or close to the surface. Using these tactics, the angler has a chance of discovering the taking fly and the best depth. Much skill is needed to cast a team of flies effectively, and one mistake in casting, or a puff of cross wind at the wrong moment, can tangle the team almost inextricably. And by the time this has been cleared or replaced, the rise may well be over!

Nymphs

Slow in gaining acceptance, fishing for trout with artificial nymphs is now common with the stillwater trout man. Even the diehards now agree it is as satisfying as dry fly work

Before beginning to tie a nymph, it is essential to know what we mean by the term. It is used to describe the larval forms of the various aquatic insects that form part of the diet of the trout.

There was a time when the angler used the word to refer only to the larvae of mayflies, *Ephemeroptera*—the mayfly, olives, and others—but the term now encompasses all the infant larvae, including damselflies, stoneflies, and even caddis larvae. Most books that list nymph dressings also include such creatures as freshwater shrimps, waterlice, and the larval and pupal forms of the various midges—in fact, all artificials designed with a natural aquatic creature in mind, as opposed to the traditional wet fly dressing.

One of the first anglers to realize the importance of fishing nymph artificials was GAM Skues, the great chalkstream expert. His success with his nymphs provoked much argument among 'dry fly only' anglers. Following Skues, two of the best known exponents of fishing the nymph on rivers were the late Frank Sawyer and the late Oliver Kite, who both wrote books about it.

Basic body shape
Nymph fishing is not confined to the placid chalkstreams of southern England; the modern reservoir angler has evolved his own techniques and patterns to take trout.

Ninety per cent of all nymph patterns are of the same basic shape, variations being found in their size and colour, and the materials used. The body comprises five parts—the tail, abdomen, rib, thorax and wingcase—and, to simulate legs, a hackle can be added, although many patterns dispense with this.

To tie a simple nymph, you need wool hackle fibres, silver or gold tinsel, a turkey or mottled brown hen feather, taken from the wing, a hackle feather, and, of course, tying silk. So far as colour is concerned, try to match the body colour to the colour of the hackle feather you are using—for example, olive wool for an olive hackle and so on. The hook should be size 10-14, with a medium sized shank.

Nymphs are among the easiest of flies to tie and an effective nymph is well within the capabilities of the beginner who uses the following step-by-step instructions.

First, wind silk down the shank in close, even turns, from the eye as far as the bend of the hook. At this point tie in a small bunch of hackle fibres. Then tie in a thin strand of wool and a piece of tinsel. The tying silk should be taken back to two thirds of the hook shank and the wool follows the silk up the shank, in tight turns, making the abdomen of the nymph. Tie off the wool. The rib should be wound in the opposite direction, and tied off where you tied off the wool. The body of the fly is then complete. The next stage is the thorax and wingcase.

Thorax and wingcase
Tie in a slip of turkey feather fibre for the wingcase with the pointed end of the feather facing the bend of the hook. This should be tied flat on top of the hook as it is going to be taken up over the thorax. At the same point, tie in a fresh piece of wool which can be the same colour as the body wool or perhaps a shade darker for effect. For example, for an olive-coloured body try a brown wool thorax.

To shape the thorax, wind the wool in a ball shape slightly thicker than the body, and tie off the wool, clipping off any excess strands. The

COMPONENTS OF A NYMPH

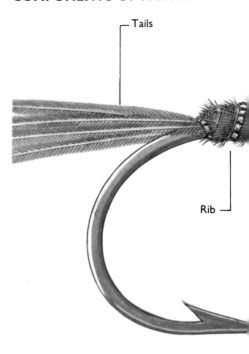

Above: *The majority of nymphs share the same basic shape, varying only in size and colour. The body comprises tail, abdomen, rib, thorax, wingcase and hackle.*

turkey feather should be taken over the thorax and tied off, and a hackle tied in at this stage.

Then wind on the hackle just one or two turns, and finish off the fly with a whip finish, and varnish. If you choose not to add a hackle, end with a whip finish.

There you have a simple nymph, easily constructed from inexpensive, readily available materials, and one that can be used for both river and stillwater fishing.

Cove's Pheasant Tail
One of the most effective stillwater patterns is the Coves Pheasant Tail—a versatile nymphal fly, for it can imitate anything from a damsel nymph to a large midge pupa. It is also extremely easy to tie.

Materials needed are a cock pheasant tail, rabbit fur (although any fur will suffice), gold or silver tinsel, and tying silk.

This time a long-shanked hook is used, about size 10. Start by winding tying silk in close, even turns to just around the bend of the hook. Then tie in a bunch of cock pheasant tail fibres and a piece of tinsel. Wind

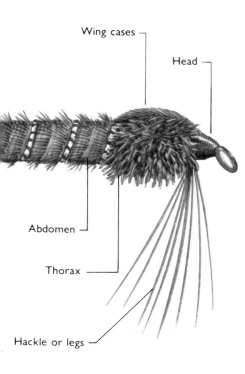

Wing cases

Head

Abdomen

Thorax

Hackle or legs

Below: A selection of imitations to represent midge pupae (top row), ephemerid nymphs (middle row) and sedge pupae and larvae (bottom row).

the silk back two-thirds of the length of the shank, and coat the silk with a little varnish this will ensure extra durability.

The pheasant tail fibres should then be wound along the shank and tied off, but do not cut off the excess fibres as these can be used to form the wingcase.

The tinsel rib should be wound in the opposite way to the pheasant tail fibres, as this prevents the tinsel slipping into the turns of the body material. Tie off the tinsel and clip off any excess strands.

To make the thorax, coat the tying silk with some wax, cut off some fur fibres and spin these on to the waxed silk.

Wind the furred tying silk into a balled shape to form the thorax. Then take the pheasant tail fibres that remained from the body and place them over the thorax, tying and clipping off the excess strands. Whip finish the fly and finish it with a coat of varnish.

To give some mobility to your nymph, pick out a few fibres of the fur thorax. These will move in the water and give quite a good simula-tion of the living nymph's legs.

You will notice that this version of a nymph has no tail. Arthur Cove, the originator, did not think it neces-sary, as in this form it imitates very well some of the larger midge pupae. A tailed version of the same fly, tied on a long-shanked size 8 hook, makes an acceptable imitation of a damsel larva.

In the last few years many effec-tive and highly realistic flies have been dressed using rubber latex sheet—that used, under the trade name Rubber Dam, by dentists. It is used the same way as any other body material. When it is wound tightly, a succulent grub-like fly is achieved, and when applied in overlapping layers, an attractive, segmented body is created.

Gold-ribbed Hare's Ear

One of the most effective traditional flies makes a fine nymph—the Gold-ribbed Hare's Ear, thought to repre-sent a hatching medium olive. It can be dressed and used either as a dry fly or as a nymph.

Materials needed for tying the Gold-ribbed Hare's Ear are fur from a hare's ear, gold wire, copper wire for weight, and well-waxed tying silk. The hook can be anything from size 16 upwards, and is weighted with copper wire.

As for the first stage of making the simple nymph, a few hare's ear fibres are tied in to form a tail. Then, for the ribbing, tie in the gold wire. The body fur is spun on to the waxed silk as for the middle stage of the Cove's Pheasant Tail nymph in-struction. Wind the fur down the hook shank to form a tapered ab-domen, and follow this with the rib.

As with any fly, continual practice will ensure that you tie good nym-phs. Always try to tie at least a dozen of a pattern at a time, and do not jump from pattern to pattern. One of the failings of many shop-bought nymphs is that they fall to bits with very little use, so when you make your own, always remember to keep the tying silk and material neat and tight. A neat fly is a secure fly which will not fall apart.

When fishing with the artificial nymph always remember that you are using an imitation of an aquatic insect – and fish accordingly.

Sea trout flies

Because the highest proportion of sea trout are caught soon after they enter a river from the sea, not all the flies are imitations of winged insects: many are intended to represent small, darting fish

The life cycle of the sea trout is almost the same as that of the salmon, with the important difference that whereas salmon do not feed in freshwater, sea trout perhaps occasionally do. Consequently, when tying flies to tempt the sea trout, try to offer them something appetizing as well as attractive.

The first flies to concentrate on are those that represent the sea trout's main diet while at sea—small fish. These are still uppermost in its mind when it enters freshwater. Sea trout also feed on prawns, shrimps, sandeels, and small crabs, but small fish of $\frac{1}{2}$in–3in—interest it most.

Standard successful flies
There are several established patterns that are always worth a place in the fly box. Teal Blue and Silver is one of the most successful the author has come across, and it

should be tied in sizes of 10 or 12 through to long-shanked flies or tandem lures of up to 3in. Other successful flies are Peter Ross, Silver Wilkinson, Teal and Red, Mallard-and-Silver, Mallard-and-Gold, and other bright patterns, all tied in the styles, to imitate small fish.

In his book *Sea Trout Fishing*, Hugh Falkus gives details of seven types of sea trout fly to suit different conditions. The first kind, which he calls 'Medicines', are effective all night but are best fished before midnight. They are big silver/blue patterns such as the Silver Blue or the Mallard-and-Silver, and are tied lightly on low water salmon hooks longer-shanked and lighter than normal hooks.

The second group, 'Sunk Lures', are good late night flies. They consist of two size 8 or 10 short-shanked

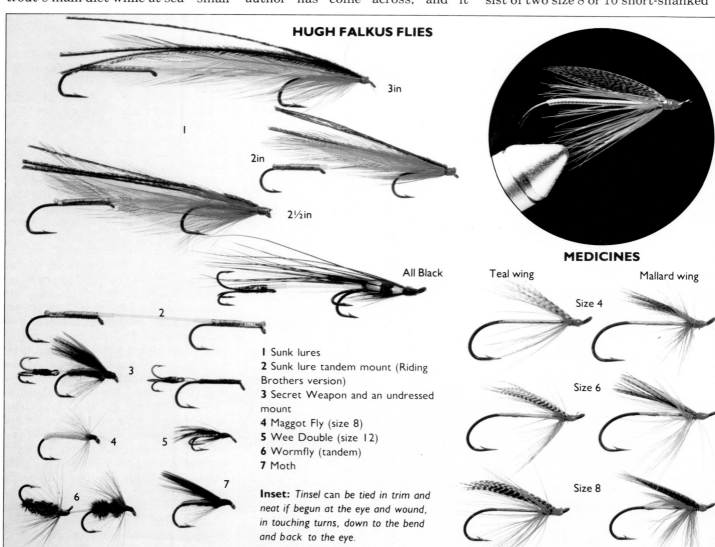

HUGH FALKUS FLIES

3in

2in

2½in

All Black

MEDICINES

Teal wing　　　Mallard wing

Size 4

Size 6

Size 8

1 Sunk lures
2 Sunk lure tandem mount (Riding Brothers version)
3 Secret Weapon and an undressed mount
4 Maggot Fly (size 8)
5 Wee Double (size 12)
6 Wormfly (tandem)
7 Moth

Inset: *Tinsel can be tied in trim and neat if begun at the eye and wound, in touching turns, down to the bend and back to the eye.*

hooks tied in tandem. The overall length of the lure should be about $2\frac{1}{2}$in. The wings are constructed of blue hackle feathers, strands of peacock herl, or blue-dyed fur. No hackles are wound in front of these lures, nor do they have tails. In fact, Falkus states that tails are unnecessary on most sea trout flies.

The third group, 'Maggot Flies', is a well-established method of sea trout fishing, and the pattern recommended by Falkus is: hook, short-shanked and snecked; body, white thread or silk; hackle, brown hen. Use these flies in conjunction with two or three maggots.

Falkus's 'Secret weapon'
Fourth is Falkus's specially constructed pattern—the 'Secret Weapon'. These flies are designed to overcome the frustration caused by

fish that are 'taking short', nibbling at the end of the bait without getting near the hook. Their secret is a flying treble extending beyond the bend (and parallel to the wings) of a normally baited maggot fly.

Falkus lists two other flies. The 'Small Double' consists of a size 12 double-iron hook, silver body, teal or mallard wing, and a black hen hackle. It is recommended when the fish are in a finicky mood in low water. The other lure, the 'Worm Fly', consists of a peacock herl body, about $1\frac{1}{4}$in-$1\frac{1}{2}$in long, with brown or black hen hackles. It is very good in low water, fished in tandem.

Sea trout continue to feed after entering freshwater. As the season progresses other types of flies, representing freshwater food, can be used with success. Such patterns as 'March Brown', 'March Brown

Silver', 'Invicta', 'Mallard and Claret', 'Butcher', and 'Zulu' all catch fish. Double hooks are useful when the fish are in a fussy mood.

The size of a fly is more important than its shape, and a great deal depends on the weather and water conditions. Standard patterns should be about size 8–10 under normal conditions, with 6–8 being used on windy days. Colour is also important. Dark flies are best in waters with dark, rocky bottoms, such as Irish lakes and rivers, and suggested patterns for these conditions are 'Black Pennell', 'Connemara Black', 'Butcher', and 'Black Zulu'. If you fish a team of three flies, the 'Black Pennell' seems to be the most successful as the tail fly on any water, although the body should be varied in colour from time to time. Use claret or yellow for example, but always with plenty of bright silver or gold ribbing.

Whether to use a large fish imitation or a smaller freshwater fly depends largely on the season. In the early season you may well adopt the maxim that a big fly will catch more fish than a small fly used at the same time in the same water. But the longer a fish stays in a river on its return from the sea, the more it is likely to return to the food available in its new environment. As its instinct for sea food fades, it will turn to eating the nymphs and flies found in freshwater.

Learn the feeding habits
Having learnt the feeding habits of sea trout, the angler who ties his own flies has all the advantages. He can make lures resembling small fish based on his own observations, and which are not the creation of someone else's imagination (very often that someone has never fished for sea trout in his life), and flies that represent the insect life in the particular water he fishes. With his own individually designed flies he is far more likely to succeed. One of the author's friends had six sea trout on one outing, the largest 11lb. All were taken on a 'Teal Blue and Silver' of his own design, tied on very long shanked hooks, very sparsely and with no tails, the wings being of widgeon feather, not the usual teal. The mark of a thinking angler.

Below: *A surface lure must float. Though a $1\frac{1}{2}$in piece of cork is the usual basis, some alternatives are given here. Results vary dramatically: sometimes these lures will take the largest fish in the pool; on other seemingly perfect nights they will be ignored entirely.*

SURFACE LURES
Cork

Muddler Minnow

Dapping fly

Deerhair Moths

Water Vole

COMMERCIAL TRADITIONAL WET PATTERNS

Butcher

Bloody Butcher

Kingfisher Butcher

Teal, Blue & Silver

Connemara Black

Peter Ross

Mallard & Claret

Dunkeld

Alexandra

Blue Zulu

Black Zulu

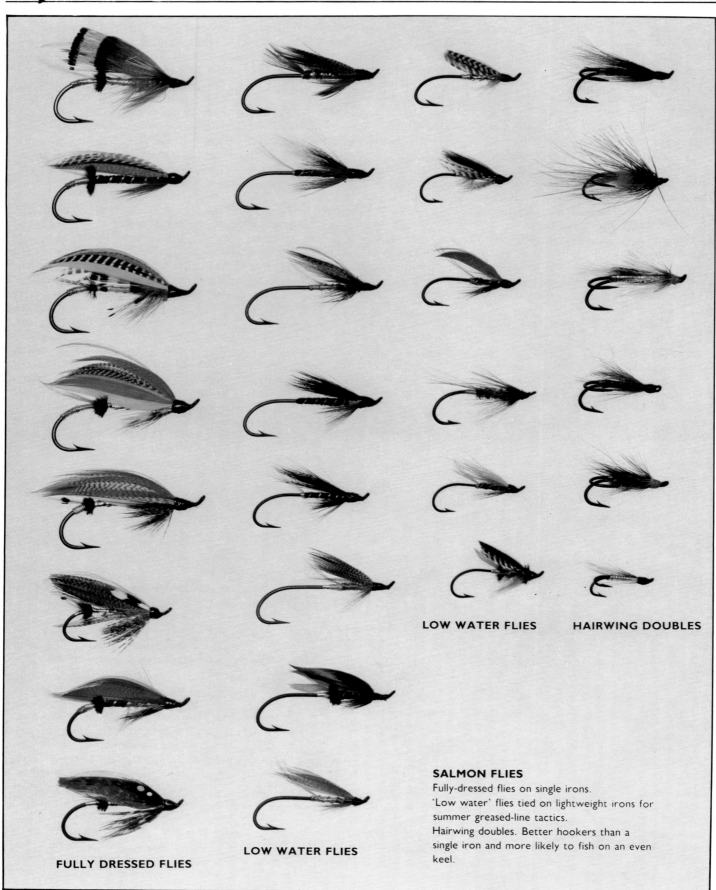

LOW WATER FLIES

HAIRWING DOUBLES

FULLY DRESSED FLIES

LOW WATER FLIES

SALMON FLIES
Fully-dressed flies on single irons.
'Low water' flies tied on lightweight irons for summer greased-line tactics.
Hairwing doubles. Better hookers than a single iron and more likely to fish on an even keel.

Salmon flies

In the days when salmon were abundant, flies were gorgeous extravagancies which bore little relation to natural insects. Today's more functional fly retains this richness of colour

Evolving from the early trout flies, the contemporary salmon fly shows little evidence to associate it with the imitation of natural insects. It is generally considered that early salmon flies were tied in ignorance of what the salmon actually thought they were, and only recently has it been realized that salmon do not feed while travelling to their spawning grounds in freshwater.

Shape, style and character
Colour has always been considered important of course, but as the ideas of one fly dresser are not necessarily those of his contemporaries, almost every known combination became available. In spite of this variety of colour, a great similarity among the patterns as to shape, style and character emerged. Type, size and presentation were considered less important than they are today: the reason being, perhaps, the greater abundance of salmon in the earlier part of this century.

The gaudy fly is still produced, though more as a fly tying exercise than anything else. The more durable and easily produced hair-winged fly is brightly coloured, and provides a better imitation of a natural insect. Indeed, the gaudy fly will always win over a drab one.

Such names as 'Jock Scott', 'Black Doctor', 'Blue Doctor', 'Blue Charm', 'Chalmers', 'Dunkeld', 'Thunder and Lightning', 'Durham Ranger' and 'Dusty Miller', 'Green Highlander' and 'Green King', the 'Logie', and many others, have become well known to salmon fishermen over the years.

Art form
An object as colourful as the traditional salmon fly lends itself as an art form, and probably for this reason alone its survival is assured, even though it has lost much of its practical popularity on the game fishing scene.

Modern flies with hair wings still retain the original brightness of the traditional ones, particularly regarding bodies, tails and hackles. In most instances these are retained in their entirety, only the wings being different. The hairs used for these wings are usually dyed the same bright shades of red, blue, yellow, green and orange, but in some instances they are left in their natural state. The 'Blue Charm' is a good illustration of this, as the teal and mallard flank feathers of the original patterns are replaced by either brown bucktail fibres or brown squirrel tail fibres, according to the size of hook. To distinguish between the two dressings, the hair-winged version of the 'Blue Charm' was called 'Hairy Mary'.

Size of fly
Having decided on the kind of fly, you then have to choose how it shall be fished. The size of a salmon fly is most important; colour only secondary. The size used will depend largely on the height, temperature and colour of the water and on weather conditions. If a salmon follows your fly or rises short this usually means that the fly is too big or your leader is too thick. The best way to start is to use a small fly—you can always increase the size later.

As a general rule: the bigger the river, the larger the fly. A larger fly would also be used in coloured water, in very rough or broken water, or in deep holes that have a dark bottom. In conditions where wind, light and temperature are constant, a medium-sized fly is recommended. Low, clear water, usually referred to as 'summer' conditions, favours a much smaller fly, and usually one of a more sombre hue.

General and specific patterns
Flies tied on what are called 'Ordinary' or 'Rational' hooks are referred to as 'Standard' patterns, whereas those used for summer conditions are called 'Low Water' patterns. These latter patterns are often merely scaled down versions of Standard patterns, tied on hooks of a lighter gauge wire, and the dressings are taken well forward of the hook bend.

Double hooks preferred
Double hooks are preferred by many anglers, not only because of the extra weight, but also because they provide a more even keel to the fly, thus enabling it to float upright. This is most important if the fly is to be presented to the fish in the proper manner.

In addition to these general patterns there are others which are designed for specific rivers. Two of the best known are the 'Spey' and the 'Dee' patterns (named after the rivers), which are made with rather sombre materials.

Spey and Dee patterns
These flies are used in the early part of the season when the temperature can be at almost freezing point. They are dressed lightly on very large hooks, 3in being quite common, and this combination of lightness of dressing and heaviness of hook means that the flies sink deeper. They are therefore more likely to come within the field of view of the fish which lies close to the bottom when the temperature of the water is very low. In addition to the suitability of these large flies for the particular circumstances in which they are used, one of their best features is the extreme mobility of their hackles and wings, giving them a very lifelike appearance when they are worked in the water.

In contrast to the gaudy flies described earlier, 'Spey' and 'Dee' flies are a very practical kind of pattern. The now very popular 'Tube' and 'Waddington' flies lend themselves particularly to these styles of dressings, as the long flowing hackles can be wound very easily, and hair fibres applied to give a very symmetrical aspect.

Tube flies

A tube fly often escapes the jaws of the fish it hooks, flying up the line in a flash of colour. That doesn't mean that its tying can afford to be any the less robust or businesslike

Above: *A simple tube fly, the Hairy Mary. It is tied from bucktail hair, floss silk and tinsel onto a long-shanked hook.*

Although the tube fly is not a modern innovation, its worldwide popularity is only recent. And although it will probably never oust the standard and low-water flies tied on normal single and double hooks, there is no doubt that it is here to stay. The tube fly, as its name suggests, consists of a length of polythene or metal tubing, round which are whipped hair fibres from the tails of many different animals. Orthodox salmon fly bodies are generally added to the tubes, and long-fibred hackles may be used in conjunction with the hair fibres, or even in place of them.

The history of the tube fly is vague, and in fact there was at one time a great deal of discussion as to who was its originator. The history of the salmon fly itself was dealt with in Part 14 of New Fisherman's Handbook, so it is sufficient to say that the tube fly is an extension of the traditional salmon fly.

One of the first to reach the attention of salmon anglers was the Parker tube fly, since when all tube flies have followed a very similar style and method of construction. One of the earliest to earn a name was the Stoat Tail which, in its original form, consisted merely of fibres from the tail of a stoat, whipped round one end of a piece of tubing. As with all patterns which

achieve a measure of popularity, variations soon began to appear, and these usually either took the form of additions to the tube body itself, using silk and tinsel as coverings, or by the addition of different coloured hairs to those used on the original Stoat Tail.

Heron breast and guinea fowl body feathers are good examples of the feathers which are now used for tying tube flies, as they have long, flowing fibres which work well in the water when the fly is fished. Some tubes are made of brass in which a polythene tube has been inserted, thus giving weight for deep winter fishing without creating too much wear and tear on the leader.

Tube flies are used in conjunction with a treble hook which is tied to the end of the leader. The tube is then slid down the leader tail-end first, until it is stopped by the eye of the treble hook. From this you will see that the tube runs free on the leader, which has a double advantage. When the fly is being fished, the pressure of water holds it tight to the treble hook, whereas when the hook is taken by a fish the reverse applies, and the drag caused by the fish's run drives the tube up the leader. This prevents damage to tube and dressing.

For colour variations or for increased size, two made-up tubes may be used together.

Conventional fly tying equipment can be used to make tube flies, plus one or two sizes of tapered, eyeless salmon hooks on which the tubes can be slid to facilitate tying. Hook sizes 4, 2, 2/0 and 4/0 should cope with most tube diameters.

Above: *A Stoat-tail tube fly still lodged in the scissors of a salmon's jaws.*
Right: *The basic tube flying free after the strike. Don't neglect its uses in trout as well as salmon fishing.*

Treble Hook

Tube running free along leader

Chapter 7
COARSE TACKLE

Two hundred years ago and more anglers used ash and hazel poles as rods, and plaited strands of hair from the tail of a white horse to use as line, tied direct to the tip of the pole. And with this tackle, desperately crude to modern eyes, they caught their fish!

So what would those anglers of bygone days make of the huge range of sophisticated gear to be seen in tackle shops now!

They would pick a veritable wand and wonder at its weight — or the lack of it. Not of wood or metal, its material of carbon fibre would mystify them. Today's intricate reels, closed face, multiplier, skirted spool, automatic, would defeat their imagination. Their fishing lines, horse hair, twine and, later, silk, seem crude compared with today's extruded monofilament. Nylon is available in breaking strains down to a ½ lb.

The mere technicalities of design, manufacture, materials, of which past anglers would understand nothing, can be set aside. What is important is would they be able to catch more fish with modern tackle than with the crude gear they had?

Probably not, at least until the finesse of today's angling techniques had been grasped. In their day, the rivers were unpolluted, full of fish, those that we now call coarse and the trout and salmon. They were sought only in small part for sport, the real intent was for supplying the table.

This meant that fishing was a straightforward means of pulling fish from the river, with no pretence of 'giving them a chance'. Some of the means by which pike were taken are now illegal; the gorge and trimmer, for example are cruel – but effective.

The gorge was a short length of wood sharpened at both ends, imbedded in a dead fish. This was suspended by strong line from a large piece of cork, and simply left to float in the pike swim. When the pike took the bait, the short wooden stake lodged in the pike's mouth or throat and as it struggled so would the sharp points become embedded deeper. The cork prevented the fish diving into cover and acted as a buoy, indicating where the fish lay beneath.

Netting was also done. These are not sporting means, of course, and today, apart from trout and salmon we eat very little of the fish taken. Pike and perch, when sizeable, can be eaten.

Those olden-day anglers, then, had fish aplenty. But to come was the Industrial Revolution, which was to make fortunes for some and at the same time poison many of our rivers with effluent and chemicals. Once, salmon ran up the Thames and trout were plentiful in its small tributaries. But in the 19th Century the Pool of London, haven of vast numbers of trading ships, was in such a disgusting state that brass on ships' fittings turned green overnight because of the noxious fumes arising from the Thames. It was so polluted that anyone diving in to save a life was in severe danger of death from poisoning!

Now, the salmon are running again, albeit slowly. It is sad that the shipping has gone and it is a high price to pay for a clean Thames. But fishermen can now fish London's river almost anywhere.

We can make good use of the high quality fishing tackle the manufacturers produce. And today's rods really are competitive in price and terrific value. When rod blanks of solid glassfibre first appeared they made up into rods that quickly received the description of 'liquorice sticks' — they were floppy and had nothing of the life and action of built-cane.

When playing a fish, the rod would, depending on its diameter, either resist flexion or bend near in half. Something had to be done and soon hollowglass rods appeared, and this medium was lighter and had more of the action of the built cane rods. At first, hollowglass was expensive, as are all innovations (remember the first calculators?) but now their price is truly competitive and rods in hollowglass are available for all kinds of fishing from salmon spinning to float-fishing.

After glass, came carbon fibre, an improvement on the fibreglass models, being even lighter and at the same time retaining a classic action.

The number of fishing tackle accessories is legion; some are essential, such as landing nets, holdalls, rodbags (nowadays plastic tubes, which really do protect your rods), forceps for removing hooks, for the old-fashioned disgorger can inflict a nasty wound when wielded in clumsy fingers; and an item not originally intended for anglers — polarized glasses. These, by cutting out rays of light hitting the eye at odd angles, enable one to see through the surface film and spot fish movement. No angler should ignore their usefulness.

Float rods

Fishing with float tackle has evolved into a complicated science and the conscientious angler can take full advantage of modern developments in the manufacture of float rods

Rods for float fishing should be 12-13ft long, able to handle lines of 3-5lb b.s., and have a slow action. Other types of coarse fishing rod may be used: the specimen hunter, for example, may find a light carp rod best when float fishing for tench or carp in weedy conditions and with the expectation of a big fish. The beginner will often use a glassfibre spinning rod because it is cheap,

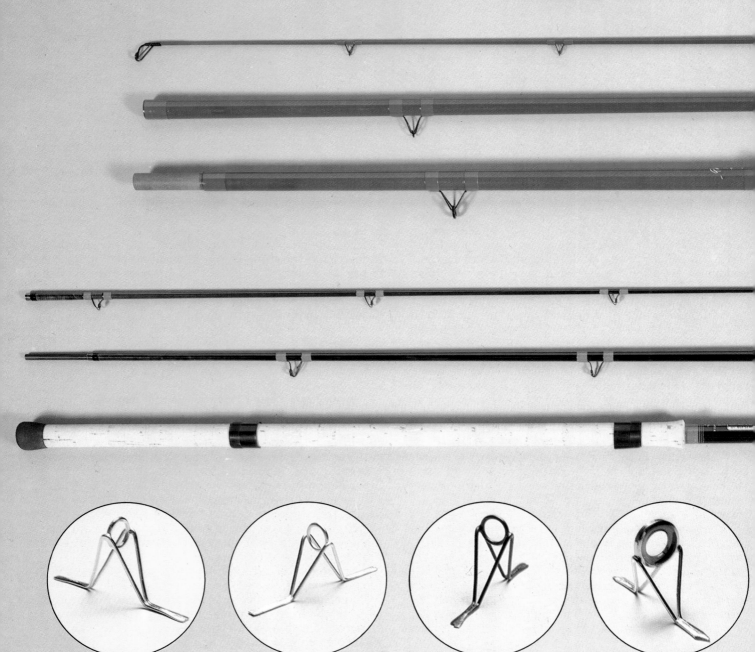

Bright chrome 'stand off' intermediate.

Satin chrome 'stand off' intermediate.

Black chrome 'stand off' intermediate.

Bright chrome intermediate lined with 'Aqualite'.

adaptable and sturdy. But the term 'float rod' is usually applied to the longer rods used for general and match fishing.

These two uses have resulted in the development of two distinct kinds of float rod: slow-action rods, which bend along much of their length when playing a fish or casting; and fast-action rods, usually rigid to within 25 per cent of their length with the action concentrated in the tip.

General-purpose float rods are slower in action than match rods and have stronger tips, usually made of glassfibre and 2½-3mm in diameter. The tip of a match rod is nearer 2½mm in diameter to allow their use with lines of 1½-2lb b.s. In addition, the match rod is usually stiffer in the butt to give quicker

These two masterpieces could never have been envisaged in the bad old days of heavy, sluggish float rods. The top rod is a 'Fibatube' 12ft hollow glassfibre match rod. Like most modern match rods, it has a fast tip action and the high 'stand off' rings are effective in preventing wet line clinging to the rod. The bottom rod is a 'Graphlex' GXL made by Don's of Edmonton: a 13ft match rod with a fast tip action constructed, unusually, of carbonfibre all the way through.

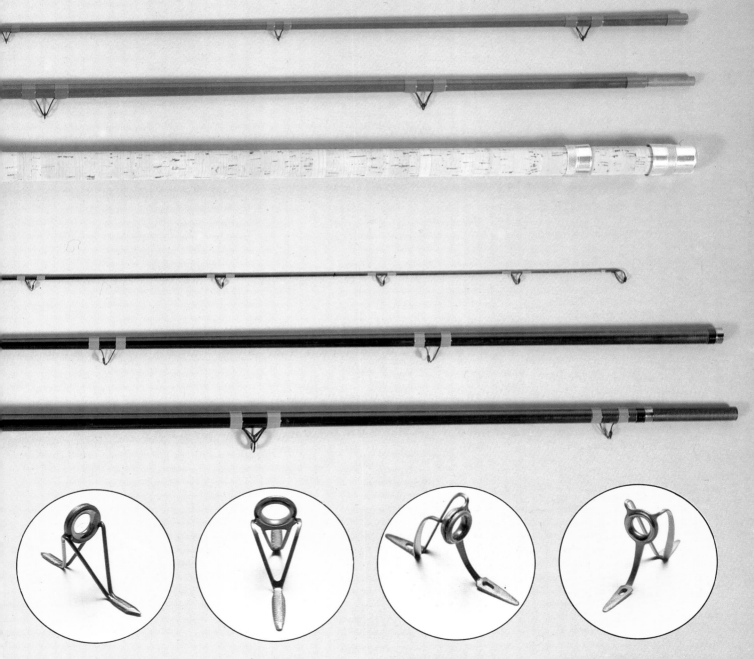

Black chrome intermediate lined with 'Aqualite'.

'Seymo' 3 leg intermediate, aluminium oxide lined.

'Fuji' 3 leg intermediate, aluminium oxide lined.

'Fuji' intermediate lined with silicon carbide.

striking. Fish control, however, is more difficult with a stiffer rod, but as a rule, matchmen are not pursuing large fish. There are exceptions to this, such as on the Severn where matches are won with good sized chub and barbel. These fish demand a stronger rod than that used by the average match fisherman.

Match rod development

Due to the changing demands of match fishing, the match rod is constantly being developed. Different areas of fishing call for different actions so there are variations in the type of rod in use.

Most float rods today are made of tubular glassfibre, though carbonfibre rods are increasingly popular.

Float rods are usually equipped with cork handles fitted with sliding rings for holding the reel. This keeps the weight to a minimum.

With a threaded tip ring fitted, the float rod may be used with various screw attachments, such as a swing tip for ledgering. Care should be taken, however, to ensure that the tip of the rod will stand up to the casting weight.

A rod of this description is also suited to long trotting, when float tackle is allowed to trot down with the current of a river or stream and the fish are hooked and played some way downstream from the angler.

Specimen hunters tend to use the longer, lighter ledgering rods—those designed by Peter Stone, for example—since they are capable of casting tackle long distances and controlling heavy fish.

The ideal match rod

Match rods, too, have a specific job to perform. They must be light and well-balanced enough to be held comfortably for the duration of a contest. They must be capable of casting float tackle with precision

Above right: *Roach pole fishing is now coming back with a vengeance. It is a very sensitive method of taking small coarse fish and demands a particular expertise. Here Peter Ward is attaching a section of a Shakespeare roach pole before fishing.*
Right: *Peter Ward demonstrates two types of float rod. In his right hand he holds a 13ft tip-action match rod and in his left a 13ft soft-action float rod.*

and sometimes over a considerable distance, and they must be able to strike close-to and at a distance.

This has resulted in the use of a fast-action rod with a soft top which helps to overcome line breakage by acting as a shock absorber. Commonly made of glassfibre, some match rods are now constructed in part of carbonfibre. While retaining a glassfibre top, the carbonfibre butt and middle of the rod have added stiffness where it is needed—but such power can prove too strong for use with fine lines.

The most popular lengths for match rods are between 12 and 13ft as these appear to provide the best compromise between length and ease of handling. Shorter rods cannot control fish as well, while longer rods are difficult to manage. Further development of carbonfibre rods, may well change this.

Pole fishing

Pole fishing has recently become very popular in this country. With this style of sport, a rod in the region of 20-28ft long is used and the line is fixed direct to the end of the rod without the niceties of reel or rod rings. The float tackle—often very small and sensitive—is fished extremely close to the top of the rod. This makes it easier for the angler to strike at very small bite indications, since he is in almost direct contact with the bait. Because of the stiffness of the pole, a shock absorber of fine elastic may be fitted between the rod and line so that, on striking, the line does not snap. This type of fishing is becoming more popular, particularly where bleak are the quarry, as the pole can be used to strike quickly and to place the bait very accurately.

An angler hoping to make a name for himself in the matchfishing world must certainly practice hard to become proficient in fishing with pole. Matches on the Continent are notable for almost total reliance on the pole for the control and distance this method gives.

Above left: *This is the correct way to attach a reel to a match rod.* **Left:** *A long match rod and fine tackle means that a landing net is necessary even though the fish may not be in the specimen category.*

173

Ledger rods

Today's wide range of specialist ledger rods have evolved from—but are quite dissimilar to—the built-cane rods designed by Richard Walker, inventor of the Arlesey bomb

The term ledgering is applied to the style of fishing where the bait is allowed to rest on the bed of the river or lake and a float is not used for bite indication. Rods specially designed to be used for ledgering are comparative newcomers to the angling scene.

Until quite recently, the art of ledgering was undeveloped and a fairly heavy rod was commonly used. Probably the earliest rod which was used for ledgering was the traditional Avon-type rod used for fishing the Hampshire Avon and other fast flowing rivers. It has a length of 11ft, is in three pieces with a built-cane middle section and top with a tonkin cane butt. It was followed by the built cane MK IV Avon and MK IV Carp designs by Richard Walker.

The carp rod was obviously designed for carp fishing but found ready acceptance by the specimen barbel hunters. The lighter MK IV Avon was a scaled-down version suitable for general fishing for tench, chub, barbel and perch in flowing or stillwaters. Both were very successful designs from which have evolved today's wide range of specialist ledger rods.

Types of rod

Today these rods are manufactured mainly of tubular glassfibre, although a few rods in built-cane of the MK IV type are still made and no doubt carbonfibre rods will be further developed.

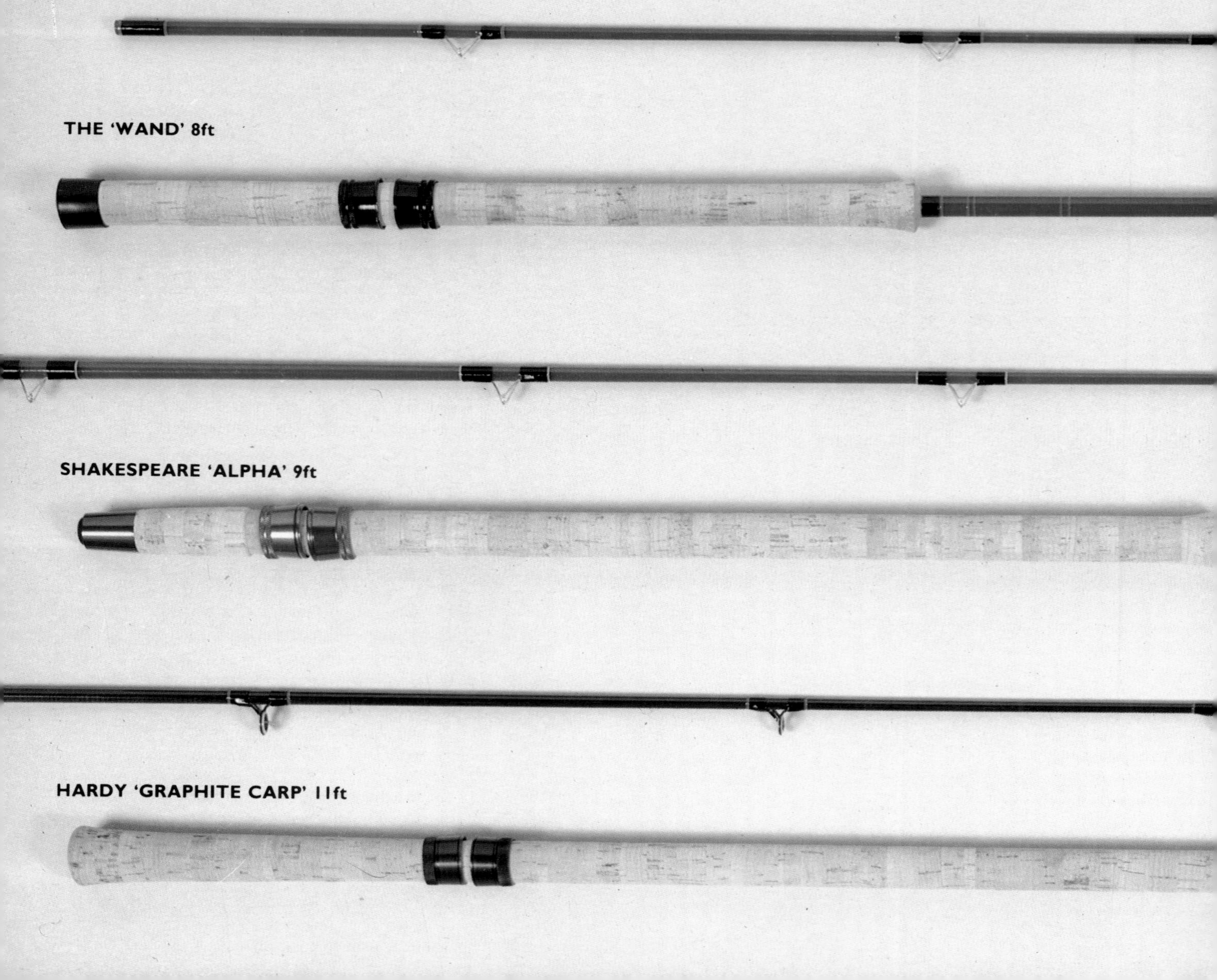

THE 'WAND' 8ft

SHAKESPEARE 'ALPHA' 9ft

HARDY 'GRAPHITE CARP' 11ft

Two-rod ledgering for barbel on the Swale at Thornton Bridge

Present-day ledger rods vary from 9ft to 11½ft, the longer rods being used more by the specimen hunter and the shorter kinds usually by the competition angler. They are also used with various types of bite indicators, although some rods have a built-in bite indicator called a quivertip, which consists of a finely tapered piece of solid glass which, because of its small diameter, is very sensitive. This type, known as a quivertip rod, is usually between 9½ and 10ft in length.

Below: *Three excellent ledger rods. From top to bottom: the 'Wand', an 8ft long hollow glassfibre rod with a spliced-in quivertip, used for light match fishing; the Shakespeare 'Alpha', a 9ft long hollow glassfibre match rod; the Hardy 'Graphite Carp', an 11ft long carbonfibre rod*

Spinning rods

The range of rods which fall within the one category begins with the small, handy wand used by a roving fisherman on tiny streams to weapons capable of landing a salmon

Spinning rods may usually be classified by the weights they can cast and the line strengths the rod can handle, their basic function being to cast a lure and to control a hooked fish.

As a general rule, the lighter the lure or spinner to be cast, the lighter and shorter the rod. In general also, the lighter the lure, the finer will be the line used with it. This is because the heavier and thicker the line the more weight is required in the lure to overcome the drag of the line, which is to be avoided especially when long casts are needed.

Most rods designed for use with the lighter spinning lure (up to ½oz)

are 6-8ft long and are teamed with fixed-spool reels and relatively light lines of 4-8lb b.s. Rods for the heavier lures are more often 8-10½ft long and may be used with fixed-spool or multiplier reels loaded with lines up to 20lb b.s. These heavier spinning rods are very often used with two hands when casting and so have naturally been referred to as double-handed.

In addition to the standard patterns of spinning rods, there is a special type which originated in the US and is known as a 'baitcasting' rod. This rod, designed to be used in conjunction with a multiplier, features a pistol-grip, cranked han-

dle to allow the fisherman to cast and control the reel using one hand. It is made with a one-piece top 5-6ft long, and the reel is mounted on top of the rod. This arrangement enables accurate casting but has the disadvantage that long-distance casts are not possible.

Baitcasting rods
These outfits are used extensively in America for freshwater black bass fishing, but are not popular in Britain as they are best used with plug baits which, by contrast with spinners, spoons, Devon minnows and similar lures, have not yet gained wide acceptance here. Baitcasting rods also require a fairly heavy plug or lure to cast well and it is still more usual in Britain to use longer rods in this situation.

For light spinning for trout, sea trout, perch and pike, a rod of 7-8ft long, capable of casting up to ¾oz, makes a good all-round tool when coupled with a small-to-medium fixed-spool reel carrying line of 4-8lb b.s. depending on the type of

Spinning rods (from top to bottom): the Abu Caster—6ft long and suited to weights of less than ½oz; the medium-weight Fibatube 9ft Special; the Shakespeare 1570–270—8ft 10in of powerful action.

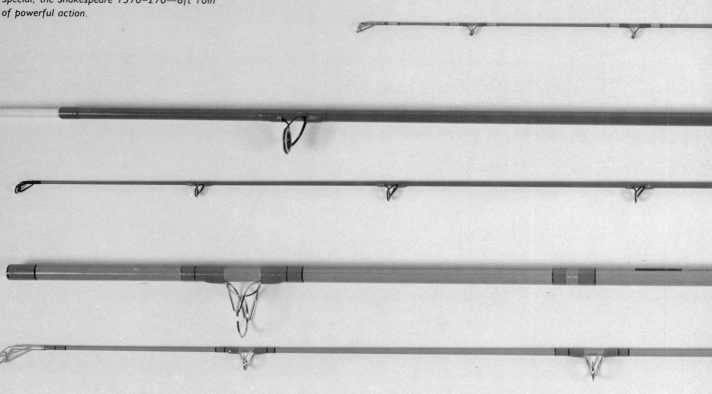

fishing. This pattern of rod is usually made of hollow glassfibre, with cheaper rods in solid glass.

A cork handle about 18in long, fitted with a screw winch-fitting to hold the reel securely is the basis of all spinning rods. The size of rod rings should be graduated to aid casting by ensuring smooth line flow from the spool.

A rod suitable for heavier types of lures in the ½-1oz range should be 8½-9ft long. The handle should be about 24in long, with a screw winch-fitting about 14in from the bottom of the handle when used with a fixed-spool reel, and 2-3in higher with a multiplier. This substitution of lines of 9-15lb b.s. makes the outfit suitable for the heavier types of freshwater spinning—salmon and pike—and for lighter saltwater spinning for bass, pollack, mackerel and other species.

Heavy-duty spinning rods

The heaviest patterns of rod are required for spinning with deadbaits for salmon and large pike in very un-favourable water conditions. The deadbaits can weigh up to 4oz, and lines up to 20lb b.s. are needed.

A rod capable of handling heavy lures and weights should be 9½-10ft long and fairly strong, with a test curve of 1½-2¼lb. This type of rod is very often used with a multiplier, for heavy spinning. The handles are usually 24-28in long.

Greenheart rods

The design of spinning rods has altered considerably over the past 50 years. The original rods were heavy and long, and made for salmon spinning. They were usually of greenheart (a special type of hardwood), or built cane. The centrepin reel used with these rods required them to be slow in action to assist the revolving drum to accelerate evenly and allow line to flow off without jamming.

With the introduction of the fixed-spool reel, rod action could be improved. They could be faster in action, as well as lighter. The fixed-spool reel could casts lighter baits and, because the spool of the reel did not revolve, the line did not jam or overrun, making casting easier.

The multiplier became popular at about the same time, and was an improvement over the centrepin so far as casting was concerned. However, it is only in the last 10 years or so that the multiplier's braking systems for casting have been developed enough to allow rod-makers to match them with the lighter, faster-actioned rods now favoured. The latest material to be used in spinning rods is carbonfibre. These rods are expensive, but perform well.

Prices for the various types of spinning rod vary considerably, depending on the quality of the materials and workmanship. A good tubular glass rod by a reputable maker costs from £30-£80 while imported rods may be bought for as little as £10.

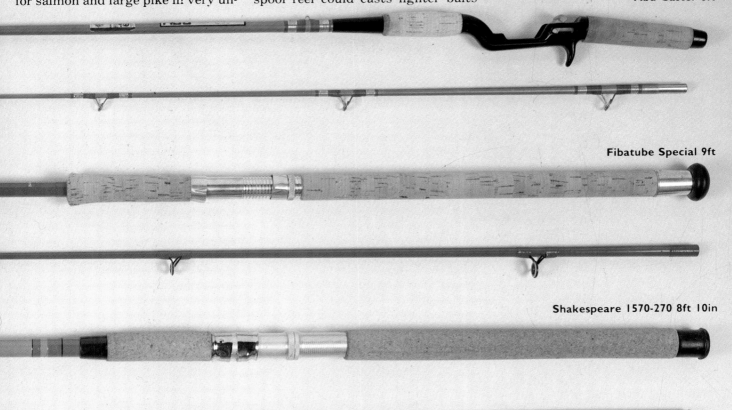

Abu Caster 6ft

Fibatube Special 9ft

Shakespeare 1570-270 8ft 10in

Fixed-spool reel

No other piece of tackle has revolutionized the art of angling quite as much as the fixed-spool reel. Knowing how to handle it properly can save time and effort and improve your fishing

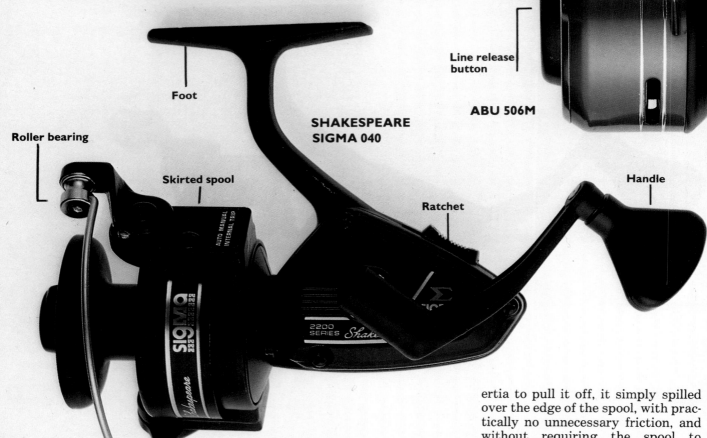

Winding cap cover

Oscillating spool

Line release button

ABU 506M

Foot

SHAKESPEARE SIGMA 040

Roller bearing

Skirted spool

Ratchet

Handle

The modern fixed-spool reel is a masterpiece of engineering design. It has banished one of the angler's oldest problems, that of casting to the required spot, and has doubled, or even trebled the distances over which the average angler can hope to cast accurately. At the same time, it has reduced the problem of tangled line to a minimum.

Despite this, we still occasionally hear the reel's critics bemoaning the fact that it has taken the skill out of casting. Even if this were wholly true, it would be no more a cause for regret than the fact that the washing machine has taken the drudgery out of washing day.

The first fixed-spool reel was patented by Alfred Illingworth in 1905. It incorporated all the basic principles of the modern reel, which still hold good today. The line spool was fixed with its axis at right angles to the direction of casting. When line was released, as long as the tackle provided the necessary in-

ertia to pull it off, it simply spilled over the edge of the spool, with practically no unnecessary friction, and without requiring the spool to revolve. Hence the modern name—fixed-spool.

Line was retrieved simply by hooking it onto a primitive bale-arm, which revolved around the fixed-spool, laying line back when the reel handle was turned.

Slipping clutches

To provide the faster retrieval desired for spinning, Illingworth geared the reel handle to the bale-arm to provide a retrieval ratio of approximately 3:1. The fixed-spool reel has come a long way since those days, and, not long after Ill-

Shakespeare Sigma 2200

The three fixed-spool reels shown here represent the results of the efforts of the manufacturers to solve the problem of casting line at right angles to the spool. The Sigma range has the skirted spool which prevents loops in the line from tangling around the spindle. This is a problem which can occur just after a cast (before the arm is closed), or when ledgering with the arm open when the wind can pick loops off the spool.

Abu 506

This Swedish reel has taken the concept a stage further with its completely closed face. There is no bale arm to operate manually. Line is released for casting by the pressure of a finger on the face of the boss on the front of the reel. Line recovery is engaged immediately by a turn of the handle. For match fishing, when terminal tackle must be out of the water for as little time as possible, this kind of action is ideal.

Mitchell 300A

This range of French reels, all noted for their quality and precision, does not have a skirted spool, but the design of the spool rims aids clean recovery of line. The amount of line a spool can accommodate depends upon the diameter of the line. Many other models of fixed-spool reels can be changed from right-to left-hand wind by unscrewing the handle and attaching it on the other side of the reel body.

Auto syncro-drag

MITCHELL 300A

Bale arm

Tension nut

Unskirted spool

Spool release button

Ratchet

Bale arm trip

ingworth's first reel, slipping clutches and crosswind reels were developed, although these only entered the market in the early 1930s, not really coming into common usage until after the war.

Now it is possible to buy such reels with a wide variety of retrieval ratios suitable for every possible kind of fishing. All have adjustable clutch mechanisms, a reciprocating reel movement which provides even laying of line, and in some cases a crosswind action to prevent the line from jamming.

To be effective, such a reel must be properly used. Most manufacturers' instructions today refer to the loading capacity of the various spools, which varies with the b.s. of the line required. Many manufacturers provide a spare spool, and since most spools are quickly detachable the angler can change spool and line in a moment.

Loading the spool

When loading the spool it must be borne in mind that the rotary action of the bale-arm around the spool im-

parts twist to the line, and that over a hundred yards of line this becomes considerable, especially when medium-weight lines, which are fairly springy, are employed.

This twist in the line is largely responsible for the manner in which the monofilament lines often tend to spring off the spool. To prevent twist it is recommended that the line be pulled off the manufacturer's spool not by letting it turn on a pencil as you wind, but over the flange of the manufacturer's spool in much the same way as the line spills over the edge of the fixed-spool itself. Since pulling line off and laying it on both impart twist to the line, the tactic is to impart opposite twist to

CLEANING A FIXED-SPOOL REEL

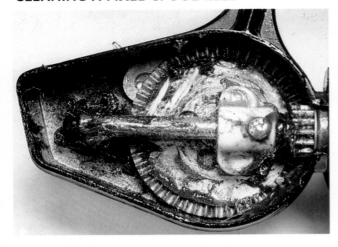

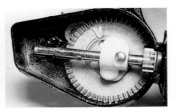

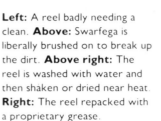

Left: A reel badly needing a clean. **Above:** Swarfega is liberally brushed on to break up the dirt. **Above right:** The reel is washed with water and then shaken or dried near heat. **Right:** The reel repacked with a proprietary grease.

the line as the bale-arm lays it on to the spool.

When the slipping clutch is set, this must be done so that if a dangerous strain is put on your line, the clutch will slip before the line breaks. This also implies that you must select a line b.s. suitable for the rod you intend to use. If, for example, your line is of 20lb b.s. and you set the clutch at, say, 18lb, you have a margin of safety of roughly 2lb. However, if you are using a rod of a ½lb test curve there is considerable danger that you will already have strained or damaged, or even broken your rod before the clutch will start to slip. To allow this to happen is clearly absurd, and so lines must be selected to suit the rod. If you must use heavy lines on a light rod you would be better to set the clutch to give when the rod is entering the test curve position, or somewhat before.

Long trotting

Long trotting is a fishing method for which many anglers prefer an ordinary centrepin reel, but this does not mean that they cannot practice it perfectly well with a fixed-spool reel. The technique is to take up slack after casting, and then open the bale-arm so that as the float drifts down through the swim it pulls line off the spool freely. If line is running out too freely, the extended finger comes into play, not on the spool, but close by it so that line in slipping off brushes against the finger, the friction slowing the rate

of flow. When the float disappears, the finger is clamped hard on the reel spool, stopping the line flow at the same time as the rod is raised swiftly to strike.

One of the minor problems of the fixed-spool reel is that line occasionally springs off the spool without warning. Sometimes this is due to the wind, sometimes to twisted line, and sometimes to overloading. Whatever the cause, this has been the subject of criticism by anglers fishing with fine tackle over long distances. Others complain that for long trotting it does not give instant control.

The closed-face reel was designed to overcome these problems and to provide easier reel control. This kind of reel is closely related to the fixed-spool and works on the same principle in that the drum itself remains stationary.

The same problems of casting light weights are involved, and as the line spirals off the drum and out through the vent of the reel face the friction is slightly greater.

Most closed-face reels are sold with line of about 6lb b.s. already wound on. The optimum b.s. for these reels should be 15lb of monofilament. Do not use braided line. It tends to bunch and pile up inside the reel facing, wasting line and fishing time.

Fixed-spool v. closed-face

Opinions differ as to whether this reel is better than the fixed-spool, but many anglers prefer the closed-

face reel's simpler mechanism. Instead of a bale-arm, a rotating metal cap fits over the spool. This carries a retractable metal stud against which line is trapped. A second metal case over the stud prevents line slipping over the top of it. The inner case revolves when the reel handle is turned and the stud acts exactly like the bale-arm, laying line evenly on the reciprocating inner spool. The stud is linked to a release catch. Pressure on this retracts the stud, allowing the line to run out.

The casting action is very similar to that of the fixed-spool reel. However, instead of having to hold the line across a crooked finger and manually releasing it, the thumb button or front-plate catch is pressed to free the line.

Like the fixed-spool reel, the closed-face model has an adjustable clutch mechanism, although in most cases this operates on the winding handle rather than the spool itself. The result is much the same.

So, fixed-spool or closed face, this style of reel has certainly solved many of the purely mechanical casting problems once faced by anglers. It will not cure clumsy casting, and it will not help catch fish if the angler casts to the wrong places. Nevertheless, used properly and in conjunction with watercraft and other basic angling skills, investment in one of the reels, or both types, is certainly worthwhile. Careful handling and regular maintenance of the reel will be repaid by years of use.

Centrepins and multipliers

Fixed-spool reels are appropriate for light-tackle fishing, but when using some specialized techniques and for big-game fishing centrepins and multipliers may be essential

A centrepin is a reel acting as a line reservoir with its axis at right angles to the rod. Good centrepins consist of a flanged drum, machined to very fine tolerances, which revolves freely on a precision-engineered steel axle. Many models have appeared over the years, ranging from the cheap and simple kind in Bakelite to the comparatively expensive models manufactured from stainless steel or enamelled metal. Wooden models have also been produced, but are now not so common.

The centrepin is simple in construction, and—by virtue of this—reliable, as well as being easy to operate and to maintain. Once the use of the centrepin has been mastered many anglers prefer it to the fixed-spool reel.

Trotting
The centrepin is used mainly for 'trotting'—allowing the river's current to carry float-tackle smoothly downstream, allowing the bait to cover long stretches of water at one cast. It is with this method that the free-running centrepin drum is put to best advantage. To recover line quickly, the drum is given a series of taps with all four fingers in a practice called 'batting'.

The diameter of the reel can vary, but most are between 3½in and 4½in. The drum's diameter will be

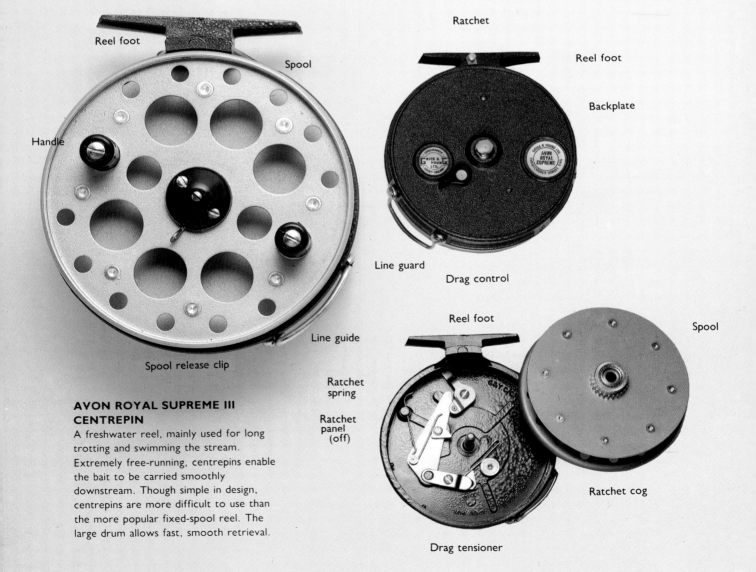

Reel foot · Spool · Handle · Spool release clip · Line guide · Ratchet · Reel foot · Backplate · Line guard · Drag control · Reel foot · Ratchet spring · Ratchet panel (off) · Drag tensioner · Ratchet cog · Spool

AVON ROYAL SUPREME III CENTREPIN
A freshwater reel, mainly used for long trotting and swimming the stream. Extremely free-running, centrepins enable the bait to be carried smoothly downstream. Though simple in design, centrepins are more difficult to use than the more popular fixed-spool reel. The large drum allows fast, smooth retrieval.

almost as large, and the larger the drum the more rapid will be the line recovery. Most centrepins have a line guard and optional ratchet, while some also have a drag mechanism. An exposed smooth rim, which allows finger-pressure to be applied to control the line when casting or playing a fish, is a

valuable feature. Many of the older centrepin reels are now very much in demand for their fine, free action.

Although the centrepin is still used —and indeed has made a come-back in recent years—its popularity suffered greatly when the fixed-spool reel was introduced 40 years ago. This reel permits almost effortless

long casting, because the drum is parallel to the rod. To achieve similar distances with a centrepin is a satisfying accomplishment. Nevertheless, the centrepin is still unrivalled in two circumstances. In water where the fishing is virtually under the rod end and there are likely to be big fish which go off at high

Handle · Cage · End plate · Ratchet · Counter balance · Level wind · Bearing cap · Reel foot · Spool release control · Reel foot · High Speed · Star drag · Bearing cap · Star drag · Level wind

AMBASSADEUR 6600 MULTIPLIER

Freshwater multiplier reels like the Ambassadeur cast further than the fixed-spool reel, but are more difficult to master. The star drag controls the amount of tension exerted on the line when playing a fish.

PENN 65 MULTIPLIER

A heavy duty reel used for boat fishing. A lever disengages the handle and gears to allow line to run freely. But apply gentle thumb pressure to prevent line running too fast and tangling.

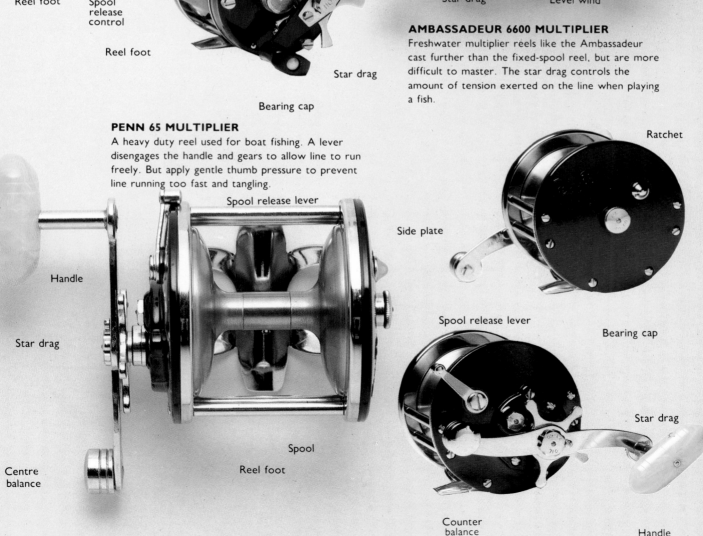

Spool release lever · Side plate · Ratchet · Handle · Star drag · Spool release lever · Bearing cap · Centre balance · Reel foot · Spool · Star drag · Counter balance · Handle

speed, such as carp; and where the fishing is close-in.

The centrepin scores in both conditions for the same reason—the perfect control which can be exercised by the thumb on the drum of the reel. A point in favour of this method is that the alternative—using the slipping clutch of a fixed-spool reel—was not designed for use with the fine lines normally used by the matchman.

In 1977 a centrepin reel for fly fishing, made entirely of carbon fibre, made its appearance. This, the 'Line-Shooter', is a big reel with a wide drum and exposed rim, allowing rapid line recovery by winding or 'batting'. It is also the lightest centrepin reel ever made, weighing only 5oz. The ratchet is optional and, by contrast with many other models, is reasonably quiet. It also incorporates an extremely sensitive drag control. Although built as a fly reel it has found favour with coarse fishermen, who use it for trotting. For this, the drag should be set so that the reel revolves with the current's pull. For 'laying-on' (float fishing but with about 18in of line on the bottom, which gives a clear bite indication) or 'stret-pegging' (again setting the float higher than the depth of the water and casting the tackle into a groundbaited area) the setting should not allow the line to pay out too freely and so tangle.

The multiplier reel

The multiplier is essentially a reel with a small-diameter drum geared to a ratio of 3 or 4:1 so that line is retrieved rapidly by winding. Models with automatic gears are available, but are far more expensive. These have ratios of about 2½ and 4½:1. As with the fixed-spool reel, there is a wide variety.

To the beginner the multiplier may appear complicated. But you should become familiar with its star-drag, brake and other parts before going fishing with it. Most multipliers are right-handed and cannot be adapted for left-handers.

The main problem with the multiplier reel is that of the line over-running and tangling into 'bird's nests'. To reduce the possibility of this, whether when lowering the bait over the side of a

A rare wooden starback centrepin reel, used for deep sea fishing in the Shetlands.

boat and down to the sea-bed or casting up to 100 yards from the shore, the thumb must rest gently on the line as it pays out. Various devices have been incorporated by manufacturers in some of their models to overcome this difficulty. These include spool tensioners, centrifugal governors, oil 'drag' retarders and 'lift' and 'brake' gadgets, but bird's nests can be avoided by the angler if he learns how to use his reel properly.

The more expensive multipliers have ball bearings set in both end-plates. Leading from one spindle is a governing mechanism, usually consisting of fibre blocks, which are thrown outwards by centrifugal force, thus acting as a brake when the bait hits the water. To stop the line from running with the weight while casting, a manual brake on the side of the reel can be employed. Another feature of superior reels is a 'line-spreader', which ensures the even distribution of line on recovery.

The mechanism of the freshwater multiplier is extremely delicate, and

sand, dust, and, worse still, salt-water, are to be avoided at all costs. The heavier saltwater models still need to be kept clean and oiled, but they are usually rust-proof. Unlike other reels, which are fixed to the underside of the rod handle, the multiplier is used with the rod reversed and the reel uppermost.

Maintenance

It is essential after each outing to rinse the reel thoroughly in freshwater and, after drying it, to apply a recommended lubricant, especially if the reel is not to be used again for some time. Periodical inspection is also advisable, for sand or grit in the gears can wreak havoc and a jammed reel while playing a strong fish is an event no angler wants to experience.

The multiplier used in pike fishing will, with practice, allow baits, spinners and plugs to be cast as far as with a fixed-spool model. As a bonus, playing fish on a drum reel, which demands special skills, can be a real delight.

Remember, too, that sea water is a very corrosive liquid. It will soon cause rusting on most metals.

183

Nylon line

Popular with both freshwater and sea fishermen, nylon line is strong, long lasting and dependable. But it does have its drawbacks and needs to be handled with care

Fishing line is one of the most sophisticated and important items of tackle. For many years anglers had to use lines of such materials as braided flax or silk, with a hook link of gut made from the stretched silk-glands of the silkworm. No other material suitable for a hook line could be made in sufficient lengths for use as a continuous line, and no material which was made in lengths of over about 15 yards was fine or strong enough. The invention of nylon in the 1930s and its subsequent development gave anglers a tool suited to the job.

Artificial silk

An angler writing in 1949, having tried the 'new' line for the first time, said that the monofilament he had bought had increased his casting distances amazingly. It had enabled him to catch 34 perch up to 2lb using spinners tied to 5½lb b.s. nylon.

Nylon was first developed as an artificial silk, imitating its molecular structure, but capable of manufacture in much greater quantities than could be produced by the silkworm.

This was achieved by joining simple molecules into long 'chains'. The addition of other elements can be used to change the structure of the nylon, so producing different physical properties.

Monofilament line

Nylon monofilament line, the kind used by most anglers, is manufactured by first drawing the nylon into a thread while in a semi-molten state and then straightening out the molecular chains by drawing it out a second time. Its value to the angler lies in its great strength, fineness, and resistance to kinking. All these qualities are supplemented by nylon's natural elasticity.

Nylon line has the property of absorbing between 3 and 13 per cent of its own weight of water. This has the effect of decreasing the breaking strain, in some cases by 10 per cent.

Another advantage is that it deteriorates very slowly, if at all, even with frequent use. There used to be a suspicion that if not stored in the dark, nylon tended to weaken quickly because of the ultra-violet

rays in daylight. Certainly the lower breaking strains of line, up to about 3lb, were likely to snap very easily after a season's fishing. But it is debatable whether this was due to continued strain or ultra-violet light. Another boon to anglers is that nylon line does not need stripping off the reel and drying after use, a tiresome chore for users of silk.

It should be mentioned that the elasticity which aids strength also has a definite disadvantage in that a strike is softened by the line stretching, especially if it is of low breaking strain. This must be borne in mind and a strike over long distance made correspondingly forceful if the fish is not to be missed. Braided nylon, which stretches less, is sometimes used in sea fishing to overcome this difficulty.

When nylon is retrieved onto the spool under pressure, as when playing a large fish or drawing a heavy specimen up through perhaps 30 fathoms of heavy sea, it winds back very tightly, especially with a multiplier reel. After fishing, the line should be wound at normal speed onto another reel, for if left on the first it can distort the spool and ruin the reel.

It is also worthwhile to wind off your line occasionally and then wind it back onto the spool, making sure that it is distributed evenly. When tying hooks directly to your nylon, be careful to remember that one of the properties of nylon is that the old-fashioned 'granny knot' will not hold.

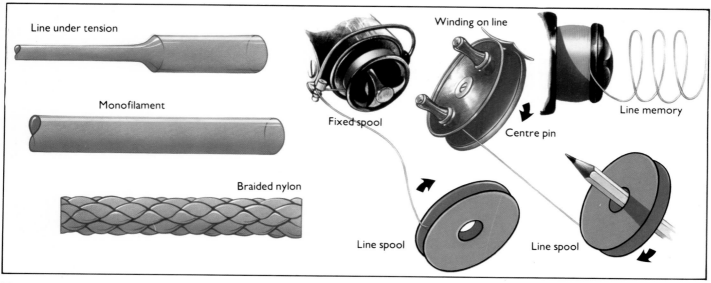

Line under tension

Monofilament

Braided nylon

Winding on line

Fixed spool

Centre pin

Line memory

Line spool

Line spool

Braided line

Braided line can be easily knotted without slipping, it is easy to wind from the spool on to the reel, it is strong, robust and long lasting. But it does have its drawbacks

Braided lines are twisted from polyester fibre, a synthetic substance manufactured from raw materials which include coal, water and petroleum. It is the petroleum ingredient that in part accounts for the steady rise in price of this line over the past few years. Like monofilament, the polyester fibre is extruded under pressure, but any similarity ends here.

Braided lines are soft, pliable, and can be purchased in continuous lengths of up to 1,000 yards. Unlike monofilament, however, the line is not translucent. Nor is it now manufactured in breaking strains of less than 10lb—a great loss to the angling world. In the sizes sold, its circumference is greater than that of monofilament, and it naturally follows that less line can be wound on to a normal reel which is, of course a severe disadvantage.

The stretch problem
Every angler who has tried to pull his hook free from a snag will vouch for the fact that monofilament line stretches astronomically under pressure. In fact, it stretches by 17 to 80 per cent, depending on its method of manufacture. Overstretching leads to distortion in the line's shape, and causes permanent weakness, often over considerable distances. In use, the braided line will only stretch a maximum of 10 per cent, and only does this in the period immediately before breaking occurs. Thus the risk of permanent damage is small.

This almost complete lack of stretch is a great help in preventing line from jamming on the spool of your reel, where a direct pull with monofilament line can often force

one strand under others below it and bring the whole reel to a halt.

Undoubtedly, it is the stretch factor that has endeared the braided line to anglers who need a strong and reliable line for really hard work.

Terylene and Dacron lines
It must be noted that braided Terylene and Dacron lines are not suitable for general boat fishing. Their large diameter (even in the lowest breaking strains) and the considerable amount of water the materials absorb, means the boat angler must use much heavier weights than with monofilament. This is especially true when a bait must be kept in one place, hard on the bottom. Such is the material's resistance to moving water that a neap tide will cause the line to 'belly'

out. This has the immediate effect of putting the angler out of touch with the fish. When a spring tide is running (which at the very minimum means the water is moving at 3 to 4 knots) a braided line's resistance is sufficient to lift 2lb or more of weight away from the bottom, and shift your bait many hundreds of yards away from its intended fishing position.

The biggest spring tides, which in many places around the British Isles create a water speed of at least 7 knots, therefore make it impossible to fish with braided lines.

While monofilament line is incredibly resistant to damage over rough ground, the same is not true of braided lines. They fray very easily, and it is vitally important to examine carefully the final 10ft frequently during a trip. If it shows signs of wear, the suspect length must be cut away.

Unlike the much thinner monofilaments which can be joined very easily, tying lengths of braided line together inevitably results in a large knot, which can jam on the tip ring.

While the initial outlay may cause many anglers to think twice before purchasing a braided line, there is a strong case for its use as a longterm money-saver.

Three popular brands of braided line. Though versatile, those made of Terylene or Dacron are not suitable for boat fishing.

Knots

For every angling occasion there is a wide range of knots to choose from. Knowing which knot to use and when is an indispensable skill which every angler should master

Thirty years ago you might have seen an angler attaching a hook with deceptive ease. He would have been using cotton, silk or flax lines with a short gut cast. A clove hitch in rope or yarn can be quite loose but, strained, it tightens upon itself and holds fast. Nylon lines are far more elastic, flexible and slippery than the older fibres and an untightened nylon knot, especially if not designed for this material, will begin to slip as soon as strain is exerted upon it.

With the advent of nylon monofilament and braided lines, many anglers had trouble with knots coming adrift, but the manufacturers soon designed several basic knots and loops for attaching hooks, for interconnections and for joining two lines of different thickness (with or without droppers). Anglers played some part in developing and making up knots for this exciting new material and now hardly anything else is used for fishing lines.

Choice of knots

For each occasion there is a choice of knot. The angler selects not merely for strength but also for ease of tying at a particular moment. For example, towards evening, in half-light, you could still manage a tucked half blood or a blood bight but might hesitate to try a two-circle turle or a dropper knot. In considering the knot-strength it is also essential to take account of the difference between the dry breaking strain of the line quoted by the manufacturer and the actual, wet breaking strain (b.s.) of the nylon in water. Something like a 10 per cent loss should be allowed for and since the knot is the weakest link in the tackle, the number of knots should be the fewest possible.

The specimen hunter prefers to have only one such weak link. He slips floats, shots and other attachments straight on to the reel line, fastening his hook at the bottom. Not for him the minor pleasure of catching small fish: he puts all his hopes on having the right bait in the right place at the right time so that when his big fish does take the bait the chances of loss are minimized.

But this is not a typical fishing situation. Trout anglers find it necessary to use casts that taper from a high breaking strain and diameter down to the finest one suitable for the water being fished. To make up such a cast, three, four, or even five dropper knots are required, although only one knot may actually have a dropper attached. Such knots must be very carefully tied and tested if the angler is to have real confidence in his tackle when a big trout takes.

Match fishermen also have to come to terms with many-knotted tackle. They need to catch as many

Knots can be the weak link in your tackle. A good fish may be lost if this Grey Wulff is not tied correctly to the leader.

KNOTS FOR HOOKS, SWIVELS, SPINNERS, ETC.

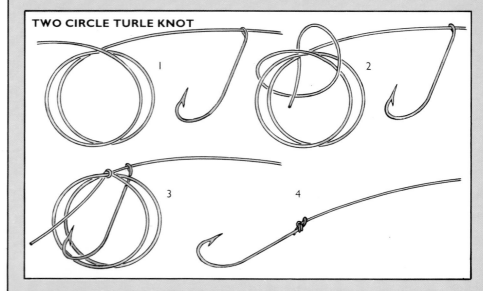

TWO CIRCLE TURLE KNOT

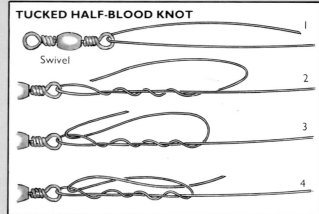

TUCKED HALF-BLOOD KNOT

Swivel

Above: 1 Thread hook up cast, make circle, over lay with another. **2** Push ends through loops, forming a slip knot. **3** Tighten, push hook and working end through circles. **4** Pull tight, snip off free end.
Right: 1 End through eye. **2** Twist four times round line. **3** and **4** Pass end through main loop, pull taut then snip off the end.

KNOTS

Universal

Hook snood

Spade whip

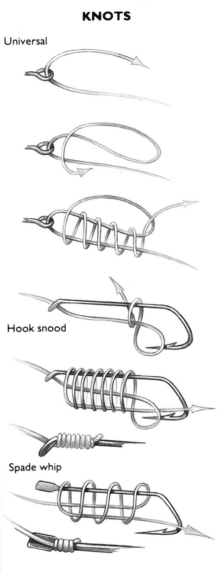

Right: 1 Pass the line through the eye and lay along the shank. **2** Make eight turns over the loop so formed, passing end through loop. **3** Pull taut, snipping off the loose end.

Below: 1 Lay a loop along the shank, holding hook. **2** Make a turn round the shank over end of hook. **3** Make a further turn, crossing firmly over first. **4** Add five or more successive turns along the shank towards the point. **5** Pull through.

DOMHOF KNOT

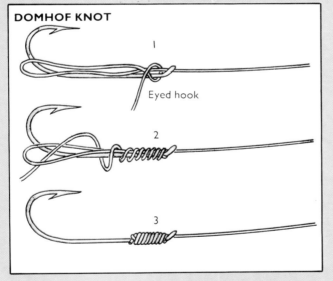

Eyed hook

1

2

3

WHIPPING KNOT (SPADE END)

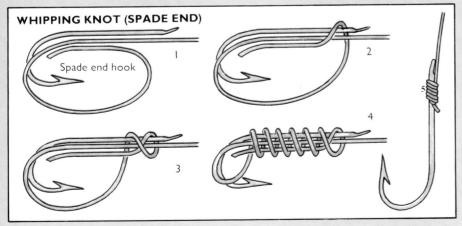

Spade end hook

1

2

3

4

5

Top: *This is a variant of the Universal Loop shown on the next page. In this knot the aim is to secure an eyed hook to nylon. It is probably the most often used knot wherever anglers tie their hooks direct to the reel line.*

Centre: *The Hook snood is a knot that provides a secure attachment to nylon line when fishing with larger hooks. It has the effect of creating a straight line from shank to nylon ensuring that the line drawn from nylon through the hook shank is continuous.*

Above: *The Spade Whip, also shown in greater detail on the left, is the answer to tying spade ended hooks. The harder the pull on the hook the tighter it grips. It is going out of favour now.*

Coarse tackle

fish as possible, big, small or indifferent, in the alloted time and swim. Should the day begin with small roach or bleak, ultra-fine float tackes may be needed but when a neighbour lands (or maybe loses) a 2lb bream, the match man must be prepared to switch tackles at a moment's notice. In order not to waste valuable time, he usually carries a number of casts of different breaking strains and shotting, with floats for different purposes made up ready on his cast winders. These generally have a loop at the top: with a similar loop at the end of the reel-line, he can substitute the whole cast and be fishing again in minutes.

Anglers fishing in snag ridden waters will use several knots on the line. The main cast with floats and shots may be on 4lb line, but the final 18in of hook-line will be attached with 2lb or 3lb line. In the event of a bad obstruction on the bottom, only the hook line will be lost.

The knots illustrated have now withstood the test of time and can be relied upon for all nylon lines, braided, twisted or monofilament. It is important to make them up properly and to give them a quick test before use, by holding the hook between finger and thumb and giving the nylon a sharp pull.

Whipping—reliable for nylon
The whipping that is illustrated deserves special mention because it is the traditional method used by sailors to whip rope ends but, provided at least five turns are made, it is completely reliable for nylon. It may look difficult but it is easier to tie than to describe or illustrate. A little practice with a piece of string whipped on a pencil stem will soon bring confidence. When using this whipping on a spade-end hook, nimble fingers and good eyesight are valuable assets. Early attempts should be tested by inserting the hook-point into a piece of wood and giving the free end of the line a couple of pulls.

The water knot is a development of the double overhand loop. Instead of forming the knot on the bight of line to make a loop, it is made on the married shorter ends of the two lines to be fastened.

KNOTS FOR FORMING LOOPS

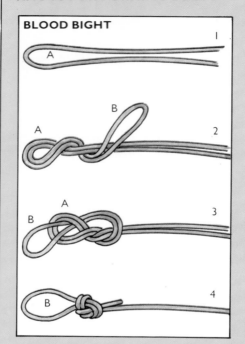

BLOOD BIGHT

Above: Blood bight, a simple knot tied in four stages and used to make loops in fly fishing leaders and sea fishing.

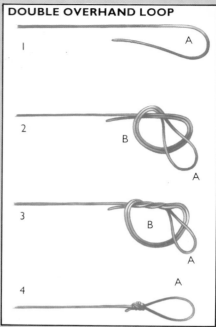

DOUBLE OVERHAND LOOP

Above: Form two knots A and B and pass A through B. Twist A around line and through B again, working knot tight.

Right: The Universal Loop. A popular knot with freshwater anglers for tying snoods. Double a length of line, wind round three times, then pass the loop through the eye of the hook, wind round and pull through.

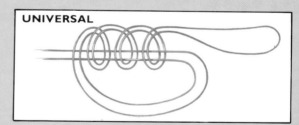

UNIVERSAL

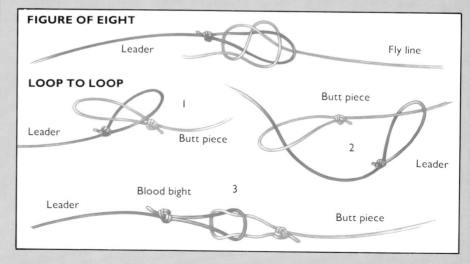

FIGURE OF EIGHT

LOOP TO LOOP

Top: The figure of eight knot will not jam as an overhand knot tends to.

Above: When tying loops make sure they are long—they will cause less jamming.

DROPPER KNOTS AND KNOTS FOR JOINING LENGTHS OF LINE

DOUBLE FOUR LOOP BLOODKNOT

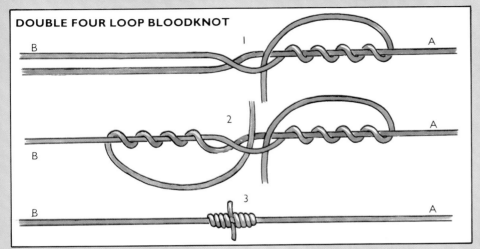

Left: Dropper or Double Four Loop bloodknot. Similar to the blood loop dropper knot, this ties two strands of nylon together neatly. **Below:** The Water Knot is useful for tying a leader containing one or more droppers. **1** Hold the ends so that there is an overlap. Draw the two ends together to form a loop. **2** Pull the right hand end through the loop from behind making an overhand knot. **3** Repeat this four times, then pull tight.

When used for making a dropper, the fly is fastened to the stalk which runs towards the rod. Because the lie of the dropper opposes the pull of the line, the fly will stand out from the leader.

BLOOD LOOP DROPPER

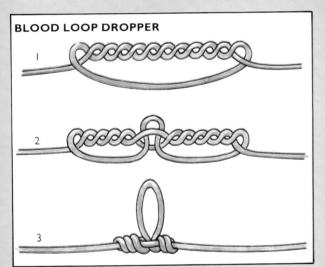

WATER KNOT

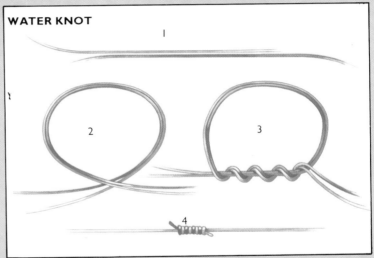

Above: Blood Loop Dropper Knot. **1** Form a circle with long overlapping ends, twist the ends round the circle, making ten smaller ones. **2** Enlarge the centre and push original circle back through. **3** Pull on the ends to tighten, holding finger in loop to prevent it slipping.

Right: Universal Knot, a popular, all-purpose knot. The loose ends may be cut off or one end left loose to make a dropper. Leader Knots and Heavy Duty Leader Knots are useful when beachcasting. After tying, all knots should be wetted before slowly tightened.

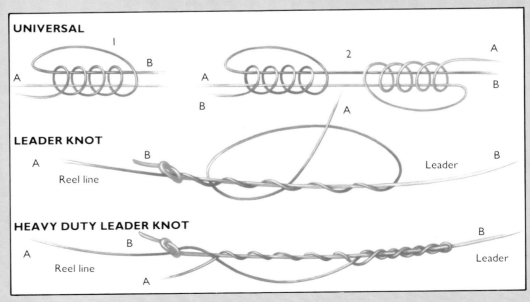

UNIVERSAL

LEADER KNOT

HEAVY DUTY LEADER KNOT

Freshwater hooks

The best fish are never the ones that are caught, but those that got away. This needn't be so, though, if you take the time and trouble to select the right kind of hook for the fish you want

Hooks are the most important items of an angler's tackle and yet, all too often, they are not chosen with enough care. Admittedly the range of hooks available is bewildering to the beginner, but in order to enjoy consistent success a reliable hook is indispensable.

Categories of hooks
Freshwater hooks fall into three categories: eyed, spade-end and ready

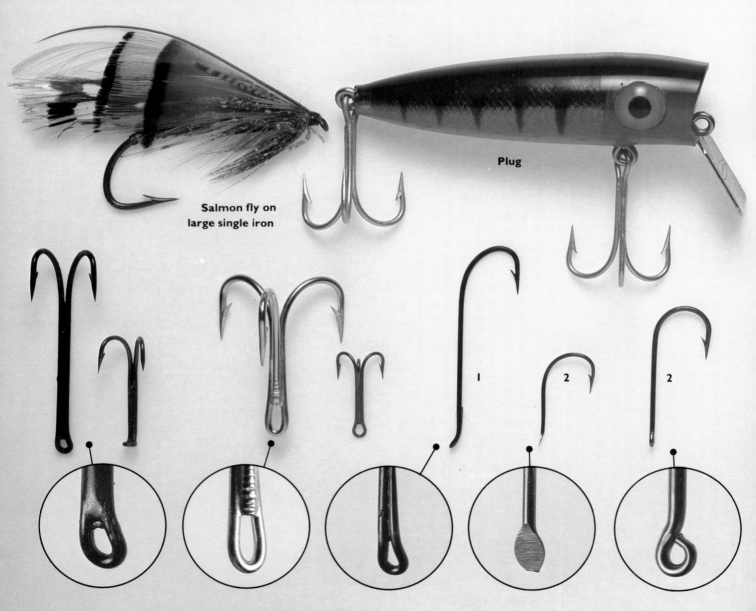

Salmon fly on large single iron

Plug

Double eye
A double hook. This hook has a japanned finish, which gives it good protection against rusting.

Needle or oblong eye
Needle eyes such as this are often used by anglers who wish to make up neat traces for pike fishing

Looped eye
A typical looped eye. This is the type of eye which is widely used on low water single salmon hooks.

Spade end
Also known as the flatted shank, this hook is useful where a neat junction of hook to nylon is required.

Tapered eye
A tapered eye on a hook with a bronzed finish. Bronzing is generally better than japanning.

tied to nylon. The first are tied to the line by the angler, who can use a variety of knots. The important thing is to be sure the knot holds, as this can easily be the weak point in your tackle which will fail when most needed. Spade-end hooks, as the name suggests, are flattened at the top end and are whipped to nylon using the method illustrated or some other reliable method. Ready tied hooks are bought already whipped to a short length of line, nowadays nylon.

There are many variations as to bend, length of shank and so on, but these are mainly variations on the three main kinds of hook. Double and treble hooks are mounted on plugs and spinners for pike, perch, chub, trout, salmon and zander. Stewart tackles comprise two single hooks set a couple of inches apart.

There is a further category of hook, the gorge hook, whose use is illegal in Britain. This is simply a straight hook, pointed at both ends. Inserted sideways in deadbait, when swal- lowed by a fish it becomes firmly lodged in the stomach.

The basic requirements
The essential requirements of a hook are the same for all kinds. It should be well-tempered and thin in the body (or 'wire'); the point and barb should be sharp; the barb should be set close to the point and not stand out at too great an angle from the body.

The thickness of the 'wire' is very important. The weight of a thick hook can cause a bait, especially a

1 The Limerick bend. Note the rather sharp angle of the bend.

2 Often used with lobworm bait, the round bend has a wide 'gape'.

3 The Viking is simply a Mustad trade name for one of their hooks.

4 The Sproat bend is similar to the Limerick but rounder in shape.

5 Crystal bend, used mainly with maggots.
6 The Sneck bend is squarer than most.

Barbless point
Though demanding a tight line, barbless points make unhooking easier.

Hollow point
Note how straight the outer edge is in comparison with the other hooks.

Curved-in point
The point of this hook curves inwards towards the shank.

Dublin point
This one curves outwards, away from the shank of the hook.

Turned-down eye
See turned-up eye.

Ball eye
When using ball eye hooks, make sure that the ball is closed or the hook may leave the line.

Straight eye
A Viking hook with a straight eye (also known as a ring eye) The eye is set in line with the shank.

Straight bend
A straight bend. Note how the point runs parallel to the shank of the hook; this is not always the case.

Kirbed bend
The point is offset to the right with the hook held bend downwards and the point facing you.

Turned-up eye
A turned-up, as opposed to a turned-down, eye is turned away from the point.

Right: *The technical terms for the various parts of a hook, and the cross-section of a regular hook compared with that of the flatter, stronger forged hook.*

light one such as maggot or caster, to sink too quickly when 'freelining' — using no float but allowing the bait to sink naturally down to the fish. An additional disadvantage of a hook that is too thick is that it can burst a bait instead of entering it cleanly.

Before using a hook, test the temper of the wire. Under pressure it should bend but not remain bent, and it certainly should not snap. To test it, hold the hook by the shank and pull just above the point with pliers.

Barbs

The barb is most often the trouble-spot in a hook. Most are cut too deep (stand out too far from the body), which causes weakness at that point. This, coupled with the common fault of the barb being set too far from the point, means that undue force is required to drive home both point and barb, sometimes causing the line to break. If the strike is less forceful, a hook of this sort will not fully penetrate the fish's skin, particularly if it is a hard-boned and tough-skinned species like the pike, perch or barbel. A big, deeply-cut barb may look effective but is not.

The eyes on eyed hooks should be examined. The size of the eye will depend on the gauge of the hook but always try to pick one which will just take the thickness of the line you intend to use — there is no point in having a gaping, obtrusive eye which causes the hook to hang from the line at an odd angle.

Shanks

The length of the shank is important where some baits are concerned. For crust, paste, lobworms and sweetcorn a long shank is best; for maggots a short one. For casters, the variety with a long shank, known as a 'caster hook', is favoured. It should be remembered, however, that the longer the shank relative to the eye, the smaller will be the angle of penetration. This means that the hook will penetrate more easily but to a lesser depth. With short-shanked hooks it takes a stronger strike but the hook

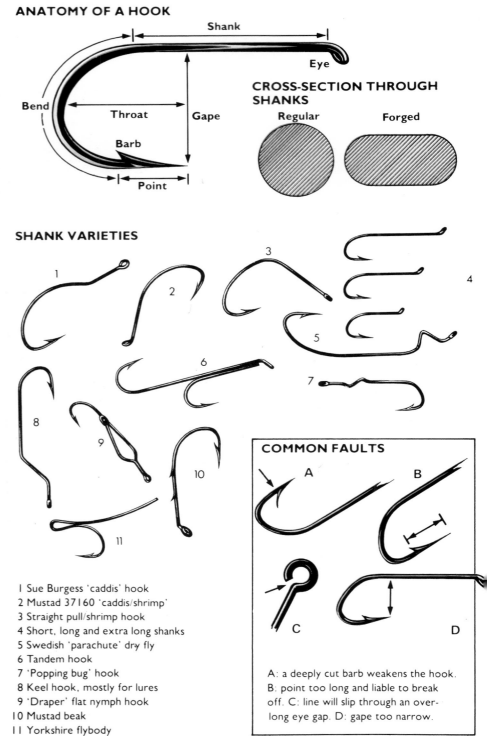

ANATOMY OF A HOOK

Shank, Eye, Bend, Throat, Gape, Barb, Point

CROSS-SECTION THROUGH SHANKS

Regular   Forged

SHANK VARIETIES

1 Sue Burgess 'caddis' hook
2 Mustad 37160 'caddis/shrimp'
3 Straight pull/shrimp hook
4 Short, long and extra long shanks
5 Swedish 'parachute' dry fly
6 Tandem hook
7 'Popping bug' hook
8 Keel hook, mostly for lures
9 'Draper' flat nymph hook
10 Mustad beak
11 Yorkshire flybody

COMMON FAULTS

A: a deeply cut barb weakens the hook. B: point too long and liable to break off. C: line will slip through an over-long eye gap. D: gape too narrow.

will drive home deeper.

Hooks to nylon should always be treated with caution. First, see whether the whipping reaches the top of the shank. On some hooks it is too short, thus causing the hook to turn over when making contact with a fish and preventing proper penetration.

Make sure that there is sufficient varnish on the whipping, as if there is too little the whipping may fall apart (eyed and spade end hooks do not require varnished whipping). Check the loop at the end of the trace. If it is not straight it has been tied badly and may be unreliable.

Shots and shotting

Split shot is one of the principal forms of weight used in freshwater fishing. The correct choice and use of shot will make a great contribution to the success of your angling.

Shot or split-shot: what does it mean to the average angler? Probably not very much. But these humble pieces of lead substitute do so many things: they help in casting and presenting the bait correctly, they carry the main responsibility for bite-detection and can on many occasions act as a substitute for a float.

Let us first consider the shot itself: what you need, how to care for it and its basic uses. Many years ago, shot was kept in sacks behind tackle shop counters. Anglers bought it by the ounce or pound. Nowadays it comes pre-packed in a variety of containers and dispensers. The author's preference is for the plastic tray with slide-on lid, moulded to provide compartments for eight different sizes of shot. Apart from a pack of micro-dust, this holds all the sizes of shot that are likely to be needed for an average day's fishing—Nos 8 (commonly known as 'Dust'), 5, 4, 3, 1, BB, AAA and the largest, swan shot. There are more, but they will not be considered here.

Quality of shot

No matter what its size, or how packed, it is the quality of the shot that counts. The shot must be soft enough to open and close easily to make alteration of terminal tackle a quick and simple operation. It should be soft enough to be pinched onto the line, with emphasis on the word 'pinched'! If you have to squeeze it very hard or even bite on it with your teeth or use pliers then it is too hard. Having to force the halves together can—and very often does—damage the line as the edges of the shot are closed. Also, shot that is too hard cannot be prised open again without breaking it. Ideally it should open so easily that it can be moved on the line when necessary and just pinched tight again by hand in the new position.

Never slide shot in its 'pinched' state up and down the line. Sliding tight shot creates tremendous heat. Try putting, say, a swan shot on a length of 6lb b.s. line—run it up and down very quickly and you will literally feel the heat that has been generated. Open the shot, move it and pinch it shut again.

You can improve on the basic split-shot which you buy. For example, chamfer the edges of the split to take away any sharp edges that may damage the line, and to make it easier to insert the thumb-nail to open the shot when removing it at the end of a day's fishing.

Shotting patterns vary with methods, and this feature is designed to show how the proper use of shot can help your fishing. At a fishing match in Northern Ireland, for example, a pole float was used which carried three No. 4 shot. This proved to be too light for the existing conditions; a float with a cork 'collar' mounted on it was chosen instead, converting it to a three-AA-carrying float. With the three No. 4 shot the bait was probably taking six seconds to reach the bottom. Not a significant change you might think, but in fact that shotting change resulted in 800 fish being caught, creating a new world match record.

Allowing for the fact that fish were not caught on every cast, it can be said that there was a saving of two seconds per fish. That works out

| SPLIT SHOT (actual size) | SSG | AAA | BB | 1 | 3 | 4 | 5 | 6 | 7 | 8 |

at a total saving of 1,600 seconds, or 26½ minutes. No one can afford to lose 26½ minutes in a match, yet thousands of anglers must do so every week by not realizing the full value of shot.

If the shotting is too light it just cannot do the vital job of emphasizing bites. Irish anglers fishing the Newry Canal and using sliding-floats with dust shot as a 'tell-tale' were getting their baits mangled without seeing the bite. The solution was not to fine down, but to use heavier shotting.

Get the bait down quickly
The explanation is simple. Fishing in deep water requires quite a bit of weight to get the bait down reasonably quickly. This is the job of the bulk shot which, on a slider, can be anything up to three or even four swan shot. So the float has to be bulky. With a light weight the float will not react either as quickly or as positively as with a heavy one. The effect of the fish lifting that dust shot was too small to be detectable by the anglers. When they hit upon the answer to the problem they put a BB near the hook as a tell-tale. This gave obvious unmissable 'lift' bites, with the float rising as the fish takes the weight of the shot with the bait.

Copy the falling rate
Casters thrown in as feed must all be 'sinkers', that is, taken and stored soon after they cast. Those we use on the hook are the darker 'floaters'. The art is to copy, perfectly if possible, the falling rate and action of the loose-fed caster. This is something you can try out and prove in the bathroom at home. Throw in a few

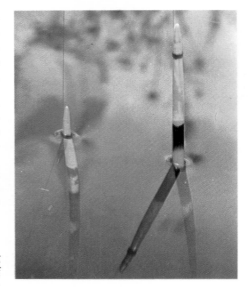

Above: *When the lift method is being used, the float will sit well down in the water if it is correctly shotted.*

casters and watch them sink; now try putting a fine wire hook, size 20, in one of the sinkers. You will notice the difference in rate of descent. This is also somehow recognized by the fish. Now repeat the test with a floating caster on the hook. Again, you will see a difference, but by balancing your terminal tackle with micro-micro dust you should be able to achieve a rate of descent of your bait so similar that it will be accepted by 90 per cent of the fish.

Lead and swan fatalities
In the early 1980's controversy surrounded the contention that lead shot used by anglers was swallowed

Below: *Three useful shot patterns—methods of grouping split shot on the line between the float and the hook.*

by swans, leading to their deaths by lead poisoning.

Anglers protested vehemently that the accusations were not founded on fact and not proven. A counter argument was that one 12-bore cartridge as used for game bird shooting, wild fowl, duck, pigeon, and so on carried as much shot as twenty anglers will use in a day.

In October 1983 the National Anglers' Council (NAC) issued a statement on the subject, basing it on the Report of the Nature Conservancy Council's (NCC) Working Group on Lead Poisoning in Swans, published in 1981. This report recommended that lead shot should be phased out by 1986, urging that research into alternatives be undertaken. At the same time, the National Commission on Environmental Pollution, investigating a wide spectrum of lead in the environment, also came to the conclusion that lead in angling be replaced.

Angling's main representative, the NAC, were party to the NCC's working group along with the National Federation of Anglers and the fishing tackle industry. They collectively supported the ultimate phasing out of lead shot but had strong reservations about the true extent of swan fatalities due to anglers' discarded or used lead shot.

A Code of Conduct was formulated by the NAC and circulated among freshwater anglers. At the same time the NAC pointed out that the amount of lead deposited in the environment by anglers was about one **fifth of the amount published in the figures alleged in 1981.**

It has been possible to avoid using lead since substitutes were introduced in response to the Control Pollution (Anglers' Lead Weights) Regulations 1986. This made it illegal to import or sell any lead weight for freshwater fishing unless it weighed less than 0.06 grams or more than 28.35 grams. Lead may still be used in the core of a line, swimfeeders, self-cocking floats and fishing flies.

Lead substitutes can be used for float fishing of all kinds, pole fishing, swimfeeder weighting, ledgering or plumbing. They should solve this unfortunate problem.

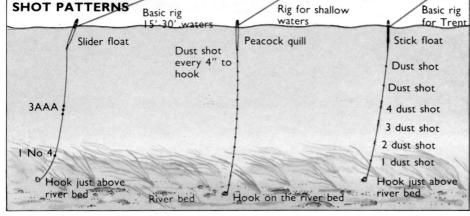

SHOT PATTERNS

Basic rig 15'-30' waters
Slider float
Dust shot every 4" to hook
3AAA
1 No 4
Hook just above river bed
River bed

Rig for shallow waters
Peacock quill
Hook on the river bed

Basic rig for Trent
Stick float
Dust shot
Dust shot
4 dust shot
3 dust shot
2 dust shot
1 dust shot
Hook just above river bed

Catapults

The principle is simple—to throw loosefeed accurately into a distant swim. But to maximize power and accuracy, these simple items have evolved into quite sophisticated tools

The best groundbait in the world is useless unless it can be accurately placed into the swim that the angler is fishing. Where his selected swim is close in to the bank he is sitting on, it is a simple matter to estimate the speed of the stream and then throw the bait, by hand, towards the head of the swim so that it will be carried down into it. But where the swim is some distance away—under the opposite bank for instance—difficulties will arise, more especially if the groundbait cannot be pressed into a heavy ball. For these the catapult is an excellent solution.

The fishing catapult has made its appearance as an angling aid in the last few years and is now available in various designs, both good and bad.

Right shape for accuracy

Too big is better than too small, and this particularly applies to the spacing of the forks themselves. A large 'U'-shape, with the ends of the forks turning slightly outwards will give the greatest accuracy. The elastic should be secured through holes at the fork ends, either by a large knot (which makes for easy replacement) or by crimped metal tubes. The elastic should be soft and able to return to its original length after stretching. Before buying elastic flex it once or twice to ensure that its pull is within your capability. The cup into which the bait is placed should be rigid and have a large, well-shaped flange at the rear which enables you to keep a firm grip when it is pulled back.

While most anglers are well aware of what a catapult can do, it is sensible to know its limitations before starting to use one. It cannot place large amounts of groundbait at any one time, nor can it manage very heavy baits such as saturated and stiffened cereals with any degree of accuracy. It will not cope with extremely light cereal baits—the spring of the elastic and forward propulsion make it break up in mid-air and scatter over a wide area. It is most successful with pellet and grain baits, which include maggots, casters, hemp, wheat, tares and so on. These should be kept damp or, in the case of cereals, wet. This will provide the weight and 'cling' needed to keep the bait intact.

The purpose, once the cup of the catapult is loaded, is to drop the bait into the swim by means of a gentle curve through the air.

A final word of warning concerns the temptation to hold the catapult at face level and to sight along the elastic and through the fork. Should the elastic break or pull free (and this happens) the result can only be face or eye injuries. It is essential to keep the cup with its load well down below the face and to keep the forks on a level with it. Then if anything should break, only the body will receive the impact.

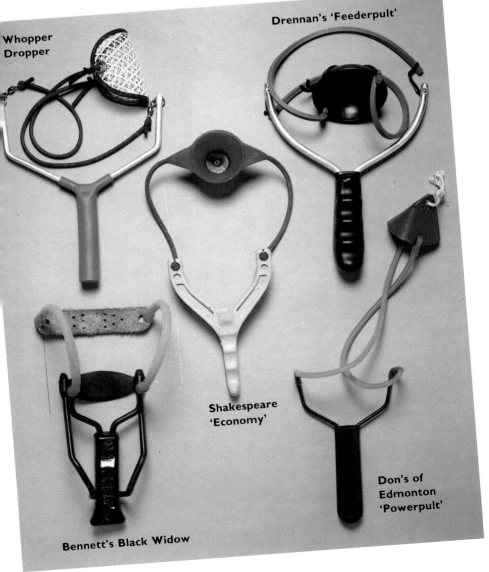

Whopper Dropper

Drennan's 'Feederpult'

Shakespeare 'Economy'

Don's of Edmonton 'Powerpult'

Bennett's Black Widow

A variety of catapults showing the different cups available for such differing groundbaits as maggots, dough, particle baits, potatoes, breadpaste, black magic and high protein.

195

Swivels

While a twisted line cannot be completely eradicated by a swivel—even when used in conjunction with an anti-kink weight or vane—it may save you the catch of a lifetime

One of the most useful, but most neglected accessories for the angler is the swivel. It is primarily used to prevent fishing line from becoming twisted, and whether the angler employs any of the various forms of spinning, or merely retrieves a dead-bait, the turning action of the bait spiralling through the water will be transferred to the line. If monofilament is allowed to twist, it begins to kink, and at best becomes a tangled mess—at worst the line weakens so badly that it will most likely break at the first strain.

The only preventative is the use of one or more efficient swivels mounted between the line and lure, working in conjunction with an anti-kink weight or vane. Such devices are attached to the reel line by means of a bloodknot or grinner knot. But efficiency is difficult to achieve in a swivel. Early traces had two, three or more swivels, operating on the principle that the more that were added, the better the chance of at least one working. Those early mechanisms were in the form of an open, oblong box with eyes mounted through each end. A little corrosion or rust plus an accumulation of grit and mud quickly impaired their efficiency.

Different types of swivel
Today, the angler has the choice of several types of swivel, all working on the same basic principle but with varying refinements. The plain barrel swivel is the most popular and probably the tackle dealer's best seller especially since many anglers simply ask for 'a swivel' and leave the choice to the assistant. Its construction is simple, with two eyes (through which trace and line are mounted) allowed to revolve independently on their separate beads of metal carefully shaped to fit the inside of the barrel. The free rotation

of the eyes depends on tolerances left when the thin metal is compressed during machining; nine times out of ten, the tolerances are adequate and the swivel revolves freely. The tenth case is where trouble sets in, and before leaving the shop it is worth checking each swivel that is purchased, and again before fishing.

An improvement on the plain barrel is the American Berkley swivel. It differs only in that a good grade of metal is used and the eyes are flattened slghtly at the terminal ends to ensure that trace and line stay in place, free from a natural tendency to pull to either side when an unequal strain is applied. An improvement in efficiency which costs little more, is the Hardy ball-bearing swivel. Again, there is the barrel type of construction but with exacting tolerances and incorporating small ball-races that ensure that the eyed pieces revolve freely.

One swivel remains in this category—the Diamond swivel, in which the loops are not round but diamond-shaped and are fastened by means of an expanded link. Usually manufactured from fine steel, they appear rather flimsy, but in fact are equal in strength to other types. They are considerably lighter and rarely jam.

Swivels for freshwater fishing are usually made of brass or blued steel, and if you have any choice it is better to purchase the steel ones because they are harder and last longer before wearing out. Brass, a much softer metal, suffers from wear and tear quite quickly. Neither brass nor ordinary steel are used in sea swivels as salt water is particularly corrosive to these metals, and stainless steel is now more commonly used.

Sea water is very abrasive too, because of the particles of sand suspended in it, so the rather open

construction of a barrel swivel will allow sand to enter and cause damage to the moving parts. This is not very important if the swivels are bought cheaply and thrown away after use, as is often the case with sea anglers who fish for the smaller, weaker species around our coastline, so that it is not too serious if a swivel jams.

Matters can be very different if you are fishing for big conger eels, skate, or shark. And the angler who is lucky enough to fish for such hard-fighting, powerful species as marlin, or broadbill swordfish, or the very biggest sharks, should never use anything but the very best tackle, —including swivels which are engineering marvels.

These swivels are made of stainless steel or a really hard alloy not affected by sea water. All moving parts are machined to very fine tolerances, so that it is almost impossible for abrasive particles to enter and will probably be grease-filled as a further protection. Miniature ball-races can be built in to ensure the smoothest possible rotation by minimizing friction, and modern developments have produced swivels which are far in advance of the simple barrel-type device.

Ball-bearing swivels
Ball-bearing swivels are now being manufactured in England. They bring a new dimension to fishing for the larger species. High quality ball bearings locked into a machined cage of stainless steel ensure that the swivel will not jam, no matter how much pressure is applied. It is the perfect link between reel line and trace when dealing with tough fighters like conger, common skate, porbeagle and mako shark. All that is needed to keep the swivel in first class working order is a drop of sewing machine oil applied periodically through the gap between body and turning eye. This eye is big enough to accept the tough wire needed to combat powerful jaws and teeth.

Pirk fishing over deep water wrecks and, to a lesser extent, snaggy reefs can take a heavy toll of end tackle. With 20-26oz pirks costing up to £4, it is also expensive. A recent solution to the problem is a 'positive poundage link', which can

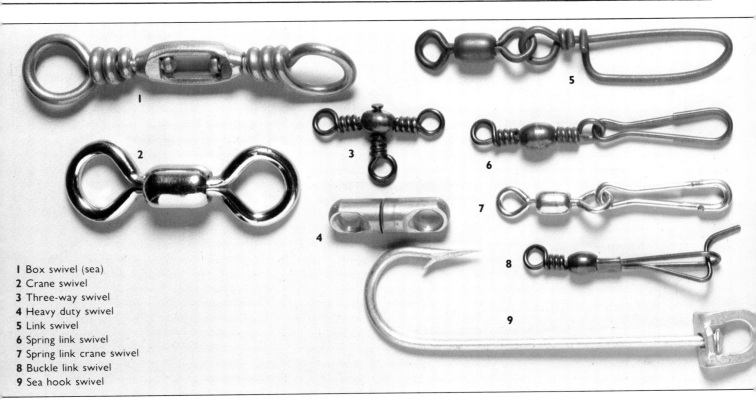

1 Box swivel (sea)
2 Crane swivel
3 Three-way swivel
4 Heavy duty swivel
5 Link swivel
6 Spring link swivel
7 Spring link crane swivel
8 Buckle link swivel
9 Sea hook swivel

be positioned between the body of the pirk and the treble hook. When a hang-up occurs, the link will open under pressure so that only the hook is lost.

The links (which can be swivelled with the aid of split rings) are available in 15, 25 and 45lb breaking strains. The accurate breaking out pressure of the link is achieved by carefully balancing tensile strength in the steel wire to the radius of the hook circlet.

How many swivels to use?

How many swivels should be used when fishing? Generally, the fewer the better; every swivel requires a join either to the line or cast, which weakens it. On most occasions just one is enough, provided that is has been properly maintained and is used with an efficient anti-kink vane. But there are arguable exceptions to this rule. Some would say that the choice depends upon the length of the trace: a short trace needing two swivels, one at each end, while a longer trace needs another built in about the mid-point.

Eels have the habit of spinning in the water, causing severe line twist. Because they also have sharp teeth, it is advisable to make up a number

10 Snap link swivel
11 Snap link diamond eye
12 Buckle link box
13 Don's diamond eye link swivel
14 Hardy's ball-bearing swivel
15 Don's diamond eye
16 Box (freshwater)
17 Barrel swivel
18 Ball bearing with plastic anti-kink vane
19 Barrel swivel with celluloid a.k.v.

of short fine wire traces, with the hook at one end and a swivel at the other. If you slip a ledger weight on to the reel line before tying the hook link on, the swivel acts as the stop and prevents the weight slipping down to the hook.

Necessity of having casting-weight
As for anti-kink weights, since some spinners are too light for efficient casting, the weight added to prevent line-twist also contributes the extra weight needed.

The simple half moon weight folds over the leader and is squeezed firmly into position. The Jardine spiral weight twists on to the line—fine in principle, but prone to untwist at the most inopportune moments. The Hillman weight is a round bullet with a wire clip that fastens to the eye of the swivel above the trace attachment; highly efficient if it were not inclined to catch on every patch of weed, clog up and bring everything to a standstill. The boat-shaped Wye weight, with a wire loop for attaching to the line and a swivel mounted to its other end to take the trace, is also an efficient item but inclined to snag on the bottom or in weed. The answer is to use the anti-kink device best suited to the water.

Swingtips and quivertips

With the vast array of rod tip bite indicators now available it is hardly surprising that the average angler is left baffled about which to choose. Here we suggest some guidelines

Above: *The target shield is a sheet of gridded plastic against which the movements of a tip indicator are more easily seen.*
Left: *A swingtip in action on a ledger rod. It can reduce casting length and efficiency.*

Ledgering was once considered the lazy man's method, a crude, last resort for most anglers. But the invention of effective bite indicators has changed all this. The swingtip in particular has brought that vital touch of refinment to the method. Anglers such as the late Fred Foster have developed into an art form.

Since Jack Clayton first introduced the swingtip to Lincolnshire waters, a host of bite indicators have been invented and sold. Many are efficient, others can only be described as wierd and wonderful—and are often unjustifiably expensive.

Three kinds of indicator
The wide range of bite indicators available to today's angler can be divided into three main categories—swingtips, quivertips (including donkey tops), and butt indicators. Butt indicators are dealt with in *New Fisherman's Handbook* pp 114-116 and this article deals with swingtips and quivertips.

The swingtip is probably the most efficient indicator of them all. It is a piece of cane or light metal, with rings for the line to pass through, which is attached to the rod end by a flexible piece of plastic or rubber.

Pendulum effect
A common fault is that many swingtips are too short. A swingtip of less than 6in in length just cannot do its job properly, as, within practical limits, the longer a swingtip is, the easier it is to obtain a 'pendulum' effect and less effort is required by a fish to produce a detectable movement.

The swingtip does have its drawbacks however. First, and most importantly, it reduces the length of the cast since the energy required to overcome the swingtip's tendency to drop and wag during casting detracts from the force of the cast.

Swingtip resistance
Secondly, the resistance of a swingtip increases immediately following a bite, when it is lifted and more of its weight bears directly on the line. Third, it cannot be used when fishing a river or when the wind is really high. Stiff rubber links or weights added to the tip are favoured by many anglers to beat these conditions, but although many have used them successfully, they do have a tendency to counteract some of the tip's effectiveness.

Virtually weightless action

Nevertheless, given reasonable conditions and no need for long casting, the swingtip is the most sensitive indicator. It is virtually weightless as far as the fish is concerned, and is in direct line of contact with the ledger weight. Only in windy conditions and running waters do the quivertip, or donkey top, really come into their own as indicators.

The quivertip and donkey top are basically the same, except that the donkey top is spliced into the rod tip, while the quivertip is screwed on. Both consist of a piece of solid glassfibre, with a fine, flexible tip, gradually thickening in section towards the base and, naturally, becoming less flexible.

Fished in a river, the flexible quivertip absorbs the force of the current on the line, bending slightly to do so. If a fish moves the bait, it alters the balance of forces between the current and the quivertip so altering the quivertip's position to register a bite.

Increased resistance

The basic drawback of the quivertip is that as tension in the line increases, the tip pulls over, increasing resistance. A great advantage that it has over the swingtip is that casting is virtually unimpaired. There is no evidence of drag on the line once the cast is underway, as the quivertip remains straight and therefore exerts minimum friction on the line.

As quivertips are detachable, they come in different lengths of various thicknesses. For close-range ledgering on a lake or a river with little flow, a short, thin tip is far more effective than the bigger version. The opposite is true when you are trying to fish a heavy swimfeeder at long range on a fast-flowing river, such as the Severn or Trent. A useful pointer when selecting the right tip for the conditions is that the force of the current on the line should result in the tip bending to approximately 30 degrees, any more than this requires a stronger tip, any less a finer, weaker one.

Even so, it has great value, particularly on rivers with a heavy flow, such as the Severn. One revolutionary version of the swingtip is

Above: *Swingtip set to register a bite.*
Inset: *The qivertip under tension. It is ideal for fishing close-to in still ponds.*

even better in rough conditions than the quivertip. It was designed by Eric Antill, an engineer. While the majority of anglers use heavyweight swingtips purely to beat windy conditions, Eric realized that weight in the swingtip could be a positive advantage—even in still conditions.

He made his swingtip out of brass rod which he threaded inside so that additional weights could be screwed in, even though bite indicators are traditionally as light and sensitve as possible. In Eric's rig, however, the weight of the swingtip was balanced against the ledger weight, with the swingtip being slightly heavier.

Irresistible action

The result was that once cast out, the heavy tip made the ledger weight 'creep' along the bottom, giving an action to the bait which was often irresistible. Furthermore, the balance between ledger weight and swingtip was such that any interference with the bait registered as a bite despite the weight of the tip.

Eric's idea has never gone much further, although we have proved that it worked. In particular, he had one or two wins under gale-force conditions when conventional swing-

tipping was virtually impossible.

Springtips

A fairly recent indicator proving increasingly popular among ledger anglers, is the springtip. Obtainable at most tackle shops, matchmen in particular have found it an ideal compromise between the floppy swingtip, and the fairly rigid quivertip. Whereas a swingtip hangs at 90 degrees to the rod, (and therefore reduces the casting range) a springtip remains in line with the rod throughout the cast, limiting friction and increasing the range.

Once a fish pulls a springtip, the resistance does not increase as it does with a quivertip. In fact the opposite is true: the spring simply collapses, resulting in more confident takes and fewer missed bites.

Effective as a springtip may be, it too has its limitations and the thoughtful angler will travel equipped with all three types of tip to meet any situation that arises.

Summary

The spring and quivertip rod indicators are useful items, but it should not be forgotten that ultimately the strike depends upon the reactions of the man at the other end of the rod. It doesn't matter how clear the bite is recorded, if he doesn't act he will undoubtedly lose the fish.

Keepnets

Before the introduction of keepnets matchmen would fling their catch on the bank to be collected at the end of the match. Today, keepnets provide a humane alternative

Most modern coarse-species anglers use keepnets whether for specimen hunting, pleasure angling, or competition fishing. The match-man obviously needs to weigh in his catch at the end of the match to establish who wins the prize. The keepnet enables him to do so without killing the fish. Pleasure anglers once used to return fish as soon as they were unhooked. Nowadays we often carry a camera and record the catch in photographs. The keepnet enables us to do this with no damage to the fish. Specimen hunters often keep a very detailed log of their catches, recording weight, girth and length and other details. They too find the keepnet a valuable accessory.

The important thing about these differing groups of anglers is that they all return their catch alive as soon as possible. All are strongly conservation minded, not only carrying out the law with regard to immature fish, but returning also the big ones which, a couple of decades ago would probably have been knocked on the head and finished up in glass cases.

Introduction of the keepnet
The match fisherman was responsible for the introduction of the keepnet. Before its arrival, every fish caught during a contest was thrown on the bank to be collected and weighed when fishing ceased. The drain on the fish population, even in the best-stocked waters, eventually led to the use of a net to keep fish alive for the duration of the match. Although those early nets were small and made from heavy twine, they were of vital importance.

Today's nets are available in a vast choice of sizes. Naturally, the bigger the net, the less risk of damage to fish through overcrowding. Although most anglers favour a round net, there is a distinct advantage in using a rectangular one when shallow waters are fished. These models will allow a greater area to remain submerged,

thus providing more water space for their inhabitants.

In many areas Water Authorities now specify the minimum size of keepnets to be used in their waters. Where the Water Authorities fail to do so, most of the larger and forward-thinking clubs themselves specify minimum keepnet sizes to be used by their members. Some clubs go even further and specify how many fish of each species may be kept in the net. A dozen roach in a net 6ft long with 18in hoops would seem to be in no danger, but a dozen bream, or even carp or pike, would suffer. Bream are especially vulnerable to overcrowding as their narrow body cross-section causes those at the bottom of the net to be forced on their sides and crushed if they are overcrowded. They are also the most sought-after quarry of the competition fisherman.

Vulnerable species
Barbel and carp are also vulnerable to keepnets because both species bear large serrated-edged spines on the dorsal and anal fins, and these often tend to tangle in the mesh during movement, resulting in considerable damage if the fish struggle to free themselves.

The organized match-angling world is also very concerned with this problem. To prevent overcrowding in certain well-organized matches the stewards are required to patrol the bank at regular intervals to individually weigh the big fish and record the contents.

MINNOW MESH (same size)

GUDGEON MESH (same size)

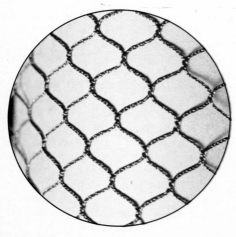

MICROMESH (same size)

Today keepnets are made with a variety of mesh sizes. Pictured are three kinds of mesh manufactured by Steadefast. From left to right: gudgeon mesh, minnow mesh and micromesh. Steadefast also produce a superfine mesh. Their keepnets range from 5ft-12ft long, and have differing widths.

Rod rests

Not long ago a rod rest was thought of as the sign of a lazy angler. Nowadays sophisticated angling styles have made a rest an essential part of the angler's equipment

Until recently a rod rest was a length of stick with a forked end, often cut from a hedge by the water and sometimes referred to by the term 'idleback'. Its best use was as a support for the rod while eating a snack, but today any attempt at ledgering, swing tip work, or laying-on is certainly pointless without a firm base on which the rod can be securely cradled.

Strength, lightness, adaptability and simplicity are the four essentials of a good rod rest. Strength sufficient to penetrate deeply a hard bank or gravel pit edge so that the rod will be firmly held, especially in

a wind, suggests the use of a metal support. But when one considers that two sets (four rests) may have to be carried, lightness prohibits the use of thick steel or iron bars.

Various kinds of thin, light alloy rod rests are available in the shops, but most are likely to bend if full body pressure is applied to drive them into the ground. Better models are thick, hollow, well pointed, and without a seam or join along the side through which water can seep and leak over tackle or the angler.

One or two models, made from a hard metal and shaped into a 'T' or 'I' section, have recently appeared

on the market. They are remarkably strong and by virtue of their shape are easy to mount into the bank. But they do cost a lot more than the average rest and are just as likely to be left behind as their cheaper counterparts. One suggestion for the forgetful angler is to paint a part of the rest a bright colour to act as a visual reminder.

Adaptability includes adjustable length and several angles of use apart from the upright position. Telescopic rests that can be held open to the required length by a thumbscrew are popular, but rather more delicate than the one-piece variety. Unfortunately, they tend to collect water and mud in the hollow section, to the detriment of rod bags or hold-alls.

There are a few rests that have adjustable heads, but most have vertical grips for holding the rod. A model with an inclined head is available, however, which can support a rod with the tip pointing downwards for swing-tip ledgering.

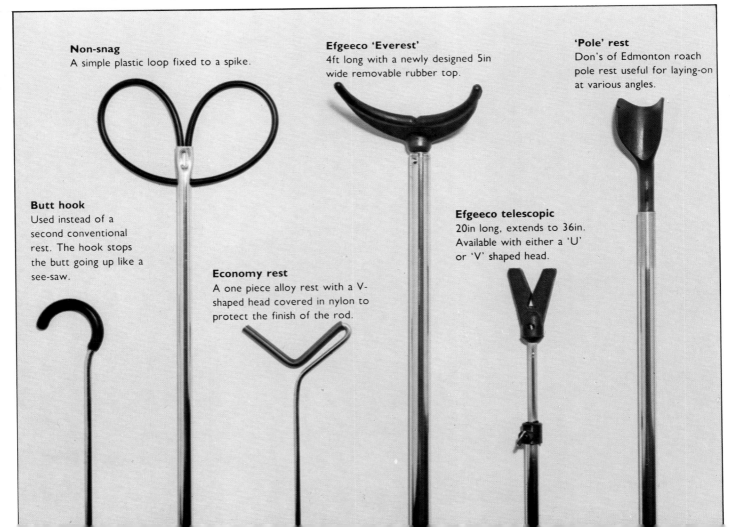

Non-snag
A simple plastic loop fixed to a spike.

Efgeeco 'Everest'
4ft long with a newly designed 5in wide removable rubber top.

'Pole' rest
Don's of Edmonton roach pole rest useful for laying-on at various angles.

Butt hook
Used instead of a second conventional rest. The hook stops the butt going up like a see-saw.

Economy rest
A one piece alloy rest with a V-shaped head covered in nylon to protect the finish of the rod.

Efgeeco telescopic
20in long, extends to 36in. Available with either a 'U' or 'V' shaped head.

Forceps and disgorgers

If you like to picture yourself as a humane fisherman, you must carry the equipment to unhook catches quickly, cleanly and with a good chance of returning fish to the water unharmed

Of the many tackle items that the angler will invest in, disgorgers, gags, forceps and pliers will be the cheapest, most essential, and generally the most easily mislaid. These simple pieces of equipment enable him to remove a deeply embedded hook and are vital to fish life and fisherman alike. They are important time savers too. There is a bewildering array on sale.

Despite their usefulness, the angler should be aware that, in many situations, these tools only become necessary because of bad fishing techniques and that deep-hooking can often be avoided.

Of course there are times when a fish bolts the bait with such speed that throat or cheek hooking is unavoidable, but many such cases could be avoided if proper attention were paid to the rod, with the angler close at hand and not several yards

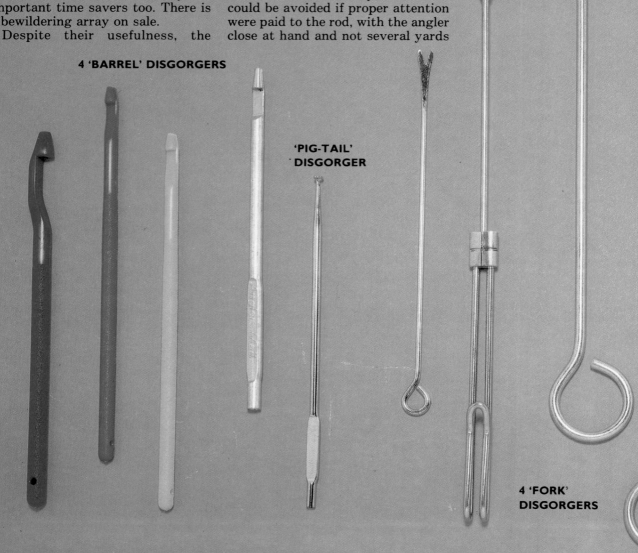

4 'BARREL' DISGORGERS

'PIG-TAIL' DISGORGER

4 'FORK' DISGORGERS

away from it. A small hook is another cause of deephooking.

A rank barb—one that protrudes too far from the body of the hook—can cause further disgorging problems, and each hook that is tied to the line should be inspected and a few strokes of a file or sharpening stone used to remove excess metal. Badly tempered or soft hooks that straighten under pressure can also present difficulties: a few seconds should be spent in examining hooks. Reject any that distort when flexed against the thumb nail.

It is in the realm of pike fishing where most unnecessary disgorging is seen. Reasons for it include bad timing of the strike ('give him a few seconds more to make sure he has really taken it'), and the use of fancy dead-bait rigs that are reminiscent of gorge tackle.

If all these precautions have been observed and the angler is still presented with a deeply hooked fish, quick action with the correct unhooking aid will prevent a death.

Disgorgers

Many anglers wrongly believe that one type of disgorger will release a hook from any fish. At least two types will be required depending on where the hook has lodged and on the type of hook being used. Where the hook is deep inside the mouth, but still visible, then the straight-forward flattened 'V'-shaped disgorger, with a long handle, may be used to ease the barb back through the skin. Where the hook is deep and cannot be seen, a disgorger with some sort of loop or ring will be necessary. This can be slid down the line to the bend of the hook.

Several of the ring and guide types are available, but most fail in practice either because they do not slip easily onto the line, or more generally because they jam at the eye or spade of the hook. Only one type will slide onto the line and ride easily onto the bend of the hook, and that is the simplest design of them all—the open wire loop or 'pigtail'.

Simply sliding the disgorger down the line and blindly stabbing with it will, in many instances, push the barb further into the flesh. The easiest method—and the safest for the fish—is to support the creature

with one hand gently but firmly behind the gills. If it is too large, lay it along the bank with the head raised against a tackle box or rod handle. Hold taut the line leading into the mouth, put the disgorger onto the line, slide it down and ease it over the eye or spade of the hook and onto the bend. Press directly downwards until the hook moves freely and withdraw from the mouth—still supported in the disgorger—taking special care not to catch it against the tongue.

The disgorger is ridiculously easy to lose, but there are two things you

can do to reduce the number that you mislay. One is to tie the handle by a piece of thin, strong line to your jacket lapel or through a buttonhole. The other is to paint the whole object either bright red or yellow, preferably with luminous paint. This also makes the business end easier to see inside a fishes mouth.

A lost disgorger can be replaced, in an emergency, by a small, forked twig or a twig into which a groove has been cut or filed. But such a crude tool can very easily do mortal harm to a fish, so use one only as a last resort.

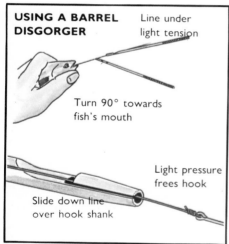

USING A BARREL DISGORGER

Line under light tension

Turn 90° towards fish's mouth

Light pressure frees hook

Slide down line over hook shank

Top: *This is what results from not having the right tools to hand. This tench's mouth has been mangled by clumsy and inept unhooking.*

Above: *A barrel disgorger runs down the line to dislodge an eyed or spade-end shank hook. But be careful not to harm the fish.*

Forceps

Within the last few years, medical artery forceps have become popular as a means of releasing a deeply-embedded hook, and several firms have produced them specifically for the angler. They are useful, but like most pieces of equipment, they have their limitations.

Some fish have a relatively small mouth opening even though the actual mouth cavity is quite large. The width of a pair of forceps, particularly when they are open, can block the view of the mouth, and if they are opened widely, can cause actual

damage. It is all too easy to grasp a portion of flesh, together with the hook, and tear it in the process of unhooking. For fish with bony or leathery mouths, therefore, artery forceps are an efficient means of freeing most hooks. Even so, the very large treble hooks used, for example in pike fishing, need a lot of leverage, and forceps are not always adequate. Choose a pair with strong, long handles and a fine nose that can grip very small hooks.

Pliers are infinitely better for removing treble hooks than either forceps or disgorgers—even the king-sized, foot-long models sold as 'pike disgorgers'. Obviously, those with a long and narrow nose are best, and stainless metal preferable to cheap tools that rust. There is at least one pair on the market that are especially designed for this heavy work on large and 'toothy' fish.

Like disgorgers, forceps are best tied to the jacket with a length of line and not clipped on to a lapel.

Gags

These are usually thought of as pike disgorging aids, and there is no doubt that they beome essential where large pike have been deeply hooked. But their use is not appropriate with small fish. In fact, considerable damage can be caused to both mouth and tongue where gags are forced and stretched into immature mouths. That gag is a simple, safety-pin-style piece of

sprung steel that, when opened, will hold the jaws of a pike apart. This enables the angler to use two hands to remove the hook without fear of the mouth closing and damaging a finger. Small ones are useless—and big ones brutal. Six inches is about right, and the first thing you should do is to crimp one of the loops on the keeper that holds the gag closed. This prevents the gag springing open at the wrong moment.

Masking the prongs

Next, the prongs at the jaws — those parts that are actually going to be pushed inside the pike's mouth—should be filed down until they are completely round, then either covered with pieces of plastic sleeving or bound round with electrician's tape until well padded.

When used correctly on a fish, the two protected prongs on the gag are wedged against the hard ridge of teeth just inside the upper and lower jaw—not into the outer lip, or halfway down the throat. By keeping them in the centre maximum space will be created through which a disgorger can be operated.

Where hooks are well down towards the throat area in a pike, a careful approach can always be made through the gill openings, avoiding the actual gills themselves.

Where hooks are well down in the entrance to the stomach, great care is needed, and rather than pull and push against the soft skin, it is better to use a pair of pliers to crush the barb to withdraw it easily.

The last resort

Some kinds of fish are more prone to swallowing hooks than others; worst are small perch and large bream. The small perch can sometimes be a greedy feeder and baits intended for bigger fish disappear well down its gullet. A 6in perch can completely swallow a 3in worm. Before trying to unhook, try a careful exploratory feel with the disgorger and if the hook is too deep to be retrieved without damaging the fish, snip off the line as near to the hook as possible. If this is done, there will be few fatalities, whereas a perch that has had a disgorger poked around its throat almost always dies within minutes.

Swimfeeders

An established part of ledgering is tempting fish to the spot where you are fishing with groundbait or samples of the hookbait. Swimfeeders enable you to do that with accuracy

Swimfeeders and blockends are perforated plastic cylinders, approximately 2-3in long and 1in diameter. Swimfeeders are open at both ends and are used mainly for groundbaiting with cereal or cereal mixed with samples of the hookbait—maggots, casters, worms, and in recent years, sweetcorn. Used in rivers by bream and chub fishermen, a swimfeeder is particularly effective. Blockends have closed ends and are usually packed with either maggots or casters.

Pegley-Davis open end feeders

Open-ended swimfeeders are used mainly with cereal groundbaits. Blockend feeders have closed ends and are used with maggots and casters. Both types of feeder have a strip of lead running through the centre: this might make them heavy and clumsy. The greatly refined Drennan 'Feederlink' does away with this strip of lead, substituting instead a strip of nylon with swan shot at one end. Swivel feeders reduce tangling of the line close to the feeder.

Hobby Crafts swivel feeders

ATTACHING SWIMFEEDERS
With feeders which have swivel attachments, the main line is passed through the swivel and a split shot, ledger stop or swivel is used to keep the feeder at the required distance from the hook. Feeders with wire or nylon loop attachments can be attached to the line with swivels.

The shape and size of both blockends and swimfeeders is important. A blockend with cone-shaped ends (like the Drennan Feederlink), for example, will cast further and more easily, resulting, in some situations, in a bigger and better catch. A large feeder is usually better than a small one when attempting to hold a large shoal of chub or bream in a swim, but when seeking specimen roach in a small, shallow river a small feeder is probably better.

Swimfeeders and blockends come in many different shapes, each designed for a specific use. Some are cone-shaped, some short but stout, some long and stout, some short and thin. Some models set up considerable resistance when retrieved, which in stillwaters particularly can have an adverse effect on both fish and tackle. The Drennan Feederlink, on the other hand, with its cone-shaped ends, cuts through the water more cleanly and reduces resistance to a minimum.

Past deficiencies

Until just a few years ago most swimfeeders and blockends were big and crude, with a large strip of lead attached to one side. Since no adjustment to the lead was possible in running water, the angler was placed at a considerable disadvantage. And because of the strip of lead, feeders were too heavy and clumsy for stillwater fishing.

Experiments with blockends began several years ago when two Oxford anglers, Fred Towns and John Everard, ran a length of nylon through the centre of a small plastic container of the type in which screws and nails used to be sold. Holes were made with a small file heated over a gas or electric ring, and swan shots (SSG) attached to the end of the nylon. The line was then passed through a swivel which was tied to the other end of the nylon.

With this new-style feeder, casting was found to be both easier and more accurate, with less resistance in running water. Another important feature of this feeder was that the weight was adjustable. If insufficient weight is used in rivers a feeder will roll, which in most situations defeats its

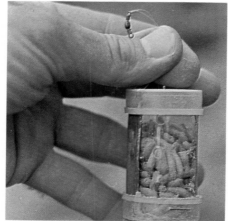

Above: *Filling a blockend swimfeeder with uncoloured maggots.*
Left: *The maggot-filled blockend is ready to be attached to the line by the use of a swivel. The lead strip acts as a ledger weight. The blockend should be cast as soon as it is filled to prevent the maggots dispersing before or during the cast.*
Below: *Swimfeeders are plastic tubes with holes through which maggots can wriggle. Groundbait is used to plug the ends until it crumbles and allows the maggots to emerge near the baited hook.*
Bottom: *A blockend swimfeeder packed with groundbait and maggots was used to tempt this fine tench.*

SWIMFEEDER · Groundbait and maggots · Maggot bait

Above: *Bait droppers come in various designs, all working on the principle of getting samples of the hookbait down to where the fish are feeding instead of being allowed to sink naturally as when using a swimfeeder or blockend. It is usually necessary to use another rod to cast out the bait dropper: this prevents tangling and allows you to position the bait dropper precisely.*

Right: *The bait dropper incorporates a container with a lid held in place by a metal rod attached to a weighted plunger. The container is packed with maggots and cast out; when the weighted plunger touches the bottom the lid is released and the maggots are deposited in the correct place. The hookbait is cast nearby.*

BAITDROPPER

object. By adding or subtracting shots, the weight could be adjusted to just hold the bottom, or roll at whatever speed the angler considered necessary.

Modern developments
The idea of passing a length of nylon through the centre of a plastic cylinder was taken further by Oxford tackle manufacturer Peter Drennan, who produced the now famous Drennan Feederlink. The 'blockends' were a vast improvement on what had previously been a simple 'chuck it and chance it' method, and today are used widely throughout the country.

After passing the main line through the swivel, the feeder is stopped at the required distance from the hook by either a split shot, ledger stop, or swivel. One of the best methods is to take a length of monofilament the required length of the tail (the distance between hook and feeder) and on one end attach the hook, on the other a swivel. Push the main line through the swivel on the feeder and tie it to the swivel on the tail. The feeder now rests against the swivel. This arrangement results in less tangling of the line close to the feeder.

When retrieving in stillwaters, the feeder should be wound in slowly with the rod tip kept low so it does not bounce across the surface. If retrieved quickly, tangling will occur. This is especially true of fast-retrieve reels.

When a fish picks up the bait, the line should pull through the ring or swivel. If it does not, do not worry, for when empty, providing the minimum of weight is used, little resistance will be felt by the fish.

In running water, feeders are fish-ed either stationary or allowed to roll along the bottom according to the whim of the angler—or fish. In fast water, the stationary method is usually adopted to avoid the contents being scattered. Only in water of moderate flow—and then not in every situation—should the feeder be allowed to roll or move.

Importance of accurate casting
In stillwaters, cast the feeder into the same spot every time: if you do not, the contents will be scattered around like a rolling feeder in rivers. Accurate casting is essential. It is also important when casting to keep the line straight, especially in a side wind.

As the swim feeder is punched forward, bring the top of the rod down to eye level then, as the feeder hits the surface, quickly thrust the top under the water to a depth of three feet. The feeder is allowed to sink on a slack line. Should it sink on a tight line, it will fall out and away from the swim.

Overhead casts
Whether fishing still or running water, overhead casts are recommended. When packed with bait, a feeder is heavy and can be cast considerable distances. Weight makes for accurate casting too.

In gravel pits, a blockend is extremely effective when seeking tench and bream. By ensuring the feeder lands in the same spot every time, a hotspot is quickly formed and the fish, once they discover the bed of maggots and casters, will remain in the area for a considerable time mopping up the loose feed. On the other hand, this may result in minute bites which though difficult to see, are often easy to hook.

Swimfeeders and blockends can be used to catch a variety of fish. The swimfeeder is especially effective for bream, barbel, roach and chub, where a cereal groundbait is necessary; the blockend when fishing maggots for tench, bream, roach and barbel.

Swimfeeders and blockends are normally used only when ledgering, only rarely are they used in conjunction with a float. Too much disturbance may be caused. Groundbaiting and floats work together.

Plugs

Here's a bait which resembles a fish or insect or waterside creature ready equipped with spinning mount, hooks and a lifelike movement to attract the shyest predator

The best description of a plug is a cross between a spinner and a dead-bait. In shape it resembles a dead fish with hooks ready-set. In use it is retrieved in much the same way as a spinner. But a plug possesses advantages that neither spinner nor dead-bait have—it can be made to work with innumerable variations on a straight retrieve at any of many

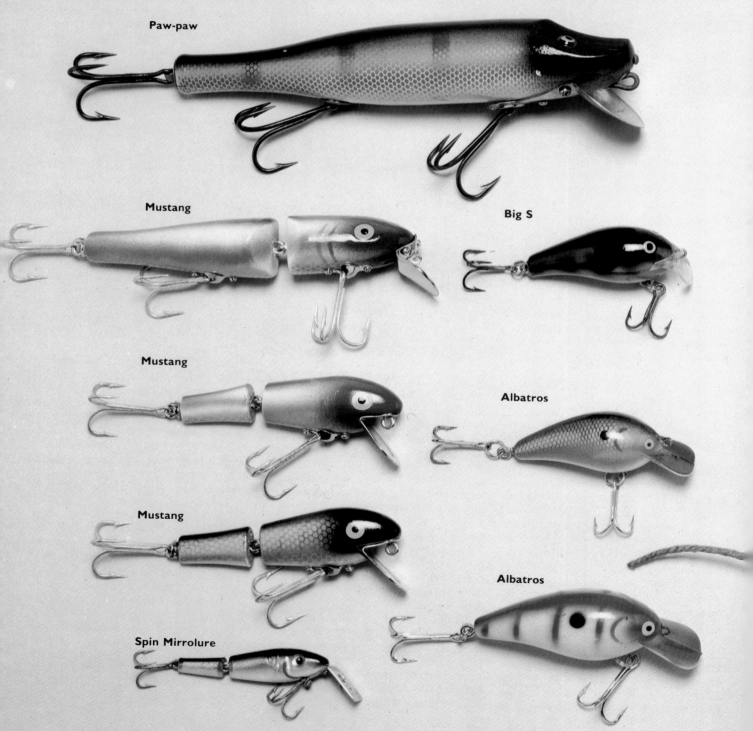

Paw-paw

Mustang

Big S

Mustang

Albatros

Mustang

Albatros

Spin Mirrolure

chosen depths. The astute angler can impart sharp, darting, erratic movements, and the series of vibrations produced in this way will travel several yards. The vibrations serve to stimulate the urge to hunt: so much so that a plug may be savagely attacked when a seemingly enticing livebait has been completely ignored in the same swim.

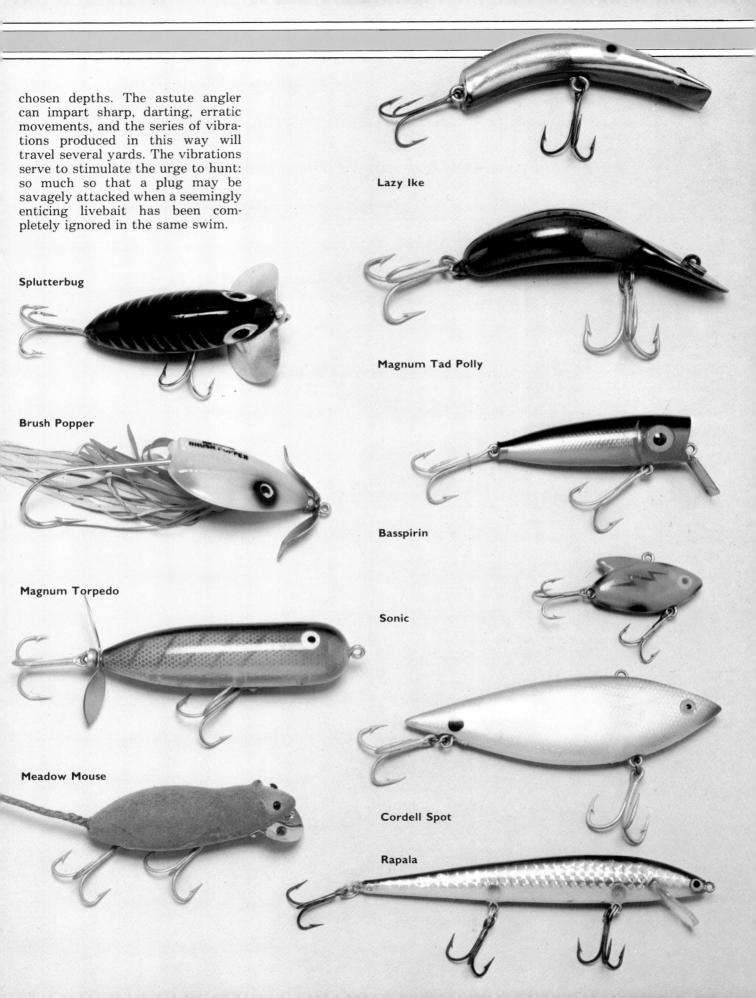

Lazy Ike

Magnum Tad Polly

Splutterbug

Brush Popper

Basspirin

Magnum Torpedo

Sonic

Meadow Mouse

Cordell Spot

Rapala

Spinners

Fishing with a whirling, seductively flashing spinner can be a deadly way of catching predatory fish—but the variety of spinners on the market is overwhelming

A spinner can be defined as an artificial lure that comprises a blade or body which rotates quickly about a straight line axis consisting often of a wire bar. Spoons, in contrast, have a wobbly retrieve and do not usually spin. Plugs are artificial fish-like objects, made of various materials, which wobble on retrieve. These distinctions are not clear-cut, and it

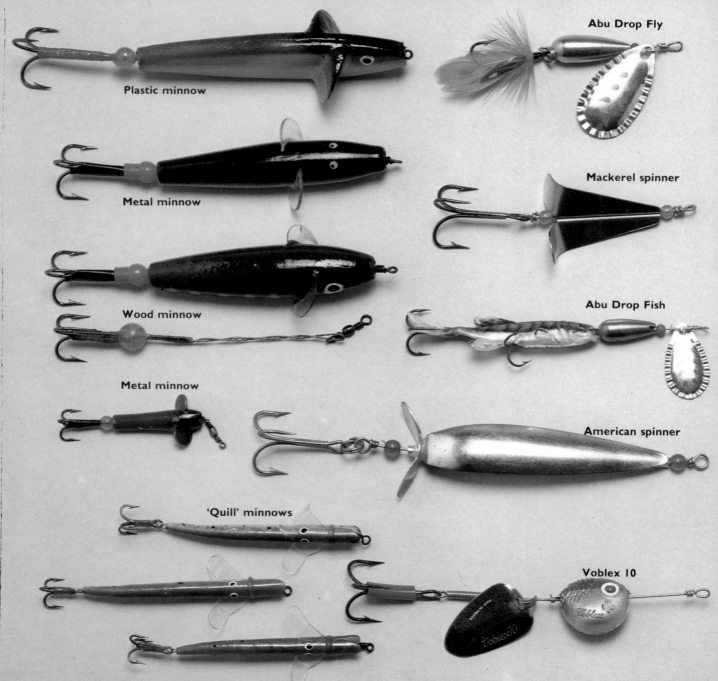

Plastic minnow

Abu Drop Fly

Metal minnow

Mackerel spinner

Wood minnow

Abu Drop Fish

Metal minnow

American spinner

'Quill' minnows

Voblex 10

is possible to buy, or make, spinners that are headed by a sizeable body and are therefore halfway between spinners and plugs (such as the famous Voblex), and spinners with so much hair or feather that they approach flies in construction, but with the added flash of a small rotating blade. There is great scope for inventiveness among anglers and many new combinations are possible, if not many new basic designs.

There are five basic kinds of spinner—artifical minnows, wagtails, mackerel spinners, fly spoons, and barspoons. It is unfortunate that the last two incorporate the word 'spoon' in their names, for they are in fact spinners with a straight axis around which the blade spins.

Artificial minnows

Of all the kinds of spinners, artificial minnows most closely represent fish, both still and on the move. The body, made of either wood, plastic or metal, is round in cross section, minnow-like in profile, and has a hole along its length through which a metal bar or wire trace passes. At the tail is a treble hook and at the

Intrepid Flectolite

Abu Drop Flex

Mepps Aglia Longue

Mepps Black Fury

Normark Vibrax

Daiwa

Veltic 6

Ondex 6

Mepps Aglia

Abu Reflex

Abu Droppen

head a swivel which can be attached to the reel line or, if fishing for pike, to a wire trace link swivel. Generally, the swivel at the head has a smaller overall diameter than the hole through the middle of the lure so that on the take the fish tends to blow the lure up the line, giving itself nothing to lever against as it tries to throw the hook. This is an excellent feature of the design which is occasionally incorporated in such other lures as plugs.

The head of the minnow has a pair of vanes which cause it to rotate. Some makes have adjustable vanes so that the spin can be reversed, and line twist reduced.

A variation on the minnow theme is the quill minnow, a superb lure for fishing for trout in hill streams. The whole body of the quill minnow rotates, often including the bar wire through its middle, so that the swivel has to work well to avoid line twist, and an anti-kink vane is usually necessary. These lures normally have up to three sets of treble hooks and since many hill trout take the spinner crossways, this is an advantage despite the tendency of the lure to become hooked up in rocks or weeds and other snags.

Wagtail movement

Wagtails look more lifelike when moving than when still. They usually have a head complete with eyes, spinning vanes, a swivel and tube-like body hidden inside two long rubber flaps which are pointed at the tail end, close to the treble hook. The name comes from these loose, flapping strips of rubber. All this detail disappears, however, when the whole body rotates quickly and, other than in body softness, the wagtail probably differs little from the various minnows. Wagtails can be made to quite large sizes and with a slow spin. This can occasionally be an advantage over commercial minnows. Like minnows, wagtails are mostly used when fishing for salmon, sea trout and trout, but can be very effective for pike.

Mackerel spinners

Mackerel spinners are superb lures for any predatory fish. They do not work well if more than 2½in long, but most commercial ones are 2in or less. They have a tube around the axial wire, and this tube is brazed to a triangular-shaped plate that has the spinning vanes at the rear, near the treble hook. Mackerel spinners can be retrieved in very shallow water and with extreme slowness at any depth. For catching large numbers of perch and pike they are perhaps the best lures ever designed, and should be fished on lines of 6-8lb b.s. to obtain the best casting results from their aerodynamic shape.

Mackerel spinners have many advantages over other spinners, as they are very cheap and nearly indestructible but they are not easy to make unless you dispense with the tube and make do with a couple of bent eyes at the front and at the back of the blade.

Anti-kink vanes

There is one more thing the spinning angler needs—anti-kink vanes to prevent line twist. Half moon leads which can be clamped to the reel line or trace are amongst the best. They range in size from minute to very large and for really heavy spinning they can always be used in multiples. Many more anti-kink devices are available, and it is wise to try them all, but make sure they are firmly fixed to the line or trace, otherwise you may well find that they are totally ineffective.

Weighing-in scales

Having caught a large bag of fish or one substantial specimen, the successful angler will want to weigh his catch. There are many types of scales that can be purchased, some of them bulky, some pocket-sized.

There are four kinds of scales: the clock or dial type, the pan design, the beam design and spring balance. The clock or dial type is the most popular for competition use and can also be purchased in handsets. The pan type is usually preferred by sea anglers as they do not usually have to worry about weighing-in live fish.

The beam type are the most accurate and will weigh to a single dram. Because of their weight and problems of carrying, they are less popular with clubs. Beam scales can be transported along the bank during matches and are ideal for weighing small specimens accurately, but two scalesmen are needed. The pocket spring balance is carried by many individual anglers.

When weighing live fish, great care should be take to cause as little harm to the fish as possible. Most clock or dial scales now have a plastic-covered wire basket with a loose-fitting lid under which to place the fish.

Before even beginning to fish, the scales should be set up on their tripod and adjusted by using the small screw on the clock. The scalesman should check that all is completely ready before asking the angler to take the fish from the water for weighing. Return the fish as quickly as possible.

Chapter 8
SEA TACKLE

A little over a hundred years ago sea fishing as a sport was confined to the use of those handlines mentioned earlier. Not only mackerel were caught with them, for cod, pollack, garfish and other species can all be taken on feathers.

Those square frames now carry nylon, but they originally held a twisted flax called cuttyhunk. Today's rig, six for mackerel, and tied with coloured feathers, is used on the reel line, attached by a swivel and with an old weight on the bottom. In spring and summer the charterboats head out for the mackerel in order to catch bait for the day's fishing.

When fishing rods began to be used, they really were the thick, unyielding posts derided by the matchman with his wand and ultra-fine tackle. Reels held 200 yards of line which by its diameter could be used to anchor the boat. But slowly it dawned on the sea angling fraternity that sport was to be had from all the sea species if the tackle was fined down.

Now, line of 10 lb b.s., rods no stronger than those used for big-carp fishing, are the in-thing, and quite large sea fish are caught on this tackle.

One must remember, when considering sea fishing tackle that the forces acting on it are very different from those experienced by the freshwater angler.

Bottom fishing the sea can mean that your terminal tackle is up to 150ft down, and even with a medium tide running the accumulated pressure on 150ft of even 15 lb b.s. nylon is considerable. It will bow your line right out even with 8 oz of lead on the end.

Now, suppose a cod of 10 lb takes your bait. It has spent its life swimming in strong tides and has plenty of strength; add to that the pull of the tide and that ½ lb lead — all to be hauled up from 150ft. No wonder that a sea rod has to be stronger, with a higher test curve, than most freshwater rods. It is proof of their skills that sea fishermen can bring to the boat cod a good deal larger than 10 lb on scaled-down gear.

Boat rods in general are best kept to about 6 ft long. But there is a tendency today for an increase in length, due to the interest shown in uptide fishing. This is a method of casting the terminal tackle uptide while fishing from an anchored boat. The extra rod length is needed to gain casting distance, but care should be taken not to cause injury to other anglers as the tackle is cast out.

The beachcaster, armed with his 16ft rod, can now throw his griplead and baited hook over 200 yards. This demands a high degree of skill, much of it gained by practising on a local field with lead but no hook. Distance casting tournaments might have little to do with fishing, but they have led to improved casting techniques in general.

The accessories every sea angler should take with him (he cannot go back to the car if he is 15 miles out!) include a stainless steel, floatable, knife, a pair of forceps, a waterproof bag for the fish he hopes to take home, at least one spare rod and reel, nylon of lesser breaking strain on the reel for making up traces and snoods, weights, plenty of hooks of varying sizes, swivels, booms, and (if he is using wire) a crimping outfit.

No matter what the weather, always have warm clothing and waterproofs. Food, too, is essential, even for those who may well lose it later on. Hours spent on the deck of an open boat in hot weather will reduce body liquids which must be replaced. Soft drinks are ideal, alcohol is not recommended. Keep the food simple, for the moment you relax your rod will dip violently.

At times, one has the impression that the fish are just waiting for your attention to be diverted. A sandwich can be put down quickly, but a 'bits and pieces' meal will be scattered about the boat if you panic.

A word about *mal de mer*. Many anglers suffer, many beat it, many never experience it. But for the newcomer to sea fishing a few words might help. When a boat is heading out in a calm sea the motion is negligible. Few people are affected at this time. But at anchor, it can adopt a wallowing, near circular motion that can be fatal to a queasy stomach. Spike Milligan's advice to a sea sickness sufferer: 'Go and sit under a tree' is very funny but absolutely accurate.

The best advice is to take one of the standard pills just before boarding and after a wholesome breakfast. If the sensation becomes fraught, keep in the fresh air and stare at the horizon. The worst thing to do is to look down, especially at a heap of old bait.

Sea fishing is the best get-away-from-it-all therapy there is — and the catch tastes terrific!

Boat rods

A boat rod is either the gantry of a crane for hauling passive fish off the seabed, or a weapon for doing battle with fighting fish. Which do you need, and what should its dimensions be?

The sea angler's boat fishing rod is simply an extension to his arm. The rod acts as a lever, converting the pulling power of a handline to lifting strength. What has happened, over half a century or so, is that anglers have applied sporting techniques to the business of deep sea fishing.

Sea angling is probably the newest of the forms of angling. Certainly, fishing with rods for really big fish only got underway at the turn of the century. Before that, it was easier, and possibly more productive, to use a hand or fixed line. Anglers went to sea as onlookers: showing an interest in the professionals' livelihood would gain anyone a place in the boat. They used handlines, so it was inevitable that the intending sport angler should follow suit. But a need grew to extend the sport beyond taking fish for the pot.

Beginning of sea angling

Sea angling was born. The knowledge that freshwater rods were unsuitable for sea fishing led to the production of sea rods in cane. These were clumsy compared with their modern glassfibre equivalents, but they advanced sea fishing considerably. At the time it was believed that rods had to be strong. Rods were at first short because cane came in relatively short, useful lengths, and nobody wanted to introduce a metal or spliced join. Some had steel cores to give them more power for fighting big specimens. The more expensive rod was made of split cane, with cheaper versions made from whole cane sections often with whole wood handles.

Need for flexibility

Gradually it dawned on sea anglers that what was needed was a measure of flexibility. The ultra-strong, extremely stiff rod failed on two counts: it did not transmit the vibrations of a fighting fish to the angler at all well, neither could it flex to absorb a fish's wild rushes. Most of the movements of the fish resulted in a bending of the whole length of the rod. With the advent of extruded, solid glass rods, there was at last a material that could be relied on for bending freely; it rarely broke under pressure. This asset, however, was not a complete answer to the sea angler's prayers—solid glass bent under a load but did not have the liveliness of recovery that built cane had. The material was cheap, so there was a flood of inexpensive rods on the market, and, although far from perfect, these brought fishing to many more people.

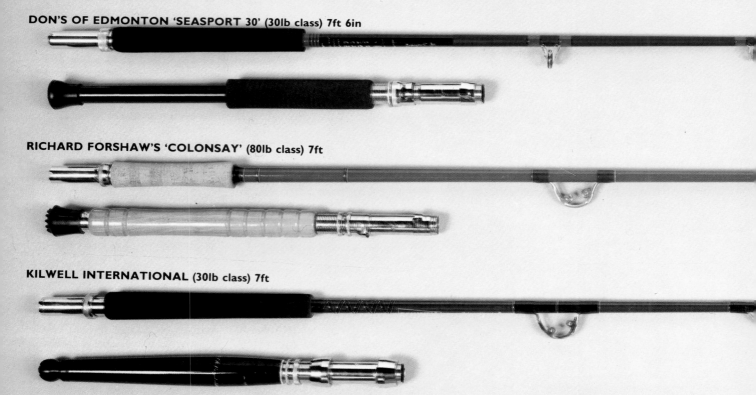

DON'S OF EDMONTON 'SEASPORT 30' (30lb class) 7ft 6in

RICHARD FORSHAW'S 'COLONSAY' (80lb class) 7ft

KILWELL INTERNATIONAL (30lb class) 7ft

Controllable glassfibre

The natural progression in the glassfibre industry from drawing out glass fibres to weaving them into a cloth or mat was quick. Rod makers realized that they now had a material that could be controlled. There was enough demand for the more expensive rod for manufacturers to set up tube rolling plants. The Americans led for a number of years, but soon a British industry emerged. The simple technique involved impregnating a cloth, woven from glass fibres, rolling it around a steel mandrel to give it the shape and taper of the required blank, and then binding it tightly before placing the mandrel into an oven, where high temperatures set the glass. After releasing the glass tube from the mandrel, the blank was then ground to produce a clean, even, smooth, tapered tube that produced a superb rod.

Action, the true requirement in the angler's boat rod, can be built into a rod in two ways. First, through the taper of the mandrel on which the glassfibre is wrapped and, second, according to the amount of

material used in a particular area of the rod. With these two factors settled, a curve of almost any power and compression can be put into the rod. There are differences in the type of glass and the resins that bind the whole thing together, but these have long been familiar to manufacturers.

Unbreakable

Glassfibre rods are not only light and powerful; they are also almost unbreakable in sensible use. They are not affected by oil, saltwater and

extremes of temperature. These features give the glassfibre rod tremendous advantages over the older, more traditional materials used for rod-making.

Above: *A variety of rods in use, mostly 6ft or 8ft long. It is very risky to balance a rod against the side with a bait out.*

Below: *Three glassfibre sea rods. The Kilwell has a gimbal fitting for use with a harness. The Colonsay sections are joined by a stainless steel Modalock fitting; the others by Varmac fittings.*

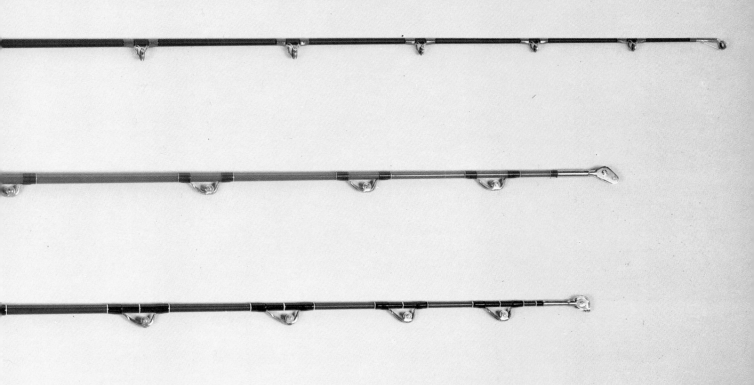

Increasingly, carbonfibre is being used for the construction of boat rods. This space age material combines incredible lightness and great strength with first rate sensitivity. As yet carbon rods are extremely expensive, which does restrict their use. Nevertheless, £60 or so is not a great sum to pay for an article that will give many years of service. Like glassfibre rods, carbon-based rods are virtually unaffected by saltwater or strong sunlight.

Unfortunately there is still development work needed, too, on carbonfibre, as it can be unstable. An American development called the Howald process mixes carbonfibre and glassfibre. Rod blanks produced from it are truthfully described as unbreakable in almost all kinds of fishing situations.

Top quality boat rods conform to specifications laid down by the International Game Fish Association, which has its headquarters at Fort Lauderdale, USA. The body is responsible for all World Record claims in 6lb, 12lb, 20lb, 30lb, 50lb, 80lb and 130lb tackle classes.

No standard boat rod
There is no standard boat rod, nor can there be, for fish vary tremendously in size and the conditions under which they are fished for alter constantly. A rod of the 20lb class is suitable for small species in sea areas with light tidal flow and allows the use of light leads of 2-8oz. This means that the rod blank is balanced for use with a 20lb line. It will have a test curve of around 4lb, which means that a pull at the rod tip of this weight will bend the rod at right angles. It does not mean that the rod is only capable of handling a fish that weighs or pulls to 4lb. In any case, a fish weighs only about one third of its true weight when in the water. The test curve given for a sea rod is multiplied by five to arrive at the correct b.s. of line to match it.

Selecting a boat rod
When selecting a boat rod it is very misleading to wave it about in the manner usually adopted with freshwater rods, which do have a flexibility that can be assessed, even if not accurately. A boat rod only proves its worth under the stress of

a sizeable fish coupled with the dead weight of a pound lead in a moderate run of tide.

A 30lb class rod will cope with fish up to 50lb, leads up to 20oz and quite hard tides—anything up to four or five knots—when fishing from an anchored boat. The rod is intended to be used for tope and big shoal fish such as cod, pollack, ling, and rays, but would still handle the smaller species. A 50lb class rod will enable anybody to hook, fight, and land most of our larger species. Porbeagle shark, all but the largest of common skate, and the average

Play a fish from the most comfortable position possible. It could take a long time.

deep sea conger, are all within the competence of a rod of this strength.

Skate and shark rods
Then there are the outlying fish —the huge common skate found off Shetland, Orkney and the West of Ireland and conger from the deep sea wrecks, where tides are fierce and the depth around 50 fathoms. This sort of fishing places a terrible stress on any rod, so the angler has to consider moving up to an 80lb class weapon. Big shark do not fall into this category because they are a free-moving species; the strain is caused by speed and a sustained fight rather than by a continuous, dead weight on the angler and rod of a fish clamped to the seabed.

The rod's fittings
No glassfibre blank can perform as a rod without the right fittings. The quality of the glass and its design must be matched by a perfect winch fitting and rod rings.

Boat rod lengths
Rods are becoming longer. At one time a 5 or 6ft rod was normal; now 7-8ft rods are commonplace. The longer rod gives better control of a fighting fish, especially when it comes close to the boat. At the same time it possesses more travel during compression, absorbing the wild lunges that can break a line when the angler is fishing with lightweight fishing tackle.

One further class of rod is rapidly gaining popularity. With a 15lb test curve and a length of 9ft, it is the longest two-piece boat rod available in this country and is being much used for a technique known as 'uptide fishing'. This method requires a longer rod in order that a bait can be cast away at right angles across the tide. There is considerable merit in it, although its practice demands disciplined fishing. Some charter skippers wisely prohibit uptide fishing from a crowded boat, on the grounds of safety.

Rod maintenance
The finish on a boat rod is not a complicated matter. Boat rods are subjected to knocks and hard usage that would soon destroy other fishing equipment. A seasonal rub down with a cleaning agent, followed by a gentle smoothing with 'wet and dry' sandpaper, will remove all the dirt and dross. It is then a matter of applying enough coats of polyurethane varnish to effectively seal the whipping on the rings and give the finish that the owner needs. Before varnishing, inspect the rings closely, looking for scuffing within the ring itself. Any ring that is worn must be replaced.

The best attention you can give to any rod used at sea is to wash it down after every fishing trip with clean tap water and store it on a rack, however improvized. to prevent 'torque' or permanent warping. Last, never lay it flat on the bottom of the boat. It is easily trodden on and fractured.

Wire line

It's a pity so many sea anglers were deterred from using wire by early rumours of rust and breakage. Wire line has long since evolved into a faultlessly efficient aid to deepwater fishing

The relatively recent introduction of wire line for boat fishing has been the most important sea angling innovation of the century. It was first introduced to this country from America a little over 10 years ago, and Leslie Moncrieff, the great sea angler, was one of the first fishermen over here to use and popularize it. It was first developed in the United States to allow big-game anglers to troll baits without the encumbrance of a heavy weight and while it is still used over there for that purpose, it is now also used extensively in conjunction with weights or a downrigger for slow trolling at depths of up to 100ft for salmon and lake trout.

It was quickly realized by sea anglers in this country that here was the answer to bottom fishing in strong tides or deep water. In fact it exceeded all expectations once the correct techniques for using it had been perfected, and some incredible bags of fish were taken by boat fishermen where other anglers using more conventional lines had very indifferent results.

Acceptance only a matter of time
So far, fishing with wire line has still to be accepted by the average sea angler, although it is surely only a matter of time before this happens. Fishing with wire requires completely different techniques and equipment, but it is not difficult to learn. With a little practice, the average angler can become proficient in its use in a comparatively short time.

The original wire also was a single strand construction from Monel metal and considerable developments and improvements have been made since that was first marketed. While the single-strand wire was very hard wearing and less prone to kinking, it was much thicker than more recent lines and rather unpleasant to use. It was followed by a

Below: *This wooden starback centrepin, though its massive diameter is ideal for wire, is no longer manufactured.*

single strand, stainless line which was beautiful to use but very prone to kinking, which once formed, was all but impossible to remove.

In efforts to overcome this problem, a very flexible seven-strand wire was evolved, and while this format succeeded to some extent, the multiple stranding produced a further problem. With constant use some of the strands were liable to fracture, and where this happened badly lacerated fingers were often the result. Apart from this, it was found in practice that salt water badly affected stainless wire over a period of time and its strength rapidly deteriorated.

Used correctly, wire line can open up a new world to the sea angler. To hold bottom, you require a fraction of the lead compared with conventional monofilament or braided lines

of Dacron or Terylene. In very strong tides, for example, and fairly deep water where you would require at least 2lb of lead on a monofilament line to hold bottom, you can achieve the same result using wire with less than ½lb. This means you are in closer touch with the fish at all times, and it is far more sporting, as, after all, the average-size sea fish of 6-7lb can hardly give of its best when it is towing a large, heavy lead and fighting the pull of the rod.

Bite indication
Bite indication with wire is a revelation in itself: bites from small fish are registered immediately and positively, where similar bites on monofilament would not be felt at all, due to its inherent stretch. So positive is the indication from wire line that an angler experienced in its use can, even in deep water, tell you the composition of the bottom—whether it is rock, sand, shingle or soft mud—just from the feel of the bouncing lead (legal for Sea Fishing).

The one disadvantage of wire line is that fishing from a crowded boat becomes inadvisable. When using wire you require plenty of room between you and the next angler, as it is absolutely essential to keep wire under tension at all times, and should you become entangled with another fisherman's line this is not possible. Wire reverts to coil form when tension is relaxed, and most efforts to straighten it result in kinks, so that it then becomes so weak that it will snap under pressure.

This brings us to the first and most important aspect of its use, and the one that causes most problems to novices. Never, *never* lower weighted wire to the bottom from a free spool, as if you do you will not know when the lead hits the seabed. The result will be a pyramid of coiled wire on the bottom which will come back full of kinks. Lower it under slight tension, with your thumb on the spool of the reel and you will then feel the lead arrive.

The angler who likes to make himself comfortable on a convenient fish-box or fitted seat during boat fishing trips, should not use wire line. It is a material that must be fished positively every second it is in the water. Propping the rod against

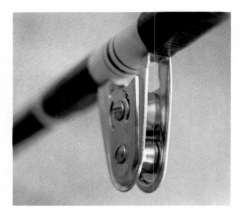

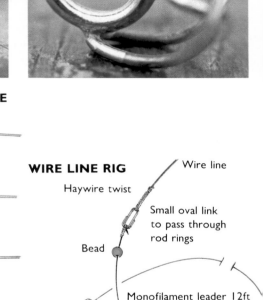

the gunwale, even for a short period while drinks are served or an item of tackle is fetched, is absolutely out of the question. To put wire over the side and not control it constantly is unfair and dangerous to others on the trip.

Use a heavy nylon leader

When using wire it is advisable to mount your running lead on a heavy monofilament leader at least 12ft long. This should be fastened to a small, oval link or split ring that is small enough to be wound through the rod guides and down on to the reel. It will mean, in effect, that when your lead with its normal flowing trace is wound in, all the wire will be back on the spool.

If you neglect to do this and mount your lead directly on to the wire, it will be left to swing like a pendulum from your rod top when moving from one anchorage to another, and this constant motion will cause metal fatigue with corresponding weakness in the line. Wire should always be connected to the metal loop or split ring with a haywire twist, but do make a double loop through the ring before commencing the twist.

A good stretch

A heavy leader serves another purpose in as much as it provides a small degree of stretch between the angler and a heavy fish. Without this cushioning effect, it is all too easy to tear the hook free.

The tackle required for wire is a reel with a large diameter, yet narrow, spool such as a Scarborough, Alvey or, ideally, a Penn Master Mariner. Normal multiplying reels with wide, small diameter spools are

HAYWIRE TWIST FOR WIRE LINE

Double turn around link

Twist line 10 times

Coil end to finish

Break off free end by twisting with pliers

Bead

Swivel

WIRE LINE RIG

Wire line

Haywire twist

Small oval link to pass through rod rings

Bead

Monofilament leader 12ft

Grip lead

Lead link

Top *(left to right): Roller-type intermediate ring designed for use with wire; Fuji's new boat ring housing an aluminium-oxide guide; ordinary ring grooved by wire.*
Above; Right: *Never allow wire line to kink.*

useless as these coil the line too tightly and it will then require a heavy lead to straighten it. For the same reason, you should use a rod with a soft action and flexible top, and it is absolutely essential that it is fitted with a roller top or better still, roller guides all the way down the rod.

Conscious of the increase in fishing with wire line, top manufacturers are now offering rods fitted with guides with extra-tough linings—principally aluminium oxide. This material is a direct spinoff from the American space project. It is so

hard it can resist the cutting effects of wire passing over it. A roller tip is still essential, however.

Finally, one word of warning to those fishing from an achored boat, or more especially from a drifting boat.

Never ever attempt to free wire with your hands should it become snagged on the bottom. It can cut through flesh like a hot knife through butter. Loop the line around a stanchion or stem post, and let the boat pull it out. It is also sound practice to use a trace of slightly lower breaking strain than the wire so that if you do have to break out, you will only lose a hook or part of the trace and not relatively expensive wire.

Wire gives an immediate indication of a bite. But learn how to use it properly.

Rubber eels and lures

If you've lost valuable fishing time gathering baits or losing them in shreds over rough ground, you already appreciate the difference that artificial lures have made to sea fishing

For more than a hundred years, rod and line fishermen have used artificial lures to catch sea fish. Long before the start of this century, ingenious minds dreamed up many different types of baits that twisted, wobbled or travelled through the water with an undulating motion. The earliest lure was made from a length of wide rubber-band, one end whipped to the hook shank. It bore a remarkable resemblance to a worm and few refinements have bettered it in terms of its ability to attract fish.

Sophisticated lures appear
From this primitive beginning, more sophisticated lures soon evolved. Two types in particular, known as Brook's Double Twist Spinning Eel, and Captain Tom's Spinning Eel, were the first to be made from lengths of india-rubber pipe.

Movement—the secret of success
No matter how good the design of an artificial sandeel, its success is totally dependent on one thing—movement. All have a negligible action of their own, and only movement imparted by an angler gives a lure 'life'. Unfortunately, this is not always realized, and one sees artificial sandeels being used garnished with a strip of mackerel, squid or—incredibly—a natural sandeel. Anything on the lure's hook will completely ruin the action its manufacturers have laboured to achieve.

Soft plastic can easily become deformed, too, if not handled with a reasonable amount of care and it is therefore important not to crush eels into a tackle box.

Plastic lures are available in a wide range of colours, but divers tell us that below 30ft, even in clear water conditions, colour (as we know it) begins to disappear. At 100ft it has gone altogether. So what is the point in painting artificials so attractively when most are used in depths of 40 fathoms (240ft) to which no light penetrates? The clue is surely in the phrase 'colour as we know it'. The human eye may perceive quite differently from the fish's eye when it comes to awareness of colour.

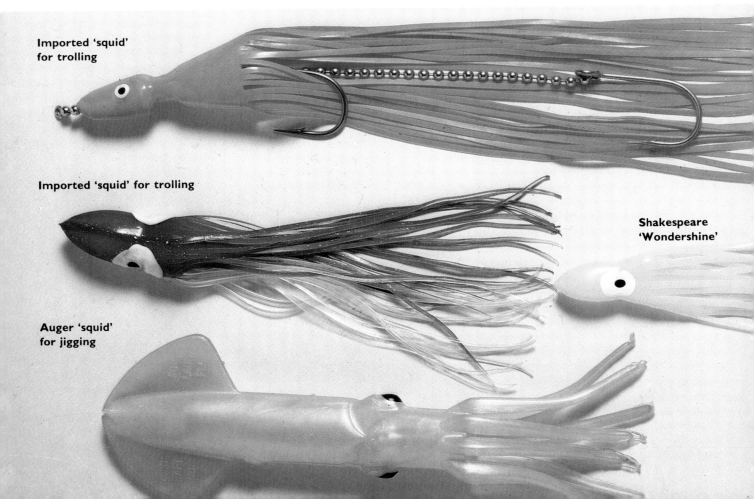

Imported 'squid' for trolling

Imported 'squid' for trolling

Shakespeare 'Wondershine'

Auger 'squid' for jigging

Beachcasting rods

A long distance cast from the shore is usually rewarded by a good catch. And for this you need a long rod. But there are other factors to consider when choosing a beachcasting rod

The first shorefishing tackle was a simple arrangement of hook, line and sinker either lowered into the sea from rocks and piers, or cast out with the aid of a pole. The line and pole are still used in parts of East Anglia and the West of Ireland. Roy Cook, a highly successful Suffolk beach fisherman, has updated the equipment to incorporate a line drum and winder which eliminate the laying out and retrieving of line by hand. He casts sinker and bait up to 140 yards, and the tackle is sensitive and powerful. For both bite detection and fighting big fish, however, the simple handline is superior to rods and reels.

At the turn of the century, shorefishing became a sport rather than the means of catching fish for the table. Rods were huge Burma canes or redundant salmon rods cut down at the tip. The emphasis was on strength. Crane-like designs continued to be employed until the late 1950s, although appearance and construction became more sophisticated. Even so, the first glassfibre rods still retained the weight and clumsiness traditionally associated with seafishing.

Glassfibre rods
Leslie Moncrieff's 'Springheel' rod heralded a new era of shorefishing, and was the first production beachcasting rod to exploit the ad-

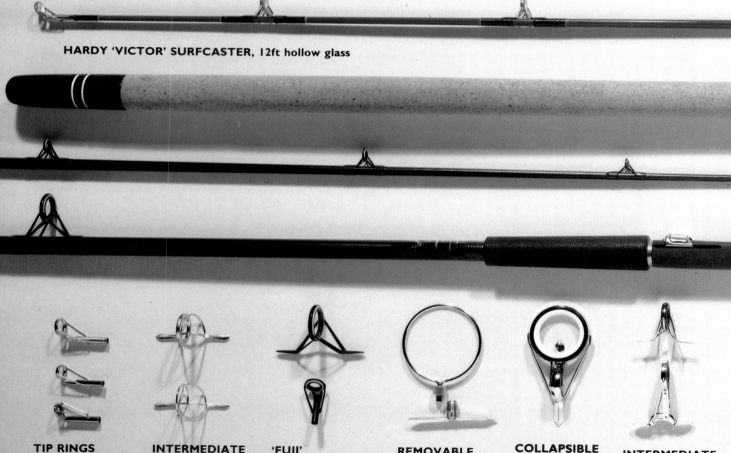

HARDY 'VICTOR' SURFCASTER, 12ft hollow glass

TIP RINGS
1 Diamite
2 Hard chrome
3 'Varmac'

INTERMEDIATE RINGS
1 'Diamite'
2 Hard chrome

'FUJI'
Intermediate and tip rings with luminous shock rings

REMOVABLE CHROME BUTT RING
An old design

COLLAPSIBLE 'FUJI' BUTT RING

INTERMEDIATE RINGS
1 'Varmac'
2 'Fuji' collapsable

vantages of glassfibre. It became a huge success, not only because of the introduction of glassfibre but because for the first time the average angler could expect to cast 100 yards. Moncrieff himself demonstrated that the rod, used with his 'Layback' casting style, would hurl 4oz and 6oz sinkers well beyond 150 yards—greatly in excess of contemporary tournament records. The effects on beachfishing were shattering—overnight the sport became highly technical and socially accepted.

The beachcasting tournaments became a battleground for designers and manufacturers. A second breakthrough arrived in the form of ABU's 484, a stiff-butted rod with a very fast action that boosted casting range beyond the 200-yard barrier. Since then tournament distances have increased marginally to the current record cast of 241 yards, using a 5¼oz weight and a multiplier reel. Perhaps it is not a coincidence that as casters and rod-makers strive for extra performance, many shorefishing rods have become excellent casting implements but at the same time are second-rate fishing tools.

Specialist rods

Carbonfibre, advanced casting techniques and finer lines open the way for experiment on rod length and power. Pendulum casters who change from glass rods to carbonfibre may find they can easily handle a blank up to 18in longer than before. The lightness, speed and slim cross-section of carbonfibre blanks

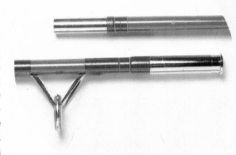

Below: *The traditional style nickel plated spigots mounted on a Hardy 'Victor' surfcasting rod.* **Bottom:** *Two sections, male and female, from the 'Graphlex' rod made by Don's of Edmonton, showing the modern internal spigot pattern.*

HARDY 'VICTOR' SURFCASTER

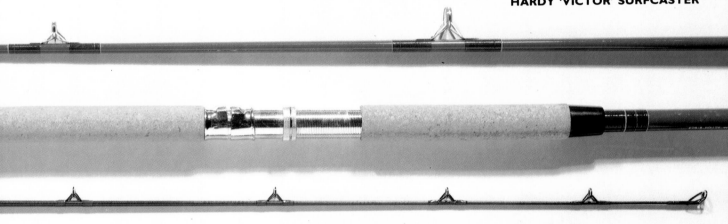

DON'S OF EDMONTON 'GRAPHLEX', 12ft carbonfibre

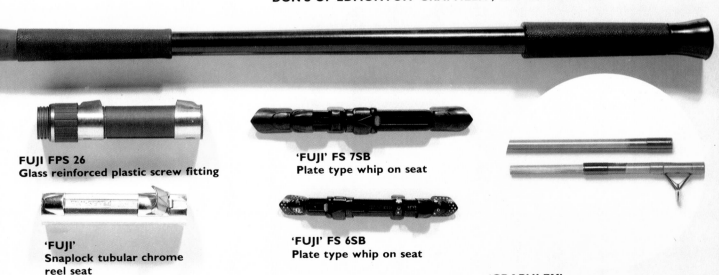

FUJI FPS 26
Glass reinforced plastic screw fitting

'FUJI'
Snaplock tubular chrome reel seat

'FUJI' FS 7SB
Plate type whip on seat

'FUJI' FS 6SB
Plate type whip on seat

'GRAPHLEX'

of the rod is the blank, which determines power and action.

When selecting a rod the best guide is to choose the kind that is best suited to the fishing you propose to do. A rod for casting 6oz sinkers and hauling big fish through fast tides needs far more power than one used to catch flounders from quiet estuaries. Power in excess of the angler's physical strength is wasted, leading only to heaviness and severe handling problems. Most manufacturers recommend a sinker weight range for their products, and this may be taken as a fair estimate of the rod's power, but it is worth remembering that most rods are deliberately under-rated to insure against abuse. Many 4-6oz casting rods handle 8oz with ease. The only confirmation of a rod's suitability is to use it. If it suits your fishing without failing under pressure, it is adequate, provided that in casting you can bend it to its full curve.

The action, or how the rod responds to load, is controlled by the taper and wall thickness of the blank. A steeply tapered rod is faster than one which slopes gradually from butt to tip. Speed and action may be further enhanced by the process of compound tapering, a design where extra glassfibre is applied at certain spots along the blank. Absolute rigidity of the butt may require the splicing on of high tensile Duralumin tubing. The merits of the various actions are debatable; there is no concensus among the world's top anglers as to which is best. Fast rods bend and flick straight in immediate response to casting and may improve distances with some styles, particularly tournament swings. They handle a wider range of sinker weights and are more sensitive to bites. On the other hand, slow rods cast far enough for fishing, are less sensitive to casting errors, and have a pleasant feel.

Action alone is unlikely to affect practical fishing but does influence rod length, the most important criterion of all. A rod is a two-way lever which allows the angler to generate high sinker speed for long casting, yet magnifies the strength of a fish so that it seems to pull harder.

encourage greater casting power, and, because the rod itself can be swung faster, extra length generates even more sinker speed without taxing the caster himself.

Rod construction

The construction of beachcasting rods follows a general pattern. A glassfibre tube, the blank, is moulded around a cylindrical rod or mandrel, hardened, removed from the mandrel and ground smooth. It is cut and spigotted or ferruled to give two or three interlocking sections. The butt is sheathed in cork, sleeved with a plastic shrink tube or fitted with grips. Traditional winch fittings or simple sliding clips secure the reel.

The important rings, preferably of stainless steel or hard-chromed steel, plain or lined with ceramics, are whipped on in a combination of sizes and spacings so that the line follows the curve of the blank. Handles, rings and other fittings, however, are almost irrelevant in terms of fishing performance except on very specialized rods. The heart

Above: *A night fisherman feeling for bites. He is using a multiplier reel, the choice of most beachcasting experts.*
Below: *A tall, spiked monopod rodrest on Southwick beach, Sussex. The rod is held high to minimize the effects on the line of pounding waves.*

Sea leads

When you consider the variety of ground that makes up our ragged coastline, you quickly appreciate why so many different sizes and models of sea leads exist

The law now states that the use of certain lead weights is illegal in freshwater angling. This law does not apply to sea angling.

Leads for sea angling range from shot to bomb weights up to 4lb which are necessary during strong tides. Each weight performs a specific task, making it imperative that the correct size and shape of weight be used.

When you have counted all the commercially manufactured leads your tackle dealer stocks, there are still the home-made and improvized varieties to consider.

Shore fishing
Split-shot, the indispensible weight used in freshwater fishing, also plays a vital role in saltwater, where it is used in float fishing and drift-lining for such species as pollack, mackerel, garfish and the wily mullet. Shot is available in a variety of sizes, and should be gently crimped on to the line with pliers.

Ball leads (also known as pierced bullets) and barrel leads, which are designed to run freely on a line, range from $\frac{1}{4}$oz to 3oz. These leads are correct for making up the sliding float rig used to suspend a bait close to the bottom in almost any depth of water. The 'slider' is popular with anglers seeking wrasse, pollack and bass over rough ground. Barrel leads weighing up to 6oz are sold in many tackle shops for bottom ledgering, but they roll around on firm sandy ground, and tend to twist the line. These larger sizes, therefore, make a poor type of lead and are best avoided.

Leads for muddy ground
For ledgering on muddy ground in tidal rivers and estuaries where the water is shallow, flat leads are by far the best. Although they make for poor long-distance casting, those with a thin profile sink to the bottom more slowly than bombs and consequently do not penetrate more than a few inches into the ooze. Extensions of the smooth, flat weight are the Circular Grip, Capta and the Six Pointed Star. These are useless as casting leads, but they hold well on firm mud, shale and sand—even when the tide pours out of rivers during spring tides.

The long-casting beach angler needs a variety of weights ranging in size from 2oz to 10oz, which offer minimum wind-resistance. Across the years numerous patterns have evolved, and present day beach fishing experts think little of putting an intact bait 160 yards out into the surf where the big fish roam. A small band of men who specialize in this fascinating branch of sea sport, using carbonfibre rods, are already casting way beyond 225 yards and, as this material becomes even more sophisticated, 300 yards may well fall within the range of normal beachcasting as opposed to tournament casting.

Wye lead **Jardine spiral**

Pierced bullets

Coffin leads

Barrel leads

Arlesey bombs

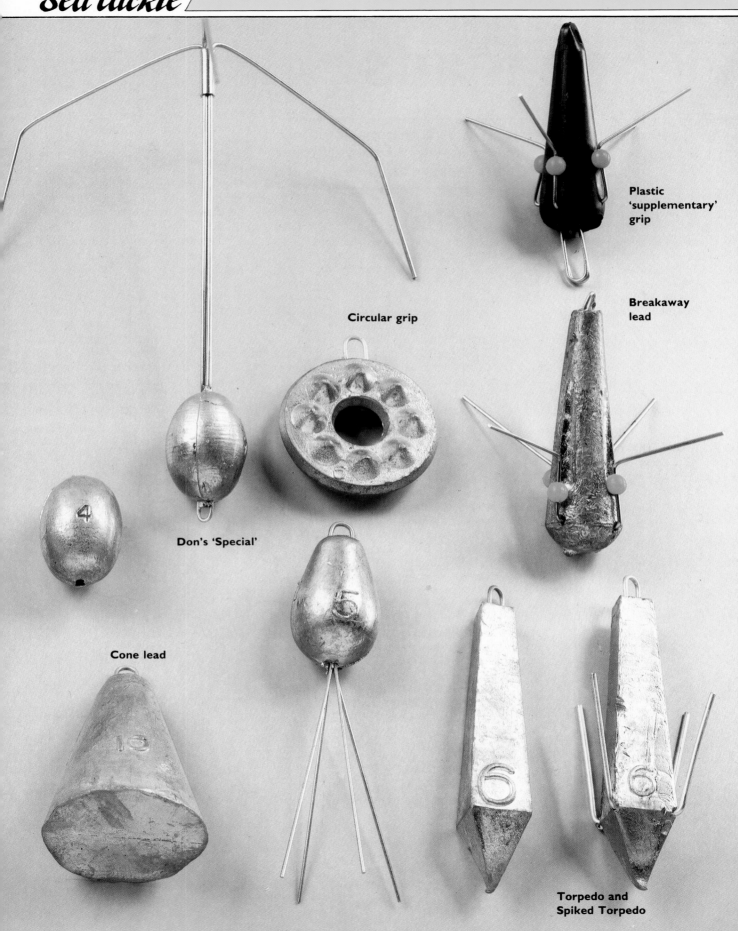

Plastic 'supplementary' grip

Circular grip

Breakaway lead

Don's 'Special'

Cone lead

Torpedo and Spiked Torpedo

The long-distance lead

Aerodynamically, the Arlesey bomb is the best lead for reaching these great distances. A swivel at the narrow end stops the reel line twisting during its flight, but once on the sea bed it is a poor holder and is easily rolled around by water movement. The compromise is a Torpedo with four flat sides and with its weight concentrated at the pointed end, which prevents the lead turning over in flight. From this lead came the Spiked Torpedo, featuring four or more soft wire arms embedded in the heavy end. These dig into the sand and prevent the lead from moving in all but the roughest weather. Under retrieving pressure, however, the arms bend backwards and the lead can be wound in easily.

An extension is the Breakaway which features grip wires each holding a small bead. These slot into depressions in the body of the lead which hold them in an upright position under tension. A rubber band is sometimes added to increase the tension. When the weight is retrieved, contact with the bottom pulls the wires down, allowing the lead to be drawn in without difficulty. This type of lead has found great favour with surf beach fishermen and is replacing the more basic and long-popular grip-wire torpedo.

Pirks also come into the category of lead weights—at least those made from a mixture of lead and zinc, which is added for toughness. Pirks range in size from a few ounces to 1½lb and feature a body moulded to a specific shape to achieve a fluttering action as it drops to the bottom and is jigged with the rod. Molten lead is also used to fill sections of chrome pipe—a cheap way of making an unsophisticated pirk. Lead poured into a length of pipe, cut for example from an old pram handle, produces a pirk at virtually no cost.

Although similar in appearance to the normal Torpedo, the Sectional Deal beach lead is made up from five 2oz pieces, moulded in a V-shape, which fit together on a central bar, fastened into a pointed bottom section of 4oz. Each piece simply lifts off the bar—giving six casting weights ranging from 4oz to 14oz.

For spinning from the shore, the weight must hug the line and present the minimum resistance to air and to water. A spiral like the Jardine takes a lot of beating. It has a continuous groove running from end to end, and twisted wires through which the line is passed. Jardines come in weights from 2oz to 8oz, the lighter versions being the most suitable for general spinning work with natural and artificial sandeel or fish-strip baits. The banana-shaped Wye lead, fitted with a link swivel, is also excellent for spinning. As with the Jardine, nothing should be placed on the line between the lead and bait. Both these types are suitable for working ultra-light metal lures, or for increasing your fishing range with the heavier models.

Leads for boat fishing

It is possible to break down boat fishing into four categories: inshore, offshore, pirking and trolling. Many types of lead and many different techniques used in shore fishing have a use when working from a boat in shallow water. Float work is exactly the same, but for drift-lining when the boat is anchored in a fair run of tide the weight must be increased to get the bait down below the surface. Two- or three-hook paternosters can be weighted with Arlesey bombs, plain bombs or small Torpedoes. For ledgering, it is best to use Cones, Circular Grip and Star types.

Offshore fishing

In offshore fishing the angler meets with the combination of deep and swift-running water, particularly during spring tide periods. The type of reel line is a most important factor when fishing in more than 20 fathoms. Monofilament creates much less drag than braided line, and less weight is needed. From an anchored boat, a 4-5 knot run of tide will push a 1lb lead connected to braided line almost to the surface. When this occurs, the lead will be some 300 yards away, down tide.

In water 35-45 fathoms deep it is impossible during spring tides to keep 3lb of lead on the bottom. This is one reason why charter skippers always drift-fish during new and full moon periods. It is as well to remember this when booking a deep-water fishing trip; working 'on the drift' can be a hard, tiring business.

Paternosters can be made to sink with bombs or torpedoes, and it is wise to have a range from 6oz to 2lb with you even when the tide is a neap. The same types are used in association with wire boom rigs for long-trace, single-hook fishing. Rarely, however, do you need more than 10oz when this method is used as the bait is fished up to 60ft above the bottom so drag on the line is less.

Deepwater leads

Leads for ledgering in deep water must have a large diameter base. The cone is the best type, but grip leads do an adequate job. Ledger leads can be rigged with a 'rotten bottom' by tying a small swivel to the eye with light nylon. If the weight gets caught up in a rock crevice or a wreck, steady pulling will free the trace end. This is a big advantage when expensive wire traces are in use.

Trolling for bass and pollack is a popular and often rewarding way of fishing. The size of the lead depends very much on the strength of tide, speed of the boat and how deep the fish are running. For deep work 1lb is about right, and for shallow fishing 8-12oz should be used. Trolling leads should have a centre of gravity below the level of the line.

Importance of swivels

This prevents any suggestion of spinning—providing, of course, that the swivels mounted behind and in front of the weight are in working order. Large Jardines rigged in the manner described earlier are also widely used and can be changed very quickly, without cutting the reel line, should a heavier or lighter one be needed as the tide alters.

The initial outlay for a set of moulds to make 2oz, 3oz, 4oz, 5oz, 6oz and 8oz weights plus a bag of grip wires will be about £12—but of course you can start with a single block and gradually build up the range.

The price of the lead varies from week to week; a modest fiver will get you enough to make several dozen leads of various sizes and, certainly, the unit cost is less than half the shop price. Over a period of time it is a worthwhile proposition.

225

Pirks and jigs

Attempting to simulate a prey worthy of the biggest predators, manufacturers market a huge range of lures—some outlandish, some amazingly lifelike, some breathtakingly expensive!

In recent years pirking or jigging for free swimming fish such as pollack, coalfish and cod, has gained ground with deepwater boat anglers, and the method is now in wide use. It entails fishing with a weighted lure, invariably fitted with a treble hook. Pirks take many forms and range from lead-filled pipes, already chromed or painted in a variety of colours,' to old plated car door handles or to sophisticated stainless steel and chrome-finished models from Scandinavia. Home-made pirks are cheap to produce, but the professional type can cost over £5.

Jigs

Jigs are generally smaller lures, often with coloured feathers set in a metal head rather than the all-metal body of a pirk. They are used in a similar way to pirks and range from 4oz to 26oz, the weight varying with the depth of water and the strength of tide. In general terms, few of less than 12oz are used in more than 20 fathoms of water.

Pirk fishing with heavy lures in the deeps requires a great deal of physical effort, which few anglers can keep up for more than half an hour. It is only with daily exercise that one builds the arms and shoulders to cope with the strain. Skippers who habitually fish wrecks in the Western Channel have the necessary physique and can keep a 26oz pirk going for hours on end, catching on average a hefty fish with every other drop. Tackle for this very specialized and rugged aspect of sea angling is a stout 7ft fast-taper hollow glass rod, with plenty of power in the butt section. Matched with a top quality high-geared multiplier of at least 6/0, filled with 50-80lb b.s. monofilament line, such a rod will suit all occasions. Braided line is never used in

this style of fishing because it creates too great a drag in flowing tidal water.

When out with charter parties, most skippers stand high on the craft's bows, well out of the angler's way, and hurl the heavy lure as far

as possible, allowing it to flutter unchecked to the bottom. When this is done over a wreck which holds a big fish population, the pirk is often grabbed on its way down while still high above the wreckage. If not, it should be retrieved from the bottom ultra-fast, until contact is made. Catches of one species are often made from one level of a wreck.

Spring tides help cover ground
For really good fishing the boat must drift and cover as much ground as possible. West Country charter skippers, who have brought pirking to a fine art, enjoy the greatest success during big spring tides, when the flow of water carries their craft along at a speed in excess of four knots.

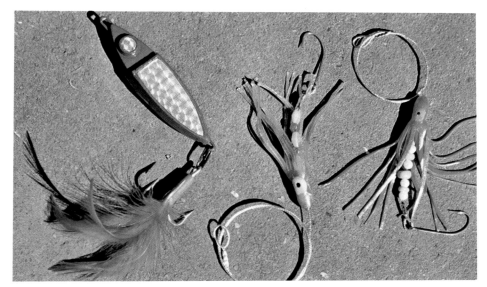

Above left: *Mike Millman displays a 20lb pollack and the lure which caught it.*
Above: *Pirks attract fish by movement or a resemblance to jerky-swimming creatures.*
Far left: *Intrepid range of Flectolite 'Jigga' deepwater pirks, 1½–16oz. Metal pirks can weigh as much as 26oz* **(below left).**
Centre: *Home-made pirks.*

Pollack and coalfish are fast-moving predators, much attracted to what appears to be a tasty meal swimming for its life. Both species invariably take the lure with a sideways slash and the treble hook usually embeds itself on the outside of the fish's jaw. Quite a few become foul-hooked in the head area, in front of the dorsal fin.

Although small pollack in the 4-6lb class go for pirks, it is more often specimen size fish up to the record size of 25lb that are caught. A few years ago the author hooked a monster of 23lb 4oz on a large Intrepid Flectolite pirk, at a depth of 42 fathoms. At that time it ranked as the fifth biggest pollack taken on rod and line, although coming from such deep water it had no chance to show its true fighting ability. Even so, pumping it up was not the easiest job in the world.

A new jig lure that is proving irrestistible to pollack, coalfish, cod and ling, is the Wondershine squid, which is available in a range of fluorescent colours. Rigged on short snoods to a paternoster, they make a deadly offering during wreck fishing expeditions, but are also proving their worth over rough ground. Such is their attraction to big predators that it is necessary to tie the paternoster from 60lb b.s. monofilament when using two or three Wondershines at a time. Anything less gets short shrift from a brace or trio of 20lb-plus pollack or a couple of 30lb ling intent on going in opposite directions. (This often happens while the weighted trace is still dropping

to the wreckage!) It must be stressed that such a rig stands its best chance when fished on-the-drift, during fast spring tides.

Pirking over reefs
Pirking over reefs and open ground, where the species are less numerous, is a different proposition. Here the drift fishing technique is even more vital to success. Cod are caught on pirks worked close to the bottom, particularly where the ground is mud or shale. In shallow water, pirking can be done from small boats or dinghies with much lighter tackle and baited lures of 4-6oz. The sporting element is high—cod hit lures hard and put up plenty of resistance by continually trying to bore down towards the bottom. Between 1970 and 1973 pirking for cod at the Ganntocks mark in Scotland produced dozens of specimen fish, some weighing over 45lb. Since then, the run of cod coming into the Clyde from the Atlantic to spawn in January and February has shrunk noticeably. This is probably due to commercial trawling, which has been understandably heavy in the area. Despite this, good fishing is still to be had, with plenty of cod reaching double-figure weights.

The majestic halibut is in the true heavyweight class. The largest species of flatfish in the world, it frequents the Pentland Firth off the northern tip of Scotland and waters around Orkney and the Shetland Islands. Large shiny pirks of up to 3lb, fitted with tough, forged No 12/0 (and larger) treble hooks, connected to wire lines, have taken several monster fish.

Drifting these large, purpose-made pirks close to the bottom in very deep water, where the tide is strong, is the most successful method for halibut. Landing a fish safely is another matter. Obviously, tackle in the 80lb class is needed before you stand any chance. But with a fish that can weigh 400lb, there is nothing unsporting about it.

Trollers
A lure suitable for shore fishing from beach, rock or a boat is the 28 gram troller which is available in a choice of colours, silver/black, gold/black, or blue/black.

Sea hooks

Sea hooks come in a bewildering variety of styles and sizes, but each type has a distinct function: the thoughtful sea angler makes the right choices and keeps them sharp

No item of the sea angler's equipment is more important than the hook which, after all, is in direct contact with the fish and so has to withstand all kinds of strain.

Despite this, hooks often receive scant attention. Many anglers will cheerfully part with £100 for a rod, reel and line, and then go out of their way to buy cheap hooks, which are brittle, poorly finished and often quite unsuited to the job they are expected to do. Others purchase good hooks, but then allow them to become rusty and blunt, with points that will hardly penetrate the softest mouth.

'O'SHAUGHNESSY'
Available in either a bronze or stainless steel finish.

MUSTAD 'BAIT HOLDER'
A sliced shank hook with hollow point, forged, reversed bend, ring eye and nickel plate finish.

DOUBLE BAIT HOOKS
Needle-eyed with detachable link, used for peeler crab bait.

Hook manufacture

Before we look at the most popular hooks for sea fishing, it is well to examine the method of manufacture that produces a good hook. Most are made from high-carbon steel wire. One machine straightens the wire from a large coil and a second cuts it to the appropriate length. The 'needles' obtained from this operation are then ground to a rough point, and another grinding imparts a fine hollow-ground point. The blunt-end of the shank may now be 'pennelled' or tapered by grinding, which allows the eye to be closed up smaller and neater.

A steel chisel cuts a barb in the needles as they move round a rotating drum, the angle and the depth of the incision being determined by the setting of the chisel.

The next step is bending, which is carried out round a mandrel or cylinder. Variations on the angle of the bend are numerous, and each style of hook and size has its own.

The eye is now formed. It is either left straight or can be set towards or away from the point. Some hooks, for example, those used in mackerel fishing, are flattened in the shank, while others have grooves for whipping on flies or feathers. For extra

strength, large hooks can be brazed, as are the Mustad Seamaster range, which are used for shark and game fishing throughout the world. This kind of hook is also subjected to anti-corrosion tests in a salt spray chamber in accordance with internationally agreed standards. To minimize corrosion, hooks are plated with either bronze, tin, nickel or even, as has been known, gold.

Treble hooks, which are now widely used for pirk fishing over deep-water wrecks, are also brazed. As much of the work is done by hand, the cost can be considerable. Hardening and tempering by heating,

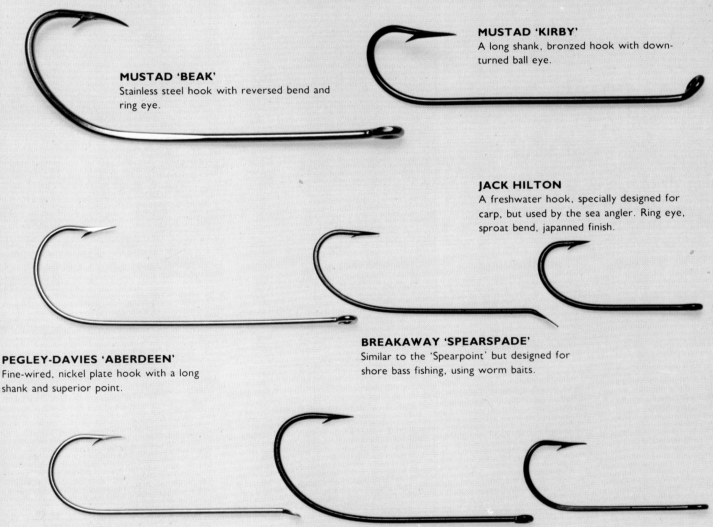

MUSTAD 'BEAK'
Stainless steel hook with reversed bend and ring eye.

MUSTAD 'KIRBY'
A long shank, bronzed hook with down-turned ball eye.

JACK HILTON
A freshwater hook, specially designed for carp, but used by the sea angler. Ring eye, sproat bend, japanned finish.

PEGLEY-DAVIES 'ABERDEEN'
Fine-wired, nickel plate hook with a long shank and superior point.

BREAKAWAY 'SPEARSPADE'
Similar to the 'Spearpoint' but designed for shore bass fishing, using worm baits.

DON'S 'LIGHTNING POINT'
A fine wire hook with spade end, round bend and nickel plate finish.

BREAKAWAY 'SPEARPOINT'
A British designed hook by Nigel Forrest used for shore cod fishing. Made of carbon steel fine wire with an ultra small eye and japanned finish.

SUNDRIDGE 'SPECIMEN'
Long shank, forged hook with reversed, round bend and bronzed finish.

and then cooling with oil, give maximum strength and resilience. Finally the hooks are scoured in revolving drums filled with an abrasive, and then polished in a similar way with a mixture of sawdust and oil.

A fair proportion of anglers are confused by the multiplicity of hook sizes, which largely stems from the traditional use of private scales. The world's fish hook manufacturers now use only the internationally-accepted British (Redditch) scale.

Hook style
So much for hook manufacture and sizes. This still leaves the bewildering array of styles of hook. For sea fishing this can be reduced conveniently to around half a dozen kinds. Among the most popular is the razor sharp, straight eyed Aberdeen hook which has a long shank made from light wire. Perfect temper prevents any straightening despite the extra leverage from the shank. This hook is used extensively for estuary fishing, particularly for bass, plaice and flounders. As it is so fine in the shank of wire the Aberdeen hook is most suitable for baiting live sandeel and prawn.

Shore anglers who fish from the precipitous rock ledges of the north Cornwall coast also swear by them for spinning with deadbaits for fast-moving mackerel, garfish, pollack and bass. Some will argue that it is the only hook for saltwater fishing. That is a bit sweeping, but every self-respecting sea fisherman should be equipped with a range of Aberdeens between the sizes No 1 and 4/0, with the emphasis on No 3/0.

For general bottom fishing three kinds stand out—Limerick, Kirby and O'Shaughnessy. The Limerick is well suited to use with a paternoster for bream, whiting, pouting, cod and ling, its pull being direct and its penetration excellent. For ledgering there is little to choose between the other varieties, which have a wide gape between the point and the shank, but the O'Shaughnessy is the strongest and particularly suitable for holding such heavy fish as the conger eel.

The conger is a fish that demands and receives respect from beginner and expert alike. In the past decade wreck fishing has produced some enormous congers, some over 100lb in weight. To cope with the strength and sawing motion of the conger's jaws and to withstand prolonged battles, a hook must be durable, and this is where the forged eye hook comes into its own. Eels over 50lb have a large appetite, and the experts think little of offering a whole bream weighing as much as 3lb. Such a bait, intended to attract huge fish, requires a forged hook of either No 10/0 or 12/0 attached to a couple of feet of cable-laid wire. No matter how much pressure this kind of hook receives, it will not straighten out.

Care of hooks
No article on hooks would be complete without reference to the care of them. While most are sharp when they leave the factory, handling can

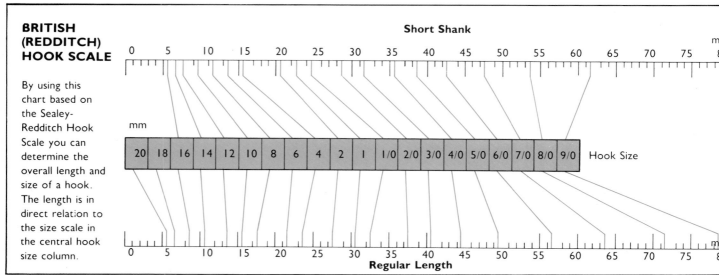

BRITISH (REDDITCH) HOOK SCALE

By using this chart based on the Sealey-Redditch Hook Scale you can determine the overall length and size of a hook. The length is in direct relation to the size scale in the central hook size column.

Short Shank

| 20 | 18 | 16 | 14 | 12 | 10 | 8 | 6 | 4 | 2 | 1 | 1/0 | 2/0 | 3/0 | 4/0 | 5/0 | 6/0 | 7/0 | 8/0 | 9/0 | Hook Size

Regular Length

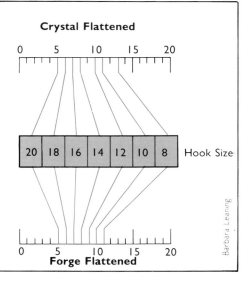

Crystal Flattened

| 20 | 18 | 16 | 14 | 12 | 10 | 8 | Hook Size |

Forge Flattened

Barbara Leaning

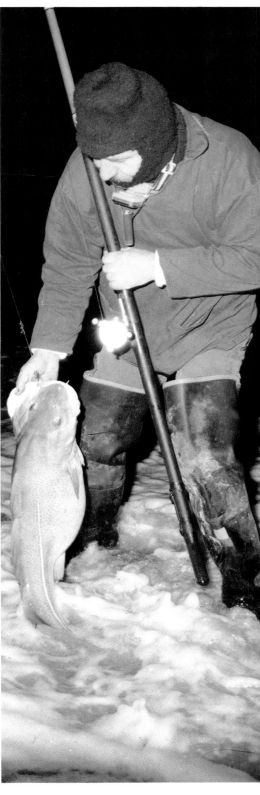

A successful night's fishing is heavily dependent on shelter, light, systematically set-up tackle and sharp, well-chosen hooks.

easily dull them, and so it is essential to examine each one before it is used, and from time to time while fishing. Any with a slightly turned point and those lacking needle sharpness should be gently honed with a good stone. Soft Arkansas whetstone, used with a light oil, is perfect for the job. Hooks that show signs of irreparable wear must be discarded after each trip. Failure to observe this simple rule could mean, in some circumstances, the loss of the fish of a lifetime – with yourself taking all the blame.

Thankfully, an angler grasps this 8lb shore-caught cod and lifts it from the surf. The last link — the hook — held. Never rely on old hooks, and always sharpen new ones before use. They hardly ever are sharp enough when bought and attention to the point will bring dividends.

Sea booms

A sea boom separates bait from reel line: if it is doing its job, it prevents tangling and presents one or more baits a little way off the bottom where they can attract the most interest

To the expert, the array of terminal tackle displayed in the sea section of a tackle shop is fascinating; but for the beginner or inexperienced angler that same array can be a nightmare of odd-shaped wire lengths. Terminal tackle for sea fishing has certainly undergone many changes in recent years, and the mixing of old and new, coupled with the barriers created when various items are identified by different names in different parts of the country, often leads to misunderstandings. Nevertheless, if the angler remembers his basic fish lore, selecting the right tackle is a matter of common sense.

French booms

The ready-made paternoster presents the hook only 2ft or so above the bottom. Where it is required to hold a bait well above the seabed, French booms should be used. These triangular wire frames can be fastened to the line by two or three twists around the central column and over the centre lug. This simple attachment means that they can be raised or lowered with ease to any depth, and that more than the normal two or three booms can be attached. But there is a disadvantage with French booms in that a heavy fish will slide them down the line, which leads to some stretching and distortion if monofilament is used.

A single-trace boom can be used either as a running or a fixed ledger and is especially useful if a long trace is to be allowed to flow with the tide. In its fixed state it will allow several feet of monofilament to lie away from the line without tangling. But it has a specific use over rocky ground in its running form, used with a length of low b.s. line with which to attach the weight. Should a snag occur, then the finer line will part, allowing the main tackle to be retrieved. The wide

Buckle line link

TWO-BOOM BRASS PATERNOSTER

STAINLESS STEEL FRENCH BOOM

Swivel

Blood loop dropper

Plastic tube provides cheap and simple boom

Corkscrew lead link

A two-boom brass paternoster, stainless steel French boom and Wessex ledger.

Bead

Bead

Swivel

Kilmore boom

angle between the points helps to keep both bait and trace from tangling around the line.

The Kilmore boom

There are several booms specially for ledgering, the best known being

the Kilmore boom. In its simple form this consists of a loop of wire leading to a swivel and lead attachment. The loop through which the line is passed can be plain, or fitted with an inner ring of porcelain, or harder-wearing metal. The latter are the better choice, for plain wire in constant use causes line damage. If the porcelain-lined model is used, take care to mount a bead stop between the eye and trace swivel, otherwise a hard knock will cause the brittle lining to fracture. A major disadvantage of the Kilmore boom is that the lead hangs from the bottom of the boom, causing the trace which hangs past it to tangle, either when the rig is descending to the bottom, or between rebaiting and casting, when the lead swings freely.

The Clement's boom is designed to prevent such tangling. The wire boom has a large eye twisted in either end, and from the end of one of these loops hangs the lead attachment. The reel line is threaded through the loops so that the lead attachment hangs farthest away from the trace. This gives a cantilever effect making it stand at right-angles to the line and holding the trace well away from the lead.

A long trace with a Clement's boom could mean that the stop had to be fastened 8ft or so from the end hook, which could lead to problems when landing a fish. There is a release Clement's boom on the market which has a small inner cylinder along the body, through which the line is passed. With the cylinder pressed against the line the boom will stop in place, but once reeled tightly against the rod tip, the cylinder will free itself, allowing the whole rig to slide down to the end of the trace. The fish can then be played to the surface and landed.

There are many other sea rigs available, but most of the new arrivals are merely variations on the basic themes described above.

Importance of swivels

Most sea tackle is designed for quick release, so that lead or reel line can be altered with the minimum of disturbance and, to counter the twisting action of the sea, swivels should be incorporated wherever possible.

Chapter 9
GAME TACKLE

Some of the best game fishermen in the world say that the traditional built-cane fly rod is still the best weapon for action, 'feel' and control of line in all difficult conditions. It is probably safe to say, too, that the tackle one prefers is that which one has learned to use to its best advantage.

There is no doubt that solid-glass rods when they first appeared were of little use to fly casting; but the advent of hollowglass did improve the action even though the material was a man-made fibre.

Now, carbon rods are available in all rod classes and perhaps the point of criticism is that for a top-class double-handed salmon fly rod in that medium the price might be high. But, then, for all top-quality tackle one must pay the appropriate amount.

For Spey casting, which tends to exert a screw-like motion to the rod at the ferrules, many salmon fishermen prefer built-cane with rods with spliced joints. This method of construction is better able to withstand the twisting force than most man-made fibres.

Fly reels used to be described as simple reservoirs for the fly line. It was said they had no part in playing the fish, were not used to reel in while the fish was still resisting, and were not involved during casting in the manner that fixed-spools and multipliers are.

There are arguments against this, of course, a run by a salmon can be very fast and extremely powerful. Since a fly line is much thicker than a coarse fishing line the reel cannot carry as much; therefore the reel is emptied much faster, the drum turning at greater speed. At this point, any defect in manufacture will tend to be enhanced, so a game fishing reel must be of higher quality.

The flyfisherman now has an automatic reel available to him. Many purists have said this is taking things too far, comparing it with that abomination the automatic-striking float, which reacts to a biting fish by exerting a sudden pull on the line.

But if one is playing a strong fish on a fly line with a fairly light leader, retrieving line can be a critical factor. The automatic reel will recover some 20 yards in five seconds and thus help to maintain a tight line between rod-tip and fish if it is making a run towards him.

Fly lines are becoming well understood these days, now that game fishing is attracting more and more anglers each season. One adjunct to fly line matters is the question of backing. It really is important, the main reason being that tightly wound nylon can exert a force of such compression that the reel drum will be smashed. Backing, taking the strain and absorbing much of the pressure, can avoid this disaster.

Leaders on fly lines were once a big problem. They had to be tied to the point of the line and almost every knot left a tiny end which protruded, enough to catch the line during the cast and ruin it. Now, knotless leaders are available that taper down smoothly, without knots.

Old fishing illustrations often showed the triumphant angler, rod held high while the ghillie was at the water's edge, gaff in hand and ready for action. In fact, when that gaff struck a good deal of salmon flesh was bruised, even ruined, apart from the suffering caused to the fish, momentarily though it would be, for the weighted priest would come quickly into action.

Unless the fish is virtually out of reach, and a gaff the only way of ensuring the fish's capture, the correct handgrip or a tailer, even a net if the fish is small enough, is always preferable.

A useful little item the trout fisherman should have with him is a little scoop with which to reveal the contents of the trout's stomach. Perhaps it is not really an inviting pastime, but the troutman is ever on the alert to know what the trout are feeding on. By studying the stomach contents he can find out. Then he selects a similar fly from the fly box, ties it on and hopes that the next trout will have similar dietary habits and accept the artificial.

Fly fishing is not often a static pastime, the exception being popular reservoirs early in the season when the banks are lined with anglers all hoping to cash in on the newly introduced trout not yet wary of human activity. The roving fly fisherman must therefore be equipped to cope with all the adjustments to tackle, flies, leaders and make emergency repairs as and when needed. This means careful planning and stowage in the haversack alongside the necessities of food and refreshment.

Salmon rods

The lordly salmon is a heavy and extremely powerful fish which will push your tackle to its limits. The right salmon rod can make a world of difference to your success rate

Salmon rods may be divided into two main types—spinning rods (sometimes known as bait casting rods) and fly rods.

Spinning rods
Spinning rods, the kind more widely used for salmon fishing, are usually 8-10ft in length. For rivers requiring the use of heavy baits and lines with

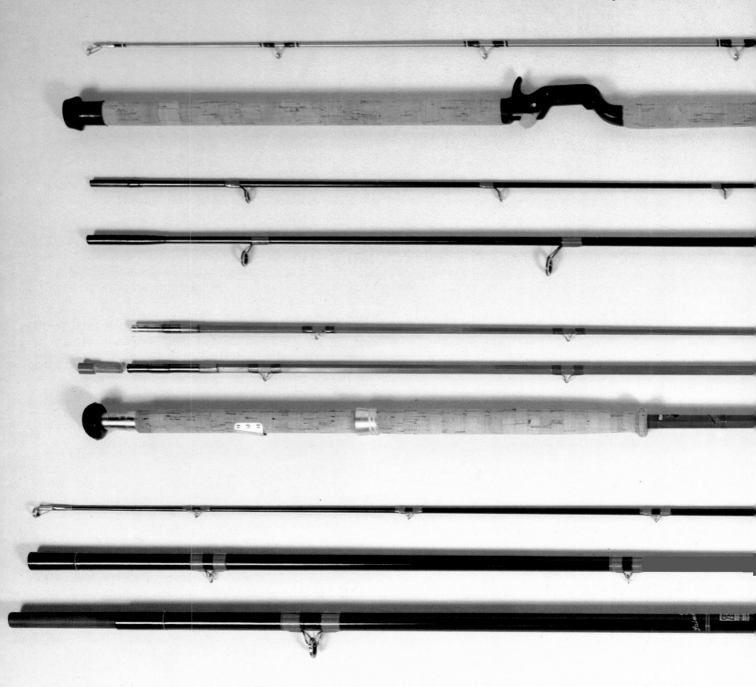

1 *The ABU 403S, a 9ft two-piece spinning rod with a pistol grip for use with multipliers.*

2 *The 'Graphlex' by Don's of Edmonton, a 9ft carbonfibre spinning rod with a screw winch fitting.*

high b.s., that is, over 15lb, a double-handed rod of 9½-10ft, used with a multiplier reel, is the best type. This combination gives good control of the bait and will handle big fish in the larger, stronger rivers such as the Hampshire Avon and the Wye. It is also suitable for fishing with a prawn bait. Smaller rivers, where lighter lines and bait may be used, call for a shorter rod, 8½-9ft long, used with a fixed-spool or multiplier style reel. Line of 10-15lb and casting weight of up to 1oz are suited to use with this combination. This outfit can be used for worming for salmon, although a longer rod is probably preferable with this technique.

Ideally, a salmon spinning rod is strong, with a medium-to-stiff action. The through action favoured in the past to assist in avoiding casting problems, such as overruns by the multiplier reel, is no longer essential as reel design has improved. The newer kind of action is preferable, even for use with the multiplier.

Spinning rods can be made from any of the usual rod-making materi-

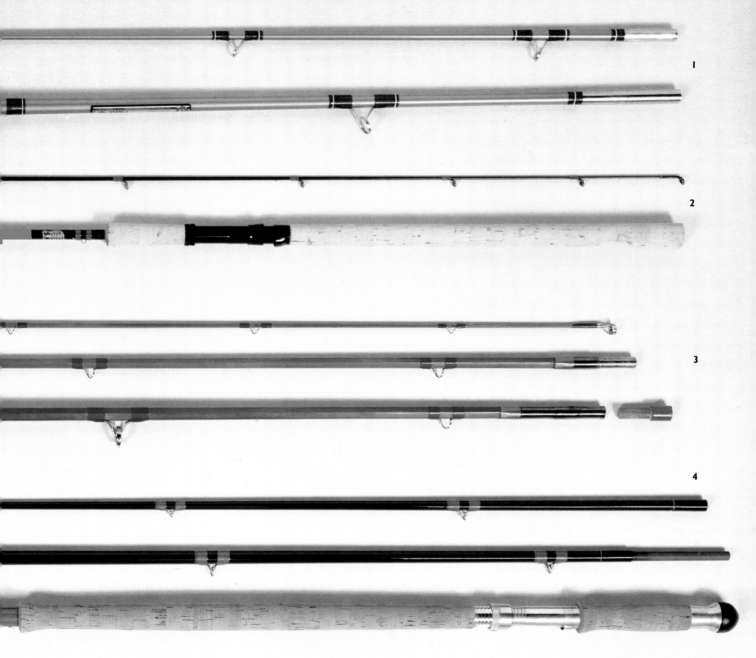

3 Sharpe's 'Aberdeen', a 12½ft, three-piece fly rod manufactured from impregnated cane.

4 The Hardy 'Fibalite', a 14ft, double-handed fly rod made from tubular glassfibre.

als—carbonfibre, tubular and solid glassfibre and built cane. The best materials are either carbonfibre or tubular glass. Solid glassfibre is strong, but is unpleasant to use because of its weight and action, while traditional built cane is no longer in common use.

Two-piece construction, with glass spigot joints in the case of carbonfibre and tubular glass, is standard in salmon spinning rods. Handles are usually of cork, with either sliding fittings or a fixed screw winch fitting to hold the reel. Stainless steel rod rings are the most commonly used. These have a hard chrome finish to withstand wear from the line. The rod should have enough rings to ensure that the strain on the line is evenly distributed along the rod's length. On rods used with the multiplier style of reel, which sits on top, the rings need to be carefully positioned so as to avoid any contact between the line and rod.

Basic outfit

A basic outfit for spinning for salmon comprises a rod of 9-9½ft and a fixed-spool or multiplying reel capable of carrying at least 100 yards of 15lb b.s. line. The reel should be held, for preference, by a screw winch fitting. This should be situated about 18-20in from the end

of the rod with a multiplying reel.

Fly rods

Salmon fly rods are designed for use by one or two hands, according to the style of casting employed. The double-handed variety are usually 12-14ft long, certainly over 11ft. The ideal length for an all-round rod is 12½-13ft, and this, coupled with a double tapered size 9 line, is suitable for fishing most of the salmon waters in this country. The principal materials used for salmon fly rods

are built cane, tubular glassfibre, carbonfibre, and greenheart, a hard but pliant wood.

Many salmon fishermen prefer a rod of built cane, particularly a model with spliced joints. These, so called because the sections are spliced together with a binding tape, form a very strong joint. The spliced joint is particularly valuable when Spey casting, which exerts a

Below: *The correct tailing grip to pick the fish up.* **Below right:** *Hold the rod tip well up to keep in touch with your fish.*

Above: *A prime Irish salmon and the double-handed spinning rod that helped tame the fish.* **Above right:** *A Spey salmon.*

twisting force along the line. Spliced joints resist the tendency of the rod section to twist at the joints.

The modern carbonfibre fly rods, although still expensive, have several advantages and are increasingly popular. Apart from casting as well as a top quality built cane model, they have the valuable assets of lightness and strength, and so may be used, where necessary, in

greater lengths without any strain on the angler. Their small diameter is a great advantage in windy conditions, where built cane would offer more wind resistance.

However, the most common material for for salmon rods is tubular glass for, apart from giving a serviceable rod, it is much cheaper than either carbonfibre or built cane. Although heavier than carbonfibre, the tubular glass rod has the advantage of lightness over the built cane variety. A 12½-13ft model makes a good all-round rod for most types of salmon fly fishing.

Action

Most salmon fly rods today have an action that may be felt right through from the heavy tip to the butt. A tip with this fairly rigid action is required because of the need to 'mend' the line or straighten it out. This need arises when the strength of the current varies at different points across the stream and the line is pulled into a bow shape as it is carried downstream. This in turn carries the fly back across the flow at an unnatural angle, making it unacceptable to the salmon. The fisherman must then roll the line to 'mend' it as the bow shape presents the fly unfavourably. A heavy tipped rod enables a weighty length of double tapered line to be lifted off the water and 'mended'.

Single-handed fly rods of 9½ft or longer are suited to fishing for salmon in small to medium sized rivers, where smaller flies are used. They should not be used, though, to lift long lines, as this subjects them, and the angler's arm, to considerable strain. Fishing in these conditions requires a light, 10ft rod of carbonfibre, tubular glass or built cane, equipped with a double tapered line, size 7, on a reel large enough to take 100 yards of 15lb b.s. backing line. This outfit should prove adequate for the salmon encountered in the smaller waters.

Left: *This fine salmon was taken on fly fishing tackle near Killin on Scotland's Tayside.*
Right: *Angling author and photographer Arthur Oglesby was fishing a big Klepper spoon when he hooked this magnificent Norwegian salmon on the Bolstad beat of the Vosso. When brought to bank it weighed 49lb.*

Fly boxes

Although the majority of boxes cost very little, the flies they carry are valuable, even if only in terms of the time spent tying them. So it is worth choosing a fly box with care

The only criterion by which to judge a good fly box is whether it caters for your needs, whether it holds all the flies that your particular brand of fishing demands. In my case this adds up to several thousand, and although this may sound unnecessary, I would hate to leave any of them behind. But each angler asks something different of a fly box, and this article can aim only to introduce the various categories of box available along with a few examples of specific models.

The firm of Richard Wheatley has been making fly boxes of all types for a considerable time, and have satisfied the needs of many fishermen. The No 1601 model from the Wheatley range is fitted with small metal clips on both sides and will hold 119 flies. On one side of the box there are large clips for the bigger flies and on the other, small clips for your nymphs and smaller patterns. The whole box is neat, will fit into most pockets, and is light, being made of aluminium.

There are other boxes in this range, some with an extra flap inside to hold even more hooks, as well as boxes that will take salmon flies, gripping them by the hooks. This method of securing the flies may be considered unsatisfactory because it spoils the hackles—which in these days are hard to come by. So Wheatley have produced a different design in model No 1607F which incorporates a neat, hinged, sprung lid to each compartment. By simply flicking the catch on each lid, it spr-

Fly box mounts

The lids of the compartments inside this plastic box are efficiently spring-loaded.

In a magnetic box, dry flies can be crushed by lengthy storage.

Nylon bristles in the Normark 'Gripstrip' box never damage or drop the flies.

Foam, although it can deteriorate with use, is simply and cheaply replaced.

ings open revealing the flies soundly protected inside. The box has 16 compartments with sprung lids and should hold 80 to 100 dry flies. In size it is only slightly thicker than the previous box. Another model has compartments on both sides and, while quite expensive, it is a first-class piece of equipment for the really keen dry fly man.

The Shakespeare Company produces an excellent range of fly boxes. Model 9133 is a wet and dry fly box with 36 clips and six dry fly compartments. Model 9132 known as the The Beatall Box has six compartments, three of them with useful transparent hinged lids and 30 spring clips. This up-market fly box is manufactured from gunmetal.

Many anglers say, however, that they crush flies putting them into or taking them out of the unyielding clips. As often as not, a fisherman's hands are cold and wet when he is making his selection—and then these clipped boxes can suddenly seem a distinctly poor choice. For this reason, too, plastic and wood, foam and bristle, are much more friendly materials than metal on a cold, wet day.

Light luggage
Without a doubt, for the man who likes to travel light, the best value for money is John Goddard's box made by Efgeeco. This box will

Ethafoam standby of the do-it-yourselfer, though it can crumble.

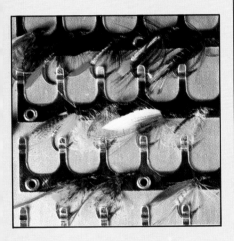

Spring clips: awkward to handle, especially with wet, cold fingers.

including the inside—a good rub down with a medium sandpaper. Put two or three coats of varnish on the outside to make the box waterproof. Next get some polythene foam from your tackle shop.

If you line the box with white Fablon before you stick the foam in, it seems to help make the flies stand out more clearly, especially when you are searching for one particular pattern at night. You can either put a complete layer of foam into strips and stick them into the box, depending on whether you want to keep just lures or hackle flies as well.

A handmade flybox
A box which answers this description is available commercially from Benwoods of London. Handmade by a skilled tool-maker, it is made from wood and lined with Fablon. Polythene foam is stuck into it in narrow strips so that the hackles of flies do not get damaged. (This can happen when the whole inside of a box has been lined with foam.) It is a model which the author can thoroughly recommend.

A recent box to come on to the market is the Gripstrip fly box. Normark manufacture and sell the box along with a free Adapta-leader. The method of holding flies is quite revolutionary; it consists of hundreds of tiny nylon fibres gripped at one end in a metal strip. Two of these strips face each other, the loose ends of the fibres facing. A fly is secured simply by pushing it in between the nylon fibre-tips.

They seem to grip the flies very well; they do not fall out even when the box is banged forcibly. It is most important that flies should not shake loose from the device holding them because otherwise you will regularly open the box to find your flies in a tangled heap.

This is the great disadvantage of the magnetic styles of fly box. When dropped, the flies shake loose from the magnetic strips or the sheet of rubber-coated magnetized metal which lines this kind of box. In addition, the sheet-magnet design tends to bend fly hackles drastically out of shape. For these reasons, the magnetic fly box cannot really be strongly recommended.

The next box can be worth every penny of its small cost. The box consists of six separate compartments, three on each side, with a sprung lid. It is manufactured in clear strong plastic and holds a good quantity of flies. It is particularly useful for river fishing when, if you know your river well, you can select the most 'likely' flies for the conditions, and leave the bigger stock of flies behind in their cumbersome boxes. An additional asset is a small ring on one end so that it can be attached to a waistcoat. These cheap, imported boxes are definitely value for money, and your local tackle dealer will probably have several in stock.

Linen waistcoats with elasticated pockets, which hold these small sprung-lid boxes snugly, are available at reasonable cost. Such an item is of enormous value to the angler who can carry everything he needs for a day's fishing.

Zippered wallets
Zippered wallets, which can be slipped into a pocket, are very popular with many fly fishermen particularly those who fish on the move working rivers and streams. This type of fly carrier is available in a variety of materials but is usually canvas, drill or soft leather. Top quality wallets are sheepskin lined, and retail at about £8. Cheaper ones have foam linings which quickly wear out—but of course these can be replaced at virtually no cost.

When buying fly boxes, decide in advance exactly what you require; whether you want to keep the various kinds separate. Several small boxes can help if you are trying to develop ranges of the same type of fly, for example, wool-bodied, seal's fur or floss-bodied buzzer nymphs. A collection of flies in a good assortment of sizes will need plenty of room if they are to stay neat.

If you buy a box that has a lot of metal inside, keep the box as dry as possible when fishing—otherwise you will find that all your carefully tied flies have rusted. You should also check the box to make sure that it is as waterproof as possible and would float if dropped into water.

One criterion – a flybox must be completely waterproof and keep the flies separated from each other.

answer all your needs if you are content to carry only a small selection of flies to the waterside safe and in good condition and leave the larger boxes behind. The box is made from a very durable plastic lined with polythene foam which acts to stop hooks rusting. It will hold about 140 flies and is very light to carry as you walk your favourite chalkstream. Perhaps the best recommendation is that the designer uses it himself.

To get away from shop-bought boxes, you can make all manner of containers if you are at all DIY minded. A wooden cigar box is often put to good use in this way. The first step is to take any paper off the outside and give the whole thing—

Reservoir rods

With the increase in reservoir fishing in recent years and the really big fish available, it is important to go equipped with the right tackle. And having the right rod for the job is essential

The purpose of a rod in any type of fishing is to act as a guide for the line and as a spring to absorb the effects of hard-fighting fish. But in fly fishing the rod must also be supple enough throughout all, or part, of its length to cast a fly which is virtually weightless. The line is weighted according to the type of fishing it is designed for and so rods will differ according to the weight of line they can carry. Rods also have different actions, and there is variation of construction as well.

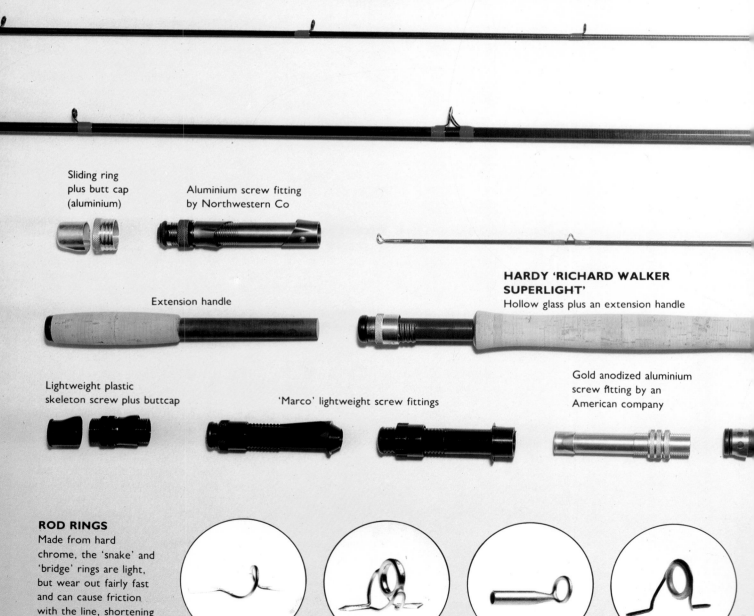

Sliding ring plus butt cap (aluminium)

Aluminium screw fitting by Northwestern Co

Extension handle

HARDY 'RICHARD WALKER SUPERLIGHT'
Hollow glass plus an extension handle

Lightweight plastic skeleton screw plus buttcap

'Marco' lightweight screw fittings

Gold anodized aluminium screw fitting by an American company

ROD RINGS
Made from hard chrome, the 'snake' and 'bridge' rings are light, but wear out fairly fast and can cause friction with the line, shortening the cast. The 'Seymo' and 'Fuji' types are tougher, but heavier.

1   2   3   4

Split cane

Wood has always been considered the best material for fly rod construction. The peak of wooden fishing rod construction is split cane, which tends to have an 'all-through' action which means that the full length of the rod will be involved when playing a fish or casting. But split cane has drawbacks in its maintenance and in its casting ability. Split cane cannot be stored even slightly wet because it will quickly warp and rot. The pro-

blem with its action is that when used for casting long distances it can take on a permanent curve, called a 'set'. But its greatest drawback is its weight when compared with to-day's man-made materials.

Glassfibre

From split cane, with its inherent disadvantages, came the development of glassfibre rods from the US. Glassfibre is less expensive than split cane; it is also lighter and requires less maintenance. But again

it will take on a 'set' if grossly abused, although not as badly as will split cane.

During the 20-odd years since it was introduced, glassfibre has progressed from the solid section to 'hollow glass'. The great advantage of hollow glassfibre rods is that they can be tailored to give any kind of action to suit individual preference. Some anglers prefer to use nymphs to tempt fish rising to the surface and would probably choose a double-taper line. Consequently a rod with a

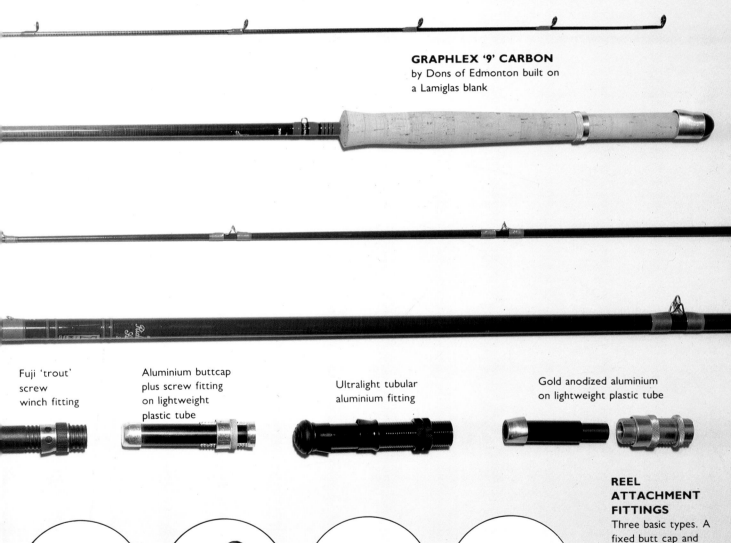

GRAPHLEX '9' CARBON
by Dons of Edmonton built on a Lamiglas blank

Fuji 'trout' screw winch fitting

Aluminium buttcap plus screw fitting on lightweight plastic tube

Ultralight tubular aluminium fitting

Gold anodized aluminium on lightweight plastic tube

REEL ATTACHMENT FITTINGS

Three basic types. A fixed butt cap and sliding ring; a fixed butt cap with a screw fitting, known as a 'skeleton', and tubular fittings with a screw thread or locking rings at one end and a fixed housing at the other.

5   6   7   8

through action will be preferred. For reservoir fishing, involving huge areas of water, long casting is essential and so, coupled with a heavy line, a fast taper rod with a tip-action will be the choice. Some reservoir anglers prefer through-action rods, but a rod with the action in its top part tends to be more powerful, propelling the line farther.

Carbonfibre

Glassfibre rods have now probably reached their peak in casting performance, but there is now a new material which has as good a casting action. This is carbonfibre, another development from the US, first introduced into Great Britain about seven years ago.

The material has all the advantages of glassfibre but is much lighter, and has a smaller diameter for the same power. There is one big difference—carbonfibre rods are much more expensive than all the others. Carbonfibre was originally seen as a short, very light fishing rod. Now a number of tackle manufacturers are offering their brands of carbonfibre rods in lengths between 7ft and 10ft 6in for trout fishing.

The selection of a rod must take into account the use to which it will be put, and the type of water to be fished. One can then choose between split cane, glassfibre or carbonfibre.

Reservoir rods

Reservoir fishing has become an important part of game fishing. Large numbers of anglers fish these waters from the banks and from boats. This type of fishing demands distance-casting and continual retrieval of the line. This means the rod will be in constant use, so the angler must choose a rod which will enable him to cast efficiently into the high winds often present on reservoirs, without becoming too tired to fish.

The rod, therefore, should be as powerful and as light as possible, so split cane is clearly unsuitable. This leaves a choice between glassfibre and carbonfibre.

A carbon rod will do all the things that a glassfibre rod can do. But it will not cast farther and will not improve an angler's skill at fly casting. The advantage of this material is

ROD ACTION

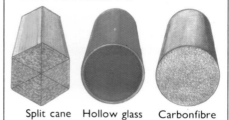

15yds

On reservoirs, distances are much greater, hence tip-action rods, with their power, work well.

30yds

Fly fishing on streams means moderate distance casting. All-through-action rods are best.

ROD MATERIALS

Split cane   Hollow glass   Carbonfibre

Now rare, cane rods have been superseded by hollow glass—itself now threatened by the lighter carbonfibre.

that less effort is needed in casting, partly because there is more 'power' in the carbonfibre sections from which the rod was made, and partly because the smaller diameter of the rod creates less air resistance.

Cost is a factor we all have to bear in mind. At present carbonfibre rods are expensive, but because inferior carbonfibre is worse than inferior glassfibre, selection must not be based purely on cheapness. Your selection of a reservoir rod must be based on sound advice from the dealer, your experience and judgement of the rods you are offered, and the style of fishing which you intend to do with it.

Above: *Fly angler on the 500-acre Ladybower Reservoir in Derbyshire. For the long casting needed, he carries a fast-taper rod with a whippy tip action, and uses heavy line.*
Right: *With the low light of late evening comes the evening rise. Trout engrossed in feeding on swarming flies seem oblivious of the angler nearby.*

CLEANING AND STORING RODS

Right: There is a right and a wrong way to store rods after a day's fishing. This one has been stored badly, with all the weight bearing downwards to create a 'set'. Cane rods are particularly susceptible to this and should always be stored correctly.

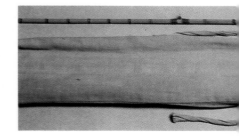

Right: Storing made-up rods. Use clip on brackets firmly secured to the wall.
Far right: Hang rods from hooks at the back of your tackle cupboard. An old wardrobe with a row of hooks screwed into the inside is ideal.

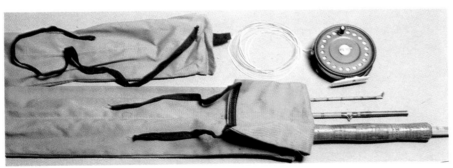

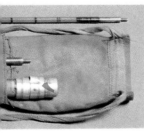

Left: *Correct storing. The heaviest parts of each section will be at the bottom of the bag. When bagging put the butt in first to carry the weight of the rod bag while inserting the finer sections.*

One of the design points of a reservoir rod is that it must be capable of long casting. Distance can also be achieved by walking as far as possible where the bank reaches out. Here, brown trout expert Geoffrey Bucknall fishes off the point of a spit at Peckham's Copse.

Fly reels

More than just a convenient way of storing your fly line, the right fly reel used in the right setting will increase your control over a struggling fish appreciably

While all anglers agree that a casting reel must be properly designed if it is to work efficiently, many feel that the fly reel is a very unimportant tackle item. This may be because in fly fishing the reel has no influence on the cast, whereas in other modes of fishing the reel has a dominant effect on distance. But the fly reel is an item which warrants careful thought, because a fly reel often does more than a fixed-spool when playing a fish.

There are several reasons for this, and one is the faster runs made by game fish when compared with most coarse and saltwater species. Fly lines are thicker than monofilament so a fly reel empties quickly and as the line pile gets smaller so the spool turns faster. Under these circumstances, if the spool is a poor fit within the reel frame it will jam and the fish will be lost.

Three basic types of fly reel

Fly reels fall into three basic categories: the single-action type where the drum moves one revolution for every turn of the handle (on a well-filled trout reel this recovers approximately 8in of line); the multiplier type where the drum performs perhaps two revolutions (thereby recovering approximately 16in of line) for every turn of the handle, and the clockwork or automatic type where the spool is driven by a spring. This spring winds itself up when you take line from the reel.

The basic function of any reel is to hold a sufficient quantity of line for the type of fishing being practised. Once that condition has been satisfied, reels become increasingly sophisticated. There are different methods of fly fishing and reel requirements will be different for each.

To illustrate this, imagine an angler fishing wet fly downstream on a small brook, where the trout average 8oz and where the record for the water is under 1lb. The angler makes short casts. He carries little slack in his hand and there is no need to give line when a fish is being played. Such a situation imposes minimal demands upon the reel.

Above: The Hardy 'Perfect'. A classic reel, basically unchanged since it was introduced in 1891. Uniquely styled in three pieces, it runs on ball bearings and is virtually frictionless. The handle is on what would normally be the backplate and the reel is right hand wind only.

Below: The Hardy 'LRH Lightweight'. This is a caged design where the spool is protected by the frame and there is no exposed spool rim to get damaged.

Above: The Shakespeare 'Speedex'. This is a multiplying or geared reel in which a simple system of gears enables the spool to turn more than one revolution for each turn of the handle.

A simple, single-action model will do all that is needed, for the reel does little beyond serving as a convenient line store. The multiplier and the automatic would also be suitable but in the situation described their more sophisticated features would not be used to full advantage and may be altogether unnecessary in this setting.

Problems on chalkstreams
Now let us imagine a different situation. Our angler is fishing a dry fly on a southern chalkstream. The distances he will cast will be greater and sometimes he will switch quickly from short to long. Because he is casting upstream he will often have a lot of slack line. The size of the fish varies from an average of 1lb, but there is a good chance of a three- or even a five-pounder. Due to the clear water a fine leader is used, so when a hooked fish makes long runs our angler sometimes has to follow.

Again the single-action reel could deal with this but anglers find that in this setting the quicker recovery afforded by a multiplier is an advantage. Other anglers may find that an automatic reel gives them still more advantages, for the automatic recovers line even faster than a multiplier. Close control can be vital, particularly when you have to get up off your knees, quickly wind up the slack and then follow a big fish down the river.

Now visualize an angler wading the shore line of a large reservoir. He is casting about 25 yards and working his flies back by bunching the line in his left hand. When the flies are two-thirds of the way back a fish takes. The angler wants to get the fish under proper control as quickly as he can but has about 16 yards of slack line to deal with.

Again the single-action reel will cope but it will take so long to wind up the slack (over 60 turns) that some anglers ignore the reel completely and resort to stripping in the line to try to keep in touch with their fish. Many highly experienced anglers find this less than satisfactory, and again use either a multiplier or an automatic to wind up the slack to get them more quickly into tight-line control.

The reel's important function
These examples show the very different settings which exist in trout fly fishing. There are lots of others, but those described show not only that the reel has an important function, but also how the requirements will vary.

The average single-action reel is around 3½in in diameter. With the aim of getting the fastest possible recovery, the spool is sometimes so narrow that you cannot get your finger between the flanges to control the spool when the fish runs. This can be a problem and is something to watch out for. To overcome this the spool edge is sometimes swept up and over the outer edge of the

Right: The Berkley 558, one of a new range of lightweight reels designed to complement carbon rods. Other than its lightness, the outstanding feature of this reel is no spool cage: merely the back plate and spindle with a couple of crossbars and a drilled plastic spool.

Below: The Hardy 'Marquis' 8/9. One of a series of 'Marquis' models featuring an exposed rim—where the spool rim overlaps the cage rim to allow for finger control of the reel.

Left: The Mitchell 710 Automatic reel which has a clockwork mechanism: when you strip line off the reel a spring is wound up, and by depressing a lever the spring is released and the line rewound at great speed.

reel frame. This 'exposed rim' makes a readily accessible braking surface but it is not without hazards.

The rim is vulnerable to bangs and knocks (aluminium is a soft material and dents easily). If the rim gets distorted it can bind on the frame and the reel will jam. Equally, the 'wrap over' flange is a trap for dirt and grit. One grain is enough to make the reel stick.

The design of the multiplying fly reel is virtually the same as the single-action, except that the handle is not fastened direct to the spool but is connected by a train of gears. These gears enable one turn of the handle to drive the spool round more than once.

Advantage of high gear-ratio

To get the quickest possible recovery a high gear ratio would seem to offer the best advantage, but beware of reels that are over-geared. The highest practicable ratio is less than 2:1, for when you go higher (faster) the gears work against the angler to such a degree that it becomes almost impossible to turn the handle.

Most single-action and multiplying fly reels have a permanent click-check to stop the spool over-running. On the best reels the tension of this check is adjustable to suit the breaking strain of the leader being used. The adjustment is made either by a milled screw, an adjustment cam, or by moving the click

spring across an adjusting rack. Each method works equally well. Another feature found on better-grade reels is the facility to change spools quickly, so affording the opportunity to switch lines (floating, sinking, and so on).

The automatic reel

The automatic reel has no handle and line is recovered by a spring. The spring is wound by the action of pulling line from the reel. When the angler wants to recover line he releases a trigger and the line is rapidly wound back (20 yards is re-

Above: *Another classic reel, the 3¾in Carter reel has three piece construction like the Hardy 'Perfect', and, made in 1925, is still going strong.*
Below: *The Intrepid Rimfly has an exposed rim and is cheap.*

wound in approximately five seconds). Some anglers find the extra weight of the automatic a disadvantage, but the enthusiastic user will tell you that the greater control he has over hooked fish more than compensates for the extra weight.

Care is needed when purchasing an automatic as some of the reels available are too small and will barely handle the most popular size lines in use today. They accept a size 4 but will not handle a double taper 6 plus a reasonable quantity of backing. Again, make sure that you choose a reel with the facility to change the spool. This gives you all the advantages of having several reels when you want to switch from one type of line to another.

Any fly reel, whether it is a single-action, a multiplier or an automatic, should be fitted with a well-designed guard. Without this, the action of stripping out line will wear a groove in the reel frame.

Maintenance a must

There are so few moving parts in a fly reel that maintenance is hardly worth mentioning. An occasional spot of oil on the spool spindle takes care of the revolving parts and a liberal smear of grease on the check pawl is all that is needed. With the automatic, follow the maker's instructions regarding oiling.

Beware of dismantling the re-wind mechanism because if the spring is disturbed getting it back can be tricky. It is advisable to leave it alone and let the maker's own service centre check it over every two or three years.

The Hardy Flyweight reel takes DT-4-F— double-taper floating line No 4—with no backing.

Fly lines

Good fly lines are expensive, but won't catch good fish unless you're prepared to expend more care in teaming them with backing, leader and point, and more time on maintaining them

In the early days of fly fishing, lines were made of plaited horsehair. This was later replaced by a lighter mixture of horsehair and silk, then by pure silk, plaited, tapered and dressed (impregnated and coated) with linseed oil.

The oil-dressed silk line was in universal use for three-quarters of a century, until it was replaced by the modern plastic-coated fly lines which consist of a plaited Dacron core with a coating of polyvinyl chloride (PVC). For sinking fly lines, the PVC is impregnated with powdered metal, the quantity used determining the rate at which the line sinks through the water.

Plasticizer
PVC is a hard material unless it contains a suitable 'plasticizer', which is introduced during manufacture.

The commonest cause of trouble with modern fly lines is loss of plasticizer from the PVC coating. This loss goes on all the time, but certain factors can accelerate it greatly. The use of grease, other than one of the special kinds that themselves contain plasticizer, will draw plasticizer out of the PVC very quickly, as will the various liquids intended to make dry-flies waterproof, should they get on the fly line.

Some of these waterproofing liquids are sold in aerosol cans, and special care should be taken when using them, to ensure that the line is not sprayed.

Another cause of plasticizer loss is leaving reel and line in hot places, such as a car parcel shelf exposed to bright sunshine, in glove pockets adjacent to car heaters, in cupboards near radiators or fires, and so on. There is little risk of ill effects from simply fishing on hot days, since the line is constantly being cooled by the water, but many a line has been ruined by being left in a closed car standing in the sun.

Fortunately it can be restored by the use of special replasticizing grease such as 'Permaplas'. But, if too much plasticizer has already been lost, the line coating becomes hard and cracks. Once that has happened there is nothing that can be done to repair the damage.

A wide variety of line is now available, identified by a code know as the AFTM (Association of Fishing Tackle Manufacturers) system. This code tells you the kind of taper the line has, the weight of the first 30ft of the line, and whether the line is a floating or a sinking one.

So-called 'level lines' are of the same thickness all along their length; they are little used and their only merit is that they are cheap. They are designated by the letter L.

Double taper lines
'Double taper lines', designated DT, have both their ends tapered for more than 10ft, giving a fine end which falls more lightly on the water. The idea of a double taper is that when one end is worn, you can reverse the line on your reel and use the other. These lines usually come in lengths of 90ft.

'Forward taper lines', otherwise known as 'weight-forward' (WF) resemble the first 30ft or so of a double taper with 40ft of very fine fly line attached. (In fact there is no actual attachment, both core and coating are continuous.) This allows more line to be 'shot' through the rings when casting. Recently, lines have been introduced with the first, heavier part longer than 30ft. These are called 'long belly lines'.

'Shooting heads' are similar in principle to 'forward taper lines', but instead of the fine shooting line being a continuation of the PVC— coated fly line, it consists of nylon monofilament attached to the fly line by a special knot. This allows even more line to be 'shot' in casting, and as the fly line is usually cut from a double taper, shooting heads are much cheaper than either double or forward taper lines.

Shooting heads
Good tackle shops will usually sell halves or 'double tapers' for making shooting heads, which will need a further reduction in length, usually to 30-36ft.

All these lines can be of different floating or sinking qualities. There are floaters, slow sinkers, medium sinkers and fast sinkers, as well as floating lines with sinking tips. They are all available in a range of weights, numbered 3 to 12. The

247

more powerful your rod, the heavier the line it will need.

Let us look at some examples of coding. A line coded DT-7-F is a double-tapered floating line, weight No 7. A WF-9-S is a forward taper sinking line, weight No 9 and so on.

The reason why the weight number refers to the first 30ft or so of the line, is that 30ft is about as much as an average fly caster can control when he whips the line back and forth in false-casting. Good casters can handle more, but in practical fishing there is no advantage in having more than about 45ft, which only very good casters can handle.

When you buy a rod you will find that its maker has specified what size line it will carry. Remember that this refers to 30ft of line in the air. If your rod has a recommendation of No 7 line, that means it will work nicely when you are switching 30ft of line through the air.

Short casting

If the kind of fishing you do involves mainly short casting, and you seldom have more than 24ft in the air, you will do better with the heavier No 8 line. If, on the other hand, you often put 35ft or more into the air, then you should use a lighter line.

For dry fly and nymph fishing, floating lines are used: the sinking lines are mainly for lake and reservoir fishing when wet flies and lures of various kinds are needed. Slow sinkers sink at a rate of about 1ft in 7 seconds: medium sinkers 1ft in 5 seconds: fast sinkers, or as they are sometimes called, 'Hi-D' lines sink about 1ft in 3 seconds. By counting the seconds after casting, you can decide how deep you allow your line to sink before starting the retrieve.

Backing line

For most kinds of fly fishing, your fly line needs backing: that is, some monofilament or braided, uncoated line is wound on to the reel first, and then the coated fly line is attached to it. Flattened monofilament of about 25lb b.s., or special monofilament sold for backing purposes, is cheaper than braided backing line, and easier to connect to fly lines.

Monofilament backing line is attached to the fly line with a needle-knot. The same knot can be used to tie a short piece of ordinary round-section monofilament to the other end of the fly line, to which in turn the tapered leader (cast) is knotted with a three-turn blood knot or a Double Grinner knot. All these knots are very secure, and have the advantage of being able to pass easily through the rod rings.

Damaged rod rings, grooved by abrasive matter or with cracked centres, can destroy lines, and these rings should be checked regularly and replaced if defective. Avoid dropping loose line on to sand or gravel, or anywhere involving the risk of its being trodden on with nailed boots or waders.

Good fly lines are expensive; they deserve care.

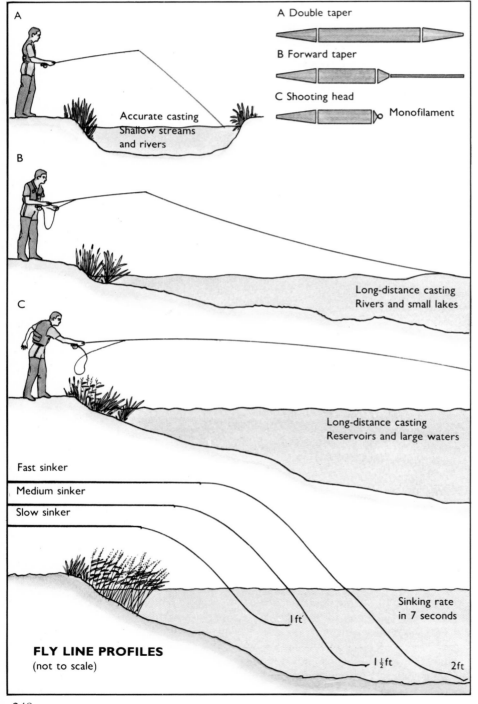

A Double taper

B Forward taper

C Shooting head — Monofilament

Accurate casting
Shallow streams and rivers

Long-distance casting
Rivers and small lakes

Long-distance casting
Reservoirs and large waters

Fast sinker

Medium sinker

Slow sinker

1ft

1½ft

2ft

Sinking rate in 7 seconds

FLY LINE PROFILES
(not to scale)

Left: *When to use the three different line profiles, and relative rates of sinking lines.*

Wet fly lines

A few decades ago wet flies were a quirk of regional game fishing: now a whole range of purpose-made lines has festooned the market and the wet fly fisher must buy intelligently

In the days when the only fly lines available to the game fisherman were of dressed silk, considerable time and trouble had to be expended to maintain or renew the oils and soft substances used in the dressing to ensure that the line remained waterproof and would continue to float on every outing.

This was particularly important for the correct presentation of the floating fly—the order of the day on very many fisheries, particularly the Southern chalk streams. In other parts of the country, fishing a sunken fly was perfectly acceptable, and many anglers discovered that they could work their sunken flies more effectively if the line dressing wore off, resulting in a waterlogging of the line and so, slow sinking.

Plastic-coated fly lines
In recent years the development of plastic-coated fly lines has proceeded apace, offering the angler a very wide choice of line profiles at varying densities. These have enabled him to fish efficiently in any water, no matter at what depth the trout (or salmon) might be feeding.

ICI Fluon coated lines have very little friction, and as a result they shoot through the rod rings positively, enabling long, effortless casts to be made. Such a line handles extremely well, and its flexibility is unaffected by cold conditions—a most important plus during winter fishing. Coated lines are available in a variety of colours. A light coloured one, particularly white when viewed from below, is less visible to the fish as it blends well against the light of the sky. From the fisherman's point of view a light floater makes it easier to see all takes, which is essential for consistent success.

Fly lines are given an AFTM (Association of Fishing Tackle Manufacturers) number. This makes it possible to match a line perfectly with a fly rod carrying a similar number itself. The AFTM number is based on the weight in grains of the first 30 feet of line.

Lines are also coded: F—floating; S—sinking; I—intermediate; WF —weight forward; DT—double taper; SH—shooting head; L—level. The selection of the correct line profile is dictated by necessity. Where casting range is short, and delicacy and accuracy essential, the correct choice will be the double taper profile or the single taper lines offered by some manufacturers. After all, if one is talking about casting a maximum distance of some 15 yards, there seems little point in loading with a line twice that length.

The use of half a double taper line, attached to a backing of nylon monofilament or braided Terylene, reduces the size of reel needed, which, in turn, reduces the weight at the butt end of the rod, leading to more efficient and comfortable casting. It should not be overlooked that half a fly line costs proportionately less than a full one, whether one purchases from a cooperative dealer, or simply buys a full line and shares it with a friend.

Forward taper line
Where longer casting is required, or the water is very deep or fast moving, the forward taper line is preferable. This has the casting weight at the forward end—hence the name—while the rest of the length is made up of fine 'running line'. Forward taper lines vary in length, ranging from the 30 yard standard up to 40 yards or more.

The shooting head is simply a variation upon the forward taper theme, whereby the actual fly line is restricted in length to that needed to give the rod the correct action —usually between 7-12 yards. This short section is spliced to the backing line, generally of nylon monofilament, which can have a circular or oval cross-section. The latter section is far more resistant to tangling, which is possibly the only disadvantage of monofilament as a backing material. This particular set-up of shooting head and monofilament backing is ideally suited to such long-distance casting techniques as the 'double haul', enabling experienced practitioners to cast 50 yards or more with accuracy and comparative ease.

A further benefit is conferred upon the angler hooking a fish at long range, or in very deep water, namely that the fly line is, by its very nature, relatively thick, offering considerable resistance to the water. Thus, there is a risk when using a full line and playing a fish at long range that the pressure exerted by the water against the line can pull the hook clean out or even cause the leader to break. This risk is greatly minimized by the use of a short line and fine backing.

'Torpedo' and 'long belly'
Just as the shooting head is merely a variation upon the forward taper profile, so are there other variations, such as the 'torpedo' taper and the 'long belly', although the principle remains virtually the same in every case. That section of the line which carries the weight necessary to action the rod correctly and enable efficient casting is found towards one end of the line, so that the line is no longer reversible, which is the case with the double taper.

Manufacturers have developed their own specific descriptions for the line densities now produced, and in order not to confuse the issue for newcomers to fly fishing, it is probably as well to discuss individually the densities in common use, offering brief comments on the function of each in turn.

Floating lines
Floating lines are ideal for the presentation of sunken flies which require little 'working' through the water, or require to be worked very close to the surface, either in

stillwater or gently flowing rivers. The depth at which a sunken fly can be fished in stillwater is restricted by the length of the leader—on average some 3-4 yards. It takes quite a long time for an unweighted nymph to sink to that depth, and when trout are feeding close to the bed of a lake, it is common practice to use a dressing containing weights to speed the sink.

On the other hand, where the fish are feeding off the bottom, application of floatant to the leader will ensure that the nymph does not sink too deep. Sometimes, when the fish are feeding and sporting at the surface—and this is particularly common in reservoirs—a lure is fished on a floating line, stripped back so quickly that it skips across the surface, creating a definite wake.

Neutral density lines

Neutral density lines are the modern equivalent of the old silk line, requiring the application of a floatant if they are to be used as a floating line, or used untreated as a slow sinking line. The main advantage of this line was that a suitable length of the tip could be left ungreased, allowing it to sink, and enabling a sunk fly to be fished at greater depth than would be possible with a standard floater. This has now been superseded by the sink tip line.

This is carefully manufactured so that the tip, which sinks at medium rate, is adequately supported by the floating body of the line. When fishing a nymph in deepish water, the 'take' is readily signalled by a movement of the floating section. It is equally efficient at indicating a take 'on the drop' (as the fly sinks), and with its use a faster retrieve of the nymph, fly or lure is possible than with the full floating line, because the pattern in use will not rise to the surface as readily as with the floater. This type of line can be very effective in deeper, or medium-flowing rivers, where it is important that depth is achieved quickly and maintained, or in stillwaters where the margins are full of snags which would tend to foul a full sinker. Some anglers claim to find difficulty in casting a sink tip line because of the imbalance between the dense tip and the less dense body, but this can

FLY LINE PROFILES

DOUBLE TAPER
A — 2ft
B — 10ft
C
D — 10ft
A — 2ft

WEIGHT FORWARD (FORWARD TAPER)
A — 2ft
B — 10ft
C — 19ft
D — 6ft
E — 53ft

SHOOTING HEAD
A — 2ft
B — 10ft
C — 18-24ft

SINK TIPS
A — 2ft
B — 10ft
C — 66ft
D — 10ft
A — 2ft

A	Tip	D	Rear taper
B	Forward taper	E	Running line
C	Belly		

Most fly fishermen, unable to afford the full range of lines available, either opt for a medium sinker in the hope of it serving most purposes, or choose one to suit the particular conditions on the water they most often fish—a fast-sinker, for example, for a large, snaggy gravel pit.

usually be overcome by practice.

Slow sinking lines

With slow sinking lines, the term 'slow' can vary in meaning from manufacturer to manufacturer, because there has never been standardization of terms in this context, but matters seem to be improving, with many firms now offering a full range of densities, so that if a slow sinker is purchased from a range which includes medium and fast sinkers the angler is on safe ground.

The use of a slow sinker does not greatly differ from that of a sink tip, in that it can be used to take fish 'on the drop', or at slow to medium speed retrieve in stillwaters, and in the medium-running or deeper rivers. Nymphs can be fished on slow sinkers, but more commonly the larger wet flies and lures are used. The take of a fish is signalled, as with all sinking lines, by that familiar tug transmitted to the

retrieving hand, and the fish is on.

Medium sinking lines

Medium sinkers, as may be expected, sink faster than the slow sinkers, and are therefore more suited to deeper or faster-flowing water, and to faster than medium speed retrieves. However, with maximum speed lure stripping, the lure itself will rise very close to the surface, which can be an advantage especially when the fish are working in the upper levels but demand a fast moving lure which does not break the surface.

Fast sinking lines

Fast sinkers enable fast working of a fly in deep water and ensure that no matter how fast the retrieve, the lure will be unlikely to rise above midwater. Obviously they are well suited to the fast-flowing rivers where the trout or salmon are taking fairly deep.

Very fast sinking lines

Very fast sinkers are fairly specialized lines, often carrying weights in the core. By their nature they are ideal for the very deepest reservoirs, lakes and lochs where the quarry is feeding deep.

Fly leaders

Which diameter to use, which knot to tie, what length to cut, when to change a leader, when it should float and when it should sink, and how to balance line, leader, point and fly

A fly is not attached direct to the fly line as the line's bulk would frighten off fish, and so a thinner line, the *leader*, joins the fly to the reel line. The leader is where the action is. The *point*, at the end of the leader, is where the action starts. Too thick a point and fish shy off or take short. Too fine, and the action is dead in seconds when a leader and point part company. With a fish on, the leader and point must withstand every surge of its muscle-packed body, fins and tail; every slash of a leaping fish jerking its head to throw the hook. It must survive the hook twisting and wrenching in its nylon-knot socket, stretching and recoiling to absorb shocks before they hit the rod tip, and certainly before the angler reacts.

All this is expected of a piece of nylon some 0.15mm in diameter if you are using a 3lb b.s. point. At 4lb the point is still only 0.18mm, and even a 7lb point has a diameter of only 0.225mm.

A hundred yards of good quality nylon costs about £2. A point costs about 2p, and if you tie your own leaders, they cost between 15p and 20p. What is the purpose of £100 worth of carbonfibre rod and magnesium reel if a pennyworth of nylon fails? Certainly you are inviting trouble if you use last year's nylon or leftover leaders.

Above all it is important to change a point or leader whenever there is reason to doubt it. If it kinks, twists, necks or gathers a wind knot, take no chances—change it immediately.

Most leaders are between 9 and 15ft long from butt to point. A tapered leader is usually composed of many pieces of nylon, each with a progressively smaller diameter and joined together with knots. One or several droppers (flies set above the terminal or point fly) may be attached to this by more knots. With so many knots, you must be utterly confident of your knotsmanship. Alternatively, you can rely on someone else's and buy made up leaders. Most competent fishermen prefer to tie their own.

Use knots in which you have faith. The ordinary dropper knot will not let you down, but it is a bit tricky to tie, especially at the waterside. If you have trouble with it, use the water knot, which is easy to make. Many people tie this latter knot with as many as a dozen turns, but four are adequate.

Knotless tapers
An expensive alternative is to use manufactured knotless tapers, either for the whole leader or just for the tail end. These tapers turn over sweetly, reduce the risk of tangles during casting in gusty weather, and are available in a variety of sizes. Altogether they are excellent—but you cannot buy them for a few pence a yard!

If you make your own leaders, a half dozen 100 yard spools of different breaking strains are all you need for a season. Breaking strains of 12, 10, 8, 6 and 4lb should be an adequate range. Store the spools in a light-proof box to prevent deterioration, or better still buy a set of special dispensers which allow easy withdrawal from the spool and prevent tangling. It is easier to make a couple of dozen leaders in the course of an evening than attempt to tie them, as needed, on the bankside.

Slip each tied leader into a transparent envelope on which you have noted the point and butt size. Before each outing you can make a selection from this stock to put in your tackle bag. Leaders that have been stored for some time take on a 'set' into the curves of the coil. By gently and slowly pulling the monofilament through your fingers, you can remove a lot of this. Better and safer still is a small piece of india rubber over which the leader is pulled gently to rid it of its set, the friction produces enough heat.

NEEDLE KNOT

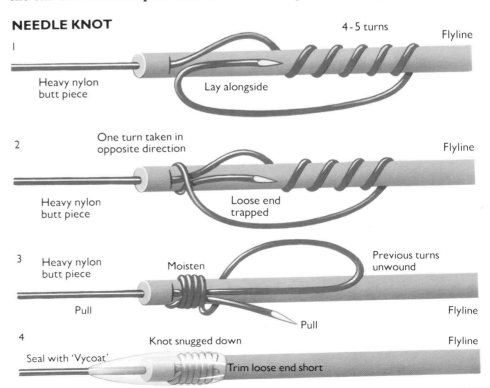

1 Heavy nylon butt piece — Lay alongside — 4-5 turns — Flyline

2 One turn taken in opposite direction — Heavy nylon butt piece — Loose end trapped — Flyline

3 Heavy nylon butt piece — Moisten — Previous turns unwound — Pull — Pull — Flyline

4 Knot snugged down — Seal with 'Vycoat' — Trim loose end short — Flyline

251

Spare line for points

Points have to be renewed occasionally on the bank, however. Carry a 50 yard spool of 3-7lb b.s. line (whatever you use) in your tackle bag for this purpose.

Opinions differ widely both about whether a leader should be tapered or not, and, if tapered, on how to taper it. Many successful reservoir anglers regularly fish simple 10-14ft level (untapered) lengths of 6lb or 7lb nylon. Others go to great trouble to taper their casts with six or seven lengths of nylon of differing diameters. In the early days of reservoir trouting, a double tapered (tapered at both ends) leader, with a heavy belly to assist turnover, was very popular. This had as many as a dozen knots in it, but in the right hands it was very successful. Nevertheless, these complex tapers are now rare, although some anglers do use a simpler form of double taper.

The level leader is quite suitable for fishing heavy flies and lures, but less effective for lighter flies and small nymphs. Generally, the leader should be tapered to suit the point size. On many small streams, a 4lb point would be rather coarse, but few anglers go below 3lb except on special occasions. On most reservoirs you can expect to hook fish up to 3lb, or even 6lb if you are fortunate. In such circumstances, a point of 6-8lb b.s. is not too heavy.

Check the connector knots

If you do not feel competent about attaching a leg smoothly, use plastic leader connectors. These sometimes have a rough finish, so rub them over with fine sandpaper before use. It is also worth colouring them to suit your line. A green or brown felt tip pen does the job admirably. Make sure the connector knots, both in the reel line and the nylon leg, are well made and do not slip through the connector under strain.

Yet another means of attaching leader to fly line is to use a fly line eyelet. This is a tiny, eyed, metal pin with barbs in its side which are inserted into the body of the fly line. Pushed well home, the line grips the barbs and the pin will not pull out. Nevertheless, a whipping of fine silk helps ensure perfect safety. Only half an inch long, these eyelets have

the advantage of not catching against rod rings, sinking the line, or in any way interfering with casting.

Some anglers advocate a loop at the end of the leg, with a similar loop to attach the leader. Two loops, however, often cause an undesirable 'wake' in the water, as well as being prone to catch up with the hook in flight during casting. The author prefers a water knot for leader attachment, although it means the legs need replacing frequently.

When not to use a dropper

Many anglers who consistently take good fish never use a dropper. Others regularly fish one or even two or three. When shortlining from bank or boat, a team of three flies can be very useful to indicate the taking fly, and sometimes the taking depth. But with long casting, things are different. Even a single dropper can drive you to distraction on a blustery day, although if you can manage it the fish often take the dropper rather than the tail fly. Perhaps it is the fly, perhaps the way it fishes on the dropper, perhaps it is the depth.

Many anglers forego the dropper after dusk, chiefly because of the hazard of fouling, but if you are shortlining with a team of buzzers, with care they are perfectly manageable even then. You can always cut them off.

When you are changing or adjusting a leader at night, use a small torch as your light source and slip a piece of thin red tissue paper under its lens. This will give enough light for the work without being strong enough to spoil your night vision.

Spacing the droppers

On professionally manufactured casts, the common practice is to fix droppers at 3ft intervals, which is fine if you fish that way. Many anglers using only one dropper, however, prefer it to be set halfway along the cast. This makes it more effective as a bobber during the last stages of the retrieve, and prevents the tail fly coming up too far at the same time. The length of the leader is probably the most important factor in deciding on how many and where to place droppers.

Colour is considered important by

some. Nylon can be bought in various shades, or you can dye it. If a leader is coiled first, you can immerse half in dye, dry it out, and then immerse the other half in a different colour. This produces a splendid camouflage, and if it gives you confidence it is worth trying.

There are no rules when it comes to leaders. Experiment with likely patterns; then make up your own to suit your style.

Importance of fly size

The size of the fly is also important. A small nymph or fly never sits well on a heavy point and often the size of the hook eye precludes the use of large diameter nylon anyway. For small flies, a 3-5lb point is suitable,

ALTERNATIVE TO NEEDLE KNOT

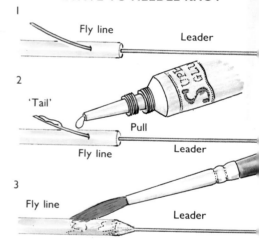

RESERVOIR LEADER FOR SINGLE FLY OR LURE

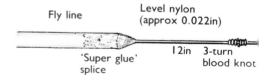

according to conditions. Conversely, a large fly or a heavy lure, especially a two- or three-hook lure, sits awkwardly on too fine a point. A heavy lure imposes severe strains on light points during casting, and it is also prone to flick back and tangle with the point. In such cases, 6-8lb b.s. should be considered, especially if big fish are expected.

Sometimes your fishing style or local water conditions demand the use a long leader, even though these can be difficult to handle.

Gaffs, tailers and priests

Gaffs are a common sight whether you are at sea or watching fly fishers work some little inland stream, while the fastidious, gentle, but difficult tailer has almost disappeared from use

The task of lifting a fish from the water and landing it safely on the bank can, in the vast majority of cases, be accomplished with a net. But a net large enough to lift a heavy fish from the water makes quite an encumbrance if it is to be carried across the shoulder or trailed from place to place by the lone angler. There are two alternatives to using the net: one is the gaff, the other a tailer. Both are lighweight, sure and convenient; each possesses disadvantages that need careful con-

Here is where the tailer would have been better used instead of the gaff. This salmon will have a large area of badly bruised flesh.

sideration before purchase.

For many anglers, especially pike fishermen, a gaff has become a status symbol which shows that the owner means business and intends to land big fish. Unfortunately, they use the gaff on every fish that is caught, regardless of size, and have no qualms about returning such fish, despite any wound that has

been inflicted. Worse still, many of the gaffs that are sold would be quite inadequate to deal with a very big fish.

Collapsible or telescopic gaffs seem to be most popular. They range from lightweight alloy to heavy models. Those made from alloy cost less but tend to corrode over the years, often resulting in their joints sticking when extended. Light oiling helps smooth running, but will not cure minor dents and distortions that so easily occur when using handles made of soft alloy.

Protecting gaff heads

Good quality gaffs have steel or heavy gauge brass sections with a firm rubber or cork handle, and the added safety precaution of a leather thong that can be looped over the wrist. Even if this is not fitted to the gaff when purchased, it can be easily added. Gaff heads are invariably made from steel, and should be kept oiled against corrosion.

Much is written about sharpening the point of a gaff at regular intervals, but if the point is adequately protected, this should not be necessary other than at the beginning of the season. Protection should be in the form of a brass safety cup into which the point will fit, and not a loose piece of cork haphazardly pushed on to the point.

The gape, or distance between the point of the gaff and its shank, is vitally important. Too little and it will be impossible to draw the point home; too much will effect balance and cause the handle to turn in use.

Fixed gaffs

Fixed gaffs consist of a wooden pole to which a head is firmly screwed and then close-whipped with copper wire. It can be carried bandolier-style across the shoulders by a cord, clipping just below the waist with a spring clip that allows immediate release. Many anglers construct their own with a large sea hook and a broom handle—a practical approach provided that a large-enough hook is used. A tope hook is only just big enough and conger hooks are worse than useless. Every trace of the barb must be removed and any sneck, or offset angle, at the bend should be straightened out in a vice.

Game tackle

Correct use of the gaff

To gaff a fish once it is played out needs a steady hand and a lot of common sense. Movement made by the gaff as it approaches the fish will often cause the creature to lunge away, and all temptation to strike at the fish should be resisted at that critical moment. Only when the fish is lying prone on the surface should the point be introduced, and then at the point of the jaw, where there is likely to be less movement than along the stomach or shoulder.

Once the point is well home, the fish should be lifted straight on to the bank in a single movement, taking care to lift with the handle and shaft held vertically. A horizontal lift will throw an enormous strain on the handle and is the prime cause of gaffs bending and distorting. Several steps should be taken away from the water's edge before any move to release the fish—many premature struggles result in a fish's escape.

The sea angler requires a much more powerful gaff, particularly when boat fishing for such species as conger, ling, skate and shark. Though professionally made gaffs are available, most deep water charter skippers, and many of the fishermen they take out, prefer to construct their own from a steel gaff head and a 6ft handle of ash or oak.

The gaff head

The gaff head is securely fixed to the pole with three jubilee clips: the surplus metal of the bands can be cut away after the screwing down. The clips are then given several coats of lead paint to prevent rusting—though such is the effect of saltwater that they need replacing at least every two years. Such a gaff should cost you no more than £7.

The shore angler, especially the specimen hunter, also resorts to making his own gaff when he finds those sold in tackle shops are often inadequate. A gaff head made by the famous hook manufacturers Mustad, is sold by many retailers and takes only a few minutes to clip to a suitable handle. A gaff with a screw-in head quickly comes adrift when a frantic conger begins to spin on the line: avoid the design.

Shore anglers who fish from

Applied with a sharp rap, the priest kills cleanly and quickly. Lead piping can be weighted to make an effective alternative.

vaulting cliff ledges many dozens of feet above the sea require specialist gaffs. On the north Cornish coast, gaffs 30ft long are used to secure ray and other big species close in. To achieve this kind of length five custom-made sections are screwed together, like the ferruled rods of a chimney sweep's brush.

Tailers

While the gaff relies on penetration in order to land the fish, the tailer uses a grip around the 'wrist', just before the caudal fin, to hold and lift a fish on to the bank. Its business end consists of a heavy length of stiff, cabled steel, bent and held open by a thin, flexible wire that connects to the handle. When the fish is played out, the open wire loop is slid carefully over the tail and back on to the 'wrist' immediately in front of the caudal fin.

How to use the tailer

Once in place the handle of the tailer is raised sharply; the wire noose will immediately clamp tightly (but not cut) into the flesh, rather like a snare around a rabbit's neck. The fish can be lifted clear of the water by the same vertical lift that would be used with a gaff.

The advantage of a tailer is that,

with sensible use, an undersized or out-of-season fish can be released with little or no damage—something that is impossible when a gaff has been used. But there is one annoying disadvantage in the tailer, and that is the tendency of the trip wire that holds the loop open to slip off its support every time it is knocked, closing the noose. The device needs constantly to be reset.

The humane priest

Killing a fish should be carried out as quickly and humanely as possible. Most anglers realize that the easiest way is to strike the head with a heavy object, but often this simple action is carried to extremes and anglers are seen using large pieces of wood, bottles, and even kicks from an angler's heavy boot to despatch the fish. Incidents like this are fuel for the anti-blood sport lobby and as likely to bring discredit to the sport as does the sight of fish left to die on the bank.

For a very small price it is possible to purchase a priest—a short length of weighted wood, metal or horn, that can apply the final stroke neatly and humanely—hence the angling expression 'visited by the priest'. Two or three firm blows across the top of the head, behind the eyes, and the dead fish is ready for wrapping in the damp leaves or rushes that will keep it fresh until it is time for cooking or storing in a deep freeze.

Index